THE CONQUEST OF THE REICH

OTHER MILITARY TITLES BY ROBIN NEILLANDS

By Sea & Land: The Royal Marine Commandos

D-Day: Voices from Normandy (with R. de Normann)

The Desert Rats

The Hundred Years War

Napoleon & Wellington: 1807–1815

The Raiders: The Army Commandos

The Wars of the Roses

THE CONQUEST
OF THE REICH

D–Day to VE–Day: A Soldiers' History

Robin Neillands

NEW YORK UNIVERSITY PRESS
Washington Square, New York

Library of Congress Cataloging-in-Publication Data

The Conquest of the Reich : D-Day to VE-Day, a soldiers' history /
[compiled by] Robin Neillands.
        p.   cm.
Includes bibliographical references and index.
ISBN 0-8147-5781-2
1. World War, 1939-1945--Campaigns--Western. I. Neillands.
Robin, 1935-
D755.7.C58 1995
940.54'21'0922--dc20   94-23982
                                                                 CIP

Printed in Great Britain

*The contributors to this book wish to dedicate
their stories to the memory of their friends
who fought in North-Western Europe in 1944–45
and did not come home again.*

CONTENTS

MAPS

ILLUSTRATIONS

The British and American commanders (Imperial War Museum)
American troops near St Lô (Imperial War Museum)
British infantry advance (Imperial War Museum)
German prisoners cross the Siegfried Line (Imperial War Museum)
British troops in Reichwald (Imperial War Museum)
Sgt J. Holmes, 35th Infantry (Imperial War Museum)
9th Bn Durham Light Infantry advance through Echt
  (Imperial War Museum)
British, American and Canadian troops meet for a bath
  (Imperial War Museum)
British tank crew host American troops (Imperial War Museum)
The liberation of Brussels by the British Guards
  (Imperial War Museum)
F/Sgt Vic Polichek standing by his Halifax Bomber
  (V. Polichek, private collection)
Young 'Volksturm' soldiers with British guard (Imperial War Museum)
An American soldier of 12th Armoured Division with his prisoners
  (Imperial War Museum)
The aircrew of Ed Stermer's B17 (E. Stermer, private collection)
The aircrew of Vic Polichek's Halifax Bomber
  (V. Polichek, private collection)
Sgt Ralph Teeters, 4th Infantry Division (R. Teeters, private collection)
Lt Quentin R. Rowland (Q.R. Rowland, private collection)
Lt Robert M. Brook, 9th Armoured Engineers
  (R.M. Brook, private collection)
Lt Don Nielsen, 8th USAAF (D. Nielsen, private collection)
British paratroopers of 6th Airborne Division in Hamminkeln
  (Imperial War Museum)
Graffiti on the ruins of a house in Munich (Imperial War Museum)

ILLUSTRATIONS

Morning parade of 1st Bn 134 Regt, 35th Infantry, 9th Army
 (Imperial War Museum)

SS troops in the Ardennes (Imperial War Museum)

Lt Everett Lindsey, USAAF (E. Lindsey, private collection)

Lt Lindsey after release from a German prison camp
 (E. Lindsey, private collection)

The body of General Deutch, April 1945 (Imperial War Museum)

British 1st Commando Brigade, Wesel, March 1945
 (Imperial War Museum)

Concentration camp victim (Imperial War Museum)

A survivor, Belsen (Imperial War Museum)

Wounded Russian prisoners of war in Austria (Amicale Francais, Paris)

German civilians inspect a mass grave near Solingen
 (Imperial War Museum)

Russian and American troops meet on the Elbe (Imperial War Museum)

The symbols of Hitler's Reich come down, May 1945

American troops at Berchtesgaden (Imperial War Museum)

Heinrich Himmler commits suicide (Imperial War Museum)

ACKNOWLEDGEMENTS

'War's a game which, were their subjects wise,
Kings would not play at.'

William Cowper

This book is not an 'official history'. This is the story of five months in a long, bitter war, told in the words of the men and women who fought it – or suffered because of it. The contributors to this book are not great captains or politicians but ordinary people – and proud of it – yet they saw or did, or endured, extraordinary things. They know the truth of Cowper's dictum better than most, and their stories of the Second World War ought to be remembered.

This book could not have been written without the help of many people, institutions and organizations, and I am very grateful to them all. These range from newspapers, which carried appeals for contributors; to museums, who opened long-forgotten files, to libraries, willing to hunt down obscure works of reference or find some long out-of-print account; and to more than a thousand people who sent in personal accounts of this time, the last five months of the Second World War in Western Europe.

My thanks go therefore to the London Library, the Imperial War Museum, the RAF Museum and the National Army Museum, London; the Holocaust Museum, Washington; the Canadian Army Museum, Ottawa; the *Daily Telegraph*; the *Jewish Chronicle*; the *Boston Globe*; the *Miami Herald*; the *Toronto Star*; and a host of newspapers and magazines in many parts of the world. I would like to thank Jane Whigham of Air Canada and Anne Checkley and her team from Canadian Pacific Hotels for their support on three trips to Canada, and Northwest Airlines for their help on visits to the United States.

Among regular helpers in this and other books I must mention Estelle Huxley for help in preparing the manuscript; Terry Brown, late of 42 Commando for the maps; and Major-General Julian Thompson, also of the Royal Marines, for reading the text and picking up points I had failed to clarify or had even overlooked. Other regular contributors include Jack Capell of Portland, Oregon (4th US Infantry Division); Zane Schlemmer of Hawaii (82nd US Airborne Division); and an old friend from the Royal Marines, Joe Cartwright of Johannesburg, South Africa. I would also like to thank Mrs Christine Barker of Portsmouth for trusting me with the fascinating diary of her father, Erwin Freppel of the 355th Wehrmacht Grenadier Regiment from 1943–45.

Many of the veterans have written extensive accounts of their war in Europe – and I wish more would do so. Among many such, I am grateful to Lt-Colonel Philip Whitehead for permission to quote extracts from his forthcoming book on the 94th Infantry Division, to H. Martin of the RAMC for sending in the account of his work as a medical orderly in Stalag 9C in Germany, and to Ralph Teeters of the 4th US Infantry Division for his accounts of the Hurtgen Forest fighting. Freddie Fish, RAF, was tireless in explaining the day-to-day details of life on a bombing squadron in 1945, as was Bill Morrison of the USAAF. Thanks also to Kenneth McKee, British 2nd Army, for permission to use his personal account of the capture and suicide of Heinrich Himmler, head of the SS; and Patrick Hennessey of the 13th/18th Hussars for permission to reproduce extracts from his excellent memoir, *Young Man in a Tank*.

Jack Ariola of the 17th US Airborne Division filled in a gap about the Rhine crossings of 23/24 March, and Fred and Helga Rhambo provided useful accounts of life as a teenager in Hitler's Germany. J. E. Thompson filled in a gap concerning the 7th US Armoured Division; and Patrick Devlin (Royal Ulster Rifles, 6th Airborne Division) of Moygallen, County Galway, reminds us how many Irishmen fought with the British Army during the Second World War.

Thanks also to Ted Smith of the Grenadier Guards, Guards Armoured Division, and J. Robert Slaughter of the 29th US Infantry Division, Virginia, for their accounts of the ground fighting, and Dennis Bolesworth of 105 Squadron RAF for his account of 'Oboe' operations. Thanks also go to George Butler of the Parachute Regiment for his account of the 13th Parachute Battalion's fight at Bure in the Battle of the Bulge.

I could not, alas, include all the accounts I received, but each contribution was useful, even when there was no space to include it in the text, for every account either filled in a little bit of background or acted as a check on the rest. My great regret remains that there was not space to include them all.

Among veterans' organizations, I would like to thank the Royal British Legion, the Canadian Legion, the American Legion and the Veterans of Foreign Wars, the Returned Serviceman's Association of Australia and New Zealand, and the Normandy Veterans' Association. Help also came from the 508th Parachute Infantry Regiment Association, the 435th Troop Carrier Group, USAAF, the 'Talon' (17th US Airborne Association), the 3rd US Armoured Division Association, with special thanks to Hayes Dugan, the divisional historian. Contacts in the United States were facilitated by the generous help of the Office of the Chief of Public Affairs, Department of the Army, Washington, DC.

Others who helped include the Buddies of the 9th (Airforce) Association in the UK, the Society of the 3rd Infantry Division, the 5th Armoured Division Association, the 86th (Blackhawk) Division, the Veterans of the Battle of the Bulge, Arlington, Virginia, the 36th Division News, the 44th Bomb Group Log Book, the 8th Air Force News, Edwin Ned Humphries of 'Crosshairs' and the Bombardiers, the 7th Photo Recon Group, many chapters of the 8th Air Force Historical Society, the 740th Tank Battalion, 'The Ragged Irregular', 91st Bomb Group, Hugh Brehm of the 78th Division Association, the 4th Armoured Division Association, the 11th Engineer Combat battalion, the 76th Infantry Division.

Thanks also to General Sir Michael Grey of the Parachute Regiment; Frank Ockenden of the 3rd Battalion, the Parachute Regiment; Captain Tony Newing, RM, editor of the *Globe and Laurel*, journal of the Royal Marines; the White Cliff Veterans' Association; the Airborne Forces Security Fund; the Glider Pilot Regimental Association; the Parachute Regiment Association; the 7th Armoured Division Officers; the Gordon Highlanders Association; the D-Day and Normandy Fellowship; the Royal Highland Fusiliers; the Royal Scots Fusiliers Old Comrades Association; the Scots Guards Association; the 51st (Highland) and 15th (Scottish) Division; the Commando Association; an the Ex-POW Association.

Many contributions came in from the RAF, the RCAF, the RAAF and the RNZAF. Among squadron and RAF contributors I must mention Air Vice Marshal Geoffrey Eveleigh of Bomber Command HQ; the Little Staughton Pathfinder Association (109 and 582 Squadron, RAF); Ted Jenner (142 Mosquito Squadron); the Editor of the *Marker*, journal of the RAF Pathfinder Force; the RAF Historical Society; Trevor Walmsley, DFC, No. 77 Squadron Association; 514 Squadron Association; 466 Squadron Association; Royal Australian Air Force; the XC Bomber Association; the Middleton St George Association (Nos 428, 419, 420 Squadrons); Royal Canadian Air Force; Eric Atkins, DFC, the Mosquito Association; 613 (City of Manchester) Squadron Association; the Wickenby Register (Nos. 12 and 626 Squadrons); No. 2 Group Officers Association; Jim Brookbank of 9 Squadron; *Touch Down*, the newsletter of 6 (RCAF) Group; John Moyles, editor of *Short Bursts*, the journal of the Canadian Air Gunners Association; the 426 Thunderbird Association, RCAF.

My thanks to the officers of all these associations, whose help in publishing my appeal for stories led to many individual contributions which I would not like to acknowledge.

Australia and New Zealand

The RSA (Returned Servicemen's Associations) of Australia and New Zealand; H. A. Coleman, Ohope, New Zealand; J. D. Dunlop, 166 Squadron, RAF, Napier, New Zealand; Bert Falley, ex-POW, 2nd NZAF, Rotorua, New Zealand; Eric Foulkes, Royal Marines, East Geelong, Australia; Eric Gallagher, ex-POW, Maunganui, New Zealand; Squadron Leader Allan George, DFC, DFM, 115 and 139 Squadron, Manaia, New Zealand; John Kelly, ex-POW, North Island, New Zealand; B. R. Lethbridge, 166 Squadron, Bay of Islands, New Zealand; W. G. Pearce, RAAF, Brisbane, Australia; G. Yerbury, ex-POW, Timaru, New Zealand.

The United Kingdom

Ken Adams, 45 (Royal Marine) Commando; Michael Allen, 141 Sqdn, RAF; Eric Atkins, DFC, 305 Sqdn, 2nd Tactical Air Force; Frank Barnes, 2nd Devons; V. Besley, 7th Armoured Div.; E. T. Beswick, 61 Sqdn SOAR; D. Bolesworth, Bomber Command; Tom Buckingham, 45 (Royal Marine) Commando; George Butler, 13th Bn, the Parachute Regt; N. F. Carpenter, 9th Bn, the Parachute Regt; H. E. E. Carter, Amersham, Bucks; N. R. Chaffey, RAF; Capt. R. H. Clark, MC, 2nd Bn, Ox. and Bucks L.I.; H. Covington, A Platoon, 76 Co., RASC; Lt-Col. Crookenden, 6th Airborne; Robert Davey, 2nd Devons; Dixie Dean, 13th Lancashire Parachute Bn; Dr A. P. Derrington, DFC, 466 Sqdn, RAF; Phil Diamond, 233 Sqdn, RAF; Tom Downey, Navigator, RAF; Dennis Duffey, 12 Squadron, RAF; Ron Eeles, 49 Sqdn, RAF; Major John Evans, 7th Armoured Div.; Major John Evans, DSO, MC, South Staffordshire Regt; Peter Elliot Forbes, 9th Bn, the Parachute Regt; Mrs Barbara E. Fozzard, for the letters from her brother, Corporal J. Thornton Hitchin, 2nd Lincolns; W. B. Garnowski, Polish 300 Sqdn; Alan Gibson, Royal Marines; C. S. Gilliatt, DFC, 107 Sqdn, RAF; Colin Goodall, HQ Co. 1st RUR, 6th Air Landing Brig.; H. S. Gray, 9th Bn, 6th Airborne Div.; Lt Gush, 7th Bn, the Parachute Regt; Frank Haddock, RAFVR; George Haggard, 466 Sqdn, RAF; D. P. Haines, 27th Bn, Royal Marines; Dennis Halfin, King's Royal Rifle Corps; F. G. Hall, 67 Co., RASC, 7th Armoured Div.; Brian Harrison, 466 Sqdn, RAF; Raymond P. Heard, Navigator, RAF; Alastair Heggie, 162 (Mosquito) Sqdn, RAF; Harry Holder, 6th Bn, Royal Scots Fusiliers; Major James Howe, MBE, Royal Scots Regt; W. F. Hurst, 51 Sqdn, RAF; H. E. Jackson, 151 Repair Unit; E. J. Jenner, 142 (Mosquito) Sqdn, RAF; Robert Law,

ACKNOWLEDGEMENTS

109 Sqdn, RAF; J. K. Lehman, 1st Bn, Royal Ulster Rifles; Alfred Lodge, 45 (Royal Marine) Commando; John Lough, Gordon Highlanders; Reg Lutwyche, 8th Parachute Bn; Henry McCarthy, 116th Infantry Brig., Royal Marines; Maurice MacKay, Royal Tank Regiment; H. L. 'Bert' Martin, Poole, Dorset, with thanks for allowing me to read his memoirs; John Melmoth, 1st/5th Queen's RR; George Morrice, MM, 1st Gordon Highlanders; Dr V. J. Murphy, 35 Sqdn, RAF; Lt-Col. Clifford Norbury, MBE, MC, 6th Airborne Div.; C. J. O'Connor, 2nd Bn, the Parachute Regt; Ron Palmer, 1st Bn, Royal Ulster Rifles; N. Payne, Royal Marines; Elizabeth Pirie, 721 Car Co., RASC; Ronnie Plunkett, Pathfinder Force; Christopher Portway; Dr J. R. Purser, Royal Artillery (Airborne); Frank Roberts, 76 Squadron Association; W. Southworth, 76 Sqdn, RAF; Bill Spence, 44 (Rhodesia) Sqdn, RAF; W. E. Sutton, Pathfinder Sqdn; F. Swann, Coseley, West Midlands; R. M. Teasdale, 83 Pathfinder Sqdn; David Thom, C Co., 5th Bn, the Gordon Highlanders; George Tinsley, Royal Army Service Corps, 1st Armoured Div.; H. Trew, C Co., 7 Platoon, 13th Para. Bn; John Waddy, 9th Para. Bn, 6th Airborne Div.; Derrick Watson, Poole, Dorset; A. V. White, 166 Sqdn, RAF; Bill Williams, 106 and 97 Sqdn, RAF; Ian Wilson, 73 Co., Royal Engineers; S. Wood, 115 Sqdn, RAF; Hugh Woodcroft, 514 Sqdn, RAF.

Canada

William M. Baggs, 164 Sqdn, RCAF; Percy Ball, Algonquin Regt; Fred Barclay, Surrey, BC; Harry Bowes, Stouffville, Ontario; K. L. Brimacombe, Argyll and Sutherland Highlanders of Canada; Aili and LeRoy Brown, Lindsay, Ontario; Richard Clark, London, Ontario; Richard A. Copley, Milton, Ontario; P. C. Costello, RCAF; John M. Craig, Thorold, Ontario; William H. Cram, 424 Sqdn, RCAF; Anthony P. Crawford, Williamsford, Ontario; Fred Davies, DFC, 408 and 405 Sqdns, RCAF; Clem Ervine, Royal Regt of Canada; George Futer, 207 Sqdn, RCAF; Edward Gale, St Catharines, Ontario; James Garry, 2nd Anti-Tank Regt, Royal Canadian Artillery; Robert J. Geisel, 115 Sqdn, RCAF; C. S. Gilliatt, 2nd Tactical Air Force; Wm. Keith Guiltinan, St Catharines, Ontario; Lech A. Halko, Scarborough, Ontario; Sid Herbert, 109 (Mosquito) Sqdn; Alan W. Hitchman, South Saskatchewan Regt; John G. Jarvis, 427 Sqdn, RCAF; Sherman (Casey) Jones, Calgary, Alberta; T. L. Kidd, Victoria, BC; Kib Kildare, Alberta; Ray Knight, Essex Scottish, Canadian 2nd Div.; Don MacFie, 436 Sqdn, RCAF; Blair L. MacSwain, 50 Sqdn, RCAF; Jonathan (Dusty) Miller, Willowdale, Ontario; H. W. Pankratz, Oshawa, Ontario; Alvin T. Parker, for information about his brother, Louis Parker, 175 Sqdn, RAF; Vic Polichek, RCAF; Frank W. Poole, RCAF; Jack A. Poolton,

Royal Regt of Canada; Alan Pottage, Black Creek, BC; Marion E. Proulx, for information about her husband, Grove Proulx, Argyll and Sutherland Highlanders; Clifford J. Roach, Yarmouth, NS; J. E. Seary, 512 Sqdn, RAF; Reg Snell, RCAF; Frank R. Stanley, RCAF; Walter Stanyer, 48th Highland Regt; Melvyn A. Stein, for information about his father, Stan Stein, Royal Canadian Engineers; John B. Stone, Toronto Scottish Regiment; David Sutherland, 207 Sqdn, RCAF; Harry Tatchell, 1st Bn, Armoured Carrier Regt; C. Richard Taylor, 6th Airborne Div., RCAF; George Tinsley, London, Ontario; Jack Tribe, Aylmer, Ontario; Adrian Vos, Blyth, Ontario; William Walsh, Essex Scottish Regiment, Canadian Army; John G. Weir, Toronto; Frank J. Welsh, 434 Sqdn, RCAF; Joseph A. White, Centreville, NS; Thomas W. Wickham, RAFVR; Marjorie Wong, London, Ontario.

The Concentration Camps

Barbara Distel, Dachau; Prem Dobias, Mauthausen; Mr Ben Halfgott, Buchenwald; the Holocaust Museum, Washington, DC; Dr Cornelia Klose, Director, KZ Mittelbau–Dora; the Memorial, Bergen Belsen; Jack Santcross, Bergen Belsen; Christa Schultz, the National Memorial KZ Ravensbruck, the Camp for Women, Mahn und Gedenkstatte, Ravensbruck; Herbert Schemmel, Arbeitsgemeinschaft KZ-Neuengamme; Colonel Richard R. Seibel, Robert Sheppard, (SOE) Natzweiler, Mauthausen and Dachau; the Special Forces Club, Mauthausen; Vaclava Sucha, Dept of Collections, Tersin-Thriesenstadt; Directors, Memorial Buchenwald; Anita Laskar Wallfisch, KZ-Auschwitz and Bergen-Belsen.

Germany

Patrick Agte, Trier; Erwin Freppel, 1 Grenadier Regt, 355; Mrs Annegret Hartmetz, for all her help in this and other books; Ludwig Heyman, Cuxhaven; Johann Huber, 7 Panzer; Kameradschaft der 24th Panzer Div.; Kameradschaftsbund, 1st Panzer Div.; Mrs Lanna Milton, of Königsberg; die Neue Brucke (293, 333, 278 Infanterie Divs); Mrs Inga Pertwee, for translating many letters and diaries; Joachim Pohle, 10 Panzer; Fred Rhambo, for his accounts of Hamburg and the *Hitler Jugend*; Oberst Helmut Ritgen; Helmut Rix, 1/JG 2, Luftwaffe; Walter Schindler, Battalion 33; 16 Panzer and Infanterie Kameradschaft; Helmut Stocker, 16 Panzer; Traditionsverband 19 Infanterie und Panzer Div.; the Verband Deutscher Soldaten, Cologne; War Diary, 24 Panzer; Wilhelm Wirtz.

ACKNOWLEDGEMENTS

The United States

Norman Abookire, 3rd Armoured Div.; Arthur W. Adams, 384th Brigade, 546th Bomb Squadron; Alfred Alvarez, 7th Field Artillery Bn, 1st US Infantry Div.; Jack Ariola, 17th Airborne Div.; Julian Van Buren, 9th Armoured Engineers; Lyn Goldsmith Barrett, American Red Cross; W. Kenneth Bell, 2nd Platoon, 1303 Army Engineers, 3rd Army; Dr Arden Bomeli, Pittsburg, PA; Rodney W. Bond, 335th Regt, 84th Infantry Div.; Robert M. Brooker, Corps of Engineers; Philip Reed Brooks, 3rd Div., 3rd Army; Daniel J. Burke, USAAF; Doug Calkott, 94th Infantry Div.; Nicholas J. Cappuccino, Harrison, NJ; Larry Christian, 36th Div.; Harper Coleman, 8th Infantry Regt, 4th Infantry Div.; Haynes W. Dugan, 3rd Armoured Div.; John Forster, 419 Repair and Salvage Unit, 2nd Tactical Air Force; Norman H. Friedman, 84th Infantry Div.; Robert E. Gemmill, 749 Sqdn, 457th Bomb Group; William Gill, 48th Armoured Infantry Bn; Neil Glover, 492nd Bomb Group; Arley L. Goodenkauf, 377th Parachute Field Artillery Bn, 101st Airborne Div.; Thomas P. Grant, Newark, Detroit; Arnold L. Gray, 8th Air Force; James H. Harris, 84th Infantry Div., 335th Regt; Patrick D. Hegerty, 15th Infantry Regt, 3rd Infantry Div.; Alan Howenstein, 376th Infantry Regt, 94th Infantry Div.; Howard G. Keller, 94th Infantry Div.; Doris W. Kennet, Maine, for help with photographs and letters from her husband, Ken Kennet, 341st Infantry, 86th Div.; James Q. Kurtz, 508 Para., 82nd Airborne Div.; Dean Leyerly, 385th Bomb Group, 549 Sqdn; Frank McKee, 508th Parachute Infantry Regt, 82nd Airborne Div; John E. Merkel, 76th Division; T. W. Miller, 358th 'Orange Tails' Sqdn, USAAF; Stuart Moak, 313 Sqdn, 50th Fighter Group, 9th Air Force; Wm. C. Montgomery, 8th Regt, 4th Infantry Div.; Bill Morrison, 8th Air Force; Emil K. Natalle, Perry, IA; Lester M. Nichols, 3rd Army; Donald L. Nielsen, 457th Bomb Group; Lt-Col. Roderick Nielson, 90th Div.; Samuel E. Parr, 2nd Armoured Div., 66th Armoured Regt; Anthony Pellegrino, 2nd Bn, 12th Infantry; Dean Peterson, 14th Armoured Div.; Richard H. Pierce, 76th TC Sqdn; Charles A. Powell, 508th Parachute Infantry, 82nd Airborne; John Price, 33rd Armoured (Tank) Regt, 3rd Armoured Div., 1st Army; Fred L. Rau, 9th Troop Carrier Command, USAAF; Eugene N. Robison, 358th Regt, 90th Div., 3rd Army; Thor Ronningen, 395th Infantry, 99th Div.; George M. Rosie, 101st Div.; Richard J. Roush, 84th Div, 3rd Bn Medical Section, 333rd Infantry; Major Quentin R. Rowland, 104th Infantry Div.; Peter N. Russo, 4th Infantry Div.; Albert I. Schantz, 4th Infantry Div.; Walter Shuster, 7th Armoured Div.; Carl Simpler, 3rd Platoon, 78th Infantry Div.; Gene Solfelt, 84th Infantry Div.; Gladys Staley, Oregon, for help in locating veterans; Ed Stermer, 385th Bomb Group; Donald B. Straith, 101st Airborne Div.; Ralph Teeters, 4th

Infantry Div. (22nd Infantry); James E. 'Ed' Thompson, 3rd Armoured
Infantry Bn, 7th Armoured Div.; Richard W. Tillery, Knoxville, TN, 334
Fighter Group; Wayne S. Traynham, 311 Infantry Reg, 78th Infantry Div.,
1st Army; J. Upham, 78th Infantry, 2nd Btn, 'F' Coy; Eugene K. Urban,
9th Air Force; Col. Hugh Walker, 9th Air Force; Kenneth T. Waters, 96th
Bomb Group, 8th Air Force; Clyde W. Weidner, 390th Bombardment
Group (H); Lt-Col. G. Philip Whitman, 3rd US Army; C. Wills, 99th
Infantry Div.; Monroe Wood, 696th Armoured Field Artillery, 3rd Army;
Frederick D. 'Dusty' Worthen, 93rd Bomb Group, 328 and 329 Sqdn.

Other Countries

John C. Ausland, Norway; Janine and Gorden Carter, Brittany; Paddy
Devlin, Ireland; E. Grasser, Fraternelle, Brigade d'Infanterie; André Heinz,
Caen, Normandy, France; Danielle Clement Heinz, 2nd Demi-Brigade, 1st
French Army; J.P.. van't Hoff, Ymuiden, Holland; the Polish Air Force
Association; Otto Sulek, RAF, Czechoslovakia.

Bren Gun

1 D-Day to the Bulge

6 JUNE 1944–1 JANUARY 1945

'Reportin' for duty, Company D,
  I got hit in Normandy;
Although I'm not entirely healed,
  I've heard the quota isn't filled.
Bodies needed to finish the Hun,
  While we've got him on the run.
First the Roer and Rhine river too,
  Many more battles 'fore we're through.'

Sgt Robert J. Slaughter
116th Infantry Regt, 29th Div.
January 1945

New Year's Day 1945 was not a day for rest or rejoicing on the embattled continent of Europe. Hard winter gripped the land, from the Channel coast to the distant Urals, a chill enemy reinforced by the heavy hand of war. Only the thought of victory warmed the half-frozen soldiers huddled in their tanks and fox holes as the New Year dawned.

This is the story of the last five months of the Second World War in Western Europe, from New Year's Day to VE Day, 8 May 1945. This is not an official history but the story of that time told as far as possible in the words of the people who lived through it – soldier and civilian, 'Aryan' and Jew, prisoner-of-war or concentration camp inmate – men and women and those who were little more than children when the war entered their lives.

On 1 January 1945 the war was entering its final year, but six months after the Allied invasion of Normandy the rapid advance through France, Belgium and Holland to the western frontier of Germany had run out of steam. The Allied advance from the Seine had not been made without setbacks. There had been a defeat at Arnhem in September, bitter fighting in the Hurtgen Forest in October and November, the Wehrmacht had counter-attacked through the Ardennes in December, pushing the American 1st Army back for fifty miles, and the Russian winter offensive was still weeks away. Thus there was no immediate prospect of an end to the European war. That it would end in Allied victory was certain and that it would end in 1945 was equally sure, but the question was exactly when and how. The German armies were fighting well along the German frontier, desperation giving an extra edge to their battle-honed skills and natural tenacity. On both fronts, east and west, they had scope to regroup and prepare themselves for spring.

On the other hand, the military and political situation within Germany was critical. That much was obvious, even to those inside the close circle of cronies surrounding the Führer of the German Reich, Adolf Hitler. William Shirer has described this entourage as 'a grotesque assortment of misfits'; they now clung to the Führer from a mixture of hope and fear. Resistance to the Führer was in any case hopeless. The plot against Hitler's life in July 1944 had been a failure, with the participants rapidly shot or hanged, and the Nazi leaders were now committed to sharing the Führer's fate. The German people were rather more hopeful, for their faith in the Führer was as yet undented, as Ham Coleman, then a New Zealand POW in Germany, remembers clearly: 'I was a prisoner-of-war for three and a half years, the last eighteen months in Germany. We have all been told of the terrible effects of Hitler's madness and of the millions of lives that were lost or damaged as the result of it; but the Germans were, to my mind, very honest, patient and hard working, and their respect for the call of duty is unequalled by any other race.

'This last characteristic probably contributed to their ultimate downfall. They were so intent on carrying out orders that they could not see the mess they were being led into. As far as Hitler was concerned, I never heard a bad word said against him, though Goering, Himmler, Goebbels and the others were often maligned.

'Military reversals and defeats were blamed on the German High Command, the OKW, but it was never Hitler's fault in the minds of his subjects. Hitler was respected as someone above and beyond the common people, his power like that of a god. He could do no wrong. He gave them visions of Germany as the home of the great Master Race which yet would rule the world, and they believed him. The German Army had not yet given in; they were not a rabble and those units that had arms and ammunition fought on. Perhaps they believed that their Führer would save them.'

Even at this late stage in the war, the people of Germany were spared many of the measures taken by the other nations caught up in this six-year struggle. Food, though rationed, was adequate. Children went to school and on holiday, though boys were recruited at age thirteen into the Hitler

Youth. Women stayed at home and enjoyed the help of domestic servants, for there was enough slave or forced labour available in Germany to man the factories. On the surface there were still reasons for optimism as the New Year arrived.

Over the New Year the leaders of Nazi Germany gathered to review the progress of the war and hear a situation report from the Chief-of-Staff of the Wehrmacht, General Heinz Guderian. Guderian knew that the war was lost and in the winter of 1944–45 his only aim was to shore up the Eastern Front while the leaders of Nazi Germany negotiated a surrender with the Western Allies. These now stood in strength along the West Wall or 'Siegfried Line' as the Allies called it, the penultimate bastion of the Reich, a fortification system running all the way from the Lower Rhine south to the frontier of Switzerland, an interlinked system of minefields and pillboxes, strongly held and seemingly impregnable (see map on page 29).

German military strength though was now in terminal decline. The Wehrmacht was fighting on three fronts – in Russia, Western Europe and Italy – and there was simply not enough men, equipment or munitions to go round. In December 1944, Field Marshal Von Rundstedt, commanding the German forces in the West, could muster about forty-eight infantry divisions, fifteen panzer (tank) divisions and several independent panzer brigades, but these were tired formations, rarely up to strength or properly equipped. Rundstedt's own estimate was that his strength was only half that of the Western armies poised on the West Wall.

Air power was now the decisive factor in war and in the air the German position was even worse. The only German Tactical Air Force – Luftflotte 3 – could muster about six hundred aircraft, many of them obsolete. The three Allied Tactical Air Forces – the British 2nd Tactical Air Force (2nd TAF) and the IX and XIX US Tactical Air Commands – could put up nearly eight thousand aircraft and to this could be added thousands of transport aircraft and the heavy bombers of the 8th US Air Force and RAF Bomber Command. The Luftwaffe had about 4,500 aircraft but the bulk of the fighter arm was devoted to defending the Reich against Allied bombers. The new German jets were just coming into service, but there would never be enough to make a difference. It would all depend on the ground fighting and, knowing that, the German armies dug in for battle.

The Overlord operation of 6 June 1944 had been an outstanding, if qualified, success. The Allied armies had got ashore without great loss and there was no real likelihood that they could be dislodged. Then came delay, and with delay, dissension.

Delays in exploiting the D-Day successes had been expected, for few battles ever go exactly as planned. It took time to build up supplies and reserves within the beach-head and some D-Day objectives, like the city of Caen, had not been taken, as planned, on the first day. Caen was not actually taken for another seven weeks and by the middle of July the Americans felt, and continued to feel, that the British were not putting enough real effort into gaining ground and pushing out of the beach-head.

When the efforts of Montgomery's 21st Army Group of British and Canadian forces were compared with the advances to the Loire and Brittany made by General Omar Bradley's 12th US Army Group, and in particular by the 3rd US Army under General George Patton, there seemed to be some substance to this charge. General Sir Bernard Montgomery, the Allied Land Force Commander at this time, countered with the claim that he had pulled the German panzer forces onto the 21st Army Group front and so freed the Americans for 'Operation Cobra', the breakout from the beach-head through St Lô, on 25 July 1944.

Jack Capell was then serving with the 8th Infantry Regiment of the 4th US Division. 'Memories of the hedgerow fighting after D-Day include "Bedcheck Charlie" or "Washing Machine Charlie", a German light aircraft that came over the lines almost every night, dropping flares and anti-personnel bombs, and the Germans stretching wires across the roads at neck level to decapitate drivers. Eventually our jeep carried angle-irons welded to the front fender to cut them.

'The St Lô breakout – Cobra – began on 24 July when three thousand US bombers and dive-bombers started to blast a path through the German defences. Visibility was bad that day and some bombs fell on our positions. My regiment, the 8th Infantry Regiment of the 4th Division, was spearhead for the attack, and next day when 2,700 bombers came over, we caught most of it.

'First there was this tremendous, gigantic, earth-shaking sound, the roar of thousands of engines. The dive-bombers hit the German defences to our front, right on time and right on target, and I thought we were doing pretty well. Then came the B17s...

'Their first bombs fell right on the German line. I was watching from my foxhole and I got out for a better view. The bombs were going off like machine-gun fire. Then a bomb fell in my field, knocking me off my feet, and I got back into my hole fast.

'From then on it was indescribable. The whole earth was shaking, the air was full of dust and smoke and bits of steel and lumps of earth, and the roar of engines overhead went on and on.

'We had about 600 casualties in the 4th Division from that "short bombing", with over 100 killed, including Lt-General McNair. The ground ahead looked like the surface of the moon, but our B Company attacked anyway and we all followed.'

British forces also suffered from Allied air attacks. Patrick Hennessey was a tank commander in the 13th/18th Hussars: 'Now we found ourselves in the *bocage*. A maze of sunken roads were lined with high, tough hedgerows, which made very difficult and dangerous going for tanks. Visibility was poor and there was little room for manoeuvre. The opposition had increased; we were now facing a variety of first-class panzer units, some of them Waffen SS who were experienced and persistent in their resistance. Nevertheless, we were gaining ground, although we had to fight hard for every advance we made. Frequently we came across fields of standing corn wherein we found concealed enemy infantry, some of whom could prove very dangerous, while others were only too anxious to stand up and surrender at our approach. We became used to the sight of dead cows and the sickly stench of their bloated and rotting carcasses. This smell became an enduring memory of Normandy in the summer of 1944.

'Our advance would have been much more difficult, if not impossible, had we not had air supremacy. Weather permitting, the Royal Air Force provided almost constant air cover, so that any movement by the enemy in daylight attracted immediate response from RAF fighter bombers. They did a magnificent job on our behalf, and on one occasion we were given the chance to see how it felt from the Germans' point of view. We were in a clearing near a wood when we saw a section of two aircraft circling in the sky. Suddenly, to our horror, they dived on us with cannon and machine-guns firing. I hastily threw out the yellow smoke aircraft recognition canisters and frantically waved the large yellow silk recognition panels we had for just such an event.

'Fortunately, they must have seen our signals, because they stopped their attack and flew away. No damage had been done but we thought ourselves lucky that they were not using their tank-busting rockets; they were Spitfires, not Typhoons. Nevertheless, it had been a very near thing. No doubt it is difficult to tell one type of tank from another from the cockpit of a fast-moving aircraft, but we could not help wishing that the airmen would become a little more expert at it.'

Harper Coleman, of the 4th Infantry Division also remembers this post D-Day period: 'After we had been in Cherbourg for about six or seven days we went by truck to the hedgerow country west of Carentan, where we took over the positions of the 83rd Division. The 4th Division was to lead out to the west of St Lô.

'It was hedgerow and swamp country and we were often facing SS troops, who fought for every inch of ground. The first day we made only 400 yards and during the next week only about four miles. Everything was destroyed, buildings, bridges, equipment of all kinds. The roads looked like a junkyard, dead animals in all the fields. Some of the civilians were not able to escape and on occasions we would find dead people in the buildings.

'The artillery barrages from both sides were some of the heaviest of any time that I remember. There were the German rockets called "Screaming Meemies", the 88 mm guns, German tanks and others. This went on for about three weeks, and during this time we lost quite a few people. How anyone made it I still do not know. I saw one of the battalion commanders killed by a sniper as was one of my squad. As I was on the machine-gun, a bullet came across my shoulder and cut the top of my hand, nothing serious but too close. During this period we came across a column of German troops who had been caught in an artillery barrage and they were on the road when our tanks went through. There was no time to move any of them out of the way. This was not a pretty sight but I don't think we gave it much thought at the time.

'I also saw one of our lieutenants shoot a wounded German in the head as he was begging for water. The lieutenant just seemed to have lost all control. He just said, "Water, hell!" Nothing we could do about it, just keep moving on.

'After the Cobra breakthrough things went faster. There would be skirmishes every day, mostly in the late afternoon, then during the night the Germans would pull out. We had many vehicles close by and everyone would pile onto trucks until we caught up with them the next day or whenever. This continued until we reached the outskirts of Paris on either 23 or 24 August. In Paris we did not do much other than wait for the French Armoured Division which was with us to clear the city. As I recall, we lay around in a large park somewhere near the centre. This lasted only till 25 August then we were on the move again. This chase-and-catch went on until early September, when we reached the Siegfried Line. There we stopped for some time for supplies to catch up with us.'

The bulk of the German armour was indeed opposing the British and Canadians, so the Americans swept south from St Lô to cut around the German rear and trap the German VII Army in the slaughterhouse of the Falaise Pocket. There was then heated debate among the generals, for the Americans felt that the British and Canadian advance on Falaise from the north had been too slow and allowed the Germans to escape across the Seine, though most of their equipment was lost or left behind.

Patrick Hennessey again: 'The city of Caen had now fallen, but not without some hard fighting despite the chastisement the defenders had suffered at the hands of the Allied bombers. We pressed on south, still against fierce opposition. The main obstacle was Mount Pinçon, a feature some 1,200 feet high which dominated the surrounding area, the possession of which gave the Germans a great tactical advantage. The capture of Mount Pinçon became a priority. The task fell to the 5th Battalion of the

6

Wiltshire Regiment, with A Squadron, 13th/18th Hussars in support.

'On 6 August we had fought our way to the foot of the hill against very heavy machine-gun and mortar fire, which was taking a steady toll on the infantry. The day was hot and sultry and the air was laden with dust and the stench of dead cattle. Every movement of a vehicle stirred up more dust, which drew fire from the enemy and curses from the infantry, who lay in shallow slit trenches, waiting for word to move across the river and up the steep scarp. The pioneers were working to clear the mines on the bridge under cover of a smoke screen and in the face of considerable enemy fire. As soon as the bridge was clear, our artillery put down a barrage on the far bank and we went across the bridge in tanks with the infantry following. They were half way across when the enemy came to life with machine-guns and mortars, catching them in the open. Within minutes, the two leading companies were practically wiped out, and the commanding officer of the 5th Wilts, who had personally come forward to rally them, was killed. The attack petered out.

'We were now on the far side of the river, at the base of the mountain, which seemed impossibly steep and covered with bushes and scrub. We milled around, dealing with pockets of enemy infantry in the undergrowth when, about 6 p.m., we spotted a track which looked as if it might lead to the top. I reported this over the radio and was told to press on up it as fast as possible. Two troops of tanks were sent with us under the command of Captain Noel Denny. Away we went, crashing up the steep narrow path. There was a bank on our right and a steep drop on the left. Passing a quarry, Sergeant Rattle's tank slithered in and almost overturned, but we kept going. It was a good cavalry action, a direct hell-for-leather dash up the path until we reached the top to the surprise and alarm of the few Germans we found there. We quickly sorted ourselves into a position of all-round defence, and we felt pretty lonely as there were only seven or eight tanks, with no infantry support as yet.

'A thick mist had come down, and although we could not see very far, we could hear Germans nearby. Eventually the infantry arrived to consolidate the position, and we were very pleased to see them. They had been in action all day and were absolutely exhausted by the time they reached the top of the mountain.'

The British approach to war was always bound to clash with that of the hard-driving, go-getting Americans. The United States had men to spare and wanted a swift decision in Europe in order to turn their might against Japan. The British and Canadians simply did not have the men to throw away, but the situation was aggravated by the manner and demands of the British Commander, General Montgomery. Montgomery had been appointed Land Force Commander for the D-Day operation and commander of all the Allied armies in France until the Supreme Commander, US General Dwight D. Eisenhower, the Commander at SHAEF (Supreme Headquarters, Allied Expeditionary Force), chose to take over command of the armies in the field.

When that time came, on 1 September 1944, Montgomery was very reluctant to give up his appointment. Apart from the reduction in authority, Montgomery and his British Commanders-in-Chief felt that no man could be both overall commander of every element in the Allied Expeditionary Force, land, sea and air, and still exercise control over seven separate armies. The British continued to push for the appointment of a Land Force Commander and for Sir Bernard Montgomery – appointed a Field Marshal in September 1944 – to fill that position.

There was never any real likelihood that the Americans would accede to this demand. By September 1944 the Americans already had forty-eight divisions in France, more than all the other Western Allies combined, and many American politicians and generals had already developed a strong dislike of the vain and argumentative – though successful – Field Marshal Montgomery. One of the few who did tolerate him was Eisenhower, who had also to endure carping from the 3rd US Army Commander, General George Patton. Patton and Montgomery were, said Eisenhower wryly, 'my two prima donnas'.

On 1 September, the British 2nd Army crossed the river Somme and began to race north into Belgium and Holland, reaching Brussels on 3 September, and the vital port of Antwerp on 12 September, after an advance of over 300 miles. Meanwhile the Canadian 1st Army was sweeping along the Channel coast and clearing ports like Dieppe (where the Canadians had experienced a bloody reversal in August 1942), but failing to take Dunkirk, which held out until the end of the war.

Pat Hennessey describes life in his tank regiment: 'A typical day would start early in the morning. About 6 a.m. the crew member who was still on guard duty would light the cooker to make tea, and then go round waking the rest of the crew. We would struggle out of our blankets, wash and shave (every day!), tackle a breakfast of tinned bacon, baked beans and perhaps an egg from Henrietta (the troop hen), and pack the tank ready for movement. Radios were switched on and tested to make sure they were all 'on net' and we could communicate, gun sights and ammunition were checked. The drivers and co-drivers would start and run the engines. Meanwhile, the crew commanders were summoned to a briefing by the troop leader who had already attended a Squadron Commander's Order Group. Armed with map boards, talc and chinagraph pencils, the three of us NCOs would gather round the young officer, who would tell us of our action during the day to come.

'On one particular day we were told we were to support infantry whose task it was to take a ridge of high ground surmounted by a dense wood which was believed to be held in strength by the enemy. The division of armour was to be one troop of tanks to one company of infantry (which was generous), and we were given our point of contact and time of meeting up with our infantry.

'The Start Line was some four miles distant and we were told our order of march. Each tank had a code letter. For instance, we were 4 Troop, A Squadron, so the troop leader would be referred to by the squadron's code for the day, say "Mike", and his troop number; therefore he would be "Mike 4". The troop sergeant would be "Mike 4 Able", the troop corporal (me), would be "Mike 4 Baker" and the 17 pdr gun Firefly tank would be "Mike 4 Charlie". On this day the order of march was to be 4 Baker, 4 Able, 4 Charlie, which meant that I was to lead, followed by Lieutenant Garlick, then Sergeant Rattle with the 17 pdr bringing up the rear of the troop. Synchronize watches, any questions, move off in twenty minutes.

'Back to our tanks to brief the crews, last-minute stowage and load guns with HE (high explosive) ammunition in anticipation of soft-skinned targets and move off to meet our infantry on time at the Start Line. The attack went in with the infantry leading across fairly open ground. The ridge with the trees could be seen clearly some 800 yards ahead, and to start with all was quiet. Suddenly, machine-guns opened up from the left and our infantry went to ground. We were called forward, but we could not exactly locate from where the enemy fire was coming. The platoon commander came over to my tank and said he would send a section forward to draw more fire and then indicate the machine-gun post by firing tracer at it from his Bren-gun. This ruse worked and we could now see our target to which we delivered several rounds of 75 mm HE and a liberal dose of machine-gun fire from the Brownings.

'The enemy fire stopped, our infantry went in with the bayonet and the advance continued. A volume of fire was coming from the wood itself. Our infantry worked their way to about 100 yards from the crest and were faced with an uphill assault. We pulled back to a fold in the ground which provided us with a degree of cover in that we could face the wood from a hull-down position at a range of 200 yards.

'We loaded HE, set to air burst, and began a concentrated fire from the 75 mm guns into the treetops. This setting ensured that the shells would explode on contact with the trees and rain shrapnel down on those below. After several minutes of this the infantry went forward. We followed with Brownings firing and the wood was taken. Our tree burst fire had certainly reduced the enemy concentration and had enabled our infantry to make the assault. There were heavy casualties on both sides but we were lucky that no anti-tank weapons had been encountered. We followed the infantry to consolidate the objective, but were not keen to stay around too long because we expected some retaliation and sure enough, within 10 minutes, shells and mortar bombs began to fall in the wood. By then we were through and beyond, heading for our new assembly area, while the infantry dug in to consolidate on the forward slope, well beyond the wood.'

Sergeant Ted Smith, MM, of the 2nd Armoured Battalion of the Grenadier Guards, part of the Guards Armoured Division, remembers the whirlwind advance to Brussels: 'I was in the Recce Troop, with fast Honey tanks, so we led the way from Tournai to Brussels. The German Army still used horse transport and the road was littered with dead horses. Nor was there much resistance. I remember telling my gunner to put a burst into some trees – just in case. His gun jammed after one round, but about forty Wehrmacht soldiers came out of the wood with their hands up.

'Anyway – Brussels ... We drove in during the afternoon and I have never heard cheering like it. The citizens were ten-deep along the road, throwing fruit and offering wine, clambering onto the tank to kiss us. It was all very different from Dunkirk in 1940. Then our Sergeant-Major, CSM Rousell, 2nd Battalion, Grenadier Guards, actually fell us in on the beach and *marched* us in column-of-threes, rifles at the slope, lef' right, lef' right, down to the Dunkirk docks, but that was the Grenadier Guards for you.'

The American armies were also on the move at this time. Lt-General Omar Bradley's 12th US Army Group – Hodges' 1st Army and Patton's 3rd Army, later to include Simpson's 9th Army – freed Brittany, entered Paris on 25 August and swept across France to the Meuse with the 1st Army en route for Aachen just inside Germany, and the 3rd Army headed towards Metz, Nancy and the Saar. Meanwhile, the 6th US Army Group – a Franco-American force under Lt-General Jacob Devers, consisting of the French 1st Army under General Lattre de Tassigny and the 7th US Army commanded by General Patch – having landed in the South of France on 15 August, advanced rapidly north towards Alsace and the Vosges, which they reached by late September. Then their advance slowed. For some weeks in July and August, though, the Allied armies in the west were advancing rapidly on every front and carrying all before them.

This was an exhilarating time, as Pat Hennessey remembers: 'We had now swung to the east and were heading for the river Seine, which we crossed on 27 August, at Vernon, with less opposition than we had expected.

'Suddenly the tempo of our life changed. We found that the enemy was in full retreat, more anxious to get away from us than to stand and make a fight of it. We set off up the main axis of our advance at high speed, travelling in column and taking it in turns, squadron by squadron, to take the lead. Day after day we would motor on for miles, only occasionally meeting any resistance. Then the leading troop, and a company of our infantry battalion, would deal with it, sometimes with the help of the RAF if enemy armour was involved; then on we would go again.

'The sights we saw were stupendous. Mile after mile, the road was littered with the impedimenta of a retreating German army. Tanks, lorries, staff cars and guns were lying in the ditches, all abandoned. There were the dead bodies of men and horses and pitiful groups of wounded German soldiers cowering at the roadside. I was surprised to see the large amount of horse-drawn transport which had been used by the Germans and had always thought that their army was as mechanized as our own.

'Dreadful as the sights were, this particular period of relentless pursuit of a stricken army was the most exciting and exhilarating time I have ever experienced. I could understand the fierce pride and elation which must have been felt by the young German soldiers in 1940 as they swept across Europe behind the retreating Allies. Now it was our turn, and we pressed on, hard and fast. There were some who tried to make a stand to fight it out, but they were quickly overcome and taken prisoner. They were at a great disadvantage as their organization had completely broken down. They had no re-supply of fuel, ammunition or rations, and they were at the mercy of the RAF from the air and us on the ground.

'By now we were going so far and so fast that we were in danger of outdistancing our own supply columns, so from time to time we had to stop to let them catch up with us. It has truly been said that there is no greater boost to morale than success in battle. We had the smell of success in our nostrils, but we were never free from danger. Before the Germans pulled out from a farm or village, they would, if they had time, leave booby traps and mines. We could never be sure that a village was completely clear, even though it might seem deserted when we arrived, because frequently snipers would be left behind to delay us.

'Now and again we would hear the distinctive sound of a Schmeisser sub-machine-gun. Our own Bren-guns and Brownings would fire with the sound of "rat-tat-tat", but the noise of a Schmeisser was more like a piece of calico being torn. The sniper's mission was usually suicidal, but they managed to inflict a number of casualties and presented us with a considerable problem.'

Quintain Rowlands was a first lieutenant in the 1st Battalion, 413th Infantry Regiment of the 104th US Division – the Timberwolves. 'In October 1944 we were under command of the 1st Canadian Army, clearing the Germans from the Scheldt around Breda, and in November we took part in the Maark river crossing. I remember a German prisoner here. His leg was so badly broken, his foot was tucked up by his armpit, and he was

11

in mortal pain. I gave him all I had to kill the pain – some aspirin tablets – but he begged me to shoot him, it was so bad. Then, thank God, some medics came by, filled him up with morphine and straightened out his leg. He even thanked me for not shooting him as they carried him away.'

The Allied armies were forging ahead on all fronts from mid-July to the end of August. Then in early September came a pause. This was partly caused by a stiffening of resistance as Hitler's retreating armies reached the frontiers of the Reich, but there were two more serious factors: a shortage of fuel and a lack of ports. Modern armies need fuel for their tanks, for their armoured cars and for the soft-skinned transport carrying supplies of food, ammunition and reinforcements to the divisions at the front. The fighting divisions had been too successful, advanced more rapidly than anticipated, and the logistical backup could not cope. Furthermore, by the end of August (nearly three months after D-Day), the Allied armies had still to rely on the prefabricated Mulberry harbour at Arromanches, the port of Cherbourg and some of the smaller Channel ports. Most of these were now more than 300 miles behind the front, and their facilities were inadequate to supply armies which now totalled almost fifty divisions and needed at least 700 tons of supplies *per division per day*, if they were to maintain the impetus of their advance. The Allies had plenty of supplies; landing them and bringing them forward was the problem.

The French railway system had been shattered by Allied air operations prior to D-Day. The main roads were being rapidly worn out by the weight of tanks and traffic. Many bridges had been destroyed. The fighting troops were supplied on an *ad hoc* basis by air transport and the 'Red Ball Express' – an endless convoy of trucks and lorries which ferried supplies to keep the armies moving. It was not enough. To save fuel, some divisions were held back and those at the front had to leave their transport behind. There was soon great competition, and not a little sharp practice, especially among the various American commanders, as each attempted to find fuel and keep his regiments advancing.

Ralph Teeters of the 4th Infantry Division remembers one effect of this fuel shortage: 'We had been living on K and C rations for what seemed like months, because our field kitchens had been left behind in Paris, to save on fuel, I guess. Anyway, when they finally caught up with us, the company commander urged the mess sergeant to cook us a hot meal ... and the cooks had nothing, *but nothing*, to cook.

'They had given away everything in exchange for a good time in Paris – the booze and the women. I can't say I blamed them but the company commander *chewed* on the mess sergeant for a good fifteen minutes; you could hear him all over the company area. When those cooks finally found something to feed to us they could hardly look us in the eye.'

Shortage of fuel was also a problem for the Germans. The vital oil fields in the east had either been destroyed by bombing or captured by the Russians. The synthetic fuel plants in Germany were not large enough to cope with the demand, and anyway were under constant attack from the air. The erosion of German transport facilities meant that even when fuel was available it could not be shipped to airfields or the front.

The key to a continued Allied advance in the west was the port of Antwerp. However, though Antwerp had been captured on 12 September with the port facilities intact, it lay forty miles up the Scheldt from the sea, and the banks and islands of the Scheldt estuary were still in the hands of the German XV Army.

James Neville was fighting along the Scheldt in 1944. 'I was with the 2nd Anti-Tank Regiment, Royal Canadian Artillery, supporting the 2nd Canadian Infantry Division. Our purpose was to engage enemy tanks. After leaving Antwerp on 2 October 1944, we had the task of clearing the enemy from the Scheldt estuary, which was vital to the reopening of the port of Antwerp. This took a long, miserable, wet and murderous time, before North and South Beveland, plus Walcheren Island, were secured in November, at a very heavy cost in lives.

'After rest and refit, we were sent to positions in the Reichwald Forest, close to a town called Grosbeek. We were dug-in on the west side of a clearing with Germans to the east. Both sides attacked with mortars, machine-gun and artillery fire and there were nightly skirmishes by the infantry.

'We remained there from mid-November until New Year's Eve 1944, when we moved to billets in Nijmegen. There we had much-needed baths, clean clothes and our Christmas and New Year dinner served together on 1 January. We shared our rations with the Dutch as food was desperately scarce for the civilian population.'

The Allied supply problems in the autumn of 1944 would have been greatly eased by the swift clearance of the Scheldt estuary, but this was not captured and swept of mines until late November, after British commandos had captured the island of Walcheren and Canadian troops had cleared the enemy from both banks. This long delay brought several simmering problems to the boil at SHAEF.

The overall strategy for the western advance into Germany had been laid down before the D-Day landings. Having crossed the German frontier, the next objective was to overrun the two industrial regions of the Ruhr and Saar. This would destroy much of the German capacity to wage war before the final Allied push east to 'the ultimate prize', Berlin. These advances would be co-ordinated with Soviet progress across Germany from the east.

Without the heavy industries of the Ruhr and Saar to supply their armies with weaponry, the Germans would have to surrender. To capture – or at least to encircle – these areas, Eisenhower favoured a 'Broad Front' approach in several phases, first bringing all his armies up to the German frontier, then crossing the West Wall to reach the Rhine, then crossing that river to overrun the Ruhr. By September 1944 this strategy was being questioned, mainly because of problems of supply. The chronic fuel shortage made it impossible for all the Western armies to keep advancing, and Eisenhower was soon put under pressure to amend his 'Broad Front' strategy. Most of the pressure came from Field Marshal Montgomery.

Without the facilities of Antwerp there were not sufficient supplies to maintain the advance of all four northern armies – one British, one Canadian, two American – towards the Rhine, though Devers' Franco-American Armies in the 6th Army Group were being adequately supplied through Marseilles.

Wishing to maintain the impetus of the advance on Germany while the Scheldt was being cleared, Field Marshal Montgomery's first proposal was that Eisenhower should halt the advance of Patton's army along the Moselle to the Saar and divert Patton's fuel to Montgomery's 21st Army Group in the north. This proposal having been swiftly rejected, Montgomery then suggested a 'narrow thrust' attack into Germany; a swift advance through Holland and across the Rhine, spearheaded by a drop by three parachute and glider divisions of the Allied Airborne Army, followed by a rapid advance by tanks and 'heavy' infantry of XXX Corps of the British 2nd Army. This surprising proposal from the usually cautious Montgomery met with Eisenhower's approval and led to the 'Market Garden' operation in September 1944, and the destruction of the British 1st Airborne Division at Arnhem.

'Market Garden' was not a total failure. The American 82nd and 101st Airborne took their bridges as planned, and this gave the British and Canadian Armies a foothold at Nijmegen from which they would later sweep south and clear the west bank of the Rhine. There was now, however, a further snag, the onset of winter, which came early in 1944. With heavy rain turning the fields into quagmires, low cloud hampering air operations and ever more stubborn German resistance, the Allied advance virtually stopped.

To give Montgomery due credit, his Market Garden plan was founded on the notion that the German armies were in full retreat and could be kept that way, hustled up to and beyond the German frontier, in no position to offer serious resistance. This was wishful thinking. The German capacity to regroup and fight back was not fully appreciated at SHAEF in September, and in October, November and December, the German Army in the west put up a fierce fight all along the Siegfried Line, most notably in the

Hurtgen Forest, a bitter resistance culminating in the Ardennes offensive of December 1944 – the Battle of the Bulge.

Whatever the opinions held at SHAEF, the troops in the line were well aware that the Germans were still willing to fight. Horace Covington remembers a small but significant German action during the winter of 1944–45: 'I was a "Don-R" – a despatch rider in 75 Company, RASC, 52nd Division, based near Maastricht, close to the German border.

'Volunteers were required for an infantry company to go "up the line" for forty-eight hours to allow the resident infantry, who had been there for some time in appalling conditions, to get a much-needed bath and rest. I volunteered with Nobby Clarke, a Scot. We were taken to a village called Hatterath near Geilinkirchen, and then guided through minefields to our position. We went in during darkness so the Germans would not know that the infantry had been replaced by Service Corps personnel.

'Nobby and I were allocated a two-man trench with an old door over the top, straw in the bottom and a Bren-gun to the front. When daylight came we saw an unpleasant sight: dozens of German and British corpses lying around. A number had been booby-trapped with grenades, as one or two of our company found out.

'The German positions were half a mile away and we were not to fire except in self-defence. Night came, and I was doing my two-hour guard while Nobby was trying to sleep when I heard footsteps approaching. I kicked Nobby awake and we listened and watched. All went quiet after some minutes. We kept still and saw shapes going away from us.

'Come daylight we were called to Company HQ and asked if we had heard anything during the night. It turned out that a German patrol had come through our lines, penetrated a Royal Artillery defence behind us and taken an entire Royal Artillery gun crew prisoner. The "forty-eight hours" developed into ten days and nights before we went back to our company, happy that we had given the infantry a helping hand.'

Although the airborne fight at Arnhem was a great feat of arms and the Nijmegen bridgehead useful, Market Garden was a strategic error. In spite of Monty's understandable desire to keep the Hun on the run, the first task of 21st Army Group after taking Antwerp should have been to clear the Scheldt estuary and so unblock the port. Subsequent attempts by the Germans to destroy the port facilities with V-1 and V-2 rockets met with little success, but it was not until 28 November – nearly three months after the city fell – that the first ships started to unload supplies at Antwerp docks. Meanwhile, there were further disputes at SHAEF.

The failure of 'Market Garden' and the destruction of the British 1st Airborne Division did not deter Montgomery from pressing his other proposal: that General Eisenhower should appoint a Field Commander to control all the Allied armies moving towards Germany – American, British, Canadian and French. Montgomery even stated that so essential was this appointment, that if Eisenhower wished to appoint General Omar Bradley to this vital post, he would happily serve under him. This last suggestion did nothing to stem the rising tide of irritation at what was felt to be an excessive amount of British influence at SHAEF, especially in view of the ever-increasing disparity of numbers in the field. Although Monty had commanded Bradley's troops in Normandy – with a very loose rein – and was to command General Simpson's 9th US Army for some time and without rancour, there was no serious possibility of the American armies being placed under a British general. Field Marshal Montgomery, however, was not a man to abandon an idea without a fight and he continued to press the point as autumn drew on into winter.

Flushed with their success at Arnhem, and relieved by the slackening of Allied pressure, the Germans began to re-form and muster more divisions for the coming battles. The last manpower resources of the Reich were now called forward for the armies. Heinrich Himmler, head of the SS and Commander of the Reserve Army, raised no less than forty Volksgrenadier Divisions from the Hitler Youth and Nazi Party sources. Men over the age of fifty were called up, the ranks of rear-echelon troops were culled, and naval ratings and Luftwaffe ground personnel were retrained as infantry reinforcements. The most significant contribution was 20,000 paratroops from the Luftwaffe, which eventually became the nucleus of the elite hard-fighting German 1st Parachute Army under General Kurt Student.

German resolve to continue the war was stiffened by two political blunders in Washington. The first was a demand for an unconditional surrender by the Axis Powers, without debate or guarantees for the German people or the Nazi leaders. The second, more serious blunder was the Morgenthau Plan which, recalling that Germany had plunged Europe into war three times in seventy years, proposed that Germany's capacity ever to wage war again should be finally eliminated. Factories would be dismantled, coal mines destroyed, industrial infrastructure removed, and Germany 'turned into a country primarily agricultural and pastoral'. This plan was put forward by Henry Morgenthau, the US Treasury Secretary, and together with the demand for unconditional surrender was endorsed by the Allied leaders at the Quebec Conference in September 1944.

Such proposals were a propaganda gift to Joseph Goebbels, the Reich's Minister of Information. Goebbels told the German people of these schemes without adding that both proposals had met with strong opposition in Allied military and political circles. The effect was to stiffen German resistance both along the battlefront and within the Reich.

On 2 October 1944 the Americans surged forward again with a major assault into Germany by Lt-General Courtney Hodges' 1st Army, which swept across the Siegfried Line (or 'West Wall') to Aachen. The Americans surrounded Aachen on 14 October and on 21 October the German garrison capitulated. The first German city had fallen to the Allied armies, but this success was overshadowed by a terrible battle developing in the woods to the south.

During October and November the American 1st Army was engaged in attempting to clear the Hurtgen Forest, a thick woodland area south east of Aachen, and so reach their next objective, the dams controlling the waters of the river Roer. These dams had to be taken or destroyed before the Americans could advance across the Roer towards Cologne and the Rhine.

The battle for the Hurtgen Forest was one of the fiercest and most testing struggles the Americans had to face in northwest Europe. While enduring terrible weather, the US infantry in the Hurtgen met well-prepared defences, minefields and pillboxes, machine-gun nests and intense mortar and shell fire. It took the Americans six weeks of bitter fighting and 31,000 casualties to clear the Hurtgen before they broke through and reached the Roer on 3 December 1944.

Ralph Teeters of Portland, Oregon, fought in the Hurtgen Forest with the 22nd Regiment, 4th US Infantry Division. 'The 4th Division had landed on Utah Beach on D-Day and the 22nd Infantry was involved in the terrible hedgerow fighting in the Cotentin throughout June and July. When we were brought up as replacements, G Company was down to about eighty men (200 is the number of fighting men in an infantry company, so their casualties were about 50 percent). A weary sergeant asked if any of us could set up a 60 mm mortar and I said I'd try.

'I was put in the weapons platoon and I learned fast. It wasn't long before we could set up a 60 mm mortar in less than 30 seconds and I spent the rest of the war in the weapons platoon.

'In 1944 an American infantry battalion was made up of three rifle companies and a heavy weapons company; the heavy weapons company fired medium or heavy machine-guns and 81 mm mortars. There was also a weapons platoon in each of the rifle companies but often we were detached as a squad under the direction of a platoon leader. An infantry company was organized in three rifle platoons and a weapons platoon, plus a Company HQ.

'The weapons platoon consisted of three 60 mm mortars with a squad leader, a sergeant, a gunner, assistant gunner and four, five or six GIs who packed ammunition. There were also two light machine-guns in a machine-gun section under the direction of the company commander.

'I was nineteen; the only person older than me was Carl Delafield, and like me he never got hit. The brunt of the fighting was done by the infantry squads up ahead, so it was an advantage to be 100 or 200 yards behind. We were also being trained to ride tanks. The 22nd Regiment was designated to ride tanks out of St Lô in what is called the "St Lô Breakthrough", and was later given a Unit Citation, describing the Armoured Infantry Combat Command which "successfully effected a breakthrough of the German line of resistance west of St Lô".

'This is all a prelude to the last five months of the war, but I think it's important. After St Lô we headed for Paris. The 4th was the first US division to march through Paris on 25 August 1944. We got a great greeting from a flag-waving, cheering, champagne-drinking, hysterical population, but we went through the city and ended up near Rheims. Then in early October we were involved in the first break of the Siegfried Line.

'Our regimental commander was a man named Lanham. Ernest Hemingway knew 'Buck' Lanham and once described the 22nd Regiment taking some pillboxes on the Siegfried Line with the help of a tank destroyer.

'After the conquest of Aachen we went into a holding position along the Ardennes, somewhere along the Belgian–Luxembourg border. I mention this now because there are three towns that feature in the Battle of the Bulge: Houffaliaze, Bastogne (of 101st Airborne fame) and St Vith. St Vith, near the German border, was a beautiful little town when we first saw it. When we saw it again, as the Bulge was rolled back in December, it looked as though someone had taken a giant plough and just scooped it up; just a few half-walls were standing. Our medium-bombers did that at the height of the Bulge ... but I'm getting ahead of myself a little. After a lull in October, our next action was the Hurtgen Forest.

'According to our Regimental History, our battle in Hurtgen Forest began on 16 November. The Hurtgen battle was complicated by long evacuation routes and *tremendous* casualties. In the 22nd Regiment, our 2nd Battalion once had three commanding officers in one day. The Germans knew our routes and had Hurtgen Forest well mapped. Maybe our mistake was to follow the trails and fire breaks, but a lot of times the casualties going back down the trail from Company HQ were even more severe than on the fighting line. The Germans had guns and mortars zeroed in on everything.

'We faced more heavy and light machine-guns, the usual infantry weapons, but most effective of all, tree bursts from mortar and artillery fire. The Hurtgen was hell – it truly was hell! The first day there our 3rd Platoon was sent forward to take a fire trail 200 yards ahead. All hell broke loose when they got up to make the attack. At the end of the afternoon we were just cowering in our foxholes. We had been assigned as a mortar squad – by this time I was a mortar gunner – to back up the 3rd Platoon, but the platoon leader had no use for our mortars ... we couldn't set them up

18

under the trees because we needed some kind of clearing to fire.

'By the end of that afternoon we were stretcher-bearers, taking out some of the wounded. There were only five members of the 3rd Platoon left and it went in at full strength. We thought, well, now we'll be relieved, maybe someone else will come up, we were so decimated. Instead, a flow of replacements began and didn't end until this was all over for us on 29 November 1944.

'The Germans had a great railroad gun firing on us and that thing clipped branches off the trees. You'd have hunks of shrapnel falling through the trees, lopping off branches as they fell. It was also raining a lot of the time; we were wet, we were dirty, we were isolated. It was almost impossible to get rations and ammunition and I don't think we ever fired our mortars. It was a matter of being pressed into service in other ways, doing outpost duty, being eyes and ears for the outfit and all the time we kept getting these replacements. They'd come in at night and sometimes they wouldn't last one day. That was when I realized that you did learn from some of this, because the older men seemed to survive better than the young ones who were just coming in.

'There were a lot of people my age, but I aged very rapidly then. When we broke out of the Hurtgen Forest, after they sent in planes and armour to our assistance, we went onto this exposed knoll and come under the most withering fire I ever experienced. It was so bad that I could not raise my head. It consisted of machine-gun fire, mortars, 88 mm ... everything. They waited until they got our whole company in formation before they started. Finally we got some tank destroyers or tanks up behind us and started firing into the woods where the fire was coming from. What I remember about that afternoon was not that I expected to be hit, but *when* I was going to be hit and how badly. It didn't seem that anyone could live through that day.

'One of the replacements had joined us a day or two before; we hardly knew his name and he hardly knew who his sergeant was. He got into a shallow shell-hole and called for help. We heard a shot and I believe he inflicted a wound upon himself to try and get back, but the German fire was landing behind us. All we could do was curse him "You goddamn fool! Why don't you take it like the rest of us?"

'We had 2,500 replacements in the 22nd Regiment alone during the Hurtgen fighting, in a regiment that probably only had about 2,500 men in the line at the start. When we went back into reserve in Luxembourg City we slept on beds, in houses, for the first time I could remember since Normandy. All those who had been in Hurtgen developed trench foot, very painful; most of us found it impossible to have even the weight of a blanket on our feet, but after a week or so we went back to the Bulge.'

Harper Coleman was also in the Hurtgen, with the 8th Infantry Regiment of the 4th US Division. 'During this time the weather turned cold and rainy, and there were mines. Some of our people were hurt by these mines and could not get out on their own, so one of our officers convinced some German prisoners that it would be good for their health if they went into the minefield and brought our people out. In the end they did but I have little doubt that they would have been shot if they had refused.'

James Upham of the 78th Infantry remembers evacuating one wounded man in the Hurtgen: 'I came to this foxhole where a man was crying. I asked him where he was hurting but he said he did not know, though he was sitting in his own dried or frozen blood. He was a replacement and had only been up two days. I had to use my bayonet to chip around his body before I could lift him from the hole. Then I heard a medic jeep in the distance and when we lifted him into it he smiled for the first time, and that was a good feeling.'

The stiffening of German resistance had been noticed by the British, as Patrick Hennessey of the 13th/18th Hussars recalls: 'It was clear now that any hopes of a quick finish to the war had been dashed with the failure of Arnhem. The weather was cloudy and becoming much colder. Short 48-hour leave breaks were introduced when a few of us at a time were allowed to go back to Brussels, where we enjoyed egg and chips, ice cream, which we had not seen in England for years, and a haircut and shave from a professional barber. We were also exposed to a degree of hero-worship, which we found to be much to our liking, if a bit embarrassing.

'The fighting was becoming far more difficult with the Germans putting up a much more determined defence, no doubt because we were actually fighting on German soil. We had a number of sharp encounters which cost us dearly, and in one instance we learned a very sombre lesson. It was laid down as standard procedure that when it was necessary to abandon a tank, the turret should be traversed so that the gun was pointing forward, directly over the front of the tank. If this was not done, either the gun mantle or part of the turret would prevent the driver or co-driver from opening his hatch to make his escape. In the Sherman there was an additional escape hatch for the driver on the floor of his compartment, through which he could get out underneath the tank.

'All this was splendid in theory, but in the instance we were obliged to witness, the tank was hit and immediately burst into flames. The turret crew instantly evacuated, leaving the gun pointing to 11 o'clock, directly over the driver's hatch. We could see the driver trying to open the hatch, which was impossible because it was fouled by the gun. The tank became an inferno, and the driver perished. In that emergency there had been no time for the turret crew to traverse to the front, and why the driver did

20

not use his floor escape hatch we will never know. Thereafter my driver Harry Bone became very thoughtful and made sure that his escape hatch was in perfect working order.

'We had now entered a phase of hard slogging against an enemy who was fighting with a renewed desperation. November had brought the onset of what was to prove a very bitter winter. Already it was extremely cold, the thick snow and ice made it practically impossible for us to leave the roads to operate across country. We were moving in column on the road south from Sittard. The road was raised on an embankment above the level of the adjoining fields. It was dead straight and lined on each side with tall trees planted close together. The squadron was strung out in single file when suddenly, on our left, a German self-propelled gun appeared some 400 yards away. It came rolling down the hill in a flurry of snow, halted, and opened fire on us. The first we knew about it was when a tank near the head of the column burst into flames, then the next one down, then the next.

'We were in a perilous position. We could not get off the road nor could we traverse the guns because of the closeness of the trees. We put down a smoke screen but only the tanks at the end of the column could return fire, and they could not traverse their guns properly. Meanwhile, we were being picked off like targets at a fairground. The third tank ahead of me was hit, then the next ... it was getting too close for comfort – there was only one thing to do.

' "Abandon tank!" I ordered. There was no argument from the crew. We leapt out, scrambled down the bank and into the freezing ditch, and not a moment too soon. The next minute a shot hit our turret, we saw the sparks and heard the sound but the tank did not burn and we were able to salvage it after the RAF had arrived and dealt with our persecutor. That German gunner must have had an absolute field day; he accounted for eight of our tanks and the squadron suffered many casualties, including our troop commander, Lieutenant Garlick, who was badly wounded.'

While the 1st and 9th US Armies were fighting for Aachen, the Hurtgen and the Roer plain, Patton's 3rd Army further south was pressing east, overrunning Lorraine and reaching the Saar river. New troops were coming up all the time, and Eugene Robison, 358th Infantry Regiment, 90th Infantry Division, recalls arriving as 3rd Army replacement:

'I arrived in the combat zone along the Moselle about noon on 16 November 1944. Fifty of us disembarked the trucks and stood aimlessly in the yard of a house which was the 3rd Battalion headquarters. An hour or so later a First Sergeant came out of the headquarters, read off some names and said, "You're in T, K or L Company." I was in L. We climbed into the truck and it took us to a small village. Here another First Sergeant ordered us to drop our duffle-bags and backpacks, which we had carried since Fort Meade, Maryland, and to put on a combat pack. We never saw our duffle-bags or packs again.

'Around 3 a.m. I was awakened by a sergeant, got up off the floor of the German farmhouse in Oberlimberg, and started putting on my combat pack with bandoliers and hand-grenades attached. The balance of the Headquarters platoon and the rifle platoons of L Company were preparing to attack across the flooded Saar river into the middle of the Siegfried Line on the frontier of Germany.

'In anticipation of crossing the river in small eight-man assault rowboats, one GI had already shot himself in the hand and another "Buckhorn" shot himself in the foot, both in hope of avoiding the attack. I opened up a box of K rations and popped the hard candies into my mouth, then fell in outside the billets. The line began walking along the main street and turned down a steep hill to the bank of the Saar. Engineers were there with the boats. I got into one and started paddling.

'All was quiet; no moon, only stars and darkness. Getting out of the boat we formed a skirmish line and started walking across a flood plain where all was mud. Soon we heard the sound of a German plane, "Bedcheck Charlie", the veterans called him. Then a green flare was dropped. We all froze as the sky lit up and we could see the pillboxes that we were to capture. Deep drainage ditches, full of water, crossed the flood plain, and we jumped over them but I fell back into the deep water with rifle, pack, field telephone, wool uniform, fatigue uniform, raincoat and heavy boots. I knew I was gone if I didn't get out so I drove my fingers straight into the mud bank, which gave me a grip to pull up from the water. Dripping wet and frozen I caught up with the line and continued advancing to the still silent pillboxes.

'Our platoon had sat down to wait for engineers to blow the door off the pillbox when the German machine-gun inside began firing. I could see tracer bullets whizzing over my head as I hit the ground. There was a loud explosion and the machine-gun ceased its rattling. Our platoon stood up and continued advancing to the village of Pachten.

'It was still not yet dawn. Before we started, we were told to fire our rifles during the attack to keep the Germans' heads down, and soon the captain told us to follow him. We started running from yard to yard and stopped at a vacant lot exposed to the street where the Germans were. The captain ran across, then Cooley, then a sergeant. I heard an M-1 rifle fire close by, then I ran across the lot. A bullet whizzed a foot from my ear, then Donelson ran, then another M-1 report. I looked around and Donelson was floundering like a headless chicken. Fortunately Donelson had only a flesh wound, the sergeant was hit in the heel, and the German sniper with a GI M-1 rifle was captured in the basement of the house we had run into.

'This sniper was taunted by his GI captors for half an hour, then sent back to the battalion prisoner cage. Dawn broke and the German artillery began laying down a barrage on the Saar river, but I was across. The shells, ours and theirs, flew over our heads but annihilated the GIs trying to get across the Saar and construct a bridge to get supplies to us. We needed tanks, artillery and ammo badly to keep us from being pushed back into the river.'

Further south, General Devers' 6th Army Group was doing well, having captured the west bank of the Upper Rhine in the Vosges, north of the Swiss frontier, with the exception of a large pocket of the German XIX Army holding out around the city of Colmar. This 'Colmar Pocket' was to cause great problems for the Allies later on.

At the end of November, with Antwerp open and the supply situation improving, the Allies sought to build up their strength for a fresh assault into Germany, but there was now another problem: reinforcements. The British had already broken up two front-line infantry divisions to supply riflemen to the rest, but now the American armies were short of combat infantry. In addition, Eisenhower's 'Broad Front' strategy, which had gained a 400-mile front from Nijmegen to the Moselle, had also made the Allied line along the German frontier perilously thin.

Each American division was responsible for about ten miles of front and many lacked the men to police this front adequately. 'It therefore seemed not unreasonable to thin out these forces still further behind the tumbled hills of the Ardennes through which the Germans struck on 16 December 1944 to begin the operation known as the 'Battle of the Bulge'.

Hitler had been planning a counter-attack through the Ardennes since August 1944. As his armies were pushed back within Germany, both the need and the ability to mount such an attack grew steadily and Hitler's intention now was to cut the Allied armies in two and reach Antwerp. To achieve this he had assembled three well-equipped armies behind the Ardennes, the V and VI Army and the VI SS Panzer Army, all somewhat short of fuel but well supplied with experienced commanders and battle-hardened troops. By early December, with bad weather affecting the use of the all-powerful Allied air forces and the Allies thinly stretched along the Belgian and Luxembourg frontier, Hitler was ready to launch his attack.

The Germans had concealed their build-up behind the Ardennes and foxed Allied Intelligence, not least by giving their build-up the code name 'Wacht am Rhin' (Watch on the Rhine). When their manoeuvres were discovered, the Allies believed that the German forces were being mustered to resist future Allied advances, not for an all-out attack to the west.

The Allies were also labouring under another disadvantage. After the British had cracked the German 'Enigma' code in 1940, the Allied commanders had been in receipt of a regular supply of information on German strengths and intentions, codenamed 'Ultra', largely culled from radio transmissions. However, as the Germans withdrew behind the West Wall, more and more of their orders were transmitted by telephone, land-line, teleprinter or despatch-rider. The volume of information available to the Allied Command abruptly declined, and the commandoes were woefully unprepared when the German panzer divisions came storming through the Ardennes in the early morning of 16 December 1944.

The Ardennes offensive took the Americans completely by surprise. Eisenhower still believed that the Wehrmacht was incapable of offensive action when in fact German morale was high, new or repaired guns and tanks were reaching their armies in quantity, their supply lines had shortened, and even the Luftwaffe had mustered a thousand aircraft to support the attack. Above all, the German soldiers were fighting to keep the invaders out of the Fatherland.

The German thrust through the Ardennes split Bradley's 12th US Army Group in two, driving the 9th Army and the 1st Army, less the 4th Division, back to the west or to the north, while Patton's 3rd US Army remained for the moment further south. Since General Bradley could not exercise command over his widely split forces, on 19 December Eisenhower attached Hodges' 1st US Army to Montgomery's 21st Army Group and it remained under Montgomery's command until the Bulge had been rolled back. The 1st Army did not revert to Bradley's command until 18 January and Simpson's 9th US Army remained with 21st Army Group until April.

The full story of the Battle of the Bulge lies outside the scope of this book but since Montgomery's time in command of the 1st US Army had repercussions later, it should be briefly explained.

The first few days were very confused, as Jack Capell remembers: 'After the Hurtgen I got a 48-hour pass to Arlon, Luxembourg, and was on the way back to our outfit when I heard on the radio that the Germans had attacked and the 4th Division had been "annihilated". Everyone on the truck was from the 4th and we said to the driver, "If our division has been wiped out, where are you taking us?" In fact, the 4th Division was not too bad. We had one company cut off near Echternach, but the division that really got overrun was the 106th, a new formation that had just moved into the Schnee Eifel, east of the Belgian Ardennes. We went into our old positions and there we stayed, with shells coming down on us at the rate of one hundred an hour or more.' The division started the Bulge 1,500 men short and finished up even more depleted, but we held the south side of the Bulge and we saved the city of Luxembourg.'

During the Bulge, the Americans had to stand and fight and many American units, cut off by the rapid enemy advance, had to be supplied by air. Daniel J. Burke was in one of these transport aircraft dropping supplies to the 101st US Airborne Division in Bastogne.

'23 December 1944 was a dreary day at Ramsbury Field, England. We lifted off at 3 p.m. in a C47 transport plane we had nicknamed "The Saint". Our mission was to resupply a surrounded unit in an area of Bastogne, Belgium. My position was at the rear door to assist the cargo unloading. In the drop area the air was so heavy with shell fire it smelled like a matchbox factory. I remember wishing we could get the hell out of there.

'As we banked left to begin our trip home, there was a loud explosion. We were hit by the ground fire in the pilot's compartment, the left engine, and our gas tanks. The entire bottom of the plane ignited. Our first pilot, Captain Wales, was killed instantly by a direct hit from the ground, and he fell across the stick causing an instantaneous dive towards the ground. I was knocked to the floor and burned my hands and knees as I tried to crawl from the cockpit to the cargo door at the rear of the plane.

'Our co-pilot, Lt Boleau, lifted the pilot from the stick and the plane levelled off at approximately 2,000 feet. He then set the autopilot but flames from the gas tanks now reached the cargo door. As the plane levelled off, I rolled out head first. The heat was so intense from the burning gasoline that it burnt my face, neck and the back of my neck, but after my count of ten, my 'chute billowed out.

'My relief was short-lived. Whizzing sounds made me realize that I was a target for the ground fire below. I thought to pull the shroud cord to accelerate my descent, looked up and saw holes burned in my canopy. I heard German voices as I approached the ground, and realized that I had bailed out into the middle of an SS panzer division. I landed hard and was met by a platoon of German infantry, who took me into a cinder-block building close to the battle zone. Inside I met Lt Boleau and we were both escorted outside by German guards. They led us to a stone wall where a firing squad of riflemen stood within 20 feet. They told us to turn our faces to the wall and I heard the action of their rifles. An SS officer came out of an adjacent building and gave what I thought would be the command to end my life, but his command was to stop the execution. Luck and the grace of God had spared our lives.

'I later discovered that I had bailed out over Malmedy, Belgium, where nearly one hundred captured American soldiers had been shot by these SS men a few days before my plane was shot down. I spent the remainder of the war in prison camps across Germany.'

The Battle of the Bulge was to rage across the frozen Belgian countryside for five weeks, but by New Year's Day 1945 the German advance had all but petered out. Shortage of fuel, stubborn American resistance, especially by the 101st Airborne Division in Bastogne, clear skies in late December after five days of bad weather and the subsequent intervention of Allied fighters and bombers, eventually brought the German offensive to a halt.

Stuart Monk was then a P47 fighter pilot with the 50th US Fighter Group: 'My first mission was on 27 December 1944 when I spun an ME109 off my ass over the Rhine river. The odds were in our favour as they lost two aircraft in the fight before they broke for home. There were twenty-five of them and only eleven of us but we found out later that a lot of these Luftwaffe pilots were just youngsters, with very little flying experience, while we had been through rigorous training before we entered combat.'

Air power was again the decisive element in victory, combined here with the tenacity in defence of many American infantry divisions. Within a week the Germans' Ardennes offensive penetrated a distance of sixty miles, to Dinant on the Meuse but any hope of reaching Antwerp was abandoned on Christmas Day 1944. It took another month of fierce fighting before the Bulge was finally eliminated at the end of January.

By New Year's Day 1945 those German tanks that still had petrol were in full retreat to the east, and the Allied armies were again in charge of events. Meanwhile, to relieve German pressure on the Western Front, the Combined Chiefs-of-Staffs and the two Western leaders, US President Franklin D. Roosevelt and the British Prime Minister, Winston Churchill, had begged the leader of Soviet Russia, Marshal Joseph Stalin, to advance the start date of the Soviet winter offensive, currently scheduled for 20 January.

Stalin was willing to do this, for with German attention and many German divisions engaged in the Ardennes, the prospects looked good for a rapid advance from the Vistula to the river Oder and the eastern frontier of Germany. It is therefore to the much-dreaded 'Ostfront' that we must briefly turn our attention.

When the armies of the Western Allies stormed ashore in Normandy on 6 June 1944, the Eastern Front was still well inside Soviet Russia. Marshal Stalin had been waiting for this 'Second Front' in the west, and only when the Normandy invasion was seen to be successful did he order his armies to advance into Poland.

The Russian summer offensive began on 10 June 1944. The Soviets came sweeping west in great force, through Smolensk, Vitebsk and Orsha, where the German Army Group Centre had just forty-two weak divisions to face a force of no less than 225 Russian divisions, seventy-five of them armoured. The German resistance soon collapsed and within three weeks the Germans had lost over 300,000 men and been pushed back to Vilna, close to the

Polish border. By early July the Russians had advanced almost 400 miles and were on the river Vistula, close to the Polish capital, Warsaw.

On 14 July the Red Army was pressing towards Warsaw. Then suddenly and surprisingly, their advance paused outside the city, to the great consternation of the Polish Home Army. This partisan force within the city, operating under the command of the Polish Government-in-Exile in London, had risen against the German garrison in Warsaw to help the Soviet advance, and anticipated the rapid arrival of the Red Army. Instead, the Russians held back. Claiming they had outrun their supply lines, the Soviets paused beyond the Vistula until the Home Army had been crushed by the Wehrmacht. Only opposite Warsaw did the Red Army pause. Elsewhere they crossed the river Nieman and reached the frontiers of East Prussia in the north, and they continued attacking along their southern Front, in Hungary and Romania.

In August their offensive in the Balkans overran Romania and captured the vital oil-fields at Ploesti. This loss was to cripple the Ardennes offensive four months later, for Ploesti was Germany's last source of natural oil. On 26 August, Bulgaria declared neutrality and the German garrisons there were forced to evacuate; the great German Reich was finally starting to fall apart.

As Germany's allies fell away Hitler's orders to hold every foot of ground limited his armies' capacity to manoeuvre. On 2 September, Finland made peace with the Allied Powers and the Finnish Army promptly attacked the German garrisons. Still the Soviet juggernaut rolled west.

By October 1944, except for some isolated garrisons in towns along the coast, the Baltic states of Estonia, Latvia and Lithuania had fallen to the Soviets amid terrible scenes of rape and murder. On 22 October 1944 the Red Army captured the towns of Goldap and Nemmenesdorf, where the fate of the German civilian population, especially the women, was a grim foretaste of things to come when the Soviet armies swept across Germany in 1945.

Winter was now coming on but the Soviets and their Communist allies continued to advance during November. By 1 November the Red Army was only fifty miles from Budapest, the capital of Hungary. In Yugoslavia the Communist partisans of Marshal Tito surged forward across Dalmatia to the Adriatic and soon controlled most of the border between Yugoslavia and Greece. Relations with the British troops in Yugoslavia, who had previously been warmly welcomed as allies and a vital source of supply, now began to deteriorate. Two weeks later the Germans evacuated southern Yugoslavia, while the Red Army closed in on Budapest. On the Baltic coast, far to the north, the Red Army advanced around the Gulf of Riga and, helped by the Finns now fighting alongside their former Russian enemies, the Red Army cleared the Germans out of Finnish Lapland.

So it went on throughout November and December, a steady advance in the east by the Soviets, a relentless crumbling of the German position, especially in the southern flank, in the Balkans, Romania and Hungary. By Christmas Eve 1944 the Soviets had almost surrounded Budapest, with the German garrison already fleeing west towards the Austrian frontier. By Christmas Eve two Soviet armies were fighting through Budapest and on New Year's Eve Hungary capitulated and also declared war on Nazi Germany. There was now a pause on the Vistula and along the Central Front as the Soviets mustered their strength for the coming winter campaign of 1945.

In the west the fighting to eliminate the Bulge continued. Allied airpower was, as usual, proving decisive, though this aerial support was not without setbacks, as Jack Capell recalls: 'When the skies cleared at the end of December, we were bombed again – by American planes. On New Year's Eve 1944, a formation of B17s bombed us; that made the third time, counting the two short bombings near St Lô back in July 1944. On New Year's Day we were strafed by American P38 fighters, and this in spite of putting out our identification panels. So began our New Year.'

The aircrews also had 'friendly fire' problems, as Canadian air gunner Vic Polichek remembers: 'I got a letter from a bomb aimer on my old crew saying they had all been killed but him. They were flying over the line in Belgium when a German ME262 jet shot them up and set one engine on fire. The pilot was setting up for a crash-landing when the American Army on the ground opened fire on them. They were at 1500 feet and only my pal, the bomb aimer, was able to jump.'

By New Year's Eve 1944, the Allied Powers held Germany in a vice-like grip between their Eastern and Western Fronts. The Western Allies, Canadian, British, American and French, were mustering along the Siegfried Line, the Russians were poised on the Vistula. Allied bombers and fighters were occupying the 'Third Front' in the sky, and two more Allied armies were coming north through Italy. In the next few months these Allied armies would sweep into Germany, crushing out the last embers of Hitler's 'Thousand-Year Reich' after just twelve years of existence.

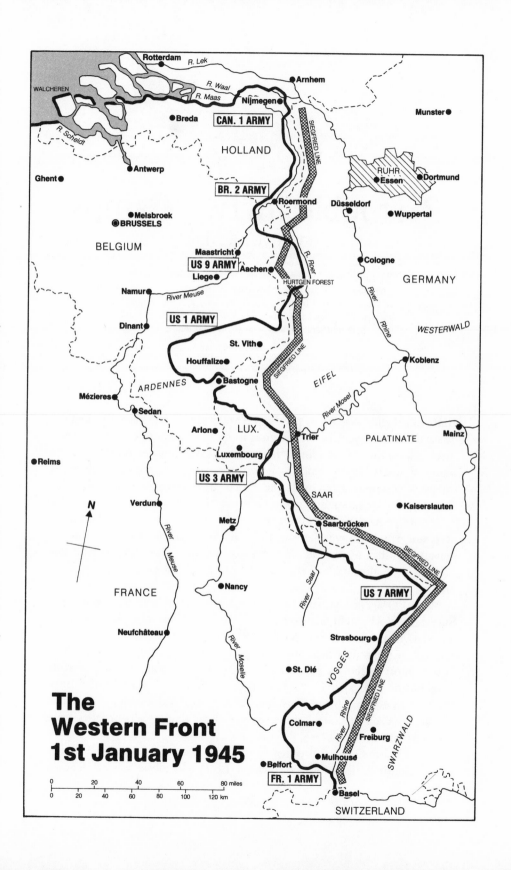

The
Western Front
1st January 1945

Mosquito fighter bomber

2 Trouble in Two Camps
1–12 JANUARY 1945

'The four best commands in the Service – a platoon,
a battalion, a division and an army. A platoon
because it is your first command, because you are young,
because if you are any good, you know the men in it better
than their mothers do, and love them as much.'

Field Marshal Sir William Slim

Guns, not bells, ushered in the New Year of 1945. Exactly at midnight a massive bombardment by all the guns in General George Patton's 3rd US Army fell on the German lines, the sound of exploding shells drowning the sound of Adolf Hitler's voice as he made a New Year radio speech to his troops and people. Even with the Allied armies poised on the German frontier, the Führer's ranting address was a blend of threats and optimism.

'We are going to fight this war to the ultimate victory ... we will destroy everyone who does not share in the common struggle ... and the world must know that we will never surrender. Germany will survive and rise again like the phoenix, and this time will be recorded as the wonder of the present century...'

Allied POWs in Germany saw in the New Year as best they could. Wilf Sutton, an RAF flight engineer shot down in 1943, recalls what happened on New Year's Eve at Stammlager IVB at Muhlberg: 'I helped form an entertainment group which put on some very ambitious plays, but my New Year memory is about a party and a powerful brew some of the boys made from raisins and potatoes. Our basic diet was now down to about three small potatoes and a bit of black bread a day, so you can imagine the effect of that brew on weakened stomachs ... in no time at all the boys were "Brahms and Liszt".

'The Theatre Group was called on to give a cabaret and my part, together with a South African "Kriegie" called Bruce Coombes, was to dance a tango. Dancing was my hobby and Bruce was the South African tango champion, so he came on dressed as a gaucho and I was dressed as a gorgeous gypsy girl. We must have impressed the audience more than usual or perhaps it was the booze and the music, but this most exotic dance brought me many offers of a bed in the corner. I therefore decided to grow a moustache, which I have to this day.'

Next morning, Monday, 1 January 1945, came 'Der Grosse Schlag', an all-out attack by some nine hundred Luftwaffe fighters and bombers against Allied airfields in Belgium and northern France. They caught the Allies completely unprepared and destroyed large numbers of aircraft on the ground.

RAF pilot Eric Atkins DFC remembers this sudden onslaught: 'I had finished my third tour of operations with 138 Wing, 2 Group, 2nd Tactical Air Force, flying Mosquitoes Mark VI. With my navigator, Lofty Eyles, I was posted to Blackbush, England, as a test and ferry pilot, and we had the impression that all the stuffing had been knocked out of the Luftwaffe. It was only a matter of time before the Army broke through and ended the war.

'December 1944 was a bad month for weather, so targets were changed and other ops cancelled. Despite this, many sorties were flown by 138 Wing. I visited the Wing in France frequently, returning patched-up Mosquitoes and picking up others for service or repair. We celebrated Christmas at Blackbush and arranged a "returning aircraft" flight over to Epinoy on 31 December. Many aircrews were on standby and could not indulge in the New Year spirit, but others had a "wee nip" and everyone was waiting for the skies to clear and the opportunity to assault the enemy in the Ardennes. I had breakfast at 0900 hrs on New Year's Day. Suddenly, the word spread throughout the mess – "Everybody on alert! The Luftwaffe has pranged Melsbroek – they are out in force."

'At the 2 Group airfield at Melsbroek many of the Mitchell aircrews had been briefed for an attack on a communications centre in the Ardennes and had taken off at 0830 hrs – just before the Germans attacked. The Luftwaffe struck with ME109s, a chaotic attack, firing indiscriminately. Some twenty aircraft, mostly Mitchells, were damaged or destroyed on the ground. Some 144 Allied aircraft were destroyed and over eighty seriously damaged, including Field Marshal Montgomery's personal Dakota.

'Since Luftwaffe raids had almost petered out, dispersal was less usual and some of our aircraft were lined up in neat rows. It did not destroy the effectiveness of the 2nd TAF. In fact the Luftwaffe, in this "Hermann" offensive, had one of the greatest losses ever in air warfare – some said over 300 German aircraft were lost. Instead of "Der Grosse Schlag" it should have been called "Der Grosse Shambles", but it was a brave last-ditch attempt and it certainly caught us unawares.'

Another witness to the '*Grosse Schlag*' was Lt Thomas Grant, an American B17 (Flying Fortress) pilot. 'My first mission was with the 706 Bomb Squadron on 1 January. After the mission we were forced to land at a British base in Brussels to refuel and while we were there the British told us that German aircraft, principally ME109s, had been strafing the airfield, gear and flaps down for more accurate gunnery. A raid was pending and announced by a jeep careering round the field with a siren on the hood. Unwittingly, we took shelter in a bomb storage area. I did thirty-three missions before the war ended, flying our aircraft back to the States after the German surrender.'

Bill Condaw, a British Typhoon pilot, has similar memories of New Year's Day: 'Following a New Year's Eve celebration we were on our way to dispersal around 5 a.m. when the Luftwaffe arrived on the scene in copious quantities. We bailed out of the truck and dug into the mud in our best uniforms, while they strafed our 'drome. My strongest feeling was that this was no fun ... I'd much rather be flying.

'Later in the day we were on our way to support the Americans in the Battle of the Bulge. Our eight aircraft were bounced by American P51s and three squadron-mates were shot down; so all in all, 1 January 1945 was not a good day.'

German losses during the '*Grosse Schlag*' were estimated at some 364 aircraft, and the damage the Luftwaffe inflicted on the Allied air forces in return was minimal. Two days later the 8th US Air Force sent 1,000 B17 and B24 bombers to scour the Ardennes battlefield and escorted them with more than 650 Thunderbolt and Mustang fighters. The Reich could not match these numbers or afford to lose any more trained pilots or aircraft, their ground forces were in sore need of air support and cover.

On 1 January 1945, the forces available to Field Marshal Gerd Von Rundstedt for the defence of the Reich in the west numbered eighty divisions, at least on paper. Many of these had been mauled in the Ardennes fighting or the headlong retreat from France and Belgium, but Von Rundstedt made the best use of his available resources, mixing experienced troops and SS formations with newly formed Volksturm (Home Guard) units. The German armies were then organized into four army groups.

In the north was General Kurt Student's Army Group H, consisting of the 1st Parachute Army and the XXV Army, opposed by the 1st Canadian and 2nd British Armies from the Dutch coast to Roermond.

From Roermond to Trier on the Moselle, Field Marshal Walter Model's Army Group B stood ready to oppose the armies of Bradley's 12th Army Group, Hodges' 1st US Army, Simpson's 9th US Army (currently attached to 21st Army Group) and Patton's 3rd US Army, currently fighting on the south side of the Bulge. Army Group B was the strongest of the German army groups and was specifically charged with the defence of the Ruhr. It contained the V and VI Panzer Armies and the VII and XV Armies, and it was supported in the north by the 1st Army of Army Group G under General Blaskowitz, which opposed elements of the 3rd and 9th US Armies. Colonel General Blaskowitz was soon to take command of Student's Army Group H.

The last German army group, the XIX Army, occupied a pocket around Colmar on the west bank of the Rhine, and was responsible for the German frontier as far as the Swiss border. As the year opened, all these armies were mustering men and arms for a desperate defence of the Reich.

In the Ardennes, matters were steadily improving for the Americans, though heavy fighting continued in bitter weather. British forces, notably the 6th Airborne Division, were also coming up.

Sergeant George Butler of the 13th Battalion, the Parachute Regiment, was involved in the fight for Bure at the forward tip of the Bulge, south east of Namur, and recalls an incident that gives a glimpse of the strange and occasional chivalry that occurs between men in battle:

'I was platoon sergeant in A Company, 13 Para. We arrived at Calais on Christmas Eve with no winter clothing and travelled up through Belgium in open trucks. Christmas dinner, cheese and a jam sandwich, was eaten on the move. We stopped that night and of the four sergeants in my billet two were killed and one seriously wounded at Bure.

'The approach march to Bure was hard work. Metal-shod army boots are not the best footwear for walking on ice and snow-covered roads, and being paras we carried everything. Our recce group reported no signs of life in Bure but when we topped the rise above the village I saw blue smoke rising from the centre. The A Company task was to clear the houses in the centre and we advanced from the right of the road.

'B Company caught a salvo right among them as they topped the rise and as we ran or slid to the village we saw a tank in the farm which opened up on us. A shell exploded on the frozen ground, caught a section on the move, killed three and wounded six instantly. Lieutenant Cavanagh and I decided that the village was safer than open ground and we got in among the houses, where we were raked with machine-gun fire from a Tiger tank. This kept us pinned and if anyone ever dictated a battle by just sitting tight, that German tank officer did. His position was protected by high walls and only the gun and a bit of turret was showing.

'However, about noon an ambulance came into the village from our lines and our RAMC sergeant, Jock Scott, began evacuating the wounded and dead. At this the Tiger advanced and came slowly up the road. Stopping by the ambulance, the officer put his head out of the turret and asked our sergeant – in perfect English – what he thought he was doing? Scott replied, "Evacuating the wounded", and the German said, "You may fill your ambulance with one load only but if you return I will fire." I could see the track of the tank and we could have got a PIAT anti-tank shot off with great accuracy, but owing to the situation with the ambulance it wasn't worth it.

'My last memory is of the Tiger heading back to its lair, and Jock Scott's ambulance, with Jock sitting on the rear steps, looking back at the tank with total indifference, the boots of the casualties seeming to fill the vehicle to the roof.'

The fight for Bure went on for three days, the 13th Parachute Battalion fighting Tiger tanks, artillery and German infantry before the village was finally captured. The 13th then withdrew from the area as the Germans also fell back. The 13th Parachute Battalion had nearly two hundred men killed and wounded in what has been described in their Regimental History as 'one of the toughest little battles of the entire Ardennes campaign'. The Allies were squeezing the 'Bulge' from north and south when, on 1 January, a fresh German attack struck the Allied lines.

Knowing that the Allies had been forced to move many 3rd US Army divisions north into the Ardennes, the Germans launched 'Operation Nordwind', with eight German divisions – three of them from the Waffen SS – falling on the American 7th Army (Lt-General Alexander Patch) in Alsace-Lorraine. The 7th Army had been obliged to thin out its front-line formations to take over ground left vacant by 3rd Army divisions moved to the Bulge, and this German attack through the hills of the Vosges met with some initial success.

The main German thrust through the Saverne Gap drove the Americans back for ten miles before it was halted, while to the east of the Vosges, General Devers, the 6th Army Group commander, ordered a tactical withdrawal to the Maginot Line, a defence position along the French frontier. The Germans then established a bridgehead across the Rhine north of Strasbourg, which led to a further American withdrawal.

These withdrawals were made at the direct orders of General Eisenhower, who had no intention of letting an American army be cut off or cut up; but the retreat was most unwelcome to the French. Alsace and Lorraine had passed to and fro between France and Germany in every war since 1870 and the French insisted that whatever happened, the newly liberated city of Strasbourg should not be given up again.

A young Frenchwoman, Daniele Clement-Heinz, was then driving an ambulance with the 2nd Demi-Brigade of the French 1st Army and remembers the fall of Strasbourg: 'Autumn in Lorraine meant heavy rain and mud and we got the impression that with autumn well advanced, the time would come to go into winter quarters, but one day we were sent to Cirey. There the sub-group Massu and our ambulance had to wait for some time until the armoured columns came rolling past, tanks and guns brushing through the German road defences arranged like great wooden doors or Arcs de Triomphe blocking the way to Strasbourg. The day wore on and still we advanced, the route climbed on through the hills all night and with dawn came the first flakes of snow. However, we were through the Vosges and advancing across the Alsace plain towards Strasbourg.

'It was still snowing but a young Alsatian in the demi-brigade said, "The Germans don't know yet that we are through the Vosges. It's worth the risk of pushing on." We moved on to Dabo, where we saw headlights, stopped a German staff car and the troops captured Wagner, the Gauleiter of Strasbourg. "Here," said the young Alsatian, coming back from the ambush, "take the helmet of the Gauleiter of Strasbourg", and he threw it to Hélène and me.

'This helmet is quite normal and has no signs that it ever belonged to the notorious Wagner, but I kept it, my son has played with it, and I have it still.'

The Nordwind offensive was the first setback for Devers' 6th Army Group, which had made good progress since coming ashore in the South of France in August. The 44th US Division had captured Saarbourg on 21 November and Strasbourg had been liberated by the French 2nd Armoured Division on 22 November. On 12 December the 44th and 79th US Divisions took Haugeway, and Devers turned his attention to mopping up pockets of resistance in his rear area and pushing on to the Rhine.

After their autumnal successes there remained one major centre of German resistance, on the west bank of the Rhine around Colmar, where strong elements of the German XIX Army still held out. In November, Eisenhower had ordered Devers to eliminate this 'Colmar Pocket' as a first priority. The task had been entrusted to African Colonial troops of Lattre de Tassigny's 1st French Army, who suffered terribly in the snow and ice-clad hills of the Vosges and made little progress. The Colmar Pocket therefore remained untaken when the Bulge fighting began, and the troops there were able to support the German advance when the Nordwind offensive began on 1 January.

Devers' withdrawal, though well-handled and tactically sound, enabled the Germans to make rapid progress to the west, enough to concern the French leader, General Charles de Gaulle. Two days later de Gaulle flew to SHAEF in Paris and told Eisenhower that unless the Allies guaranteed to hold Strasbourg, he (de Gaulle) would order the French 1st Army to act independently in defence of the city.

This threat, if carried into effect, would have been a blatant incitement to insubordination, and having almost reached the end of his patience with Montgomery, Eisenhower was in no mood to put up with further truculence from the French. He told de Gaulle bluntly that unless the French Army continued to obey his orders, it would no longer receive supplies of food, fuel or ammunition. Warming to his task, Eisenhower also pointed out that if the French Army had eliminated the Colmar Pocket and so denied the Germans a foothold in Alsace-Lorraine, this problem with Strasbourg would not have arisen.

Having put de Gaulle in his place, in so far as that was possible, Eisenhower then ordered Devers to hold Strasbourg. The decision was supported by Churchill, who was then on a visit to SHAEF. The improving weather meant that Devers was able to receive considerable support from the 9th Air Force, who had another field day here, bombing and strafing German columns on the snowbound roads. Strasbourg was held, Nordwind petered out and the XIX Army withdrew east across the Rhine from the Colmar Pocket early in February.

In early January 1945, the American armies were handing out most of the punishment while other Allied troops were having a quieter time after their battles along the Scheldt and the Maas. Sergeant J. B. Stone of the Toronto Scottish Regiment, then stationed in the Nijmegen area, kept a diary for the period:

'C Company of the Toronto Scots was equipped with Vickers .303 machine-guns, Bren-guns and infantry weapons such as grenades and rifles. We generally fought in support of other infantry units with the 2nd Canadian Division, but on occasions we were deployed as forward defence troops. At the New Year we were positioned in reserve close to Haps, fifteen miles south of Nijmegen, just west of the river Maas.

'There was a party for the sergeants in the morning and CQMS Bayes got well soused and told off Captain Dinnick and Major Grant, as well as giving a brigadier hell. Last night Langlois shot up Cuijk village and had his pistol removed. John Gilbert and Bill Cann never got home at all. Lt McKenna was so fed up with everyone that he left our house around 2030 hrs and returned about 0400 – he was pretty happy by then.

'The sergeants' party was held that afternoon and the main drink was hot buttered rum and sugar. It seemed to be pretty potent stuff. Sergeant Wally Jones and Private Alf Parrish went to Brussels on 48-hour passes. Lieutenant McKenna spent the afternoon at an officers' party. We did a hit-and-run harassing fire (HF) shoot at night but there was no return fire.

'Jan. 2: We had two HF shoots, one at midnight and then another at 0400 hrs, but they were fast affairs – about 5 minutes each. I took a bath parade out after lunch. There were no baths in Cuijk, the ones in Grave were out of order and the 30 cwt broke down in Nijmegen. We made supper but had no bath.

'Jan. 4: Two shoots tonight, one at 2230 hrs and one at 0130 hrs. The section on the late shoot was raked by MG and rifle fire. None of our people was hurt; it takes a fast bullet to beat a TSR man to a hole!'

Zane Schlemmer, a platoon sergeant in the 508th US Parachute Infantry Regiment, 82nd Airborne Division, remembers the end of the Bulge: 'January 1945 found us on the Belgium–German border, northeast of St Vith. After advancing and clearing a huge snow-flocked forest, I spotted a hunting tower, which deer or boar hunters must have used in the past. The tower was taller than the surrounding fir forest, so I climbed it for a look around. While up there the fog suddenly lifted and I could see rows and rows of "dragon's teeth", anti-tank obstacles, extending as far as I could see in the fields on the side of this forest. It was only then that I knew that we were in the middle of the Siegfried Line, Germany's "West Wall".

'The weather was intensely cold. In addition to my usual uniform I had a turtleneck wool sweater, and an American army officer's short overcoat, which I had taken from the frozen body of a 106th Infantry Division major I discovered in the forest. At times I also wore my army issue "mummy-type" sleeping bag, by cutting armholes and the bottom out of it. I had also acquired a long-haired German dog from a company of German soldiers we ambushed in a railroad cut. We called the dog Adolf and he was my sleeping companion, curling up against each other wherever we could find a place to sleep. We modified our gloves by slitting the fingers and sewing them together, except for the thumb and trigger finger, thus making them modified mittens. Even with all this damn clothing, I never was warm.

'The only nice thing about this winter war was that the snow had covered all the battlefield debris, the dead were frozen and none of the smell of the battlefield permeated. The flip-side of that was the probability of freezing before evacuation, should you become wounded.

'The only vehicle we could use, due to the lack of roads, the snow drifts and the terrain, was a small, tracked Weasel. It brought up ammunition and K rations, and took back the wounded and those with frozen feet or fingers. The weather was nearly as much an enemy as the Germans. We used the element of surprise, for the Germans were confident that no one could advance under those conditions and they didn't want to give up any shelter they were in. One night I filled my canteen completely full of water, not knowing when I would be able to get any more; during the night the water froze so solidly the ice split the seams of my canteen. When rations couldn't reach us we existed on captured German black bread and canned horse meat, along with the glass jars of bottled vegetables and fruit that we found in the cellars of the farmhouses.

'One of my fondest memories was being pulled off the line for a 24-hour break. We hiked to a road where trucks took us back to a farmhouse which had a portable rubber shower station set up beside it. The rubber exterior was frost-covered, but inside it was warm and steamy. We undressed and separated our underwear and socks, which we had worn for well over a month. We were then given soap and five luxurious minutes each under the hot showers; then we were given clean underwear and two pairs each of clean socks ... truly heaven! No other 5 minutes in my entire life gave me more pleasure. Then, clothed, we were "puffed" with DDT against lice – though God knows how any bugs could have survived that freezing weather. Then it was back to the line.'

Ralph Teeters of the 4th US Infantry Division enjoyed a longer leave – to Paris. 'How it worked was that leave came in turn to the longest serving men in the company who had not already had any. First we went back to Regiment and got cleaned up. A wise old staff-sergeant there told us to forget about money – cigarettes were the currency in Paris – and he piled my arms with cartons of Chesterfields, as many as I could carry, like a load of kindling.

'He was right. The rate of exchange in Paris was around three or four packs of cigarettes for one of those Parisienne whores, and maybe a carton for a bottle of brandy. I didn't know how long I might survive, so I was determined to have a good time. I didn't go up the Eiffel Tower or see the Louvre. I don't even know if they were open. I went to Rainbow Corner and "Pig-Alley" as we called the Pigalle, and wore myself out on drink and sex. We were tired and hung-over when we got back on the trucks after 48 hours, and they took us back to the war.'

Harper Coleman, also of the 4th US Division, even made it to London and home. 'I got back to the 4th by the first week of January. It did not seem like the unit I had left, everyone was new. I was told that the gun crew I had served with was gone; they took a direct hit on their position during the Battle of the Bulge.

'This was the time when we were pushing the Germans back. We had been in the line for more than a week, in mud and snow and rain, with no chance to change or dry socks, so I, and hundreds of others, went out with trench foot. I was unable to walk so was shipped back to Paris and then on a hospital train to London.

'One of the things about London then was the destruction of the city. Large parts of it were just ruins. During this time there were buzz-bomb raids and V-2 rocket strikes, and I was very close to a V-2 explosion on several occasions. Anyway, there was a policy at this time that anyone with a given amount of hospital time had to be sent Stateside. With a little help from several nurses my service file disappeared, and with the end of the war near I was sent in a hospital ship to North Carolina, where I was medically discharged on 6 September 1945.'

With that break in the weather that had allowed the Luftwaffe their '*Grosse Schlag*', in the first four days of January the Allied air forces flew 15,000 sorties against German forces in the Bulge, and with this assistance the Americans surged forward across the border into the Schnee Eifel (that part of the Ardennes east of the German frontier). However, if the sky was clear and the fighting successful along the Western Front, Eisenhower's tiff with de Gaulle was just a prelude to a much more serious dispute with his other Allied subordinate, Field Marshal Montgomery. The alliance that had withstood adversity was now creaking under the strains of success.

Nor was dissension confined to the Allied side. Conflicts over strategy were now breaking out in Hitler's headquarters at the Alderschloss – the Eagle's Nest – in Germany.

Ever since the Allied breakthroughs on both fronts in the summer of 1944, General Heinz Guderian, Chief-of-Staff of the German High Command (OKW), had been pressing the Führer for some changes on the Eastern Front. Even after the Soviet gains in that summer campaign, Guderian had met with little success. This time, when he arrived at Hitler's headquarters in early January 1945 with disturbing news and another request for change, he bolstered his pleas with some hard facts. Guderian's Intelligence Chief, General Gehlen, had been assembling data on the Russian build-up along the Vistula, and both men were now quite convinced that a major Russian onslaught could not be long delayed or easily resisted.

Guderian began his presentation to the Führer by laying out Gehlen's estimates of Russian strength and the German forces available to meet it. The comparisons were terrifying. In artillery the Russians had twenty guns to every German field-piece. In tanks the odds were seven to one, in infantry twelve to one. Massed on the Central Front behind the Vistula, or already in bridgeheads on the west bank, the Soviets had grouped over two million soldiers, over 6,000 tanks and nearly 50,000 artillery pieces. In some parts of the front the Russian guns stood wheel-to-wheel for miles, just waiting for the signal to deluge the German defences with a pitiless hail of shells.

Against this potential juggernaut, Guderian could put one German army group, Army Group A, under General Harpe. This consisted of three under-strength German armies, the IV, IX and XVIIth Panzer, totalling 400,000 men, in seventy-five divisions, with about 4,000 guns and just over 1,000 tanks. If these figures were correct then the odds against the Germans were far too high, even when fighting on the defensive when odds of three to one might be acceptable as a maximum. There was no hope of reinforcement from the Southern Army Group of just twenty-eight divisions, though this contained more than half the German panzers, because this army group, at Hitler's express orders, was attempting to defend the oil fields of Hungary. Guderian and Gehlen piled fact on fact but it did no good.

Hitler believed that Gehlen's estimates were hopelessly wrong. He declared that the Russians had nothing like that amount of men and material and were simply putting up 'the biggest bluff since Genghis Khan'. He therefore refused to let Guderian strengthen or shorten the eastern Front or redeploy the thirty German divisions positioned around Courland, with their backs to the Baltic Sea and in imminent danger of being surrounded. The Baltic was the last training water available to the German U-Boat fleet and the Führer would not abandon the Baltic shores to Russian troops and aircraft. Guderian then requested that some of the German divisions now re-equipping inside the Reich should be moved east to occupy the defences inside Germany, or used to stem the Western Allies pressing along the Moselle and in the Ardennes. Hitler again refused. Guderian then asked for the transfer of German divisions garrisoning Norway and Denmark. The Führer said no again and the conference ended in acrimony.

Hitler's attitude to military reversals had not changed since the defeat at Alamein in 1942. His troops were not to retreat; they were to stand and fight and die if necessary, in their existing positions. Any troops who declined to do so were either cowards or traitors and would be treated as such by the SS.

On 9 January, with the Bulge now being steadily reduced and the Russian offensive clearly looming, Guderian tried again. Before seeing Hitler he spent some time with the Commander-in-Chief West, Field Marshal Gerd Von Rundstedt. Rundstedt agreed to transfer four of his divisions to Poland and East Prussia – if the Führer agreed. The Führer did agree to the transfer, but not to Poland.

Instead, he ordered these divisions to Hungary, shouting down Guderian's protests by declaring, correctly, that it was vital to protect the Hungarian oil fields. Having failed to obtain reinforcements, Guderian again asked for the only alternative: permission to shorten his front. This produced another outburst from Hitler, who declared that Guderian, Gehlen, and anyone who believed their assessments of Russian strength were 'probably insane'.

The Führer's view of the impending Russian offensive affected more than military matters. The German Reich had expanded since he came to power, to absorb large areas of land in East Prussia, Silesia and the Sudetenland of Czechoslovakia. After their conquest of Eastern Europe the Germans had obtained their *Lebensraum* – living space. Many of these areas had had large German-speaking communities which had provided Hitler with a reason to demand these territories for the Reich during the 'Years of Appeasement' in the 1930s.

Millions more Germans had since moved east, to expand these German communities or occupy rich lands from which the Poles and Czechs or Jews had been evicted. All these 'ethnic Germans' now lay under threat from the advancing Russians and local partisans. Many of them were more than uneasy about their prospects if the Eastern Front crumbled, and wished to retreat to the elusive safety of the German frontier. The Führer again said no, and a tragedy was in the making.

Hitler regarded any suggestion of civilian evacuation as a defeatist, if not a traitorous, proposal. The local party leaders, in the Occupied Territories, the Gauleiters, were ordered to keep their people in place and prosecute any who attempted to flee. When the German army commanders in the east proposed to the Gauleiters that German civilians be moved out of the battle area, to free the roads for military convoys and to reduce the need for supplies, their requests were therefore denied.

Meanwhile, in the early days of January, the Soviet propaganda machine was spelling out the extent of German atrocities in Russian to Red Army troops on the Vistula, urging them to take a full and terrible revenge on any German they encountered, soldier or civilian, man, woman or child, in the great winter offensive that was coming. The loot of Germany, and the women of Germany, were to be the lawful booty of the Red Armies in this coming campaign.

The looming Russian campaign began to affect civilians inside Germany, many of whom had moved east to avoid the Allied bombing, as Helga Rhambo remembers: 'I was fifteen in 1945. My father was fighting with the German Army in Russia and we were in a children's camp at Klentsch in the east of Germany, having been driven out of our home in Hamburg by the British fire-storm raid of 1943. I was in school, played games, and tried to keep warm. We had grown up during the war and this was normal to us. My mother and my two brothers, then aged eight and six, were with me, and there was rationing but no shortages, at least not for children.

'Then, in January, in mid-winter, it changed. We had to leave the camp and get away to the west, how you could and to where you could. Everyone was moving west, the trains were full of wounded soldiers and refugees. We had no idea where my father was, so we simply went to the nearest town and waited for a train west. We went to a town we thought would be safe but the town was Dresden.'

Other people in Germany, Allied POWs and the inmates of the numerous concentration camps, were awaiting the end of the war in grim conditions, but with higher hopes. Edward Gale of the Canadian 4th Armoured Division was in a POW camp on New Year's Day 1945. 'My platoon was captured

41

in Holland in September 1944. The wounded went to hospital in Dordrecht, where we spent a few days, the last days of any civility we were to see for the rest of the war. There was no food to speak of, a slice or two of black bread made of 50 percent sawdust every four or five days, no heat, no doctors for the sick. Boxcar rides from one camp to another, bitter cold, no food, nothing. That's how I got to Stalag 11D on 1 January 1945.

'Things were better there. It was a Canadian camp made up mainly of Dieppe POWs and they had Red Cross parcels. I believe we got half a parcel a week and I thought we had died and gone to heaven ... they even had heat and hot water. There was a hospital there where I had the shrapnel taken out of my arm and leg. This place was no Hilton but we had some food and cigarettes and Canadians to talk to.'

Being wounded or taken prisoner was not always the end of danger, even for German prisoners on the Allied side, as Fred L. Rau, flying with the 9 Troop Carrier Command, USAAF recalls: 'This episode took place after Christmas 1944. We were on an "evac" mission during the Battle of the Bulge, loading wounded GIs. When we were loaded, a corpsman asked if we could take four litter cases and I said we could. They put the litters forward of the jump door and we didn't find out they were Germans till we had them on the plane. One helluva surprise!

'Over the Channel the flight nurse came forward and asked for help as our ambulatory GIs were going to throw the Germans out over the sea. I felt as they did, but I knew we couldn't let it happen. I went back and explained that the flight nurse was responsible for all the wounded and it would be her "butt" if anything happened, so, being chivalrous Americans, they sat down.

'I spoke some German and went over to ask the prisoners some questions. Two only gave name, rank and serial number, but one of the other two was eighteen and a pilot. The other was in his mid-thirties, from the infantry. The pilot was shot down on his first mission. From what I could gather, he went on his first and last mission right out of training and had been told that if taken prisoner he would be shot. I told him he would be treated well and his family would be informed. I then spoke to the infantryman. I asked him if he knew that the war was going badly for Germany. He said, "Yes". I asked what he thought of Hitler and his response was, "Hitler is a madman and a butcher", so I responded, "You must be glad you are a prisoner."

'His response was, "If I could escape, I would." In my surprise I could only blurt out, "Why?" and his answer was, "I don't fight for Hitler, I fight for my country."

'It was then I realized he was no different from me. We were both at war for the same reason, though not for the same principle. Some of the events have faded with time, but I will always remember what I learned on this day in the war.'

Ben Helfgodt, a Polish Jew then aged fifteen, spent New Year's Day 1945 in a concentration camp. 'I was sent from Buchenwald to another camp, one you will not have heard of – Schlieben – near Falkenburg and Kottebus. On New Year's Day I had a little bit of bread which I ground up with some corn into a sort of paste, and that is what I had to eat.

'Have I told you about Hell? Well, this was hell of a different kind. The Germans were not shooting us any more. There was no need, we were dying from starvation, neglect and disease. We travelled for two whole days from Buchenwald to Schlieben in boxcars, without food or water, and when we arrived we were given soup, but we could not eat it. It smelt like excrement; it was made from rotten potatoes or the slime of rotten potatoes. Those who even tried to eat it were sick. The camp people heard a new group had arrived and they came running to see us. They saw the cauldrons of soup and though we could not eat it, they were fighting for it. They were emaciated, their clothing was torn, lice were running all over them; these people were ghosts.

'The only reason some of us survived there was because we were then sent to work in a factory with German women. Inside it was warm and we could sit down. Our work was to make anti-tank weapons – *panzerfausts* – for the German Army, and because we worked with these women the Germans said we should be kept clean, so we had baths and a shower maybe three times a week.

'We slept in bunks 2 feet 6 inches wide, two boys to a bunk, lying on bare boards; the lice dropped on us from the ceiling, for the place was infested. I was raw from scratching. One night I felt as if I was sleeping on stones, but it was the bones in my buttocks, for all the flesh had gone. There are limits to hunger; you can starve for a long time, but we were obsessed with food and could think of nothing else. Not big spreads, or anything cooked, just bread. We thought only of bread – the greatest thing was bread. There were 300 boys in the group that went to Schlieben in December 1944 and only forty of us survived to early May 1945.'

Hitler's confidence in a successful outcome of the war was based on a variety of factors: on the development of terror weapons, on hopeful astrological forecasts, and on a few personal convictions. One of these was that dissension among the Allied nations was inevitable, given the nature of the parties, and that such dissension would eventually pull the Alliance apart and enable him to snatch victory from the jaws of defeat.

'Never has there been such a coalition', he told his generals at the end of 1944. 'Ultra-capitalistic states on the one hand, ultra-Marxist states on the other. On the one hand a dying empire, Britain; on the other hand a colony bent on that inheritance, the United States.

'Each of the partners entered this coalition to achieve their own ends. America wants to be England's heir. Russia tries to gain the Balkans. England hopes to retain her empire. Even now they are at loggerheads. We can wait to see how their antipathy develops, deliver a few more blows, show them that victory is never certain and their antagonisms will grow stronger.'

A belief that the Western Allies would eventually join the Germans to fight Soviet Russia was now common in all ranks of the German Army. Many Allied soldiers report hearing such a belief expressed by their prisoners, but there was never any real disagreement over the necessity for maintaining the Alliance among the Big Three – Roosevelt, Churchill and Marshal Stalin – the politicians or the General Staffs. There was, however, a considerable amount of argument over strategy among the officers of SHAEF and the field commanders. The cause, yet again, was Field Marshal Sir Bernard Law Montgomery, and matters came to a head at SHAEF on 1 January 1945.

The catalyst was Montgomery's persistent campaign for the appointment of a Land Force Commander. His campaign had been fuelled by his appointment to command all Allied forces, including American forces, north of the Bulge during the Ardennes campaign. Montgomery's estimates of his contribution to the elimination of the Bulge now vied both with Eisenhower's calculations and with most of the available facts.

Montgomery had handled the northern flank battles well. The American Army commanders, Hodges of the 1st US Army and Simpson of the US 9th, had no difficulties in working with him and the front was stabilized with British units, notably the 29th Armoured Brigade, the 6th Airborne Division and elements of XXX Corps coming up in support.

But the British part in the Ardennes fighting was a small part. Most of the fighting was done by American troops. The casualty figures speak for themselves. American casualties during the Battle of the Bulge totalled 75,572 killed, wounded and missing; British casualties from all units engaged totalled just 1,408.

The German advance was stemmed before it reached the Meuse, and though Montgomery's calm and capable handling of the crisis was duly noted, many of the necessary steps had already been taken before Montgomery took command; Prime Minister Winston Churchill stated as much in a speech to the House of Commons on 18 January 1945: 'Care must be taken not to claim for the British Army an undue share of what is undoubtedly the greatest American battle of the war, and will, I believe, be regarded as an ever-famous American victory.'

Churchill's statement was caused by Montgomery's remarks to the press in early January 1945, but they came at the culmination of months of barely concealed discontent between the two commanders, Montgomery being unhappy with Eisenhower's overall handling of the campaign and Eisenhower coming to the end of his patience with his most persistent critic.

Giving Montgomery command of two-thirds of Bradley's 12th Army Group revived the Field Marshal's appetite for overall Field Command, and when Eisenhower met Montgomery on 28 December to discuss the conduct of the Bulge fighting, Montgomery came away with the impression that Eisenhower had agreed to him taking command of all Bradley's forces.

On 29 December therefore, Montgomery wrote to Eisenhower on 'the matter of operational control of all forces engaged in the Northern thrust towards the Ruhr, i.e., 12th and 21st Army groups. When you and Bradley and myself met on 7 December, it was very clear that Bradley opposed any idea that I should have operational control over his Army Group, so I did not pursue the matter. I therefore consider that it will be necessary for you to be very firm on the subject, and any loosely-worded statement will be quite useless.'

Montgomery's letter contained a 'Draft Directive' which Montgomery now asked Eisenhower to issue: 'From now onwards full operational direction, control and co-ordination of these operations (the Northern front and the advance to the Ruhr) is vested in the C-in-C 21 Army Group, subject to any such instructions as may be issued by the Supreme Commander from time to time.'

Nor did Montgomery stop there. His letter concludes with a re-statement of his belief that success depended on:

(a) ... All available offensive power being assigned to the Northern line of advance to the Ruhr.
(b) A sound set-up for command, and this implies one man directing and controlling the whole tactical battle in the Northern thrust.

Montgomery's letter implied a lack of trust in Eisenhower's strategic plan and in his ability to control the campaign in Western Europe. Montgomery had been harping on this theme for four months but now he had gone too far. Eisenhower's supply of patience finally ran out for – even worse – Montgomery had leaked his views to the British press where, not surprisingly, they met with general approval.

This opinion was not shared by the American Chief-of-Staff, and Chairman of the Anglo-American Combined Chiefs-of-Staff, that formidable soldier, General George Marshall. Marshall cabled Eisenhower on 30 December, offering his full support and reiterating that there would be great and public disapproval in America if a British general were given command of American ground forces.

Numbers alone should have established the American position beyond all doubt. Even before the Bulge the Americans had sixty-five divisions in the European Theatre of Operations (ETO), compared with nineteen British and Canadian divisions and three French divisions. By the end of 1944 fresh American divisions were arriving in France at the rate of one a week while British reserves of manpower were exhausted. As Britain's contribution declined relative to that of America, so did Britain's ability to influence political or strategic decisions.

That apart, the staff at SHAEF, British and American, were solidly behind General Eisenhower. On 1 January they urged him to have a showdown with Montgomery and settle this matter once and for all. Fortunately for Montgomery, his Chief-of-Staff, Major-General Francis (Freddie) de Guingand, a man well used to the thankless task of pouring oil on troubled waters, was visiting SHAEF that day. Having gauged the situation, Guingand had a meeting with Eisenhower's Chief-of-Staff, Lt-General Bedell Smith, after which the two men went to see Eisenhower.

They found Eisenhower determined to sort out the situation one way or another. Eisenhower was tired of Montgomery's relentless campaign for the post of Land Force Commander. He was tired of stories in the British press praising Montgomery and denigrating Bradley, himself, and the American Army. He was tired of Montgomery's memoranda and cables criticizing his 'Broad Front' strategy.

He had already drafted a signal to Marshall as Chairman of the Combined Chiefs of Staff, laying out the situation with Montgomery and declaring that he would resign his command if the Combined Chiefs considered it the right decision. In other words, it was now a stark choice between Montgomery and Eisenhower. Faced with such a choice, the Combined Chiefs-of-Staff would certainly sack Field Marshal Montgomery forthwith.

Guingand was appalled. He begged Eisenhower to delay sending the cable until he had a chance to explain the situation to Montgomery. Flying back to Montgomery's HQ, Guingand found the Field Marshal in blissful ignorance of the trouble he had caused at SHAEF. The news of Eisenhower's proposed action took him aback, for Montgomery's position, even as Commander-in-Chief, 21st Army Group, was not as secure as he supposed.

Montgomery had also sorely tried the patience of Winston Churchill, and waiting in the wings was General Sir Harold Alexander, a good battlefield commander, popular with the Americans, and now commanding the Allied armies in Italy. Monty was not irreplaceable, and if he wished to continue in command of 21st Army Group there was no option but capitulation. For all his vanity, Montgomery knew how to give in gracefully and swiftly sent his regrets and an explanation to General Eisenhower:

Dear Ike,

I have seen Freddie and understand that you are greatly worried by my considerations during these difficult days. I have given you my frank views because I have felt you like this. I am sure there are many factors which have a bearing beyond anything I realise. Whatever your decision may be, you can rely on me one hundred percent to make it work and I know Brad will do the same. Very distressed to hear my letter may have upset you and I would ask you to tear it up.

Your very devoted subordinate

Monty

Eisenhower was too decent a man, too astute a politician and too well aware of the importance of the Alliance to bear grudges or press home his point. His reply was brief but magnanimous:

Dear Monty,

I received your telegram this morning. I truly appreciate the understanding attitude it indicates ... with the earnest hope that 1945 will be the most successful of your entire career.

As ever,

Ike

No more was heard of Montgomery's campaign for the post of Land Force Commander but unfortunately this matter had hardly been settled when Montgomery again upset both the American people and the American Army.

At a press conference on 7 January 1945, Montgomery gave his account of the Battle of the Bulge. His presentation was almost entirely devoted to his own decisions and the exploits of the 'British Group of Armies'; reports of the conference had the most unfortunate repercussions. His address to the assembled press began:

'Rundstedt attacked on 16 December ... and drove a deep wedge into the centre of the First US Army and spread the American forces. The situation might [have] become awkward. As soon as I saw what was happening, I took steps to ensure that if the Germans got to the Meuse they could not get over that river. I was thinking ahead...

'Then the whole Allied team rallied to the danger ... General Eisenhower

47

placed me in command of the whole Northern front. I employed the whole power of the British Group of Armies ... this power was brought into play very gradually and today British divisions are fighting hard on the right flank of the 1st US Army ...'

And so he continued. There was no mention of Bradley or Patton, or the fact that a major component of 'the British Group of Armies' was the American 1st and 9th Armies. For all his faults, of which vanity was the greatest, Montgomery was not entirely insensitive but his conference was badly reported by the British press, who omitted his fulsome praise of the American fighting man and the Supreme Commander, General Eisenhower.

Large parts of his actual address – the unreported parts – paid due and full tribute to '... the fighting qualities of the American soldier', and '... the captain of our team, General Eisenhower, who bears a great burden, needs our support, and it is up to all of us to see he gets it.' These remarks did not appear in the communique or in the subsequent newspaper articles, and the American press and public were furious.

This proved a propaganda gift to Dr Goebbels and an edited version of Monty's speech, issued by German radio, gave great offence to the American generals, whose lack of sympathy for Montgomery now hardened into active dislike.

While the commanders were arguing at SHAEF, the battles on the ground and in the air continued to eliminate the Bulge and the German gains around Colmar and in Alsace-Lorraine. The Bulge fighting cost the Germans 100,000 casualties, men they could ill spare; but the Allies were also suffering a manpower shortage. The Americans lost a lot of men in the battle, and there was an immediate shortage of front-line infantry.

The harsh winter weather and the heavy fighting had also increased the number of Allied desertions. British and Canadian deserters tended to make for Antwerp and Brussels, American deserters for Paris, where by early January 1945 there were some 15,000 American deserters in hiding, the equivalent of a full division, living by stealing supplies from Army depots to sell on the black market. Offers of an amnesty to deserters or any men in military prisons willing to return to their front-line units failed to produce much response. Some men were found in the rear echelons and sent forward, but many more volunteers came from black troops serving in the supply services who now began to appear in the fighting line, as Carl Sumpter remembers:

'After the Bulge there was a shortage of infantrymen, so it was decided to form Negro rifle squads if they could get enough volunteers. Up to this time it had been believed by the High Command that Negroes would not make adequate combat soldiers. A good many Negro soldiers volunteered from the safe assignments to become combat soldiers, and off they went to be trained. I had the unique experience to be in combat with some of the first Negroes to serve their country as combat riflemen. We were moving up to capture a village and I was given a squad of eight rookie black soldiers to move through and clear out one of the streets of the village. They were obviously rookies because they were all dressed and equipped exactly alike and everyone was brand new without a single stain of grease or mud. Each of them had an M-1 rifle, and strung criss-cross over their chest they had four bandoliers of ammunition. I laughed when I saw them because they looked like Mexican bandits. "What do they think they are going to do with all that ammo ... fight a war?" I thought. I had yet to learn how they had been trained.

'The nine of us assembled and I pointed out to them the street that we were to cover. I assumed that they would operate much the same as the usual GI infantryman, which was to move from cover to cover, with some running and some giving the runners covering fire. That was not at all the way these black GIs had been trained. They all started out at once, all of them shooting at every window, door and building. I could see now why they started out carrying all that ammo. They scared the sap out of me when they all opened up at once, and I was looking frantically around to find out what they were shooting at.

'Then I realized that they were green rookies and were firing to keep up their courage and to keep the enemy's head down. So away we went down the street through the village, shooting the sap out of everything. I didn't fire a shot because I didn't see anyone to shoot at.'

Fighting flared up all along the Western Front as the New Year began. In the north, along the rivers Waal and Maas, the Germans had intended to put in an attack on the 1st Canadian Army in support of their Ardennes thrust. Thanks to aggressive Canadian patrol activity this attack never took place. Instead, the Canadians decided to consolidate their positions by eliminating the German outposts on the island of Kapelsche Veer, west of the town of S'Hertogensbosch. The fierce fight for the Kapelsche Veer went on for nearly two weeks in early January, involving Canadians, Poles and No. 47 (Royal Marine) Commando (who lost fifty men in just one ambush on 13 January). That was one day after the Soviet Army confirmed General Guderian's worst fears and surged forward in force across the Vistula.

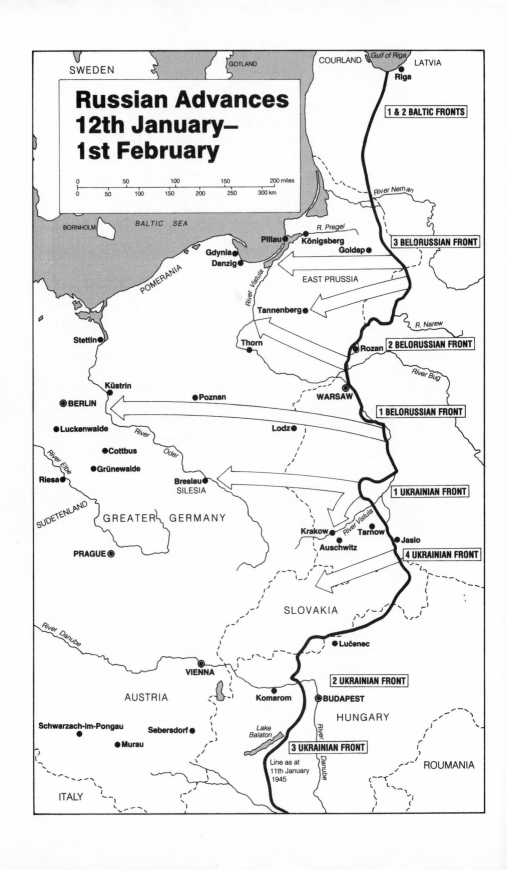

Russian Advances 12th January– 1st February

SWEDEN

GOTLAND

COURLAND

Gulf of Riga LATVIA

Riga

1 & 2 BALTIC FRONTS

| 0 | 50 | 100 | 150 | 200 miles |
| 0 | 50 | 100 | 150 | 200 | 250 | 300 km |

River Neman

BORNHOLM

BALTIC SEA

R. Pregel

Pillau

Königsberg

3 BELORUSSIAN FRONT

Gdynia

Danzig

Goldap

POMERANIA

River Vistula

EAST PRUSSIA

Tannenberg

R. Narew

Stettin

Thorn

Rozan

2 BELORUSSIAN FRONT

River Bug

Küstrin

Poznan

WARSAW

BERLIN

1 BELORUSSIAN FRONT

Luckenwalde

River Lodz

River Oder

Cottbus

Grünewalde

River Elbe

Riesa

Breslau

SILESIA

1 UKRAINIAN FRONT

SUDETENLAND

GREATER GERMANY

River Vistula

Krakow

Tarnow

Jaslo

PRAGUE

Auschwitz

4 UKRAINIAN FRONT

SLOVAKIA

River Danube

Lučenec

VIENNA

2 UKRAINIAN FRONT

AUSTRIA

Komarom

BUDAPEST

HUNGARY

Schwarzach-im-Pongau

Sebersdorf

Lake Balaton

River Danube

3 UKRAINIAN FRONT

Murau

Line as at 11th January 1945

ROUMANIA

ITALY

Russian T34 tank

3 The Winter Offensives

12 JANUARY–1 FEBRUARY 1945

'Pray that your flight be not
in the winter.'

Matthew 24:20

The major Allied participant in the European land war between 1941–45 was Soviet Russia. In January 1945 the advance of the Soviet armies, and the political future of the lands they occupied, began to concern the West. Russian army groups were referred to as 'Fronts', and no less than five Fronts were involved in the Soviet winter offensive from the Vistula to the Oder, which began on 12 January. The Russians had made no major advances on the Central Front since October, while the railway lines into Poland from Russia and the Ukraine were repaired and supplies built up for the winter offensive, but on the Southern Front they had taken Belgrade and forced Romania and Bulgaria out of the war. By mid-January the Red Armies had overrun most of Hungary and were shelling Budapest.

Following that massive military build-up noted by General Gehlen, the time came for a drive in the centre, right across Poland and into Germany. The main assault was to be made north of Warsaw by the 2nd Belorussian Front, nine armies under Marshal Rokossovsky, heading for Danzig on the Baltic. The attack on Warsaw itself and the region to the south was by the seven armies of the 1st Belorussian Front commanded by Marshal Zhukov and by Konev's 1st Ukrainian Front. The German forces in the north, in Latvia and East Prussia, were attacked by the 3rd Belorussian Front under Marshal Cherniakovsky, which would surge north to attack Konigsberg, while Army Group Courland, the German forces to the west of the Gulf of Riga, would be contained and then overwhelmed by the 1st and 2nd Baltic Fronts (see map on page 50).

Soviet Russia's almost unlimited manpower, with tanks and other weaponry supplied by the West or from its own armament factories, was not only sufficient to mount this huge assault, but was also able to continue the advance into Bohemia and Slovakia by Marshals Petrov, Malinovsky and Tolbulkin, then into Hungary and eventually into Austria and Bavaria. The principal aim of Marshal Stalin, the Soviet leader – one which was becoming increasingly apparent as the war neared its end – was for total Soviet domination of the Balkans and Eastern Europe and for the subjugation of as much of Western Europe as his armies could capture before Germany surrendered. To achieve this aim the Soviet armies had to meet their Allies as far west as possible, and huge forces were deployed to achieve that end.

The German armies waiting to meet this assault came from the Army Group Centre and Army Group A, with General Weiss's II Army facing Rokossovsky, the IX Army facing Zhukov, and the IV Panzer Army facing Konev. The Germans had just seventy-five divisions to cover a front some 600 miles long and none was fully equipped or up to strength. The German armies in the east were spread too thinly for the task that lay before them and their destruction was inevitable.

Zhukov and Rokossovsky could deploy nearly two million men in 180 divisions on the Central Front alone – a force aimed at Warsaw and the Oder – backed by 3,000 tanks and 30,000 pieces of artillery. With Hitler unwilling to rescue the isolated divisions in Courland or Latvia, by diverting divisions from the west or sending reinforcements from Germany, the plight of the German armies in the east was desperate.

Hitler could have sent men east. The Germans had trained twenty-four new Volksgrenadier divisions in the closing months of 1944, but most of these were either sent to Von Rundstedt in the west or retained in Germany. Having made his dispositions, on 16 January Hitler returned to his Chancellory in Berlin and there, in his underground bunker, he stayed until the end.

The Russian winter offensive began at dawn on 12 January with a massive artillery bombardment and the advance of Konev's forces. These were followed two days later by a massive surge forward by the tanks and infantry of Marshal Zhukov. Within days the German forces facing the Russians had been shattered, and were in full retreat towards the Oder, taking with them a great mob of German refugees and former settlers.

One of the German soldiers awaiting this attack was Erwin Freppel, who kept a rough diary. The following extracts, drawn from his jotted notes, give a good idea of what life was like for a German soldier during this retreat. 'Our positions were west of Vistula, at Baranov and Warka (bridgeheads on the Oder). After heavy fighting Russians won the battle, using 800 guns. Our company reduced to seven men at this time. Impossible to defend front because of Russian tank troops followed by motorized infantry. We are starving, eating ice. Walked out, discarding weapons to walk faster, artillery and carts sent ahead, countless casualties.

'14 Jan.: Russian air attacks on retreating column. Flak guns only fire at low flying aircraft as short of ammunition. Weather sub-zero. Snow and ice, scattered bodies. German soldiers take boots from bodies, lighting fires under them to warm the leather. Our column came across civilian refugees who joined the soldiers. Women and children now being killed together with soldiers. German aircraft drop chocolate, bread or cigarettes. Heavy snowfalls make marching difficult, sometimes a lift on a sleigh or a cart.

'End Jan.: Came across a village where a woman made coffee. She had seen endless columns of retreating Germans, also – she said – Russian tanks and trucks had passed by during the last few hours – up to a hundred. Came across German soldiers hanging from ropes on road signs. Witnessed a suicide. Commando of SS executing Germans because of 'cowardly behaviour' i.e. not fighting back, retreating. These executions were performed in front of the men. No organized columns now, Russian planes bombing the 'treks' and roads. Major Rosenberg, leader of Pz. 89, killed by Russians ... about 250 men of division sent to form new division in Reich area, all that are left.'

Eight days after the initial attack, Konev's 1st Ukrainian Front had advanced more than twenty miles on a forty-mile front and reached Cracow, while Zhukov's forces had invested Warsaw. Zhukov's Polish troops entered the city on 16 January and it was cleared of German resistance by the evening of 17 January.

The city of Thorn was surrounded on 24 January, before the civilians had time to escape, and Hitler ordered that this city was to be regarded as a fortress and held at all costs. On 1 February this order was changed and the garrison was ordered to break out to the west, marching out on 2 February, carrying the wounded and the women and children on sleighs. Five days later the survivors of the garrison, about 19,000 men came into the lines of II Army beyond the Vistula; another 13,000, many of them women and children, had perished in the snow.

Further to the north, Rokossovsky's troops had taken Tannenberg, the site of the great German victory over the Russians in 1914. The architect of that victory, Field Marshal Von Hindenburg, still lay in his marble tomb at Tannenberg as the Russians closed in; the German garrison removed the body and took it with them as they fled to the west. By 20 January the Red armies had advanced nearly 100 miles and left behind them a trail of death and devastation, wrecked and looted towns, slaughtered German soldiers, and raped, abused women. The bitter winter weather was not the only inhuman factor during this winter campaign.

In the north, Rokossovsky reached the Baltic near Danzig – now Gdansk –

cutting off twenty-five German divisions in East Prussia; while in the centre, Konev overran Upper Silesia. This was Germany's only other source of coal outside the Ruhr, and its loss was a severe blow to the German war economy.

The Russian advance on the Central Front was sweeping all before it, but a significant number of Germans were able to escape to either side of the main advance, fleeing south into the Balkans or north to the Baltic coast. By 20 January the Red Army had advanced to East Prussia in the north, taken Cracow and Lodz in the centre, and were surging forward towards the German frontier. On the way they overran the concentration camp at Auschwitz, which fell to Konev's Army on 27 January. They found very few inmates, for the survivors had already been sent to Belsen or marched away to the west. They did, however, find ample evidence of atrocities.

George Tinsley, then a POW and formerly a driver in the Royal Army Service Corps, was in Auschwitz at this time. 'In January 1945 I was one of about 200 British POWs in a prison work camp at Auschwitz in Poland. This was known as Stammlager No 711, adjacent to the Jewish concentration camp known as Camp III, all known commonly as Monovitz, named after the village that once stood on this site.

'Our "employer" was the powerful German industrial group, I. G. Farben Industrie. The factory complex took its name, "Buna", from the synthetic rubber that the factory produced. There were 30,000 prisoners of all nationalities, including 10,000 Jews and French forced labour. This vast factory was nearing completion in 1945 in spite of heavy bombing by the American and Russian air forces, with the loss of many lives, including over forty British POWs.

'The British POWs were unwilling witnesses to the horrors perpetrated on the great number of Jews, political prisoners, homosexuals, gypsies, and Russian POWs in this place. All the prisoners were supplied to I. G. Farben by the SS for a fee. In our case we were sold by the German Army but the arrangement was the same.

'In the case of the Jews their working life was short, about three months before they died from a combination of hard work, malnutrition, beatings and then the gas chamber. We saw them come and we saw them go. We British POWs were more fortunate in that we got Red Cross parcels from time to time. Without them we could not have survived on the German rations and we were able to slip the Jews a bit of chocolate.

'The winter of 1944–45 was very harsh, the Russian Air Force was becoming very active and the fighting on the Eastern Front came closer every day. Work activity slowed considerably and we noticed that the German civilian overseers and managers were thinning out in numbers, probably being evacuated before the arrival of the Russians. It was common knowledge that the Russians were not well disposed towards anyone not Russian.

'During the last days at Auschwitz the Jews seemed to disappear. We did not see them leave for they were moved at night, but their route took them past our camp and we were aware of this eerie sound of thousands of wooden clogs on the cobblestone road, in a strange kind of shuffle, as if they were too weak to lift their feet ... and so they went and disappeared from this world.'

The discovery of Auschwitz added to the fury attending on the Soviet advance. That advance was so swift and overwhelming that the Russians frequently entered towns while the shops were still open, the factories still working, and civilians were in the streets. This made the looting and burning much easier, and what the soldiers could not take they destroyed. Any house containing soldiers was burned; anyone attempting to conceal valuables or food was shot. German women falling into Russian hands were ill-used; stripped and raped and left to die in the snow beside the roads. Thousands of Germans were turned out into the streets and countryside to die in the bitter winter weather ... and still the advance went on.

As word of the Red Army's brutality spread, the Germans in the 'Warthe' district – that part of Poland incorporated into the Reich – and in East Prussia and Pomerania, took to the roads as refugees, taking anything they could carry, pressing on in long columns – or 'treks' – towards the elusive safety of the Oder. Many died in the frozen fields beside the roads.

By 24 January, twelve days after their initial attack, many Russian units were already on the Oder. Faced with this threat, on 26 January Hitler ordered the formation of another army group, Army Group Vistula, giving the command to his loyal and trusted subordinate, Heinrich Himmler, head of the SS. This appointment led to furious protests from Guderian on the not unreasonable grounds that Himmler, though head of the Gestapo and the SS and an architect of Nazi terror, had never commanded even a platoon in the field.

Himmler travelled to his new command in his private train, moving by night for fear of air attack. He arrived at the Army Group Vistula Headquarters near Poznam on 27 January without even a map. Not knowing what to do, he contented himself with issuing exhortations to his soldiers and ordering the evacuation of several outlying garrisons. His arrival did nothing to bolster the confidence of the German soldiers, but no commander could now stem the tide of the Soviet advance and the horrors that went with it. Storming on, Zhukov's forces reached the Oder on 29 January, driving the remnants of IX Army before them across the ice-bound river.

Dick Parkinson, a sergeant in the South African Army, then a POW, remembers when the Soviet Russians overran his camp in East Germany: 'At first light we anxious and bewildered prisoners spotted a long column of horse-drawn carts interspersed with clumps of Cossack cavalry, moving out of the nearby woods. There is a halt in front – a figure on the roadside is being questioned – a shot is fired – the figure slumps – the column moves on. A posse of Cossacks rides over to the camp and clatters down the main street. Impassive, Mongol-type men on shaggy ponies, festooned with ammo belts and weapons make straight for the Russian compound, from which a host of red flags are fluttering. Their message is "Get going for the Motherland". The fact that on arrival at the Motherland these starving POWs will disappear into the "Gulag Archipelago" for being contaminated by the West is mercifully withheld at that moment. Screams come from a pig farm nearby and a gaunt POW slouches by, taking bites from a raw liver.

'The camp inmates felt free to search the countryside for food. Wrecked and overturned trains, abandoned barges on the Elbe, empty and vandalized houses, terrified civilians hiding from second-wave Russian troops – all these told the tale of fearful chaos.

'Quantities of black bread were issued to the POWs who were then marched across the Elbe into what appeared to be an abandoned city – Riesa. This invading army was everywhere in evidence: sturdy women soldiers in the turrets of enormous tanks, and long lines of well-kept horses being groomed by rosy-cheeked peasant soldiers.'

Where the Red Army advanced, German men, soldiers or civilians, were murdered or shipped east to Russia as slave labour. Women of every age were raped, and everyone, men and women, was beaten and robbed of everything, from the rings on their fingers to the shoes on their feet. In the face of this terror many German men shot their wives and children and then shot themselves. There are many reports of woods and orchards thick with swinging bodies, but individual suicides were so common as to be not worthy of record. Tens of thousands died of cold or hunger on the roads or were crushed under the tracks of advancing Soviet tanks.

By 25 January the northward thrust of Rokossovsky's armies had surrounded the town of Königsberg, preventing any evacuation by land. The Germans attempted to evacuate their troops and as many civilians as possible by sea, but ships were in short supply and Russian fighters and bombers ranged at will over the port. Terrible scenes ensued on the docks of Danzig and Königsberg, where Army Group Centre held out stubbornly against the Russians as the hapless civilians, many of them women and children, tried to escape by sea. Women with babies were given priority and babies were therefore thrown back from the ships to other women on the dockside, many babies falling into the sea between the ship side and the quay.

Mrs Lanna Milton was in Königsberg in 1945: 'I was born in 1935 in Königsberg, East Prussia, the daughter of a military German family. My father fell in the final battle of Berlin, defending the Reichstag building. He died on 30 April 1945, as the Russians struggled inside this battered historic building. My mother and I fled Königsberg in the February of 1945 as Mom's company of "*Wehrmachthelferinnen*" – Wehrmacht WACs – was being evacuated by ship so that they would not fall into Russian hands.

'Now Königsberg no longer exists and what remains of the city was re-named Kaliningrad and incorporated into Russia. As a German WAC my mother worked in military communications, on teletype and telephones in the signals section. In 1943 she went to take a training course in the Polish port city of Gdynia, which Hitler had re-baptized as Gotenhafen.

'I remember very well the night of New Year's Eve 1944. My mother took me to her brother's home that evening for a social occasion. Due to the military situation it was a somewhat restrained evening. My mother was off-duty and enjoyed social events. Smoke and some alcohol filled the air. People pretended everything was going all right – and I already sensed they were deceiving themselves. My mother knew that the Russians were massing troops along the borders of East Prussia, since she was working in Army communications and administration. Yet she kept silent. It was an eerie feeling. The Soviets had completely liberated their country and had penetrated deeply into Poland, where the front stood along the Narev river.

'Everybody – I mean everybody – in the party waited for midnight as a radio speech by Hitler was eagerly awaited and some promise of fantastic new weapons which would finally turn the unfavourable military situation around. After the radio speech came the display of fireworks unleashed by the *Kriegsmarine* in the port district. The row of historic sheds along the Pregel river in Königsberg lay in ruins as the result of an air raid on the city. It all felt like the quiet before the storm.

'The great Soviet offensive was unleashed on 12 January. Mom's company was being scheduled for evacuation on 25 January. The Russians were quickly approaching the outlying districts and artillery shells were being rained on the city. We hurriedly left our beautiful apartment for ever on that afternoon. A train took us to the port of Pillau for transport to military control centre in the eastern Baltic, which was located in the port city of Gdynia. During our short stay in Pillau we learned that the Soviets had thrown a ring around Königsberg. The Nazi Party had prevented the evacuation of the civilian population. Can you imagine? – just to keep up appearances that everything was going to work out fine. Of course, the company of Wehrmachthelferinnen was evacuated in a timely fashion, and not even one day too soon. It is with deepest sorrow that I still think of the countless number of women and children left behind in the sealed-off city which now came under steady artillery fire day and night. As you may know, the city finally capitulated on 9 April 1945, practically obliterated, a sea of smoking fire and ruins.

'We were shipped to the port of Gdynia on 1 February 1945. I still remember the crowding on the ship and the penetrating cold of the Baltic Sea. In Gdynia the WAC company had to wait for military instructions to be shipped where needed. Finally the destination was set for the port of Lübeck, and from there to Frankfurt-am-Main. During our travels through the Baltic I clearly remember the sound of *Fliegeralarm*. A single British plane was heading over us while the flak crews quickly manned their stations. However, nothing happened. Most likely the plane was dropping mines into the waters of the Baltic. We had a mine-sweeper ahead of us, the ship was zigzagging on its course, and at night sailors were manning the closed iron doors separating the various compartments of the ship. We were acutely aware of the danger presented by Soviet submarines in the eastern Baltic.

'On arrival in Frankfurt-am-Main, Mom was assigned to another Signal Army unit, and she surrendered on 27 March 1945 to General George S. Patton's famous 3rd US Army.'

On 25 January, Russian troops from Konev's 1st Ukrainian Front established bridgeheads across the Oder south of Breslau. Further north, Zhukov's troops surrounded Poznam and swept on towards Küstrin, while on the Baltic coast Rokossovsky's troops entered Pomerania. On 31 January Zhukov's troops also reached the Oder and the two main Russian army groups now stood only fifty miles from Berlin. Behind them lay a devastated countryside, littered with the wreckage of the German armies and tens of thousands of frozen bodies. Still the German soldiers fought on, hungry, frozen, short of ammunition, lacking support, with a march to a slave labour camp their most likely fate if they fell into the hands of the Russians, and a 'Flying Court Martial' and a hanging by the SS awaiting anyone who fled to the rear. The German Army had ravaged Europe but it is hard not to feel sympathy, even admiration, for the German soldiers making this last hopeless stand along the Eastern Front.

It is some evidence of the lunacy taking hold in the Führer's Berlin bunker that Hitler and his deputy, Hermann Goering, were still optimistic, feeling that the Western Allies would not be prepared to let most of Eastern Europe fall to the Communists and must soon offer an armistice. 'They entered the war to prevent us capturing the East', said Goering. 'So they will not want to see the East advancing to the Atlantic ... if this goes on we shall get a telegram from the West in a few days.'

In fact, the Western Allies were busy supporting the Russian advance with massive raids on the cities of eastern Germany, including Berlin. Noel

Robinson from Oregon and Don Nielsen from Arizona were pilot and co-pilot of a B17 in 751 Squadron, flying from Glatton, near Peterborough in East Anglia. Don Nielsen kept diary notes of every mission:

'Mission No. 8. 3 February 1945. Target – Berlin: This was the roughest mission yet for us. I flew co-pilot with regular crew. We took off at 7.30 a.m. in the dark. We had a maximum gas load and 10 × 500 lb. bombs. We assembled at 9,000 feet in the dark; it was very hard to spot the right ships and at the same time keep an eye open for other planes flying in the dark. We climbed to altitude and went in across Zyder-Zee. Levelled off at 26,600 feet; the temperature was − 46°.

'Just before IP the ball-turret oxygen hose sheered off. We lost all our oxygen in the ball, waist, one side of the radio room and the tail. The boys doubled up to share what oxygen outlets were left. The ball-turret gunner Rickert got out of the ball so fast he sprang the door on it.

'We were the seventh group of planes over the target, with thirty or so groups behind us. All in all the bombers stretched for 300 miles. Just before the target I saw a B17 in the group ahead of us catch fire and blow up.

'We were hit with flak right at "Bombs away". I was flying the plane and it bounced all over the sky. I thought the controls had been shot because the nose dropped, but then came up OK. The cause was a large hole in our elevator. Flaps were out because the electrical circuit was shot out. We lost all our gas in RH feeder tanks and in RH "Tokyo" wing-tip tank ["Tokyo" tanks carried extra fuel for long-range missions]. Our inverter was shot out and the alternater would not work. Our superchargers worked off the inverter so they would not work either and we could only get 30 inches of manifold pressure out of the engines. As a result we began to drop behind the formation.

'Just after leaving Berlin I saw two more B17s blow up off to the left. The alternate inverter then kicked in and we got some power back. We flew north and then west, just below Denmark to the North Sea with a little more flak but inaccurate. We let down over the North Sea but had to watch our gas carefully. Our waist gunner discovered that an elevator control cable had been shot away but there are two of them and one was still good. We crossed the English coast and broke formation, cranked the flaps by hand to test them and let the gear down to see the tyres weren't flat. No. 3 engine cut as out of gas. The fuel gauge read 120 gallons but it was broken. We came in and Grimm cranked the flaps down for a final approach. Landed at 3.45 p.m.

'We taxied to dispersal and found that the ship was like a sieve. The hole in the elevator was the size of a man's head. The waist gunner had a piece of flak lodged in his parachute. We counted fifty-six holes in the plane but there must be many more. The plane had to go to sub depot for repair.

'Tonight I hear on the news that we bombed military targets in Berlin but that is not so. We were just there to flatten the city and ruin civilian morale so that it would be a little easier for the Russians.'

Nineteen American bombers and five fighters failed to return from this mission to Berlin, on Saturday, 3 February 1945, ten days before the Allied air forces struck at the city of Dresden.

In a little over two weeks the Soviet armies had swarmed across Poland from the Vistula to the frontiers of Germany. Here and there, in Courland, at Königsberg, Breslau and Posnam, isolated German garrisons and units of the German Army, sometimes whole divisions, still held out, but the German Eastern Front had been shattered. Then came some relief. During the last week of January a thaw reduced the roads to swamps and slowed the Soviet advance. This gave the hard-pressed defenders of the Reich a small respite and time to dig in and defend what they held. More they could not do, and while the German soldiers hung on, flayed by artillery fire and fearful of the future, the Soviet soldiers took terrible revenge on the civilian population.

Royal Marine Eric Foulkes was near the Hungarian border at this time: 'I was taken prisoner in Crete on 1 July 1941 and in 1945 was working on a small farm in the village of Sebersdorf, in Austria, near the border of Hungary. The main of the family, who owned the farm, was serving on the Russian Front, so it was left to his fourteen-year-old son and I to keep the farm going. We had to use two of the milking cows to haul the farm wagon.

'The boy's mother was busy looking after her other four children, as well as doing work around the farm, plus the cooking; it was a case of survival for everybody. Life was going along normally in the village till German troops arrived. I heard that these were part of a German army retreating through Hungary from the Russians and making their way back to Germany. Within the next two or three weeks this turned into a large-scale retreat as large sections of horse-drawn transport arrived.

'They commandeered all the hay from the farms in the surrounding area to feed their horses. In the next few days trails of refugees arrived. By this time the local people were really frightened of the fact that the Russians were so close, because of all the propaganda that these people had been given about what the Russians would do if ever they arrived. The wife was really frightened and I advised her to join the refugees. I fitted out the farm wagon with steel rods and a large canvas sheet to look like a caravan, which the boy and I loaded with all the food that was available, and off they went with the two milking cows pulling the wagon. It was just as well that they left when they did, because the army started to slaughter the available cattle as there was nothing left to feed to them.

'At night, locked in our lager, our working party of forty men were debating on what we were going to do when the Russians arrived. Sections of the Hungarian Army then came retreating from the front. These men wore khaki-coloured uniforms. We all decided that we would not stay any longer than was necessary, but the German Command decided that all POWs would be put into batches of 1,000 and sent down the road, with a one-day interval between each batch. As far as I can remember we were in about the fifth batch. The countryside was bare of food or firewood ... and so commenced our six-week march.

'It was a cold, wet and hungry march, very windy going through the snow-capped mountain passes. In about the fifth week, as we were bypassing the town of Murau, a couple of the guards took about eighty of us who were in a really sorry state of health to see a doctor. When I went into the surgery and was asked what was wrong, I could not decide what to say, as my whole body was covered in abscesses, I was having problems with my breathing, and my chest felt as tight as a drum. I noticed a spittoon on the floor so I coughed and spat blood into it. He took one look and said, "Hospital". After tests were taken I was told that I had pleurisy and allowed to spend a week resting. I am sure I would not have made it to the end of the march, which was to be outside the town of Schwerzach-im-Pongau in Austria.

'Life in this camp was really a hard and hungry one, as there were about 46,000 British prisoners there as well as some French and a few Americans, but after about three weeks the advance units of the American Army arrived.'

Accounts of this time are full of terrible incidents when Russian soldiers, knowing only two words of German: "*Frau, Komm*", would take women away to rape, shooting anyone who attempted to interfere. There was rape by every army, even on the Western Front, but on nothing like the scale which took place in the east.

The war diary of the XXIV Panzer Regiment records the state of affairs in East Prussia at this time: 'End January: Streets congested with refugees – tanks trying to plough through ... Commander von Rittmeister Fischer attacks on the night of 27/28 January and pushes ahead to Krikehnen. The bridge at Alken is blown up behind them so their support isn't able to get through. They try again next night. The village completely destroyed – it shows signs of Bolshevistic cruelty.

'30 January: Gauleiter and Reichs-Defence Commissioner Koch had to be sacrificed, due to intrigue, and General Friedrich Müller took over. Koch had insisted that the generals had tried to flee to the west.

'As planned, the tanks of Pz. Rgt 24 push towards east, deep into enemy territory. Near Grunwalde they come across enemy, who didn't expect them. A lot of refugees, who were for days captured by the Russians, are freed. Advance can't continue with attack because the infantry isn't up to it.

'Battle for Zinten: Group von Einem fights but on 9 February has to retreat. On 10 February battle around Nonnenhausen and Maraunen, east of Zinten ... more divisions turn up for battle of Zinten ... division fights in this area with the Hermann Goering Panzerkorps until 20 February. They are able to hold the Russian Army but can't win back the barracks, which are the key to the town ... Hohne, Hahn, etc. die.

'12 February: Heavy fighting. Our division is fighting the hardest battle for East Prussia; in uninterrupted fight we are defending our country. The enemy has heavy losses: 209 tanks, 149 guns, many cars and lorries; 23 of the tanks were destroyed in close action with *panzerfaust*. The Air Force shooting 23 enemy planes.

'Final battle: Heavy winter weather and continuous battles also affected the enemy – a pause on 4 March but all knew that the last and greatest attack had to be expected ... until now the ice covering the *Frischehaff* [an inlet twenty miles east of Danzig], allowed the refugees to cross it but the weather changed and the ice melted. The Russian "butchers" hunted each refugee "trek" on the front and near the coast.'

Still the Red Armies came on, giving no respite to the refugees. Danzig fell on 30 March, after heavy shelling and street fighting had reduced most of the city to rubble. The 10,000 German soldiers in the garrison were taken prisoner and marched east, while those civilians who had not been killed or committed suicide were hunted out of the ruins, robbed, stripped or raped. A further 80,000 German soldiers, many of them wounded, were captured in Königsberg, where more than 40,000 Germans had been killed before the surrender.

On the Southern Front, Budapest fell on 23 February, giving the Russians another 100,000 prisoners for the work camps and coalmines of Siberia. On 29 March the Russians crossed the frontier into Austria, capturing Vienna on 13 April. Prague fell on 8 May, the last day of the war, but not before the Czech partisans had taken a fearful revenge on the German civilians and any captured German soldiers. The war in Eastern Europe had always been marked by destruction, brutality and massacre, from the moment the German Army crossed the Polish frontier on 1 September 1939. Once across that line, common humanity perished in the frozen countryside of Poland and Russia and was still completely absent when the Russians came back into Germany in the bitter winter of 1945.

There is no need to continue this litany of terror and destruction on the Eastern Front, though the stories here illustrate just a small part of what happened to thousands of people trapped by war in the freezing wastes of Poland and East Prussia. The Russian advance in the east and the horrors that came with it had more than a military effect on the war in the west- The news of rape and murder spread across Germany, stiffening the resolve of the German Army to resist in the east, and encouraging more and more German civilians to flee west, towards the advancing American, British and Canadian armies.

The PIAT – Projectile Infantry Anti-Tank

4 Blackcock and the Saar

16–31 JANUARY 1945

'It is the men that count, not the machines.
If you tell the soldier what you want and
launch him properly into battle, he will
never let you down. Never!'

Field Marshal Sir Bernard Montgomery
21st Army Group, 1945

Before we follow the Western armies on their various thrusts into Germany, it would be as well to take a look at the map and see exactly where they stood in January 1945. It should be realised that the German Army was not yet entirely confined within the German frontier and the Rhine is not everywhere the western frontier of Germany.

Much of the north of Holland, from the north shores of the Scheldt estuary along the rivers Maas and Waal to Nijmegen, was held by the nine divisions of the 1st Canadian Army, which was facing north to oppose the German XV Army of seven divisions which still occupied Rotterdam and the rest of Holland. To the south and east of the Canadians, the British 2nd Army lay along the Siegfried Line from Nijmegen to Venlo, though there were still some German pockets west of the Siegfried Line which remained to be eliminated.

Further south still the American 9th Army lay along the river Roer, facing the towns of Jülich and Düren, and then came the 1st US Army which had already penetrated into Germany through the Aachen Gap. South of Aachen lay the hilly Ardennes and the Schnee Eifel, which was now being cleared of German troops. The front line then followed the West Wall, along the river Saar up to Lauterbourg, then south along the Rhine – here the boundary between France and Germany – and so to the Swiss frontier near Basle. The battle in progress on this front was to eliminate the Colmar Pocket, a task which Generals Patch and Lattre de Tassigny now had well in hand.

The objectives for January were to eliminate all German resistance west

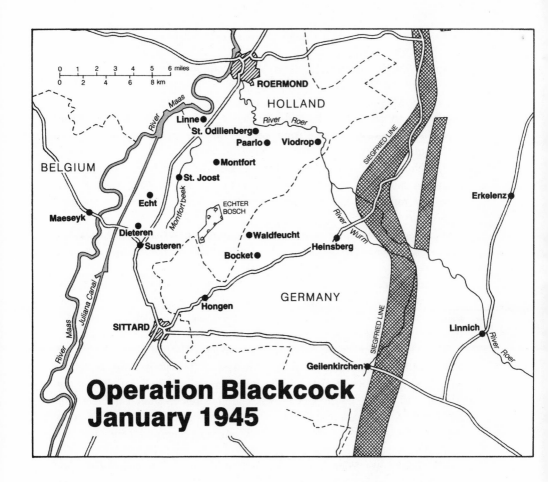

Operation Blackcock
January 1945

of the Siegfried Line, and push east across the Roer river to the Rhine. In the south the task was to push up the Moselle valley to Koblenz and clear the Germans from two regions south of the Moselle and east of the Siegfried Line, the Saar–Moselle Triangle, where the main objective was Trier, and then the rest of the Saar-Palatinate. This task would be shared between Patton's 3rd Army on the Moselle and Patch's 7th Army advancing north along the west bank of the Rhine, once the Colmar Pocket had been reduced.

Verdon Besley was an infantryman serving with the Queen's Royal Regiment in the 7th Armoured Division and he describes one January night on the Maas: 'It was very cold. During the night we were usually given a drop of rum, but in the mornings my overcoat was frozen on me. We rested most of the day but could not have a fire in our dugout as the smoke would give us away.

'One night I was told to go on a patrol of about four men, including

65

Sergeant Paddy Fortune, and an officer who was very young and had just joined us. We had orders to bring back a prisoner. It was moonlight when we went over garden fences to an open field. We hopped across the field and came to a barbed-wire fence with a house beyond. There was a lot of noise coming from the house and the young officer said we should charge, so I started to crawl under the wire, but my sergeant said, "Not with my men you don't", and the officer let fire with his Sten-gun and all hell broke loose. I managed to get back through the wire and ran like hell, zigzagging across the field, with bullets cracking around my ears.

'We stopped, fired our Bren-guns and ran again. When we got back, the officer asked what he should report. I never knew what he did report as they gave me some rum and I had to sleep it off!'

There was plenty of such patrol activity along the Western Front but as the skies cleared in early January and air support became freely available, plans were laid to eliminate some of the larger German pockets west of the frontier.

The Market Garden operation of September 1944 had given the British and Canadians a useful foothold on the Lower Rhine. Fighting along the Maas and Lower Rhine flared up in mid-January, when XII Corps of the British 2nd Army, commanded by General Ritchie, launched Operation Blackcock, to clear the Germans out of the triangular-shaped salient they had maintained west of the river Roer and the Siegfried Line, between Geilenkirchen and Roermond.

The 2nd Army front faced north into this salient, which ran for some twenty miles from the Maas and the Juliana canal east to Geilenkirchen on the river Wurm, a tributary of the Roer, and north for fifteen miles from Hongen to Roermond. Across this salient the Germans had established three defence lines, all spurs running west from the Siegfried Line, all well supplied with mines and entrenchments and manned by two strong divisions, the 183rd Volksgrenadier in the east and the 176th Infantry Division in the west. These divisions were supported by a considerable amount of artillery, including twenty of the formidable 88 mms, and could call on further gunfire support from German positions beyond the Roer and along the Siegfried Line.

The British XII Corps consisted of three divisions, the 43rd and 52nd Infantry Divisions, and the veteran 7th Armoured Division (the Desert Rats), plus two armoured brigades and strong detachments of specialized armour: the 'Funnies' – the flame-throwing and mine-clearing tanks of the 79th Armoured Division. The XII Corps contained two artillery groups from the Royal Artillery, and could call on artillery support from the guns of the VIII Corps and the XIII US Corps.

General Ritchie decided on a phased attack, with the 7th Armoured Division going in first on the left flank, up the road to Echt and St Joost, followed by the 43rd Division in the centre and then by the 52nd advancing along the western edge of the Siegfried Line on the right. At 0730 hrs on the morning of 16 January 1945 the initial advance was made by the 131st (Queen's) Brigade of 7th Armoured Division, which soon became involved in heavy fighting for the town of Susteren.

Major John Evans, DSO was in the fight for Susteren: 'At 2.30 on the cold, dark morning of 17 January 1945, B Company of the 1st/5th Queen's Royal Regiment were spread out on the snow-covered fields with orders to attack and take the small town of Susteren, two miles from the German border. "Attack by stealth," we were told, "and if you fail we have corps artillery laid on to flatten them before you rush in." Little did we think that we would experience that frightening barrage before the day was out – called down on our own position.

'Searchlights shone on clouds to provide artificial moonlight, but this "Monty's moonlight" meant that while we could see our objective half a mile away, the enemy would spot us as we started moving, so I called for the searchlights to be switched off. We were already on the "Start Line" but I refused to move until the lights were extinguished and this took quite a time, so it must have been about 4 a.m. before we moved.

'We crept forward silently and got to within 30 yards of the town before we heard a guttural shout and a single shot was fired. We then adopted our usual tactic, rushing in screaming and shouting, firing rifles and Brens from the hip. From previous experience we knew that the defenders would freeze with shock.

'This proved to be the case and we ran through the first part of the town without a single casualty, taking about thirty-seven prisoners. The platoons were placed in street corner positions to provide a field of fire down the roads, and I selected a semi-detached house as Company HQ with instructions that it should only be entered from the rear. Our elation evaporated at dawn, when we discovered that the enemy had three tanks in the town. Our own tanks had failed to reach us because of the dykes, drainage ditches and soft ground, so these German Tigers were a real problem.

'Then followed some desperate fighting. The tanks were soon patrolling the streets, demolishing the houses on top of my men; Private Howard knocked the track off one tank with a PIAT, for which he was later decorated. There was a prominent house opposite my position, which the enemy tanks thought was my HQ and promptly flattened. Pleased with themselves, the two tank commanders came up and opened their turrets to speak to one another. They were no more than 15 yards from where I was, and the target was too tempting to resist. Resting my captured Schmeisser against the side of a window, I fired two short bursts and saw hits on one commander's head.

'It was obvious that we were in for a long day and many casualties, so desperate solutions were needed. I was in contact on my 19 radio set with Major Jock Nangle, the Acting CO of the battalion, and when he suggested that they could bring down artillery fire on our position to clear the tanks out, I reluctantly agreed, provided we had half an hour to get under cover.

'I stood by the tiny cellar of the house as the seconds ticked away to the bombardment. Suddenly Lt Stone dived through the rear entrance. "My platoon are well dug-in", he said ... his last words. "Get down there", I replied. He hesitated, and I shouted, "Get down there", pointing to the stairs.

'At that moment there was a violent explosion. To this day I don't know whether it was British shelling or a shell from an enemy tank. I favour the latter because my left arm was struck with a concentrated blast. The skin only had a burn-like mark but inside everything was broken: bones, blood vessels, the lot. Although initially numb, the arm was quite useless and later gave me extreme pain.

'Lt Stone had been blown down the stairs. I followed him and the men already in the cellar seated me on a chair, where I nursed my arm. "How is Lt Stone?" I asked. "Sorry, Sir, he's had it", was the reply.

'The town above was now being reduced to rubble by our guns. The house above came crashing down, and I was slipping in and out of consciousness with the pain of my arm, when suddenly the world was ripped apart by an almighty explosion. A shell had hit the rubble and blasted into the cellar above my head. Six bits of shrapnel tore into my flesh, hitting neck, back, thigh and the remaining good arm. The wounds, some of them very large, looked worse than they were because though the shrapnel sliced the flesh, it miraculously missed the bones.

'All I knew what that I had been hit again. The shock had thrown me against a wall, where I contemplated being buried alive. It was difficult to breathe because of the dust and fumes, but I was quite calm, just amazed that it was all going to end.

'As the dust settled, I became aware of a light and it dawned on me that the last shell had blown a hole in the cellar roof. I managed to scramble half out of the cellar, which wasn't easy, but clinging on with my one good arm I saw that there was little left of the buildings. The shelling had stopped and two soldiers were behind a wall about 10 yards away. I recognized Private Street and called to him. Both soldiers were in a state of shock and it took some time for them to see me. Eventually Street crawled over. "Christ, it's the Major!" he said, and I had enough sense to say, "Get a door and put me on it." I think if I had said, "Put your head in a bucket of water", he would have done that too, such was the tension of the time.

'They put me in another cellar where I passed out after a German prisoner had attended to me. I remember that my feet had been wet from the snow and were like blocks of ice. The German lay across them, rubbing them to keep them warm. By then it was evening, our support troops had arrived and Private Seaton, my batman, was sitting at my feet when I then uttered these immortal words: "Seaton, get my camera and binoculars and put them on my stretcher." Both won from the Germans, of course, and I have them to this day.

'My company had excelled themselves, and although the British shelling was followed by German shelling and a counter-attack, the remnants of my company held on and performed incredibly well.

'Twenty years after the war I decided to visit Susteren, where I had been wounded and lost my arm. To my surprise I received a terrific welcome, for the locals had been looking for me for nearly twenty years. There was a civic reception and banquet, a special parade with the town band, and the Burgomaster said: "One day we shall build houses here and one street will bear your name." In May 1985 I was invited over to open "Major Evanslaan" and plant a tree. They gave me a greater honour when the Burgomaster said that they wished to give my name to a new school. I made it clear that I accepted their tributes on behalf of all those who fell at Susteren in 1945. This school has given me great pleasure and I am constantly in touch with the children.'

German resistance at Susteren was not quelled until midday on 18 January. By that time 7th Armoured Division had advanced four miles from their Start Line across very difficult tank terrain, a mixture of canals and deep ditches and frozen fields, and through a series of defensive positions.

Ronald Mallabar of HQ Company, 9th Battalion, the Durham Light Infantry in the 7th Armoured Division, remembers his part in Blackcock: 'The order was "Nine DLI will attack and capture Dieteren." This was an infantry operation because our advance was barred by an unbridged canal, and we would be without support until the REs (sappers) had got a bridge across for the tanks.

'We moved out early on the morning of 16 January. It was bitterly cold and there was deep snow. I was a regimental signaller attached to a rifle company, so in addition to all the other kit, I carried a No. 18 radio set weighing 56 lb. This was hot work until the shells started exploding among us – the lumps of earth thrown up by the shells were frozen hard, mostly ice, and as bad as shrapnel.

'Being a signaller in the infantry carries a number of problems. First of all the aerial marks you out for snipers. Secondly, because of the chatter in the earphones you can't hear what is going on – like mortar bombs coming down. You have to watch the rest to see what to do.

'We were soon in Dieteren, and after a brisk firefight the Germans withdrew. I found an empty house, dumped my radio on the floor and sat beside it. Then came a series of loud explosions and a message to watch out for German tanks. The next message was equally alarming. German machine-gunners had got behind us and put a stop to bridge-building over the canal, and we must send a platoon back to deal with them. I was sent along but when we got back the Germans had already been driven off. I saw a German Schmeisser machine pistol lying in the snow, which would normally have been picked up as they were in great demand, but this one had the former owner's fingers mashed in the breech. There was another dead German lying nearby with the top of his skull sliced off. I remember thinking that his brain looked just like a walnut in a half-shell.

'Then it was my turn. I heard the thump of mortar and had just turned when a bomb exploded right behind me, throwing me against a wall. My jerkin immediately turned red with the blood that was pouring down my face and I thought my skull had been sliced open. In fact a steel splinter had passed between the rim of my helmet and the top of the radio, hit me on the back of the head and emerged by my ear. Twenty-five years later a lady doctor at my local hospital removed a small piece of steel helmet from my head – and she was German.'

While the infantry units of 7th Armoured Division were fighting around Susteren, the 8th Armoured Brigade and the 155th Infantry Brigade had come forward in the centre on a night advance to clear the woods of the Echter Bosch. Here, too, they encountered stiff opposition in every village and from roving groups of German infantry operating in company strength and supported by Tiger tanks armed with the formidable 88 mm gun. The 8th Armoured Brigade could make little progress through this swampy, wooded country, and on the evening of 19 January the brigade was pulled back and attached to support the 52nd Infantry Division, which was now pushing forward.

The 52nd (Lowland) Division attack on the 18th had been led by the Scots of the 156th Infantry Brigade, supported by flame-throwing and mine-clearing tanks of the 79th Armoured Division. These came in handy during the fight to clear three villages – Hongen, Bocket and Waldfeucht – which spanned the division's front. A sudden thaw had turned the fields into mud, every stream was a swollen torrent, every village was stubbornly defended. The infantry enjoyed the support of mine-clearing and flame-throwing tanks, but it was not until nightfall on the 20th that the Germans were evicted from Hongen, where nineteen-year-old Fusilier Donnini of the 4th/5th Royal Scots Fusiliers earned a posthumous Victoria Cross in house-to-house fighting.

The 155th Brigade entered Waldfeucht early on the following day, where they were first heavily shelled and then attacked by German infantry from the 183rd Volksgrenadier Division supported by Tiger tanks. Bitter tank and infantry fighting went on throughout the day in the streets and gardens of Waldfeucht, but the Scots refused to be evicted, taking on the Tigers with PIATs and the German infantry with rifle fire, grenades and the bayonet. This fighting was house-to-house, the troops breaking through walls and roofs to evict the defenders, or fighting hand-to-hand through the gardens. The Germans finally withdrew around midnight on 19 January. With Waldfeucht taken, the second line of German defences had fallen into British hands and the advance continued.

The remaining division of XII Corps, the 43rd (Wessex) Division, had been advancing on the right, staying level with the 52nd Division to the west of Waldfeucht. Both sides were now receiving infantry reinforcements. The Germans opposing 7th Armoured were bolstered by the arrival of a parachute regiment from the German 606th Division at Roermond, while SS troops had been sent in to oppose the 52nd and 43rd Divisions to the right.

The 7th Armoured had been joined by the four Commando units of the 1st Commando Brigade under Brigadier Derek Mills-Roberts. The commandos set out to clear the right bank of the Maas, while the rest of the division began to clear the German 176th Division from the town of St Joost. These tasks took two full days and involved more heavy fighting.

The advance to the Baltic of Brigadier Mills-Roberts' 1st Commando Brigade is one of the epics of the campaign in north west Europe. 'The Brigadier would only settle for the best', recalls one Commando officer. 'If the morning's training went well, we got the afternoon off. If not, we went on training until we got it right, however long it took.'

The commandos encountered stiff opposition around the Montfortbeek stream, where Lance-Corporal Harden of the RAMC, attached to 45 (Royal Marine) Commando earned a posthumous VC for bravery under fire. A Troop of 45 Commando had lost two men killed and thirteen wounded in the attack and Corporal Harden went out three times to tend wounds or bring in wounded men. Though wounded on the second sortie, he went out again and was killed. St Joost was finally cleared at dusk on 21 January.

The Allied ground forces engaged in Blackcock had so far received little support from the air, for poor weather with low cloud, rain and snowstorms had hampered flying operations. On 22 January the skies cleared and were immediately filled by Typhoon and Mosquito fighter-bombers of 83 Group, 2nd TAF, the group attached to XII Corps. Their attacks continued, by day and by night, for the next two days. With this support, XII Corps now began to advance rapidly towards Roermond, which fell on 26 January and brought the British front line up to the Roer river.

71

Major Derrick Watson of the 1st/5th Queen's, recalls the end of Blackcock: 'In the closing stages of the battle, A Company were ordered to occupy Paarlo, a village on the Roer. I had under command a Vickers MMG section and a tank from the Royal Tank Regiment. During the night of 29/30 January about fifty German soldiers crossed the Roer to Paarlo in assault boats and attacked our forward lookout.'

Verdon Besley takes up the tale: 'Late in the evening there was a sudden barrage and a terrific bang from upstairs. Two men came down, blinded by a *panzerfaust* rocket which had been fired through the lookout window.'

Major Watson again: 'I received a wireless message from the lookout post – "Get some help up here quickly." I took two sections and set out, crawling towards the lookout. A German, apparently wounded, called out, "Friend, come and help me!" but when we stood up a Spandau machine-gun opened up on us, wounding the lance-corporal at my side. We pulled back to the tank, which opened an effective fire, first on that Spandau and then on another one. It became clear that the Germans were occupying the ground between the lookout and my Company HQ.'

Meanwhile, Verdon Besley was carrying out a defence of the lookout in spite of a stream of fire and the lobbing of German grenades through the windows. 'I had placed myself directly above the middle room with the door on my right and a window in the room facing the Germans, so that I could watch the door, the stairs and the window. I had just stopped at the top when I heard a voice below. I shouted out, "Is that you, Assi?" A reply came back in broken English, "Us, you mean us." I shouted back, "Not you, you bastard", fired my rifle and all went quiet.

'By this time I was worried about the men below in the cellar, as I could not hear a thing from them. Later I was told the corporal was keeping them quiet. I found a phosphorus grenade in my pocket and pulled the pin and threw it down the stairs, but grenades started to come through the window of the room I was guarding and I had to take cover each time I heard one come through. However, I did manage to keep the Germans out of the cellar.

'As time passed, the ammunition was running out and the Bren-gunners came down and took most of mine. After a few hours, Baker decided he would try and get help and left me to guard the front door. Now the bombardment got worse, the house shook and I was blown across the hall but was not hurt. The two men came down from upstairs and said they were out of ammunition, and the three of us were in the hall when we heard a voice outside say, in a sort of German accent, "Out!" We just said, "Yes, you bastard", and fired. I say "we" because we were all of the same mind, but it was lucky we did not hit him as he was one of our own officers who had broken through. He was a Czech, later known as Robert Maxwell, the man who owned the *Daily Mirror*. Well, with this, Major Watson came in the front door and said, "Who wants medals?" All we wanted was more ammunition.

Derrick Watson continues: 'I went back to Company HQ after we had lifted the siege on the house. The tank had opened up on the Germans and we were finally able to send them scurrying back across the river. We then fired everything we had at them, to bring the fight for Paarlo to a satisfactory conclusion.'

'Blackcock' lasted nine days, an indication that progress across this waterlogged country could not be quick. The operation cost the XII Corps 1,500 men killed and wounded as well as 100 tanks, but it cleared the way to the Roer.

While the Canadians were fighting along the Maas and Waal in northern Holland, and the British were clearing the Germans from around Roermond, the Americans were mopping up after the Bulge, advancing to the Roer and beginning their fight up the Moselle to the Rhine, starting with a thrust up the Moselle towards the town of Grevenmacher in the Saar–Moselle Triangle.

Lt-Colonel Philip Whitman of New Hampshire was then a captain in the 94th US Infantry Division. He begins his tale before Christmas 1944: 'In late December 1944 a German submarine lay waiting in the English Channel for a target to come steaming by, bringing reinforcements to the "Bulge". The 66th Infantry Division, fresh from the States, was crossing the Channel to go into the Bulge and help drive the Germans back. A single torpedo sank the *Leopoldville*, carrying the 262nd and 264th Regiments of the 66th Infantry Division. Over 700 men drowned within sight of the French shore.

'The 66th Infantry Division ended up containing the Germans in St Nazaire and Lorient, while our 94th Infantry Division went into the Bulge. The 94th Infantry Division had been in SHAEF reserve but promptly reassigned to the 3rd Army, commanded by General George S. Patton, and XX Corps commanded by General "Bulldog" Walker who, if memory serves me correctly, was outranked by General Maloney, our division commander. The XX Corps was a fighting machine and our 94th Division was the spearhead of XX Corps in the drive to the Rhine.

'On Christmas Eve many of us attended a service at the Catholic cathedral in Nantes, and to this day, though a Protestant, I consider it to be the most beautiful service I have ever attended. We all had reason to pray because we all knew, or thought we knew, what was ahead of us. Believe me, the best pacifist is a soldier going into combat.

'On that same Christmas Eve, a remarkable event was unfolding in a Catholic church in the Lorient Sector, where the 301st Regiment was in control. The incident was related to me by Lt Sel Kohrs, of L Company, 301st Infantry Regiment. He and several men decided they would attend the service in a church at Hennebont. They filed in through a side door, stacked their rifles, placed their helmets on top of the stacked rifles, genuflected, and sat down in the nearest pew. A few minutes later, through a door on the opposite side of the church, in walked a group of armed German soldiers. Somewhat shocked to see American soldiers sitting quietly in a pew, they in turn stacked their rifles, placed their helmets on top and sat down in a pew directly opposite Sel Kohrs and his men.

'For two hours these soldiers, who the day before had been trying to kill each other, sat in the same church. After the service, the Germans gathered their arms and helmets and left by the same door through which they had entered. Kohrs and his men retrieved their weapons and left at the same time. Neither group tried to intercept the other after leaving the sanctity of that beautiful church.

'Living in pup-tents did little to keep out the freezing cold, so every man was issued with a bottle of cognac. Unfortunately, one of my men, a strapping Indian, got slightly drunk and took his BAR (Browning Automatic Rifle) to a hill overlooking our bivouac area and started spraying bullets about 8 feet over our tents. I ordered my company to find him, capture him, and if necessary, kill him, but we finally collared him and I put him behind bars.

'On 15 January 1945 I received information from Lt-Colonel Martin that Company F would be making an attack on the woods just northwest of Tettingen at 0700 hrs on 16 January. By this time we knew that the 1st Battalion of the 376th had made the initial penetration of the German defensive line in Tettingen and Butsdorf and had been fighting for two days to hold their position. The woods northwest of and adjacent to Tettingen exposed their left flank and had to be taken. Company F was given the mission. I was further informed by Lt-Colonel Martin that Lieutenant Thomas Fairchild of Company G would make a reconnaissance of the area and report to me on my arrival in Wochern.

'The snow was knee-high as I took off in my jeep to find Tom Fairchild, while my executive officer, Lieutenant Richard Hawley, guided our company through the snow to Perl. Hawley lost his way in the snow and the company arrived late in the afternoon, dead tired. Meanwhile, Lieutenant Fairchild could only tell me there was an anti-tank ditch, 10 feet wide by 10 feet deep in the woods called Monkey-Wrench Woods.

'Next morning at 0700 hrs we jumped off through the woods beyond Perl. The 1st Platoon, under Lieutenant Wilfred Wilson, ran into a deep anti-tank ditch which the Germans used in wooded areas as opposed to the cement "Dragon's Teeth" they used in open areas. I sent the 3rd Platoon, under Lieutenant Stanley Mason, to follow the ditch and cross it when he could. The 2nd Platoon commanded by Lieutenant Gordon Weston was to follow the 3rd Platoon in support.

'One by one, Indian style, the 1st Platoon crossed the ditch with me right behind. On the other side we found a minefield with anti-personnel mines attached to every tree with trip wires just one inch above the snow. What I soon realized was that we were attacking the rear of the enemy position, which they considered impregnable.

'A whisper came back to me: "Captain Whitman – come forward." I did, picking my way over the trip wires until I found my lead scout, Michael Alba, kneeling beside a tree. He very quietly pointed out the moving head of a German reading a book. We had stumbled onto their Command Post. I worked my way back to the rear, carefully stepping over the trip wires until I reached Lieutenant Wilson. I briefed him on the situation and said, "Let's go."

'The rest is history, but not very well described in either our Divisional or Regimental histories. Without taking any personal credit, this attack was one of the most successful engagements in our attempts to breach the Switch Line. Many Germans were killed, sixty-two were taken prisoner, twelve machine-gun nests were reduced and a three-storey hospital bunker was captured. Our casualties were four men killed and a few men wounded.

'Sheer luck played an important role in this operation, for we caught the Germans with their pants down. Honeycutt and Davis forged ahead of the skirmish line of the 1st Platoon and promptly paid the penalty. Cleary, a bright, pink-cheeked eighteen-year-old First-Aid man was killed as he knelt to give aid to mortally wounded Honeycutt. His Red Cross helmet was ignored by the Germans. I left his body there for several hours so that every man in my company could appreciate what we were up against. Sergeant Van Dusen, a squad leader who spoke fluent German, came by, saw Cleary lying dead, turned to find two Germans approaching to surrender with their hands over their heads. He killed them both. I cannot recall, as I stood near him, whether I admonished him or not; I was somewhat upset myself. Three weeks later in Bannholz Woods, I saw Van Dusen 50 feet away, conferring with Sergeant Scopoli. Suddenly his helmet flew off and he slumped to the ground – dead.

'I, too, was tempted to shoot a German that morning. In order to follow the course of our attacking troops, I had the side of the anti-tank ditch hollowed out so I could stand and observe the actions as best I could. Meanwhile, German prisoners were streaming towards us. One, as he approached me, deliberately tripped a wire, exploding a mine on a tree 8 feet or so away from my head. He was hit and pitched headlong by me into the bottom of the ditch. I was most fortunate, and received not a scratch, but my ears rang for days.'

Allen Howenstine of Michigan City, Indiana, was wounded in the Saar–Moselle fighting. 'At this time I was twenty years old; a mortar gunner in H Company, 376th Infantry Regiment (Lt-Colonel Russell M. Miner), 94th Infantry Division. On the morning of 14 January 1945, the 2nd Battalion of the 376th jumped off from Wochern in Germany into the Siegfried Switch, a very well-fortified part of the Siegfried Line. My assignment was to order fire for our two 81 mm mortars, and I travelled with a rifle platoon of F Company.

'Late in the day of the 14th, the rifle company had pretty well cleared Monkey-Wrench Woods, so called because its shape resembled the well-known wrench with its jaws open. A squad of German soldiers came out of a pillbox and our machine-gunner decimated them. Four were killed outright and five or six more were wounded, and I think a couple got away across the draw which separated Monkey-Wrench Woods from a wood which the Germans still controlled.

'We gathered the wounded and took them back to the pillbox, which we immediately took over as our headquarters; a place to get warm. The pillbox, as I recall, was about fifteen to twenty feet underground. It was equipped as a hospital bunker, with probably twenty to thirty bunks built into the walls. When the first guys got into the pillbox they discovered a German doctor there. He had medicine and instruments in his pack, and a Red Cross arm band; he had evidently been getting ready to depart when we came in but he immediately began to assist the wounded. One German was critically wounded, shot through the upper body and lungs, and died during the night.

'We probably should have carried the wounded Germans back to our battalion aid station, about two miles to the rear, but by the time we were in a position to do so it was dark, we weren't absolutely sure the woods were cleared, and the area was heavily mined. No one was willing to run the risk of injury or death for a wounded enemy. Also, the Germans had not endeared themselves to us. Earlier in the afternoon Jamie, one of my friends, was taking two German prisoners to the rear when one kicked the trip wire of a booby trap or mine. Both Germans hit the ground, the mine went off and wounded their guard. Jamie was only superficially wounded and was able to shoot both Germans as they attempted to escape.

'The German doctor, who could speak fairly fluent English, did what he could to make his patients comfortable. The next morning the wounded prisoners were taken to the rear, and the German doctor put on his pack and indicated that he was going to rejoin his comrades in the wooded area across the draw from where the pillbox was located. He said that according to international law we had no right to hold him and he was free to go. A few rifles pointed in his direction changed his mind, and he was taken to the rear.

'There were several German counter-attacks over the next few days, especially in the Tettingen-Butsdorf village, a few hundred yards to our right. None of them was really successful, but led to heavy casualties on both sides. Usually a counter-attack consisted of one or two Tiger tanks with upwards of a hundred supporting infantrymen. When the first one was beaten back, by the next day another was mounted, and so on. I always wondered why they didn't come at us with five or six tanks and a battalion of men. In some cases I'm sure they would have been at least temporarily successful.

'On 19 January I received a shrapnel wound in the knee; a small, almost spent piece of shrapnel. I was evacuated as a walking-wounded and at the evacuation hospital, a doctor removed the shrapnel. A local anaesthetic was used and the doctor and I chatted during the operation. Upon completion he said, "Well, young man, you've messed up your knee pretty bad." I told him that I had walked to the battalion aid station, but he didn't buy any of that and put me in a cast from my ankle to my hip. I was then sent to a hospital in France where no one removed the cast for three weeks. The doctors then immediately pronounced me fit for duty and within a week or so I was back with my outfit.

'In later years, as I read about the Second World War, it is sometimes mentioned that surgeons became so sick of seeing young men coming through with all manner of injuries, that they sometimes went to extraordinary lengths to protect them. I have often wondered if that is what happened in my case. At any rate, I missed about a month of the worst fighting and the coldest weather.'

The 3rd Army's fight to clear the Saar–Moselle Triangle, which began with the attack on Tettingen, continued for another six weeks until 1 March. But we must leave them for a while and return to the 1st US Army, which was now facing a problem. Operation Blackcock was clearing one path to the Roer river, the last barrier before the Rhine plain. The American 9th Army also had to cross the Roer but their problem was the Roer river dams further south in the 1st Army sector.

These dams, which stood on various rivers but were known collectively as the 'Roer river dams', consisted of seven massive barrages controlling the waters of the Roer and its tributaries. The largest was the Schwammenauel dam, two miles south of the town of Schmidt. All the dams were important: should they be destroyed while the Allies were actually crossing the Roer, or even after they had become established on the east bank, then the forward troops would be cut off and the river crossing would be a disaster. Therefore, any advance across the Roer could only take place after the dams had been taken or destroyed. The terrible fighting in the Hurtgen had taken place to clear the way to the dams but as soon as that breakthrough was achieved, the Ardennes offensive had stalled the advance. The dams were still intact and in German hands when American troops of General Huebner's V Corps of 1st Army took up the challenge in January 1945. For this task, General Huebner had his own 2nd and 9th Infantry Divisions plus the support of the 78th Infantry Division which came under his command on 2 February. The first task of the 78th Infantry was to take Schmidt.

The V Corps attack went in on 4 February and enjoyed an immediate success when a company of the 9th Division reached the Urft dam and captured it intact. At 0300 hrs on the following day the 78th Division swept through the front line of German defences without a shot being fired. At dawn, however, resistance began to stiffen as German troops in pillboxes and trench positions put in a strong fight. The attack slowed, reinforcements failed to come up and no further progress was made by the 78th Division that day.

That night General Huebner ordered the 78th Division's commander, General Parker, to take the Schwammenauel dam the next day ... 'or else'. This advance also began at 0300 hrs, giving the 78th men a second night without sleep, and their advance was again met with intense fire and stiff resistance. Heavy fighting went on all through 6 February and the following day, but it was not until the evening of 7 February that the forward troops of the 78th Division entered the outskirts of Schmidt. The battle, however, was not yet over.

On 8 February the Americans discovered that the shattered ruins of Schmidt were strongly held by infantry and dug-in tanks. Time was running out, for a major thrust across the Roer by Simpson's 9th US Army in the north was scheduled for 10 February and the vital Schwammenauel dam was still not taken.

The 78th Division was now exhausted and the task was handed over to General Craig's veteran 9th Infantry Division. Craig took two regiments of the 79th Division under command – the 309th and 311th Infantry Regiments – and thrust his reinforced division through Schmidt towards the dam, two miles beyond.

German resistance was still fierce and even with fresh troops the pace of the advance did not quicken. The 1st Battalion, 309th Infantry Regiment, did not finally reach the dam until after nightfall on 9 February. There the men split into two groups, one to cross the top of the dam and one to edge across the spillways at the bottom. For both groups this was a nerve-racking task that led to an unfortunate discovery. The dam wall was intact but the sluice-gates, which controlled the flow of water, had been blown up and destroyed.

This was the worst possible situation. Had the dam been destroyed, the resulting flood, though destructive, would soon have passed. As it was, a steady unstoppable flow was now pouring from the dam, a flood that looked likely to continue for many days, as the Roer river burst its banks below the dam and spread out across the countryside. The 9th US Army attack – Operation Grenade – would have to be postponed, while the Anglo-Canadian attack further north in the Reichwald – Operation Veritable, planned to coincide with Grenade – had already started.

25 pdr. gun

5 Malta and Yalta

1–11 FEBRUARY 1945

'We had the world at our feet. Twenty-five
million men marching to our orders...
We seemed to be friends.'

Winston Churchill
Yalta, 1945

Wars tend to be fought on two levels: the military and the political. While
the battles of Blackcock and the Roer raged along the western borders of
the Reich and the Russian armies forged ahead in Poland and the Balkans,
the 'Big Three' Allied leaders – Churchill, Roosevelt and Stalin – were
meeting at Yalta in the Soviet Crimea to discuss the post-war world.

Ever since the United States had entered the war in December 1941 the
Big Three, sometimes accompanied by political leaders from Canada, France
or South Africa, and always with their political and military advisers, had
met from time to time to discuss the progress of the war and agree on
future strategy. In early February, with the end of the war in sight, President
Roosevelt and Prime Minister Churchill arrived in Malta to prepare for
their next meeting, the 'Argonaut' Conference at Yalta.

In previous years and at other conferences, at Casablanca, Quebec and
Teheran, the atmosphere had usually been genial and the spirit of co-
operation abounded. Now, with victory almost within their grasp, the unity
forged between the Allies in the hard years was beginning to crack. Post-
war considerations now began to fill the agenda as the naked ambition and
aggression of the Soviet Union in Eastern Europe became more obvious –
at least to Winston Churchill. On the face of it, however, in February 1945
the 'Big Three' alliance was as firm as ever.

During their preliminary meeting in Malta, Winston Churchill hoped to
persuade the US President, Franklin D. Roosevelt, that as the two demo-

cratic countries in the Alliance they should stand firm against any demands or territorial claims made by the Communist leader, Marshal Stalin.

President Roosevelt was far less interested in the post-war shape of the Continent. He intended to have all the American troops back home two years after the war ended – at the latest. He also wanted to see Russia enter the war against Japan as soon as possible after Germany was defeated, and in the longer term he hoped to see the end of the colonial empires of Britain, France and the Netherlands. Regarding Soviet Russia as a non-imperial power, he hoped for Stalin's support in achieving this ambition.

Churchill's hope at Malta was that the two Western leaders would have enough interests in common to present a united front to any unpalatable proposals put forward by Marshal Stalin, either for the immediate future or in the post-war period. Churchill was well aware the the British Empire could not endure, but he hoped to end it step by step, through a process of gradual internal self-government, leading in time to full independence. His chief concern was the relentless advance of Communist forces in the Balkans and Eastern Europe, which would, he feared, lead to Communist hegemony in Eastern Europe when the war was over. Since British troops were even now engaged in preventing a Communist takeover in Greece and the Soviets had been less than helpful to the Polish Home Army fighting in Warsaw, he had some evidence to support his fears.

While Roosevelt and Churchill were mulling over their political strategy, their military leaders, the Combined Chiefs-of-Staff, a committee composed of the British Imperial General Staff and the American Joint Chiefs-of-Staff, convened in Malta on 30 January 1945 to discuss strategy for ending the war in Western Europe. Eisenhower's proposals for the months ahead arrived on 20 January 1945, and caused dispute between the American and the British staffs in Malta.

Eisenhower's intention was to continue his 'Broad Front' strategy in three distinct phases: To destroy all German forces west of the Rhine and close up along the river; to seize bridgeheads over the river; to destroy all German forces east of the river and overrun Germany up to the limits of the western advance, when the Western armies would meet those of the Soviet Union. The dividing line between the two – the rivers Elbe and Mulde – had already been proposed and would be confirmed at Yalta. Germany would subsequently be divided into four Occupation Zones – American, British and Soviet, with the French allocated a small zone in the west, along the Saar. This arrangement put Berlin well inside the Soviet Zone, but the Four Powers had agreed to divide and rule Berlin on similar lines. For the moment, at least, Berlin was the prize of the first army to get there.

When it came to developing his three strategic objectives, Eisenhower stated his intention of making his major thrust into Germany north of the Ruhr. This important industrial area would certainly be heavily defended, and he saw no way of maintaining more than about thirty-five divisions across the Rhine in the north until the railway lines across Belgium and Holland could be repaired and supplies assured for a thrust deep into Germany. The possibility of bridgeheads across the Rhine in the south – in the 12th US Army Group area – could therefore not be overlooked.

Therefore Eisenhower intended to make certain logistical preparations in order to switch his main effort, if necessary, from the north to the south, from Montgomery's 21st Army Group to Bradley's 12th US Army Group. Eisenhower's statements were not always models of clarity and this one caused a certain amount of confusion, which led in turn to serious dispute.

The British Chiefs-of-Staff had discussed these proposals before leaving London and on arrival in Malta they placed several amendments on the table. These were, briefly, that *all* the logistical effort available should be put behind one thrust, that this thrust should be in the north and that 'the best results could be achieved if one Land Force Commander, responsible to Eisenhower, were given operational control for all Ground Forces employed in the main thrust.'

The American Combined Chiefs totally rejected the British proposals. They came less than a month after the last clash over the matter of a Ground Force Commander, and the Americans were convinced, probably correctly, that the man behind this proposal was that persistent and irritating general, Field Marshal Montgomery of Alamein.

There was a great deal of discussion. Some of it was so heated that the Combined Chiefs moved into closed session, where General Marshall, head of the American Joint Chiefs and also Chairman of the Combined Chiefs, made clear his 'total dislike and antipathy to Field Marshal Montgomery'. In the face of such antipathy the Ground Force Commander proposal was finally dropped.

Gradually tempers cooled. When Eisenhower's reply was studied in detail it began to emerge that what he was actually proposing was an attack north and south *of the Ruhr* with the object of surrounding and cutting off the Ruhr industries from the rest of Germany, rather than an all-out assault through the Ruhr itself. The main attack would be to the north, supported by a subsidiary attack along the southern flank of the Ruhr to encircle the entire area. Eisenhower's plans were therefore redrafted and accepted by the Combined Chiefs without further dispute.

The British insistence on a northern thrust was maintained not out of any desire for national glory, but for reasons of strategy and political advantage. Not only is the country south of the Ruhr unsuited to the deployment of large armoured forces, but an advance through the south of

Germany would not lead to targets of strategic importance.

The original Allied plan, agreed before D-Day, had been for the elimination of Germany's industrial base in the Ruhr, then a thrust northeast across the North German plain. This terrain was ideal for rapid advances by armoured forces, the deployment of large Allied armies, and one where the German armies had no advantage of terrain and could be easily overmatched. Finally, such a thrust could lead to the capture of the Reich's political capital – Berlin. With its political, military and industrial centres captured or destroyed, Germany must surrender and with luck and judgement would surrender to the West, with all the prestige and post-war advantages that would confer.

For the moment, all these objectives seemed attainable. The main thrust across the Rhine would be north of the Ruhr and made by 21st Army Group, the British 2nd Army, the Canadian 1st and the American 9th, with Hodges' 1st Army from 12th Army Group attacking south of the Ruhr. The two American armies, the 1st and 9th, would complete the encirclement and join forces somewhere east of the Ruhr, around Paderborn, where they would proceed to eliminate the Ruhr pocket. The Combined Chiefs left for Yalta on 3 February in a far more cordial and cheerful mood than had seemed likely a day or two before.

One of the decisions reached by the Combined Chiefs was to withdraw five divisions from Italy to reinforce Eisenhower's armies in Germany. Churchill viewed this suggestion with some dismay since he had hoped a rapid advance north through Italy would keep the Russians and Marshal Tito's Yugoslav partisans out of Austria. The Chiefs also proposed acceding to a Soviet request that, to aid the Soviet advance into East Germany, the strategic bomber forces, RAF Bomber Command and the 8th USAAF, should carry out heavy attacks as soon as possible on the communication centres of Berlin, Chemnitz, Leipzig and Dresden. This decision, which led to the now notorious Dresden raids later in February, was endorsed by the politicians assembled at Yalta.

The Yalta Conference did more than discuss policy and military strategy for the next few months. The Allied leaders had to consider what to do with Germany after the war. Germany had plunged Europe into war three times in the space of seventy years – in 1870, 1914 and 1939 – and must not be permitted to do so again. The argument now was about how to achieve this sensible ambition.

The 'Big Three' leaders now controlled a mighty military machine, a world war was raging which they were sure to win and – as Roosevelt and Churchill knew but Stalin as yet did not – the Western Allies would soon possess a weapon, the atomic bomb, which should make further world wars unthinkable.

Churchill believed that the German economy must be revitalized and rebuilt and her people shown the virtues and benefits of democracy and restored to full membership of the European community, not least as a bulwark against Communism. He believed that the fearsome cost of reparations forced on Germany by France after the 1914–18 war had contributed in no small measure to the collapse of the German economy, the fall of the Weimar Republic, massive inflation and unemployment, and the rise to power of the Nazi Party.

Roosevelt, on the other hand, had already endorsed parts of the 'Morgenthau Plan', which proposed dismantling German industry and turning the German people over to pastoral activities before the American troops went home. Roosevelt did not intend that American troops or money should guarantee the peace of Europe. That would be the task of the United Nations Organization which Roosevelt hoped to establish before the war ended.

Stalin's proposals were rather more direct. They ranged from shooting all the German leaders up to a number of around 50,000, to removing all German industrial plants to Russia and extracting massive sums from the Germans in reparation for Russian losses in the war. He also had other aims, but these had yet to appear. From these divergent views a common policy had to be evolved at Yalta.

With victory on the horizon, the common cause which had linked the Allies since 1941 – the defeat of Germany and Japan – was now only just sufficient to keep the Alliance together. National interests were beginning to reassert themselves and assume priority. The balance of power rested with the Americans but that was a problem, for Britain and America were on a collision course.

The Americans felt that they had not liberated half the world, at a vast cost in blood and money, in order to return the liberated colonies of Asia to their former imperial masters, be they British, Dutch or French. When the war ended these colonial peoples, too, must be free. These demands were not entirely altruistic. With them went the thought that the European colonies in the Far East, India and Africa, would provide lucrative markets for American goods in a post-war world, and so maintain the increased production that had pulled the United States out of the Depression.

The requirement for decolonization was not new. During the drafting of the Anglo-American 'Atlantic Charter' before America entered the war, Roosevelt had insisted on the inclusion of a decolonization clause 'ending discrimination by all States, great or small, against access to the trade and raw materials of the world', a clause that struck directly at Imperial Preference, the commercial chain that bound the British Empire to the Mother Country. Neither of the Western leaders was prepared to budge on the decolonization issue. President Roosevelt had declared as early as 1942: 'The British have signed the Atlantic Charter and the United States Government means to make them live up to it.' Churchill did not see it that way at all, growling in a speech at the Mansion House in the City of London in November 1942, 'We mean to hold our own. I did not become the King's First Minister in order to preside over the break-up of the British Empire.'

Yet in spite of Churchill's resolve and even without America's insistence, the British Empire was already doomed. Within the next twenty years it would be transformed into a Commonwealth of free and independent nations – some time before the majority of those black American soldiers now fighting on the Western Front could sit where they wished on a bus. The British had neither the means nor the will to retain their empire after a war which would leave them exhausted and impoverished. Still the colonial issue tinged Roosevelt's thinking at Yalta and made him lean more towards the views of Stalin than to those of his friend and colleague from Great Britain. Stalin was more than willing to exploit this rift between his democratic allies.

That apart, Roosevelt was dying. A polio victim, he had worn himself out during the Depression and the years of war. Roosevelt and Churchill arrived at Yalta on 1 February 1945 and all who saw Roosevelt were shocked by the change in his appearance since the Quebec Conference of the previous autumn. He had just been re-elected for an unprecedented fourth term as President of the United States, but the strains of office had finally taken their toll. He was now confined to a wheelchair and lacked his former energy. Nevertheless, the United States was far and away the dominant world power, and at Stalin's suggestion Roosevelt took the chair at Yalta where his decisions were seen to be crucial to the outcome of the talks. Roosevelt was convinced that he could handle Marshal Stalin, that the Soviet Union and the United States shared a common revolutionary origin and therefore understood each other. It took some time, and a new American president, before the United States realized that Stalin had no interests but his own.

The 'Argonaut' Conference at Yalta began on 4 February and lasted until 11 February 1945. The final declaration covered a great many subjects, including Soviet agreement to attend a conference at San Francisco in April 1945, a meeting charged with setting up the United Nations. Getting this accepted involved fending off a Soviet proposal that all sixteen Soviet Republics should have individual seats and votes at the UN. The plan to partition Germany into four Occupation Zones after the war was confirmed. But these matters, though important, were overshadowed by arguments over a more pressing consideration – Poland.

To explain the depth of feeling aroused by the Polish question we must go back to 1939. The preliminary political basis for Hitler's attack on Poland was the Soviet–German Non-Aggression Treaty, usually called the Molotov–Ribbentrop Pact after the two foreign ministers who drafted it. This pact assured Hitler that Russia would not intervene when he invaded Poland. For keeping out of the fight, Stalin had been rewarded by Hitler with large areas of Poland and the Baltic states. Until Hitler broke the Non-Aggression Treaty in 1941, Russia and Germany were virtual allies.

After the outbreak of war between Russia and Germany in June 1941, Stalin at once began to demand arms, munitions and a 'Second Front' in the West, while remaining determined to retain all he had gained by collaborating with Hitler. At the other conferences since 1941 Stalin had demanded that the Western Powers recognize and accept the new Russian frontier in territory rightly belonging to Poland. So far, no one had cared to press the point, but with the war ending the matter of Poland's frontiers could no longer be delayed.

Britain had a particular interest, for she had declared war on Germany in 1939 to fulfil her guarantees to Poland, and Churchill had often declared his commitment to 'a strong, free, independent, sovereign Poland'. Polish soldiers had been fighting for that for five long years, usually alongside the British. The Polish II Corps had fought with the 8th Army at Cassino, a Polish parachute brigade had fought at Arnhem, a Polish armoured division was even now fighting with the Canadians in Holland. Churchill was now deeply concerned over Soviet intentions towards the Polish state, for by February 1945 there were, in effect, three powers interested in governing Poland after the war.

Within Poland were the remains of the Polish Home Army, broadly democratic in character, maintaining itself in and around Warsaw. There was the Soviet and Communist-dominated 'Polish National Committee of Liberation', set up in Lublin, Russia. Finally, there was the Polish Government-in-Exile in London. Diplomatic relations between the Polish Government-in-Exile and the Soviet Union had been broken off in 1943 after the discovery of the bodies of 4,000 Polish officers murdered by the Soviets at Katyn. This had not deterred the Soviets from pressing their interest in post-war Polish affairs and on 31 December 1944, the day after Roosevelt and Churchill agreed to go to Yalta and discuss these matters, the Soviets recognized the Lublin Poles as 'the Provisional Government of liberated democratic Poland'.

Politics apart, the dispute was over frontiers and the extent of Polish territory. Russia had always had a great, and in many ways understandable, interest in Polish affairs, since armies invading Russia had usually attacked through Poland. The easiest way to shut that western gate was to absorb

Poland into Soviet Russia, which had been an aim of Russian rulers since long before Napoleon. From time to time the Russians had achieved that end, but never for long in the face of the Poles' unquenchable desire for independence.

The current frontier dispute dated back to the end of the 1914–18 war, when the collapse of the Austro-Hungarian Empire led to the establishment of an independent Polish state and an argument over frontiers, especially in the east. A frontier commission under Lord Curzon had drawn up a Russo-Polish boundary, the 'Curzon Line', running from Czechoslovakia to the southern tip of Lithuania, which the Poles would not accept because it gave Russia about a third of Poland and the important city of Lvov. By 1938 the Polish–Russian frontier still lay well east of the Curzon Line, from Latvia to Romania.

Then came the war, when the Russians seized most of the claimed land in Poland, up to and beyond the Curzon Line. All this they intended to retain, while suggesting that the Poles could compensate themselves for this loss of territory by moving their western frontier to the Oder–Neisse river line.

This territorial matter could be discussed by the Big Three but any solution would have to be ratified by the Poles. At Yalta the Soviets managed to get their creatures on the Lublin Committee accepted by the others as the 'Provisional Government of Poland', but only on the understanding that this 'Provisional Government' would include representatives from the Polish Government-in-Exile in London and other representatives of the Polish people, and that the 'Provisional Government' would exist only until there could be free elections in Poland. The condition that free elections would be held in all the liberated states of Eastern Europe was embodied in the final Yalta communique.

Poland would be the touchstone of the Soviets' good faith – or lack of it. If the Soviets broke their agreement over Poland, the hopes for democratic freedom in the other countries overrun by the Red Army or Communist partisans – the Baltic states, Hungary, Romania, Bulgaria, Czechoslovakia, even Austria, Germany and Italy – were bleak indeed. Even among already liberated nations like France and Greece, the Communist wartime partisans were prepared to use their armaments and political terror to overthrow the elected governments or get their nominees into power. Greece was in the middle of a civil war and France was only kept from one by the presence of the Western armies and the willpower of General de Gaulle. Where no such assistance was available, the Soviets acted at once to extend their rule or put their surrogates in power.

To give but one example, two weeks after Yalta the Soviet Deputy Foreign Minister, Andrei Vyshinsky, presented an ultimatum to the King of Romania, ordering him to dismiss the leader of the all-party Romanian government, General Radescu. The King was given just two hours to comply. Having done so, he was then obliged by Vyshinsky to appoint Petru Grotzu, leader of the Romanian Communists, as his next prime minister. The Communist rule of Romania forced on the people by the Soviets was to endure for the next forty-five years ... and all in spite of the 'Declaration on a Liberated Europe' signed by Stalin at Yalta only two weeks before.

Standing up to Soviet demands at Yalta, and resisting Stalin's pressure for further concessions, was an American responsibility, for Britain no longer had the economic or military clout to oppose him. President Roosevelt was too ill to make any decisive stand against the Soviet demands and was unwilling to side with Churchill, the old Imperialist. Roosevelt and his advisers, who were willing to do virtually anything to get along with the Russians, were unable to realize that their readiness to see the Soviet point of view was regarded by Stalin as weakness and a basis for further demands. The United States view was that the war was not yet over and for it to be won quickly and decisively – not least against Japan – the power of the Soviet armies was essential. Any dispute now risked a collapse of the Alliance and must be avoided, at whatever cost to the future. The Poles must either accept the Russian offer or be left to seek whatever accommodation they could with the Soviets after the war.

Yalta has been described by the historian Chester Wilmot as the place where the Western Powers 'won the war but lost the peace'. It was certainly the place where many of those East European and Balkan countries, just released from Nazi rule, were allowed to fall under the sway of Communist dictatorships. Yalta set the pattern for Eastern Europe for another forty-seven years. Yalta should have served notice on the Western Powers that they would have to forget any notional spirit of brotherhood with the Soviets, and acknowledge that the Russians intended to seize as much of Europe as they could, whatever agreements they made at the conference table. The West should have been equally firm and pragmatic, and advanced to meet the Russians as far to the east as possible. They should also have taken Berlin, the most prestigious prize of the European war.

While the Big Three conferred, their armies had not been idle. Soviet forces were now on the Oder, only forty miles from Berlin, and the Western armies were now pushing forward across the Roer and the Schnee Eifel towards the west bank of the Rhine.

Sergeant R. Godwin of the British 7th Armoured Division was wounded at this time: 'It is very misty as we turn off a road and up to a farm. My tank is a Sherman "Firefly" with the long-barrelled 75 mm gun, quite capable of taking on a Tiger. As we arrive at the farm and the other tanks carrying infantry withdraw, suddenly we are under fire. My officer backs his tank into a barn and I back mine into a pile of manure – everything has happened so fast. I see my first shot pass through and under the leading enemy tank. Then a shot hits the farmhouse three yards away. We reload and fire but nothing happens, a faulty striker. Jock has already opened the breech and tells me the cap has been struck. I throw the shell out of the turret and decide to pull the tank round the side of the farmhouse. Unfortunately, a German tank has gone round already and as we turn the corner an armour-piercing shell hits us square in the turret.

'I am severely wounded in the chest, back and left leg by splinters from the turret as the shell came through but the shell hit poor Jock full in the chest. It is more than twenty years before I can rid my memory of his screams. The gunner and Pete the driver have bailed out. I am still struggling as the plug on my headset won't part but I manage it and run to the wall of the farmhouse before I collapse. Pete runs to the tank to get the first-aid box and give me morphine and I am lifted onto the engine plates at the back of the corporal's tank. We set off across the field and as I am on the back I can see the big gun on the German tank swinging onto us. I shout to the corporal to weave about a bit and before the Germans can get a sight on, we are away. The MO (doctor) tells me the largest piece of shrapnel had gone through my lung and I had been drowning in my own blood. In the First World War I would never have made it.'

The American battles between 1 February and 27 February can be divided into three parts: the advance on Prüm and Cologne, the attack across the river Sauer on Bitburg, and the continued advance to the Rhine through the Saar–Palatinate, which will be covered in a later chapter. The attacks towards Prüm and Bitburg made by Patton's 3rd US Army commenced on 3 February, when the 4th and 90th US Infantry Divisions advanced astride the hills of the Schnee Eifel.

Prüm and Bitburg were communication centres, focal points for a network of roads. The Germans' ability to regroup rapidly was again in evidence here, for barely a week after the elimination of the Bulge, the Germans had elements of ten divisions in and around Prüm and on the Eifel, perhaps 12,000 men supported by tanks and artillery. This was a small force when compared to the numbers coming against them, but more than capable of putting up a fight.

The 4th US Division already knew the Schnee Eifel hills, for they had attacked through here in September when the division was part of Hodges' 1st US Army. Forced back south by the Bulge attack, the division was now part of Patton's 3rd US Army – which was not entirely to everyone's taste. Jack Capell again: 'We heard this rumour that General Patton had actually swum across the Sauer to get at the Germans, but I never met anyone who saw this feat so it was probably the invention of his fertile publicity team. We in the 4th Division were not admirers of General Patton. He was an accomplished battlefield commander but more reckless with the lives of his troops than other generals we had served with. He was known as "Old Blood and Guts", and we would say, "Yeah ... his guts and our blood." '

The attack of 3 February was led by the 4th Infantry Regiment of the 4th Division, who at first enjoyed considerable success against troops of the German 326th Volksgrenadier Division. The 4th overran the enemy pillboxes and positions with only one casualty, and when the 22nd Infantry Regiment came up in support, the Americans pushed on unopposed towards Brand-schild. On the following day, however, German resistance began to stiffen.

The 22nd Regiment took Brandschild on 6 February as the 8th Infantry forced their way through the German defence line to the north; but the pace of the advance had slowed. Meanwhile, the 87th US Division had cut the road at the north end of the Eifel and gained the crest of the hills, though here, too, they met heavy artillery fire and resistance from German troops operating in company strength, supported by tanks.

Ralph Teeters, of the 22nd Infantry Regiment, recalls this time. 'I had a machine-gun section sergeant named Levi McConn. He was from Washington and a hell of a good man, but he was an independent spirit. He did not march to anybody else's drum and he had some strange habits. For one thing, we used to collect all the watches and valuables from the German prisoners. We always did that as soon as we could because we couldn't send a prisoner back with anything valuable or the rear echelons took it. Well, Levi went a step further: he'd go into the burned-out tanks. He'd take watches and, I'm sorry to say, gold fillings, and I remember one time he sent a K ration box full of watches without the bands, and other things he'd taken.

'He was a good combat man and a man who could be relied on. So Levi gets hit, in this period when we were rolling back the Bulge. He was in an outpost and hit in the hand and arm. Any time you got hit that was your passport, your condition allowing you to go up the line with honour. Instead, he stayed there in the line for two or three days because he was needed so badly, and when he came back his wound had become infected and they sent him back to field hospital somewhere in Normandy. While there, he gained the confidence of the officers and the officers sent him to Paris to get their liquor ration.

'Well, Levi never got back. He stayed AWOL in Paris for thirty-six days, shacked up with a woman, trading the officers' liquor and generally getting by. He finally turned himself in because he had contracted gonorrhoea; with a case of the clap the only thing you could do was go to the medical authorities in the Army. He was court-martialled and when the whole story was out his penalty for going AWOL with the jeep and the officers' liquor was to be sent directly back to his old job with the company. Of course he was busted to private, but that made no difference. Levi became machine-gun section sergeant again as soon as an opening occurred. It's ironic that Levi's punishment was to go back to the company where we'd been all the time. Nevertheless we were very glad to see him. I hold a soft spot in my heart for Levi, a good soldier and a great man, and wish I knew what had happened to him.'

The 90th Division opened its attack on 6 February with an advance on Habscheid by the 359th and 357th Infantry Regiments. This attack began at 0400 hrs and by daylight the 359th were in Habscheid where they found many of the defenders asleep. This good luck was not to last. The roads were blocked by concrete 'dragon's teeth', which prevented tank support coming through, and heavy machine-gun fire began to sweep the American infantry before combat engineers could clear a way for their supporting armour. It was nightfall before the tanks arrived and the advance could continue.

The American 11th Armoured Division moved forward south of Habscheid on 6 February but the poor weather, a succession of heavy rain, thaw, more rain and then a freeze, confined the tanks to roads and trails where progress was inevitably slow. However, by 7 February the Americans of General Middleton's VIII Corps had punched a hole eleven miles wide in the Siegfried Line and, in spite of German resistance and local counter-attacks, their advance continued.

During this time the bombing of Germany continued, as USAAF Lieutenant Don Neilsen's diary records: 'Ninth Mission, 6 February 1945. Target: Marshalling yards at Eisfeld. Took off in the dark at 0745 hrs and got off to a bad start from the beginning. We shuffled the deck several times and ended up with the formation all over the sky. There was a little flak over the Dutch coast but we did not get hit, though because of the weather we were only at 15,000 feet. The primary target was near Mereseberg but the weather was overcast and because we were only supposed to bomb visually, the whole division broke up and each group tried to find a target of opportunity.

'Our group flew all over Germany looking for one and we finally picked this poor little town and blew the hell out of the marshalling yards. We then headed out the old way and because of the head winds it took a long time to get out of Germany. Over the Channel the weather got bad and the group split up. We came back at under 200 feet all the way, just to get under the clouds. At the field there were quite a lot of guys circling, trying to get in with visibility about 200 yards. One man crashed and blew up on his final approach. We made five passes and finally got in. Mission time $9\frac{1}{2}$ hours.'

The RAF were also in action, as Lancaster navigator Freddie Fish of 153 Squadron recalls: '8 February, Politz oil refinery, near Stettin on the Baltic coast. 475 Lancasters. Long trip over the North Sea and Denmark with a feint towards Berlin before swinging north. The entrance door came open and it was bitterly cold with a hell of a draught. The synthetic plant was severely damaged and produced no more oil. $8\frac{1}{3}$ hours flying time, 1,650 miles.'

Freddie Fish continues: 'Many crews had a good sprinkling of Canadians, Australians and New Zealanders. We had an Australian wireless op, Bill Turner, and a New Zealand bombardier, F/O E. Durman, and of course many of us had trained in Canada or Australia. I think we had a first-class crew. By 1945 we had air superiority by day but Germany was still a hell of a dangerous place to fly over at night. The flak, both barrage and radar predicted, was uncannily accurate and very dangerous and we all had a healthy respect for it. It was virtually fatal to fly over a flak area and German night fighters were still active. We were attacked quite a few times and hit by cannon fire. We found that if our gunners gave them a squirt from their Browning machine-guns and we went into our corkscrew manoeuvre, we always shook them off.

'Flak and fighters were not the only problem. There was icing, adverse winds, failure of equipment and the risk of being bombed by our own aircraft higher in the bomber stream. I know all about that because in October 1944 we had a bomb go through our starboard wing. It made a hole the size of a kitchen table but fortunately it had not fallen far enough to complete its arming cycle and did not go off.'

On the Western Front, casualties were mounting in the battle for Prüm. On 7 February, Colonel Buck Lanham of the 22nd Regiment, 4th US Division, reported more than sixty men killed, wounded or missing on that day alone, adding: 'We are now a serious threat to Prüm and the Germans may be mounting a big thing against us.'

They were indeed. The German 2nd Panzer Division was coming against Lanham's men. Though a shrunken relic of its former self, 2nd Panzer could still damage the 4th Infantry Division which had yet to recover from the fighting it had gone through in the Hurtgen Forest and the Ardennes. German reinforcements – II Panzer, 352nd Volksgrenadiers and 5th Parachute Division with seventy tanks and assault guns – arrived to stem the advance on Prüm on 8 February, and became entangled in stubborn fighting with the 4th Division around the Mon Creek and the villages of Gondenbrelt and Obermehlen throughout that day and the next. On 8 February Buck Lanham lost another 100 men from his beloved 22nd Regiment and similar losses were suffered by the 8th US Infantry Regiment and the rifle regiments of the 90th Division.

Stiff fighting continued for the next two days, with the 22nd Regiment in the van as the Americans smashed their way towards the Prüm river. The 8th Infantry Regiment reached the Prüm river on 9 February and on that day, with the 8th and 22nd Regiments now seriously depleted, General Blakeley, the new commander of the 4th US Division, committed his reserve, the 12th Infantry Regiment, which forged to the west bank of the river by early the following day. Troops of the 22nd Regiment finally entered Prüm on 11 February 1945.

While Middleton's US VIII Corps were fighting across the Schnee Eifel to Prüm, General Eddy's US XII Corps were fighting for the town of Bitburg, also in the 3rd Army sector but twenty miles to the south. Like the Schnee Eifel this was an area which the American troops had seen before, when the 5th US Armoured Division had attempted a drive on Bitburg in September. On this occasion General Patton intended a major attack on a seven-mile front between Echternacht and Wallendorf, timed to coincide with Middleton's attack on Prüm. This attack was complicated by the rivers across the front, notably the Sauer and the Prüm, both of which were in spate and over their banks, flooding the ground across which the Americans would have to advance.

On the other hand, the German defences here were relatively weak, with just two Volksgrenadier divisions, the 79th and the 212nd, to oppose the four divisions available to General Eddy: the 5th, 80th and 76th Infantry Divisions and the 4th Armoured Division. The advance across the Sauer on Bitburg began in heavy rain and snow on the night of 6 February 1945.

The flooded river was nearly 100 feet wide, and the crossing in storm-boats was perilous enough without the mortar and machine-gun fire that met the men of the 5th Infantry Division as they paddled across. Only twenty-four men got across when the first attempt was abandoned. The attack to cross the Sauer went on all night at various points around Echternacht, but very few men got across before daylight put a stop to the attempt.

The 80th Division, crossing at Wallendorf, had better luck, and strong elements of six companies were across the river by first light. This was just enough to keep the attack going and General Eddy ordered his divisional commanders to continue passing men across the river during daylight, covering their passage by moving tanks up to the riverbank. By nightfall on 7 February the 417th Infantry Regiment of the 80th Division had a battalion dug-in on high ground beyond the Sauer, while other companies of that regiment were pushing towards Echternacht.

Reinforcing these forward elements was still hindered by the flooded river which swept away any footbridge erected by the combat engineers; but the American infantry continued to cross in small contingents, sometimes in small boats, sometimes even swimming. Early on 8 February elements of two companies of the 417th Regiment crossed at Echternacht, holding a bridgehead on the far bank until boatloads of their regiment paddled across to join them.

It was not until 11 February that a bridge was finally flung across the river, and by that time sheer guts had gained the soaked and scattered elements of these various American infantry regiments a bridgehead three miles wide and a mile deep, containing some thirteen assorted battalions from the 5th and 80th Divisions.

The German resistance had been based on a thick network of pillboxes and minefields covered by machine-gun and artillery fire, but no reinforcements were available to the German defenders. The two forces were still evenly matched and it was not until 17 February that the Americans could break out from their bridgehead, by which time most of the 76th Division had crossed the river.

Their first task was to eliminate a pocket of resistance in a region on the front of the 80th and 90th Divisions known as the Vianden Bulge. This 'bulge' was eleven miles deep between the rivers Oeur and Prüm, and took in some of the most difficult terrain in the Eifel, a difficulty compounded by pillboxes, minefields and machine-gun positions with interlocking fields of fire. The Vianden Bulge was not eliminated until 22 February, and after a day to rest and re-equip the XII Corps turned their attention to their main objective – Bitburg.

The 5th US Division had been closing on Bitburg while the other divisions of the corps had been involved at Vianden. To reach Bitburg, they would have to cross the Prüm river, but the floods of early February had now subsided and the river did not delay them long. On 24 February the 5th Division crossed the river in less than an hour against light opposition, and by the 26th a battalion of the 2nd Infantry Regiment was on the outskirts of Bitburg, while other battalions cut the road to Echtenacht. The 4th US Armoured Division then crossed the river to the north of the town, and though the Germans now decided to reinforce the defenders in and around the town, it was far too late. The Americans were over both the Sauer and the Prüm rivers and had captured a wide salient inside the Siegfried Line between Prüm and Bitburg, both of which were important communications centres. Aircraft from the 9th Air Force then pounded Bitburg on 27 February and the American infantry took the town on the following day.

Further south, Captain Philip Whitman was fighting in the Saar–Moselle

Triangle with F Company, 376th Infantry Regiment, 94th US Division. His tale typifies the confusion of infantry fighting: 'On 9 February our battalion was in regimental reserve. F Company was ordered to take a section of Bannholtz Woods, with G Company in support and the help of a rolling artillery barrage. It was a dreary, dark day and hardly had we arrived at the start when I heard the thump of mortars. We scattered for cover but a shell landed next to my head, blowing my helmet off, and I heard Lt Hawley crying, "Captain, Captain!" Both his legs had been shattered and there was a gaping wound above his knee. I tried to get him away with a "Fireman's hold", but it was impossible to carry him over the fallen trees and branches, so we got him back to the aid station in a jeep.

'Returning after this disaster, sending my platoon leaders to ready their men, I met a friend, Captain "Stubby" Sinclair of the 2nd Bn, 301st Regiment, who told me that there were two German Tiger tanks lurking in the woods, covering the ground over which we must pass. I therefore sent all bazooka teams to the 3rd Platoon and had anti-tank mines ready to isolate and maybe restrict the movements of the Tigers.

'The attack began next day, 10 February at 0645 hrs, with a thunderous artillery bombardment blasting Bannholtz Woods, but by 0700 the 3rd Platoon bazooka teams had not appeared, and I needed them. They never did appear, neither did my forward artillery officer and to my horror I saw G Company attacking the wrong woods, far to the left. I screamed on my SCR 300 radio, "Heath, you are attacking the wrong woods", but my 2nd Platoon had attacked with them and got sucked into their zone of action.

'Shortly thereafter I made a dash for the woods up a draw with Lt Pierce and my radio man. We promptly drew a German mortar barrage that scared the hell out of me, but I made it, followed by the radio man. I went by wounded men who screamed that our artillery had done the damage. As I stood there I spotted a German soldier behind me and shot him with my carbine. He started screaming and the two Tiger tanks heard him. What they heard was enough for them to crank up their engines and start moving towards my temporary command post, so I looked at Lt Pierce and said, "Let's get the hell out of here."

'We took off towards our final objective, the far edge of the woods. I did not know what had happened to the 1st and 3rd Platoons but ran into the platoon sergeant of the 3rd Platoon, Sgt Scopoli, with the remnants of his men. Lt Mason had already been severely wounded and evacuated. After sweeping the right edge of the wood I had them dig in and just as I joined them all hell broke loose.

'I caught three young Germans hopping into a prepared machine-gun nest and unloaded a full clip from my carbine before I hit the ground and scurried back to Sgt Scopoli who was now involved in a full-scale firefight.

I told him he had Germans on the left instead of the 2nd Platoon, and to hold as best he could. Bullets were flying and Scopoli was talking with Sgt Van Dusen when Van Dusen's helmet flew off and he slumped over dead.

'Then Sgt Harold McGuinness appeared and told me that our 2nd Platoon had attached itself to G Company and was protecting their right flank. We also picked up a bazooka man of the 1st Platoon who had been slightly wounded but had no shells as his ammo bearer had been killed. Mortar shells were dropping in the area and we had a tree burst over our heads. Everyone, Lt Pierce, McGuinness, Roller, Jones, and I were all hit, me with shrapnel in the leg, some of which is still there fifty years later.

'I went to find Lt Weston and my 2nd Platoon, which took nearly an hour to find, round up, and send to reinforce Scopoli. We had not gone more than 100 yards when we met Sgt Scopoli and the remains of his 3rd Platoon – thirteen men. He had been attacked by infantry and Tiger tanks and Rasmussen, the BAR man, had been killed covering their withdrawal. When I heard about this much later, I tried to get Rasmussen the Silver Star, which he richly deserved, but the Department of Defence turned me down. Many more of my men deserved medals for gallantry that never came to light because so many never lived to tell their stories.'

All hell indeed. The Germans in the Bannholtz Woods were well dug-in and had the support of mortars – always lethal in woodlands – Tiger tanks, and more than enough infantry. It became a murderous, close-quarter infantry battle, often hand to hand. The Germans brought up their reserves of tanks and infantry, which were kept at bay by B Battery of the 919th Field Artillery, which fired over 33,000 rounds to hold the Germans off. With this support the American infantry hung on, though Captain Whitman reports seeing the Tigers 'lowering their gun muzzles to blast our men out of their foxholes'.

Of the 127 officers and men of Captain Whitman's F Company who fought in the Bannholtz Woods that day only twenty-seven were standing at the end of it.

P51 Mustang

6 The Air War

JANUARY–MAY 1945

'Germany is a fortress, but a fortress
without a roof.'

Franklin D. Roosevelt
President of the United States, 1944

The battle for Germany was fought not only on the ground. Throughout
the winter and spring of 1945, the Allied air forces bombed Germany by
day and by night. The Luftwaffe pilots rose to meet them, though in
declining strength and with ever less enthusiasm, hampered by poor training
and lack of fuel. Even so, they took a steady toll on Allied aircraft, adding
to the problems the aircrews experienced on every operation.

Freddie Fish, a Flight Sergeant-Navigator in 153 Squadron, RAF Bomber
Command, describes an operation in early 1945. 'The following account of
a raid is typical of what Bomber Command crews experienced in the last
months of the war:

'2.1.45: Target Nuremberg. Just after take off, Navigator's "Gee" set
caught fire and became unserviceable. We followed the bomber stream until
dark, using estimated winds to calculate our position. When the time came
to switch on another navigation aid, the H2S, this also failed to work. Then
the wireless set failed and the mid-upper gunner's helmet went up the
spout. Despite these problems, we arrived over target four minutes early.
At debriefing, when asked when he was first sure where he was, the
navigator replied, "When we were over Nuremberg, and they were bloody
well shooting at us." On the way back, the navigator's helmet failed and
the navigational aids caught fire. We crossed the English coast four miles
off track and found our way back to base by map-reading flashing beacons
called "Occults" and "Pundits". Thus ended a trip of nearly $8\frac{1}{2}$ hours,
1,670 air miles, with no navigation equipment!'

Air Marshal Sir Arthur Harris, the Chief of Bomber Command, had a
strong force trained for night operations and he intended to keep using it.

97

Although the RAF did operate by day, daylight raids were mainly in the hands of three American Army Forces: the 9th, the ground-support tactical air force; the 15th, operating out of Italy; and the 8th USAAF – the 'Mighty Eighth' – flying from bases in Britain.

Among USAAF flyers arriving in Britain in 1945 was Bill Morrison of San Francisco, an air gunner in the 91st Bomb Group. 'I entered the Army Air Force in May 1943, just after my eighteenth birthday. I qualified for pilot and went to pre-flight school, but the 8th Air Force had experienced two hard missions, to Schweinfurt and "Big Week" in early 1944, when hundreds of bombers had been shot down. When a four-engine bomber went down over Germany, the air force lost two pilots, but they also lost six gunners, so I became an air gunner.

'In December 1944 we made a stormy crossing to Liverpool and then to Combat Replacement Depot at Stone, in the middle of England. From there the crews dispersed to bombardment groups to replace men lost, or who had finished their thirty-five missions. That's how I got to the 91st Bombardment Group, 423 Bombardment Squadron (H) on Christmas Eve 1944.

'I don't think most of us were afraid or apprehensive. We loved our country and accepted the fact that we might die in the course of the next few months. I don't think any of us wondered how many of the guys waiting in the snow that night wouldn't be around after the next couple of weeks. It was a thrill to see your name and crew on the roster sheet – "The following crews will fly the next Operational Mission..."

'The crew sheet for the next mission was posted in the latrine and all air crews had to check it every night. There were always twelve crews listed who would make up the 323 Squadron for that mission. It was a Sunday morning in early January when they shook me awake and told me it was 0300 hrs. Breakfast was at 0330 hrs, briefing at 0430 hrs. So "Feet on the floor!" This was our first mission.

'We dressed quickly and quietly in the dark. It was very cold and too early to think properly but no one talked. At briefing there was not much noise as we waited for it to begin. On a stage at one end was a curtain, behind which was a large map of northwestern Germany. The briefing began and the target was revealed. "Cologne, Flak City", the third time in a row that the group had gone there. Our target was the Hohenzollern bridge in the centre of the city. My job now was to go to the armament shack and draw the 12 × 50-calibre machine-gun assemblies and have them ready when the crew truck arrived.

'I wondered whether I would be scared. I was an average GI, away from home and family for the first time, and had no idea how I was going to react but I felt very proud to be a part of all this. I think our crew were

98

very patriotic and we each knew the rest could be counted on. I can't speak for everybody and maybe there are some who would not agree with me.

'There was a brief time while waiting to start the engines when each person reflected quietly on his chances. Then there was the sound of the generator starting; the whine of the first engine starting up always brought you back to reality ... it was as noisy as hell! Then the taxi out to the end of the runway, the brakes squealing, the engine note rising and falling ... it was getting light and now I could see the faces of my crewmen.

'Then the noise of the engines rising to a peak. We could feel the tail rise and the bouncing on the runway would begin until we were airborne, the wheels came up and everyone went to his position. I helped Ernie climb into his ball-turret and slapped him on the helmet as he pulled the hatch shut. There wasn't much for me to do now except look out of the waist windows at the snowy countryside below, until we disappeared into the low cloud. As we climbed, I felt engulfed in a white veil before we burst through into sunlight, quite beautiful in the east.

'There were scores of B17s forming up all over the sky. From the different squadron leaders' aircrafts flares were being shot into the sky – red-red (ours), red-green, green-gold, etc., to identify them to their squadron. The squadrons took the best part of an hour to form up and become a group of Lead, High and Low squadrons, twelve in each. Groups would then move off to the assembly points on the coast and become a Wing. Finally, a full air division would be moving out over the Channel or North Sea, always climbing higher. At 10,000 feet we went on oxygen and I test-fired my .50 machine-guns.

'Today there was no need to put on the flak suit, a heavy, metal-armoured vest. Our formation crossed the French coast and everything below was snow-covered and the sun was shining brightly as the cloud disappeared. We reached our bombing altitude of 20,000 feet about halfway over France. Bob, the navigator, informed us when we crossed the front line and we flew to the Rhine, where our Wing swung north to the target. The bombardier called, "Flak ahead", and I put on the flak helmet and suit. I was also wearing a chest-pack parachute. Out of the waist windows smudges of spent flak smoke began and then we were in the target area.

'To say the sky was covered with exploding black flak bursts is not an exaggeration. This was my baptism of anti-aircraft fire and the sky seemed filled with boiling smoke; we were buffeted about by the close ones. We started to take hits, each a sharp crack or "bonk" when it hit us. There was nothing for me to do but stand there and look at it. I don't remember being frightened at that time. I heard "Bombs away!" over the inter-phone as Ferdie salvoed six 1,000 lb. bombs on the squadron leader's smoke bomb. Only the lead bombardier used a bomb-sight; the rest of the bombardiers and "*toggliers*" simply dropping their loads when they saw the leader's bombs fall. These bombs were equipped with smoke-markers, which you could see immediately.

'There is a small hatch behind the ball turret that you could open. I knelt and opened the hatch to watch our bombs go down on Cologne; anything was better than just watching all that flak. I could see the city and the big bridge over the Rhine and our bombs falling towards it. Then they hit, black, towering smoke followed the orange-red wink of the explosion. I remember seeing three bombs burst directly on the bridge. There were other near hits, in the river and on both sides of the river until it was covered in black smoke and some fire. Heavy flak was still coming up and our aircraft was still getting hit.

'Our bomb group dropped over 200 bombs on Cologne. There were fires, explosions and black smoke blanketing the city and I felt the aircraft turning left. I closed the hatch and went back to the waist window. We were still getting fired upon but nothing like on our bomb run and I could count eleven B17s in our group, a miracle that there were not a lot more missing. I realized later that flying the waist position could mean hours of boredom, since enemy fighter reaction was nonexistent. Hours of boredom and then minutes of terror once we started the bomb run.

'When we landed in England hours later, we looked for flak holes in the aircraft and found over two dozen in the wings, body and tail fin. All the tension of the day came out once we were on the ground everybody talking loudly and no one listening. At interrogation they gave us a two-ounce glass of bourbon whisky before we were interviewed by the officer, and at this interview I smoked my first cigarette.'

Long-range Allied fighters, like the Lightning and Mustang, had driven most German fighters from the sky by 1945, and the German air defence was constrained by the Führer's decision to develop the fast ME262 jet as a bomber rather than a fighter. In fact, Hitler's hopes of maintaining an air offensive now depended on the use of V-weapons, the V-1 flying bomb or 'Doodlebug', and the rocket-fired, supersonic V-2. Of these, the V-2 was by far the more effective.

The V-1 was a crude pilotless aircraft with a range of about 150 miles and a top speed of 300 miles an hour, the range dictated by the fuel supply. When the fuel ran out the engine stopped and the bomb fell. The V-1 was a terror weapon of no real strategic use; Allied fighter pilots could close on a V-1 and destroy it with cannon fire. Though this act was not without risk, most of the V-1s fired against London were destroyed by fighters or anti-aircraft fire as they crossed the coast of England.

Against the V-2 there was no defence whatsoever. Indeed, when the first

V-2s fell on London, causing great devastation and destroying whole streets, these disasters were put down to gas explosions for the V-2s fell silently and arrived without warning.

Most of the V-1 sites along the Channel coast were attacked by RAF Mosquitoes in the autumn of 1944, and then overrun by the Canadian Army as it advanced north towards Holland. V-weapons based further east were then turned on Antwerp with the aim of destroying the port facilities or inhibiting clearance work in the Scheldt. Between September and the end of 1944 some 5,000 V-1s were fired at Antwerp and Brussels, while London received 1,050 V-2s between September 1944 and 27 March 1945. Although these caused considerable loss of life, they were in no sense a war-winning weapon.

For the air defence of the Reich the Führer relied on three tried and tested types – the JU88, the FW190 and the Messerschmitt 110 plus the newly developed and very fast jet aircraft, the ME262. With a speed of 600 m.p.h. this jet was too fast to be engaged by even the fastest Allied fighter, but the Luftwaffe pilots had not yet learned how to handle it against massive bomber formations and were reluctant to engage. Though Allied fighters could not catch the ME262 in the air, the jets needed long concrete runways for takeoff, and when such runways were spotted, they were immediately attacked. The Luftwaffe's prospects were not improved by a steady loss of experienced pilots as the P51 Mustang fighter became operational over Germany, by a lack of training for new pilots and, above all, by a serious shortage of fuel.

Helmut Rix was a Luftwaffe fighter pilot at this time. 'I was born in 1924 near Krefeld on the Rhine. My interest in flying started at an early age and as soon as I was old enough, I took up gliding. I joined the Luftwaffe on 1 March 1943 and went to Oschatz for six weeks' basic training. We were posted to LKS [*Luftkriegschule*] near Potsdam for night flying, airfield circuits and instrument flying. My time at the Officers' Cadet School was hard but very rewarding; we got our pilot's wings and I was promoted.

'In early January 1944 I was posted to the Blind-Flying School at Kastrup, Copenhagen for instrument flying, radio navigation by day and night, long-distance flights from Denmark to southern Germany, or along the Baltic coast to Danzig and southeastern Germany. As far as the war was concerned, we had seen very little of it. When we were in the air (never armed) we got "Bandit Warnings" in good time, so we could land safely. The first time we got a taste of war was when two RAF Mosquitoes attacked our airfield and shot the place up. It was all over in a flash.

'Life wasn't all drill and instruction. Copenhagen was a very fine city and although there were ration cards in Germany, Denmark was full of surprises. Cream cakes with real cream, three or four grades of milk, salami, lots of things I had never seen before.

'My favourite aircraft was the JU88, though we had to be careful at takeoff because it had a tendency to break to the left before takeoff speed was reached. Once in the air it was a delight. At the end of our course, in July 1944, we got our extended pilot's wings and as I waited to become a night fighter pilot on the ME110 or 410, we were posted to Bad Aibling in southern Germany.

'Time went by very slowly and not much happened. There was a great uncertainty as to what was going to happen to us, and then out of the blue came the announcement that our transfer to night-fighters had been cancelled. We were given a choice: to become single-seater, all-weather fighter pilots, or go to a parachute regiment. Well, that was easy – I wanted to fly and with all the special training we had gone through, I chose to fly the FW190.

'In September 1944 we were posted to JG110 at Pretzsch for conversion training. After flying heavy twins, it was quite something to sit in an advanced single-engine trainer like the Arado 96. It's like driving a bus and then being told to drive a Formula One racing car, but I enjoyed the freedom and excitement of flying the AR96. Besides carrying on with instrument flying, we got a taste of close formation flying in "*Rotte*" (two aircraft) and "*Schwarm*" (four aircraft). Night flying was included.

'In mid-December 1944 we were posted to the I/JG2 *Ergänzungs-geschwader* at Neustadt Glewe for intensive combat training: high-altitude flights, formation flying and dogfights. Our stay here did not last long and on 12 January 1945 I was posted to the 8/11 JG301 Combat Squadron at Welzow. I was now twenty years old.

'The introduction to my fellow pilots was not a happy one. We didn't have time to get acquainted – a "Scramble" order came through and eight out of ten of my new comrades flew off and did not return. Things began to get very bad, there was a shortage of everything. We were supposed to get some flying experience with the squadron before we were sent into combat, but that never materialized. Instead, I got an order on 13 February 1945 to pick up an FW190 A9 at Niedermendig, west of Koblenz. I went by train from Welzoe via Berlin–Hanover–Essen–Cologne–Koblenz to Niedermendig, with my parachute under my arm. It was a hectic journey. I hadn't been on leave, it was the first time I came near home and I decided to make a little detour.

'Destruction was everywhere, Allied bombing by day and night. From my home village we could hear the artillery at Roermond and the fighting in Holland, just twenty miles away. After a few days, I travelled to Niedermendig, where I got stuck. Allied fighter-bombers, Thunderbolts and Lightnings, were the masters of the air, and the aircraft I was to ferry got damaged while taxiing and needed a new propeller.

'I got away on 27 February at 7.30 in the morning, before the enemy turned up. My flight order had been changed to Stendal near Magdeburg, to where the Wing had transferred. I plotted my flight over Koblenz to Giessen, where I had to stay overnight because of enemy air activity, and took off again early next morning for Eschwege. After refuelling I took off again and made for Stendal, flying low through the valleys of the Hartz Mountains. My order stated a minimum height of 50 metres, and I took full advantage of it all the way. With an unarmed fighter it would have been very foolish to tempt Providence.

'The next day should have been my first combat mission, but at the last minute I had to give my aircraft to a more experienced pilot. Finally, on 2 March I tried again – scramble at 10.15, in my FW190, Red 4. We climbed on a southeast course to 24,000 feet and were in a line-abreast formation, ready for a frontal attack when my formation leader broke away to the left into a dive. We got into a line-astern formation, with me as No. 4. It was a beautiful morning, clear blue sky, but cloud cover at about 14,000 feet. The front aircraft were just disappearing in the clouds when my plane shuddered. Flames were licking around the front of the engine. A dull thud followed and I was engulfed in flames. In the panic that followed, I got rid of my cockpit hood, but forgot to undo my straps and so air fed the flames and the aircraft was out of control. I managed to undo the straps but how I got out I shall never know. My 'chute opened perfectly and I landed in about six inches of snow, nearly blind, with severe burns to my head, face and lower arms.

'I was picked up by a farmer and taken to hospital in Aussig (then Sudeten Germany), still wearing the full leather suit which had saved my life. After seven weeks I discharged myself because things were getting rather hot; the Russians were too close for comfort and I wanted to get back to my squadron. It was a terrible journey, through the burning towns of Aussig and Dresden, and on to Berlin, where I arrived on 20 April 1945. I had to dodge Russian shells landing around the Bahnhof Friedrichstrasse, from where I made my exit to the airfield on the western outskirts of Berlin.

'I looked a mess. My head and arms were still bandaged, my leathers burned. When I got to the control tower, the commanding officer thought I was a ghost. He found out where my squadron was and arranged transport on a convoy that night. It was a precarious journey but I arrived at Newstadt-Glewe unscathed and I was reunited with my squadron. They were surprised to see me, for nobody knew what had happened to me and I had been posted missing. I found out that we had been attacked by P51 Mustangs as we were diving into the clouds.

'I never flew again, however hard I tried to persuade the medics. It broke my heart to see my comrades take off for fighter-bomber attacks into Berlin, and quite a few of them not returning. The Russians advanced further and further and in the end the whole of JG301 was transferred to Heide in Schleswig Holstein. There we were taken over by the 2nd Tactical Air Force at the end of hostilities. We were interned, the individual squadrons bivouacking on farms until we were disbanded. I arrived home on 18 August 1945, three days after the war ended.'

Allied fighters dominated the German skies but the Luftwaffe's main problem was shortage of fuel. The vital Ploesti oilfields of Romania had been overrun and by the end of December 1944 the last oilfields in Hungary were about to be captured by the Russians. Since 1942 the Germans had been developing synthetic oil and petrol plants, distilling fuel from coal and oil-bearing shale, but the amounts produced were inadequate to supply even a declining war machine. The German fighter ace, Adolf Galland, recounts that by early 1945 the shortage of aviation spirit was so critical that to save fuel fighters were towed out to the runway. Since no other method of haulage was available, the aircraft were pulled by cows.

On 15 January 1945 all the Allied air forces, Tactical and Strategic, were directed to concentrate their bombers 'as a first priority' against the petroleum industry. This directive was followed by the US air forces, who began to pulverize German oil depots, storage tanks and fuel transport links, but with less enthusiasm by Air Marshal Harris, who wished to continue attacking German cities, especially communications centres. The USAAF and Bomber Command continued to pound Germany by day and by night and in mid-February combined their strength to attack the city of Dresden, an attack which became one of the most controversial air actions of the war.

Berlin, Leipzig, Chemnitz and Dresden had been singled out for air raids, which had been agreed at Yalta. Dresden, the capital of Saxony, was a major road and rail centre, vital for the supply of troops and munitions to the Eastern Front and the evacuation of German civilians to the west. By mid-February 1945, its normal population – about 600,000 – had been swollen to twice that number by the influx of refugees. Dresden was a beautiful historic city, still untouched after five years of war. On the night of 13–14 February 1945 all that changed.

The first attack was made by 722 Lancaster aircraft of Bomber Command. This attack struck home with great accuracy and demolished or set fire to large parts of the city. The smoke of the fires started by Bomber Command still hung over the city the following day, when 1,300 aircraft of the US 8th Air Force came in to drop their bombs. This attack was followed by two more American daylight raids before Bomber Command and the 8th Air Force switched their attacks to the other centres, Chemnitz and Leipzig. The 8th returned to Dresden on 2 March, when 400 heavy bombers dropped their tonnage on the city. Civilian casualties in Dresden during the raids have been estimated at between 50,000 and 135,000.

Lieutenant Robbie Robinson, a B17 pilot in the 475th Bomb Group, 8th USAAF, kept a diary and gives some details of the Dresden raid: 'The Soviet forces were smashing their way towards Berlin during February 1945, and the Allied forces were giving them air support. Our eleventh mission was similar to the Berlin mission of 3 February, except the target was Dresden. This was an important railway centre, and with Berlin in such a disastrous state of confusion as a result of the earlier raid, Dresden was choked with traffic and refugees.

'The RAF hit the city first on the night of 13 February with 800 planes, and the 8th Air Force hit it again in daylight on 14 February, with 1,300 bombers. I was alerted at 0245, and went through the usual procedure of alerting the crew. During the briefing, it was noted that this was a long mission and that all pilots would have to use fuel conservation tactics, as we were stretching the limits of the B17's range with the load we would be carrying. We had six 600 lb. general purpose bombs and four 500 lb. incendiary bombs, as well as the maximum gas load of 2,780 gallons. My plane, No. 123, was still in maintenance undergoing repairs after the Berlin raid, so we would be flying another aircraft, No. 154, on this mission.

'We entered the Continent at the usual spot on the Zyder-Zee and were met with anti-aircraft fire from two mobile guns on the ground. We had dubbed these gunners Hans and Fritz. They were very crafty gunners and excellent marksmen. They would only fire four rounds, two apiece, so the fighter escort could not get a positive fix on them and they would normally get at least one hit. This day was no exception, and a B17 in the group behind us was knocked out of the sky. From there to the target we encountered little anti-aircraft fire and no fighters. The target was mostly covered with clouds and smoke from fires set by aircraft ahead of us, so the bombing had to be done by instruments. There was a hole in the cloud cover right over the city and we got a good look at what was going on down there. The whole city appeared to be in flames as we dropped our bomb load.

'Coming home, we were fighting a strong head wind and it seemed that we were never going to get out of enemy territory. We passed over Frankfurt, received moderate anti-aircraft fire and a B17 ahead of us was hit and went down. Another B17 with engine problems was flying by himself about five miles from the formation, just ahead of us. The German gunners started tracking him with their 88 mm cannons, and it reminded me of hunting rabbits. The pilot was moving that aeroplane all over the sky as the shells kept exploding behind him. He escaped as he was able to dodge the fire until he was out of range. We all gave him a big cheer. Around Koblenz we witnessed a town take a bomb strike from another group of the 8th Air Force, and they seemed to just obliterate that town.'

Though the Dresden raid has become notorious, Dresden was not the only city to be heavily bombed when packed with civilians. George Futer of Black Creek, British Columbia, Canada, was flying at this time and recalls the raid on Royan. 'I was an air gunner, shipped overseas in 1943 and posted to the RCAF reception centre at Bournemouth. Instead of being sent to 6 Group with the RCAF squadrons, I was posted to the RAF Operational Training Unit at Upper Heyford in Oxfordshire and then to 207 Squadron of 5 Group, Bomber Command, at Spilsby, Lincolnshire. Without implying any disrespect to the RCAF, I was proud and happy to be attached to the Royal Air Force.

'After twelve trips we were asked to join the Pathfinder Force and though it meant flying two combined tours in a row – over sixty ops in all – we immediately volunteered, but did nineteen ops before joining 97 Squadron at Coningby.

'I think it necessary to add a word here about the Lancaster bomber and the feelings it instilled in both ground and air crews. When a crew became established on a squadron, having survived the first few operations, they were granted a "kite" of their own. Along with the aircraft they inherited its dispersal area, and three fitter-riggers who cared considerably more for the "kite" than they did for the men who flew it. An irate rigger would think nothing of chewing out an aircrew officer if he thought "finger-trouble" had resulted in damage to his "kite".

'After joining 97 Squadron we acquired aircraft marked OF-G for "George", which we modified to "Grunter" because of a china pig which the mid-upper gunner carried as a talisman. We flew this "kite" through September and October to mid-November 1944, when another crew took it on ops and failed to return. We still retained OF-G, "Grunter", only now it was a new Lancaster, No. ME623. I only mention this trivia to relay the intense feeling that developed in a crew towards their aircraft, though it was, after all, only a machine . . . or was it?

'31 December 1944 was a bit of a bind for our crew. New Year's Eve, and we had to take our Lancaster up for night bombing practice. We considered it a waste of time since our bomb aimer could hit a shove-halfpenny board from 18,000 feet – well, almost. The "bind" revolved around hours of New Year's Eve revelry lost in the mess while playing silly buggers over a bombing range. Anyway, it would only be a couple of hours and we could make up for lost time once we got back. That turned out to be wishful thinking. After landing we discovered that there would be no clinking of glasses in the mess that night. "Auld Lang Syne" would have to wait, for ops were on with a daylight raid to the Dortmund-Ems canal.

'No flare-force was needed on a daylight raid, so the Pathfinders dropped only target indicators. Our crew, in the forefront of the attack, carried "route markers" [parachute flares] which we dropped at the various turning points to keep the 200-odd main force Lancasters concentrated on the prescribed "track". Straying aircraft were vulnerable to attack.

'Breaching the Dormund-Ems canal was no piece of cake. We were well aware of that since we had done it twice before, and we were going in at an altitude of only 8,000 feet, but the raid was successful, the canal was again breached and 1945 got off to a good start. Two Lancasters were lost; in one of them, Flight Sergeant Thompson, a wireless operator with 9 Squadron, was awarded a posthumous Victoria Cross.

'On 4 January we were briefed to bomb Royan, a German-held town at the mouth of the Gironde river. Some bombing attacks, even when carried out with precision, failed to have the desired effect, and Royan was one such raid. French forces surrounding Royan lacked the equipment to effect a German surrender, so an American officer apparently suggested that Royan be "softened up" by bombing. This idea filtered its way up to SHAEF and with some misgivings about civilian casualties the task was assigned to Bomber Command. It was believed that there would be no French civilians in Royan, other than collaborators.

'At briefing we were given the reason for attacking Royan and advised that the US 8th Army Air Force would also be taking part. Since 347 Lancasters were to attack this relatively small target, it was obvious that the town was slated for destruction, especially when some of the main force Lancasters were carrying "cookies". This was strange anyway, because we never dropped 4,000 lb. "cookies" – or incendiaries – on French targets.

'Our crew was "Primary Blind Marker". In other words, we would reach the target early and drop a target indicator as the aiming point for the main force bombers. After we had dropped our TI we would come around again on our own bombing run, for we carried bombs as well as markers. Bomber Command wanted photographs and we were to make at least five runs across the target to take pictures; again, not normal procedure. The Lancaster had a higher cruising speed so the American bombers left some time ahead of us and I remember passing their aircraft somewhere near the Bay of Biscay, but they never reached Royan. I am quite sure of that. We were the first aircraft over the target and we criss-crossed it for an extended period and were virtually the last to leave, so it would have been impossible to miss seeing them.

'We even joked about the matter over the intercom, assuming that the

Americans had lost their way and returned to England. Records disclose that SHAEF had cancelled the raid at the last minute because of the possibility of French civilians being in the town, but if the American bombers were recalled, why was the RAF attack not aborted as well?

'The attack virtually destroyed Royan; in excess of 600 civilians were killed. A ten-day truce was called to permit a search for survivors, but the German garrison did not surrender. Bomber Command was exonerated but accusations over the planning of the attack continued for years. Six Lancasters were lost but the aircrews had enough to contend with in the normal pattern of war, without that kind of screw-up ... and then there was Dresden.

'No one who flew on the night of 13–14 February will ever be able to erase the sight of Dresden from their mind. On this raid our crew flew as "Emergency Markers", meaning that, if necessary, we would drop new TIs to change the area of bombing. We dropped our bomb load with the first wave and then circled the city awaiting orders from the Master Bomber, and stayed over Dresden for as long as our fuel would allow before setting course for England. To this day I can still picture those flames!'

L. A. Halko, who now lives in Canada, was actually in Dresden during the Allied raids. 'I was in Dresden as a prisoner-of-war in February 1945, during the Allied bombing. I survived because I was beaten and kicked out of a shelter ... "*Raus du Kriegsgefangene Schwein*" ["Get out, you swine, prisoner-of-war"]. Then the shelter was hit and those in it were killed.

'Before being deported to Dresden I lived in Warsaw, a city as beautiful as Dresden before the Germans destroyed the city street by street, often gang-raping the women, to subdue the city once and for all. Some quarter of a million Polish civilians perished and little was left but endless mounds of rubble and shells of gutted buildings.

Donald L. Neilsen of Glendale, Arizona, a pilot of 457th Bomb Group, 8th USAAF, was on the second Dresden raid. 'I am not very proud of the fact that I was on the raid to Dresden on 14 February 1945. Killing civilians seemed so senseless, but in the military one follows orders and I have some diary notes which may be of interest:

'11th Mission – 14 February 1945 – Target – Marshalling Yards at Dresden. A long one! We took off at 8.15 after an hour's delay. We had assembled at 9,500 feet and climbed on course across the Zyder-Zee – a few bursts of flak there. We had to go to 27,000 feet because of a weather front. Part of target was visible when 1 Group went over and I could see the centre of the town in flames. This was like Berlin – more support for the Russians. There was no flak over target and the trip back was fairly uneventful. We had a strong headwind and seventeen out of our thirty-six aircraft had to land in France to refuel. We encountered a little flak at Frankfurt but weren't hit.'

Dresden was not attacked again but other east German cities were bombed continuously in February and March. The Rev. Reginald C. Snell of Brantford, Ontario, Canada, was a tail gunner in the RCAF, flying in Lancasters with Bomber Command, and recalls his last operation.

'This account of my bombing missions covers that time from 1 January 1945 to 6 March 1945, when we were shot down. During that time we bombed the following cities: Nuremberg, Nyersburg, Stuttgart, Ludwigshaven, Bottrop, Cleve, Chemnitz, Dortmund and Pforzeim. These targets were bombed daily by American bombers and nightly by RAF and RCAF in order to break the will of Nazi Germany until the Germans had no alternative but to surrender.

'On the night of 6 March our target was Dessau, southwest of Berlin. Our Lancaster was loaded with high explosives as well as incendiary bombs. Until this mission I always had confidence we would return to home base at Elsham Wolds, where 103 (Lancaster) Squadron was situated. The captain of our plane always asked me, the tail gunner, to pray before takeoff, as the crew knew I was a devout Christian.

'When I prayed that night I felt no assurance God would answer my prayer. Two of our regular crew were out of action and two inexperienced men took their place, the wireless operator and bomb aimer, and my gunnery squadron leader suggested I took a type of parachute worn on one's back. The usual parachute was the individual pack which was left near the rear escape hatch. In an emergency the tail gunner had to leave his turret and clip it on the front of his parachute harness. Why he asked me to wear this new parachute I do not know.

'Anyway, we were going into the target when I saw a night-fighter move quickly across my turret. The fighter must have banked and come back under the Lancaster, then opened fire. It set our incendiary bombs ablaze. Our captain shouted, "Emergency! Emergency! Jump! Jump!" over the intercom, but our aircraft was already a mass of flames.

'I swung the turret around, opened the door and saw a wall of fire between me and the escape hatch. I knew I would be overcome before I could reach the hatch, so I did what every tail gunner is instructed not to do – bail out of the turret. The reason is that the force of the slipstream is so great that the gunner may have his legs cut off leaving the turret. I knew there was no other way, so I prayed – "Oh Lord . . . Please help me", rolled into as tight a ball as possible, stuck my head out of the turret and was sucked out. Once I was clear of the aircraft I pulled the ripcord and the beautiful silk rolled out and billowed over me. I looked down to see whether I had all my body, and all that was missing were my flight boots!'

In February 1945 the air forces turned their attention to smashing Goering's fuel depots and communications systems, a series of attacks culminating on 22 February in Operation Clarion, a combined RAF–USAAF assault on Germany's oil supplies. Canadian Mosquito pilot C. S. Gilliat, DFC, flew with 107 Squadron RAF on Operation Clarion.

'On 22 February 1945, there was an all-out attack by Bomber Command, 8th and 9th US Air Force, and 2nd Tactical Air Force against transportation targets in Germany. Our squadron put up eighteen aircraft in three echelons of six; our squadron commander was in the lead echelon and there were three pairs in each echelon.

'We reached our target area at 1200 hrs and broke off in pairs, each pair with a specific patrol area – a road or railway. I was No. 3 in the first echelon and we went to the Flensburg area, where we fired on railway engines and a small goods train which we attacked with guns and bombs. We returned at low level, 50–100 feet, to our base at Cambrai. The only time we were shot at, other than some light flak, was when we got close to some Navy ships in the North Sea. In spite of firing the "colours of the day", they fired at us, but we were out of range. From 25 February to 21 March I carried out nine sorties and attacked a total of seven trains, three in one night near Iserbahn.'

The cities and sinews of Germany, the railways, roads, bridges, canals, were now being systematically disabled. In the first three months of 1945 the Allied air forces dropped nearly 300,000 tons of bombs on targets in Germany and German-occupied territories. The damage was terrible and the loss of life considerable, and even before the Dresden raid the question was raised: With the end of the war clearly in sight, why was the bombing offensive not halted? Since Germany was on the brink of defeat, any further loss of life, especially among the civilian population, was not only unnecessary but also inhuman. In addition, further destruction of Germany's infrastructure only added to the problems of Allied ground forces.

The short answer is that there was a war on. The Germans were still fighting hard on two fronts and would continue to do so for another three months. As the accounts in this chapter illustrate, they were still able to put up a fierce fight in the air.

In total war, civilians take the brunt during air attacks on cities, even as the soldiers in the line endure the shell and bullet. The name of Dresden must be linked with those of Guernica, Rotterdam, Warsaw, Coventry, and all the other cities previously smashed by the Luftwaffe; the Germans had sown the wind, and the whirlwind had come upon them.

Bill Spence, who flew on the Dresden raid, puts the aircrew point of view: 'I was a bomb-aimer with 44 (Rhodesia) Squadron, 5 Group, Bomber Command, based at Dunholme Lodge and Spilsby from August 1944 to April 1945, during which time I did thirty-six operational sorties.

'So much has been written about the Dresden raid, much of it biased

The commanders: Bradley, Tedder, Eisenhower, Montgomery and Simpson.

Hedgerow fighting: American troops near St Lô, 1944.

British infantry advance, supported by Churchill tanks.

German prisoners cross the Siegfried Line.

British troops in Reichwald supported by 'Crocodile' flame-throwing tank.

Sgt J. Holmes, 35th Infantry, in the Ardennes.

British infantry – 9th Bn Durham Light Infantry – advance through Echt.

Shower parade: British, American and Canadian troops meet for a bath, winter 1945.

British 'Crab' flail tank crew host American troops, 1945.

The liberation of Brussels – the British Guards drive in.

F/Sgt Vic Polichek, RCAF, standing by the rear of his Halifax bomber MK3.

Young 'Volksturm' soldiers, 13–15 years of age, with British guard, 1945.

A soldier of the 12th Armoured Division with his prisoners.

Aircrew 1: Ed Stermer's B17 crew.

Aircrew 2: Vic Polichek's Halifax Bomber crew.

SOME CONTRIBUTORS

Sgt Ralph Teeters, 45th Infantry Division.

Lt Quentin R. Rowland.

Lt Robert M. Brook, 9th Armoured Engineers.

Lt Don Nielsen, pilot, 8th USAAF.

British paratroopers of 6th Airborne Division in Hamminkeln.

'For this Hiltler needed 12 years', Munich, 1945.

Morning parade, 1st Bn 134 Regt, 35th Infantry, 9th Army, February 1945.

SS troops in the Ardennes, 1944–5.

Lt Everett Lindsey, 94th Squadron, 1st Fighter Group, 15th Air Force, USAAF.

Lt Lindsey just after release from a German prison camp.

The body of General Deutch, Wesel, 24 March 1945.

Machine-gunners of British 1st Commando Brigade in Wesel, 24 March 1945.

Concentration camp victim, Germany, 1945.

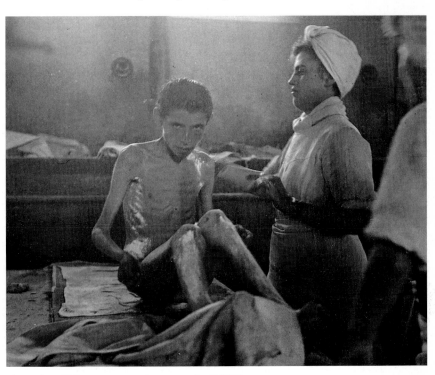

A survivor, Belsen concentration camp, April 1945.

Badly wounded Russian prisoners of war, Austria, May 1945.

German civilians are brought to inspect a mass grave near Solingen, April 1945.

Russian and American troops meet on the Elbe.

The symbols of Hitler's Reich come down, May 1945.

American troops at Berchtesgaden, Bavaria, 1945.

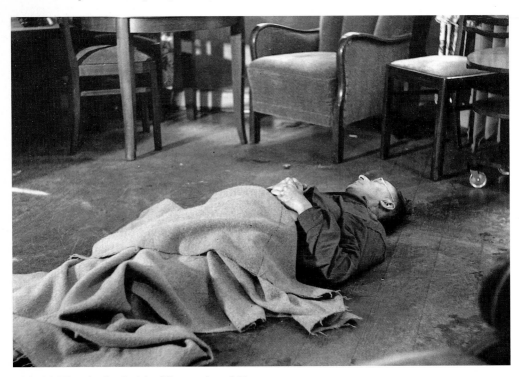

Heinrich Himmler, head of the SS, commits suicide.

and written by people who were writing after the event and misinterpreting the facts. The raid must be viewed in the context of the time, taking in the war situation and the knowledge in the hands of the planners. We were told at briefing that we were to carry out this raid to help the Russians who were advancing westward. Dresden was an important communications centre with lots of German troops passing through on their way to the Russian Front.

'Looking at the raid with the present-day viewpoint and with the privilege of facts not known at the time, one can naturally decry the raid, but the same criteria could be applied to any raid. One regrets the loss of life and the destruction of a beautiful city, but we were at total war. Civilians and military targets were close together and it was difficult to differentiate between them. The fact that we were to bomb Dresden meant nothing at the time. This was just another target in the war against Germany, a war to get rid of an evil regime.

'We were one of the first aircraft to bomb Dresden. Though there was thin cloud and haze, the markers were clearly visible: 5 Group Marker Force marked the target with 5 Group being the first Group into the attack. The Main Force would have no bother identifying the target for the city was ablaze by the time 5 Group had completed their mission. On our way back we could see the blaze for hundreds of miles. The anti-aircraft fire was not particularly heavy but there was a good deal of fighter activity and we were stalked by a fighter after leaving the target. He eventually came in on an attack but broke off without firing. Maybe his guns had jammed, maybe run out of ammunition, or maybe he was a veteran pilot who knew that with the fires of Dresden behind him he was clearly visible to our gunners, and so broke off to fight another day. By the time we got back, reports were coming in that the raid had been a great success.'

The aircrews were still taking losses in February 1945, for the German flak and night-fighters were still in action. John Jarvis of the Royal Canadian Air Force gives a summary of Bomber Command losses:

'From the beginning of the war, Bomber Command carried out a direct offensive against the German people in their homeland. Until 1942 it was not a very effective offensive, and very costly in casualties. Nevertheless, it never ceased, except for brief periods for regrouping, or because of poor weather. Speaking of casualties, there were 110,000 aircrew who were engaged in action against the enemy. Here are the statistics of their fate:

51% were killed in operations against the enemy
9% were killed in crashes in England
3% were seriously injured in crashes
12% became prisoners-of-war; many POWs were also injured
1% were shot down but evaded capture
24% survived unharmed

Thank the Lord, my crew was among the last statistic.'

During the last five months of the war, Bomber Command aircraft losses were:

January	:	133
February	:	169
March	:	215
April	:	73

This was a total of 590 RAF aircraft lost from a front-line bomber strength of some 1,600 aircraft – about a third. By April, bombing operations had largely ceased; the lower figure is an indication of fewer operations, not of any German incapacity to resist. Bombers were being shot down in quantity, even after Dresden, and claims that the Germans were incapable of resistance by the time of the raid are simply not true.

Warrant Officer William Pearce from Queensland, Australia, flew on these operations. 'I trained as a wireless operator air gunner and flew out of England in Lancaster bombers, firstly with 100 Squadron, and then with 156 Squadron, Pathfinder Force.

'I qualified for the Caterpillar Club – people who owe their lives to their parachute – on the night of 20–21 February 1945 when my squadron was detailed to mark the synthetic oil refinery at Reiszholz in the Ruhr valley, about twenty miles southeast of Dusseldorf. This was to be my forty-second op.

'Our task was to "back-up" the target markers dropped by previous Pathfinder aircraft at the direction of the Master Bomber. H-hour was 0130 hrs and we were due on target at H plus four minutes. It was to be a six-minute attack, with only some fifty aircraft involved.

'At approximately 10.25, while still short of the target, my aircraft was hit by a night-fighter. It took a burst of cannon-fire across the tail and rear turret, then into the starboard inner engine, elevators and petrol tanks. The engine immediately caught fire. We later found out that we had been hit by a burst from a JU88 night-fighter, fitted with upward-firing cannon, codenamed "Schrag-Musik". These aircraft infiltrated the bomber stream, found a target, and took their toll. The cannon-fire that hit us in 1945 hit just as hard as cannon-fire hit in 1942.

'I can still remember my feelings when I heard the cannon-fire rip across our aircraft. The explosions were quite audible and I knew immediately what had happened. In that split second my world shattered and the feeling I had in the pit of my stomach emphasized this fact. My stomach dropped to my boots and I went cold all over.

'We were still carrying our full bomb load, a 6,000 lb. blockbuster, target-indicating flares, and approximately half our petrol. With the fire in the wing our position was untenable, and our skipper, English to the core, came on the intercom and ordered us to "Bail out, chaps!"

'We didn't need to be told twice. Each crew member, with the exception of the rear gunner, who had been killed by the cannon-fire, acknowledged the skipper's command and proceeded to get out of the aircraft. I discarded my flying helmet and oxygen mask (we were hit at about 18,000 feet and were using oxygen). I picked up my parachute pack from the floor and started for the rear door on the starboard side of the aircraft, just forward of the tailplane. I can remember sitting on the wing strut, which runs across the fuselage. I was fumbling to attach the parachute pack to the clips on the front of the harness when the lack of oxygen started to have its effect. I was feeling very lightheaded due to lack of oxygen but I can remember thinking that I had better get moving.

'I eventually reached the rear door; the mid-upper gunner was standing in the open doorway, and I was just able to tap him on the shoulder as he went out. However, he made the fatal mistake of picking up his parachute pack by the ripcord and it had opened inside the aircraft. He had clipped it to his 'chute harness and gathered the canopy in his arms; I remember seeing the folds of silk as he stood in the doorway. When he left the aircraft his body went below the tailplane but the opened 'chute canopy had gone over the top. He was pulled back into the tailplane and killed. This is what I think I saw, and even in my "lack of oxygen" condition, I feel it is correct. His body was found on the ground, still attached to his parachute harness.

'The next moment I was torn out of the aircraft by the slipstream and was falling head-over-heels through space. After tumbling for what seemed an age, I can recall thinking, "Well, I had better pull it now." I found the ripcord handle, pulled it, and was left suspended in the middle of a black void.

'I could hear aircraft swishing past me and I had frightening thoughts about what would happen if one of them hit me. I hit the ground in an ungainly heap in the middle of an open paddock. There was very little wind blowing and this was fortunate as I had hurt my left shoulder and my left arm was practically useless.

'I gathered up the parachute, expecting the German Army to pounce on me at any moment. This didn't happen, so I groped my way to the edge of the field and buried the parachute under fallen leaves ...' Bill Pearce survived the war and returned safely to Australia. Not every airman was so lucky.

A significant number of aircrew were shot or lynched by the SS or enraged German civilians, or narrowly escaped such a fate, as USAAF pilot Everett Lindley recalls: 'For me, flying a Lightning fighter, all hell broke loose in the middle of a strafing run at Landshut on 15 April 1945.

I was leading the 1st Fighter Group on a low-level strike to Regensburg and Linz. Of the five (out of twenty-seven) fighter pilots shot down on this mission, only one survived.

'I was firing at a long line of freight cars when from nowhere, at about 700 feet, came a concentrated volley of twenty or thirty orange balls from 37 mm flak guns. Too late to turn, I was forced to pull out, but before I could extricate myself, my plane was struck several times.

'The first shell ricocheted off the windscreen and pulverized the glass. When it broke loose on the inside, exploding glass hit me in the left shoulder. I could move my left arm but did not want to look at my shoulder. As I pulled out, I could hear more orange balls striking my aircraft. Two hit the right engine, one the wing, and two penetrated beneath the gondola, hitting the armour-plated bucket seat. I could hear and feel those last two, and I knew that they could start a fire.

'When I could no longer see the instruments, I was forced to release the emergency panel. This cleared the cockpit of smoke but it also sucked flames in from the gondola. I glanced at the right engine and saw that most of the right wing was in flames.

'The P38 was in a right spin. I could hear someone yelling, "Red Leader, bail out! Bail out, Red Leader!" and I realized the ground was close. 'The call to "Bail out" came again and I made another effort to free myself from the fighter, but failed. Why this P38 did not explode with all that fuel aboard I shall never know. Finally, with my right hand on the ripcord, I used all my might and broke loose, instantly pulling the ripcord.

'I suddenly found myself in a delightfully cool and quiet situation. I looked up at my 'chute but saw houses, trees and farmland. As I looked down at my feet I saw only sky. Obviously I was upside down. My hands were only halfway to the shrouds when I slammed into the ground on my right side, my head hitting the surface. I was knocked unconscious momentarily, my 'chute covering me, and I was in the village of Stenging, just north of Muhldorf, Germany, with a broken right leg.

'A German civilian passed right by me, said something but did not seem belligerent. Soon after he spotted me, hostile forces surrounded me, so I drew and cocked my .45 Colt automatic and pointed it. I remember thinking that I had worn this weapon on forty-three missions to protect me from capture. Now I needed to use it.

'Someone yelled, "Hands up!" and I could hear weapons being cocked and soldiers approached. I was too busy to ask myself what I thought I could do against some thirty of the enemy. Someone else yelled, "Hands up!" and I stood there, confronting them for what seemed to be an eternity before I tossed the gun to the ground. With my hands up I was ordered to lead my captors out of the woods, put in a vehicle and driven to Muhldorf.

'When we arrived I was taken into a public building and ordered to stand, with my hands up, at the bottom of a basement stairway. After half an hour I was ordered upstairs. Just as I reached the foyer, an enraged civilian flew into me, throwing punches and screaming. He knocked me down, the guards ordered me up, then pushed me back into him with their rifles; a blow to my temple floored me a second time. I saw stars and felt dizzy. I was again ordered to stand, rifle prods helped me. The civilian beat me until he was exhausted, my nose bled, my eye was cut and my teeth were driven through my lips.

'A vehicle arrived with two German SS troopers. They were SS *Obersturmbahnführer* Colonel Mathias Zeirhut and his aide, Sergeant Johann Gilch. They took command and ordered me into their Volkswagen. I was directed to the front seat with the sergeant while the colonel took the back seat, and we drove out of Muhldorf into the countryside. I assumed they were transporting me to a POW camp, but we soon came to a stop in the boondocks. The colonel tapped the back of my head with his pistol and commanded, *"Raus mitt you!"* I obediently got out of the car with hands up and faced him. The sergeant also got out and walked in front of the left headlight, where with his back to me he seemed to be fiddling with his fly. I assumed he needed to answer a "call of nature". Instead, he was loading his pistol.

'When Colonel Zeirhut got out of the back seat he walked around me, pistol in hand; it looked like a 7 mm Mauser. At the front of the vehicle, he raised his arm and fired. I had sensed his intention and I winced when the shot was fired, but somehow it missed me. Gilch then pointed his weapon at me and Zeirhut walked around the car to within 6 feet of me before firing again.

'This time the bullet struck me in the left shoulder. It felt like the kind of straight-arm hit made in football. It pierced the bone and spun me around and to the ground. Rather than be shot to death, I decided to run for it. I ran across a pasture, hobbling on my broken right leg. Zeirhut and Gilch both fired at me, and I could hear bullets whizzing by my head and ricocheting off the ground. They must have fired at least sixteen times.

'My right leg was painful, and I could see blood pumping out of my shoulder through my flight suit. I wasn't scared – there was too much going on; I was looking for salvation. I ran zig-zagging, favouring my right leg. I saw a small bridge spanning the river and headed for it. When I got to the high point of the bridge, with no place to hide and feeling totally naked, I stopped to gather my wits.

'This was a dangerous situation. I felt completely lost and desperately sought any indication of salvation. I was eventually picked up by an elderly German farmer and his son, Wehrmacht Sergeant Joseph Kettner, who took me with them into their yard. I saw a group of people there, old folk, children, and some around my own age. Zeirhut and Gilch were lurking somewhere in the background, and I think they hoped the Kettners would turn me over to them.

'The onlookers shook their fists at Zeirhut and Gilch to harass them and during this mêlée, Wehrmacht Sergeant Kettner despatched a lad to the local Luftwaffe station for assistance.'

Everett Lindley spent the next few weeks in a POW hospital. Mathias Zeirhut and Johann Gilch were tried for the war crime of attempted murder after the war. Zeirhut received a life sentence, Gilch ten years.

Apart from bombing operations, a great many RAF sorties at this time were devoted to mine-laying in the North Sea and the Baltic. Freddie Fish again: 'On 12 March 1945, we were on mine-laying operations in the Kattegat. Mine-laying operations were called "Gardening" and were extremely dangerous as so few aircraft were involved – only nineteen on this op – and we could be plotted by the enemy individually. We carried six 1,500 lb. parachute mines and as soon as these were dropped, a German fighter appeared, obviously vectored on to us by Ground Control. We fired and "corkscrewed" and dived into cloud, but in the next thirty minutes we saw three aircraft shot down. Of the five aircraft from 153 Squadron, one was lost and one severely damaged. Owing to heavy losses on mining, the wing commander sensed a drop in morale and offered to go on the next op. His aircraft, plus another from 153 Squadron, were shot down and all crews lost, on 4/5 April 1945.

'On 16 March, 231 Lancasters of 1st Group were over Nuremberg, where we barely missed colliding with a JU88. He had not seen us and our flight engineer called to the pilot to go up. The fighter passed about 30 feet below us, on a collision course. The night-fighters were very active and twenty-four Lancasters were lost that night, 10 percent of the force and twice the norm of 5 percent. Our compass also failed, the gyro being completely out.

'On 24 March, after bombing the Harpenerweg synthetic oil plant, we were hit by predicted flak. The port and starboard inner engines were set on fire, the starboard petrol tank was holed and we were losing fuel. The fire extinguishers went off and after losing height from 20,000 feet to 12,000 feet we managed to put the fires out, but we only had petrol for about fifty miles. Fortunately the navigator had a list of emergency aerodromes. He checked and found that Eindhoven in Holland was not far away. We got there, calling "Darky" emergency on the radio transmitter and were given permission to land on a very short runway, where the pilot made a very skilful landing on two engines, the undercarriage having been blown down by the emergency compressed air system. This was a brand new aircraft, delivered in the last two weeks, but it was now a complete write-off. The crew were flown back to the UK next day, thankful to have completed a tour of thirty trips.'

The bad weather that had added to the misery of the ground forces in the winter and early spring of 1944–45, also caused problems for the aircrews. RAF navigator Brian Harrison, recalls one eventful night: 'Memories of 5 March 1945 are probably still fresh in the minds of surviving members of No. 4 Group, Bomber Command. The target that night was Chemnitz and at briefing the Met Officer had mentioned the likelihood of icing over our bases and stressed the need for pilots to climb through the icing layer as quickly as possible.

'Takeoff was uneventful but as we attempted to climb through the cloud, it became apparent from our skipper's comments that he was having problems controlling the aircraft. Power in the climb and response to the controls were absent and we were ordered to clip on our parachutes "just in case". Almost immediately came the order to "Abandon aircraft". The icing had taken such a hold that we faced the possibility of spinning out of control, and since we were only at an altitude of 2,000 feet, this would have led to disaster.

'I raised the escape hatch near my navigation table and looked down into a layer of cloud. After checking that my parachute was firmly attached to the harness, I gingerly lowered myself through the hatch. Suddenly I was whisked away and followed by a welcome deceleration as the 'chute opened. I floated gently to earth. Although darkness was approaching, I could make out two other 'chutes on the way down. I hit the ground in what could be described as a perfect "three pointer" – my two knees and my nose! A farmer was soon on the scene, having spotted parachutes, and hot tea in the farmhouse was served prior to being transported to the airfield at Lissett.

'On arrival back at Driffield, it was a relief to see four of my fellow crew members safe and sound. At that point, the only two missing crew members were the pilot and wireless operator, although we were not too concerned as only a couple of hours had passed since we had baled out. However, we became concerned when we were told that a member of the public reported a parachute falling into the North Sea just off the coast. This was very bad news, since the North Sea is no place to be in winter. Although the commanding officer of our squadron accompanied the Bridlington lifeboat on an all-night search, no trace was found of Fred, until his body was found a few days later, washed up near Hornsea.

'As we waited for news of Ron, our pilot, the telephone rang to say that he was safe and on his way to join us. His story was bizarre; satisfied that his crew had baled out, he found himself fighting to control the ice-heavy bomber and experienced difficulty in leaving his seat to reach one of the hatches, since taking his hands off the control column resulted in the aircraft rearing wildly. He was therefore obliged to stay put and await whatever fate was in store for him.

'It became clear that the Halifax had been losing height and was now below the icing layer. Slowly, Ron felt a measure of control returning and he decided to attempt a landing at Carnaby, an emergency landing field designed to receive bombers. With control restored but a full bomb load aboard, and conscious that he could afford no errors if he was to avoid blowing the Halifax, himself and a large chunk of the East Riding to Kingdom Come, he pulled off a superb landing without further incident.'

Finally, John Jarvis, an air gunner with 427 'Lion' Squadron, RCAF, gives an account of operations in the last weeks of the war: 'Our first sortie was on 14 March 1945, to the marshalling yards at Zweibruken, near the border between Germany and France. Photos taken at the time the bombs were dropped showed that the marshalling yards were destroyed; there were many casualties among the German troop concentrations in the town. No bombers were lost, though German fighters were looking for us. I saw fighter flares being dropped along the track of the bomber stream.

'On 20 March 1945 we were one of 166 aircraft that bombed the oil refinery at Hemmingstadt. The only event I can recall about this night was when we were crossing the Kiel canal, when we encountered "predicted flak". The enemy gunners used radar when aiming their guns, which much improved the chance of a hit. A direct hit was not necessary, for the shells used had proximity fuses which exploded when near an aircraft. When I saw five bursts in a row on our altitude and track, I reported it to Don, who altered course. Sure enough, almost immediately there were five more bursts right where we would have been.

'Eleven days later came a time that many crews will never forget. On 31 March we were briefed to fly at the lowest level in our "gaggle", which placed us at the rear of the formation. We were aware that this was the most vulnerable position, but the worst result would be that we would miss our rendezvous with the fighter cover before we reached the target area. Our fears were well founded, for that is exactly what happened.

'We were ten minutes late over the target at Hamburg. Not wishing to become separated from the other gaggles, our fighter cover of Mustangs did not wait. There were eight Lancasters at our level, because we had picked up three "strays". As we were beginning our bombing run, I spotted enemy fighters approaching from the rear and below. I commenced my patter, interrupting bomb aimer Fred, who had already started his patter, directing the skipper in the bombing run: I reported, "Five enemy aircraft approaching from the rear, prepare to corkscrew starboard." Because they were approaching very fast, and because I could see the muzzle flashes of their cannon, I followed with "Starboard *go!*" and commenced firing, though they were not yet within range of our guns. Five Lancasters behind and on either side of us were shot down in that first pass. None of them took evasive action, nor did I see any of them return fire.

'We still had our bomb load on, and the bomb doors were open. Performing a corskcrew manoeuvre with much load put enormous stress on the wings. The instant that we were straight and level again, Burchell called out, "Bombs gone, bomb doors closed." We were being attacked a second time, so I gave commands for a second corkscrew. I have no memory of this second attack because the one that followed was so traumatic.

'We could see the tracer coming towards us and streaking past. The instant that I said "Go!" at the beginning of the third attack, I heard a loud explosion and saw a large piece of our aircraft pass my turret. I was too busy firing at the German jet to find out where we had been hit. However, seeing he had damaged us, he must have assumed that my turret was out of action. At any rate, he came very close and gave both Jim and I an excellent chance for a good shot. As he turned away, both Jim and I saw black smoke coming from the jet and so claimed that we had "probably" destroyed him. The claim could not be further proven because we were bombing on H25 radar through ten-tenths cloud, which prevented visible proof that he crashed.

'After this attack I opened the doors of my turret to get my parachute and put it on. When I looked more closely I saw that the starboard elevator had been hit and blown right off. However, because all the damage was on one side of the aircraft, the other elevator was functioning perfectly well. Don, our skipper, said that he only needed to make a slight adjustment to the trim tabs to make our aircraft "S" Sugar perform as "sweetly" as ever. I never did get the parachute clipped on before I realized we were OK. Our ground crew later counted ninety-two other holes in the tail plane, fin and rudder and the fuselage.

'Another fragment of the shell struck the plastic lid of the Elsan – the can in the rear of the fuselage used as the crew toilet. The plastic lid shattered like glass when hit by the fragment of shell and the contents were splashed all over the rear of our Lancaster! During the trip home, most of the crew were a bit subdued, thinking how close we had come to being shot down. When we landed and I opened my turret doors, the stench from the smashed Elsan made me change my mind. I closed the doors again, rotated the turret 90 degrees and opened the doors again to the fresh air.'

The bombing of Germany that had gone on for five long years continued until the end of April. On 25 March 1945 Winston Churchill questioned the Air Staff on the necessity of further bombing. It was then agreed by the Air Staff that 'No further advantage can be expected from further attacks on the remaining industrial centres in Germany.' Therefore, on 6 April, a directive from the Air Staff was sent to the squadrons: 'The tasks given to the British and American Strategic Air Forces were to disorganize and destroy the German military, economic and industrial systems, and to offer support to our forces on land and sea. We are now on the point of achieving our object and henceforth the main task of the Strategic Air Forces will be to offer direct support to the Allied Armies . . .' This support continued until the last days of the war.

German 75 mm STUG III assault gun

7 The Reichwald and the Rhine

10 FEBRUARY–6 MARCH 1945

> 'Before attempting any major Operations
> east of the Rhine, it is essential to
> destroy the main enemy armies west of the
> river.'
>
> *General Dwight Eisenhower*
> *February 1945*

Throughout February 1945, the principal aim of the Western armies was to clear the way to the Rhine. In the north, Montgomery's 21st Army Group was already on the Rhine at Nijmegen but needed to clear the Germans away from the west bank down to the town of Wesel, a task involving a drive across the tangled forests of the Reichwald and Hochwald by the Canadian 1st Army – Operation Veritable – and another by the 9th US Army, east across the Roer – Operation Grenade. Although circumstances were to separate these attacks by nearly two weeks, it is convenient to consider them as one battle, fought in two phases, and as part of a general thrust east across Germany to the Rhine which included the 1st US Army's drive for the city of Cologne.

Hitler's gamble in the Ardennes finally ended on 27 January with the surviving and much-depleted German forces driven back to or beyond the positions they had held in mid-December 1944. The Ardennes offensive had cost the Germans dear but it had delayed a number of Allied advances, including the start of this major thrust towards the Rhine, originally planned to coincide with the Russian winter offensive. In the south, as in the north, some of the Allied forces, notably the French 1st Army, were already on the Rhine around Strasbourg. While the 'Veritable–Grenade' attack was underway there would be a further assault across the Siegfried Line by General Omar Bradley's 12th US Army Group, with Hodges pushing for Cologne while Patton's men drove on through the Saar–Moselle Triangle to Trier, then pushed up the Moselle valley to Koblenz on the Rhine.

The division between the Anglo-Canadian and American assaults for 'Veritable–Grenade' was along a line running northeast from Aachen to Wesel, with the 9th US Army operating to the south. These two main assaults, 'Veritable' and 'Grenade', were scheduled for early February 1945, before the first of the spring thaws had turned the ground into a quagmire.

The first troops to engage were the British and Canadians of the 21st Army Group, who attacked through the Reichwald – a large forested area south of Nijmegen, between the rivers Meuse (or Maas) and the Lower Rhine (or Waal). This assault was to begin on 8 February 1945 and would be followed two days later by an attack across the Roer river in the south by the 9th US Army, which was currently under command of 21st Army

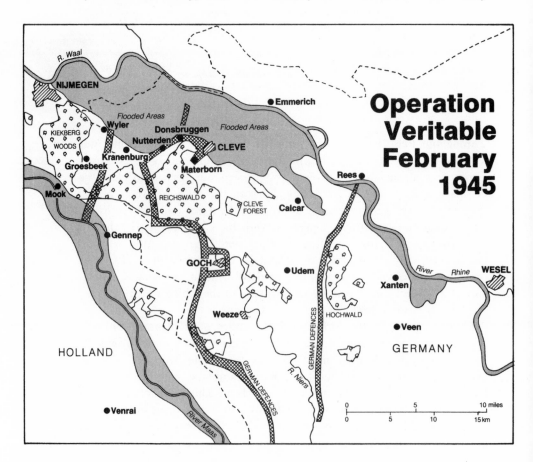

Group. The 9th Army would be supported by two divisions of General Hodges' 1st US Army and the aim of both attacks, 'Grenade' and 'Veritable', was to reach the Rhine around Wesel and Duisburg. The start date of 'Grenade' was then compromised by the failure to destroy or capture the Roer dams before the sluices were damaged and the Roer valley vanished under floods, as related in Chapter 4.

These floods caused many problems for the advancing Allied troops and called for the skills of the sappers. Colonel Ian Wilson, was a twenty-year-old lieutenant in the Royal Engineers in February 1945, and recalls his time as Platoon Commander of 3rd Platoon, 73 Field Company RE:

'Our platoon had been attached to a Canadian engineer unit near Lanklaar in Belgium, building a bridge across the river Maas. We reached our company location in Holland close to the river Maas after dark and found billets in a village named Wanroi. The Canadian 1st Army, which included the British XXX Corps, had a foothold across the Maas in the Grave–Nijmegen area and was preparing to clear the way to the river Rhine. Our task was to keep open the roads under the heavy traffic of the coming offensive. The company employed 200 Dutch civilians as a road maintenance force as well as soldiers of the Pioneer Corps. The main attraction for our Dutchmen was that they were given a midday meal, sparing their meagre rations for their families. Another company responsibility was patrolling the bank of the river Maas, with the enemy on the other side, and there were a few alarms when enemy river crossings were attempted.

'Our defence of the river line was very thin and it was fortunate that no determined German attack developed. I well remember feeling very isolated on one occasion and being very pleased to see a Pioneer Corps sergeant arriving with his section; he was a thrice-wounded infantryman who had transferred to the Pioneers but had "marched to the sound of the guns". This uncomfortable existence continued throughout January, but as it moved into February the thaw arrived and made us wish for the frost again. The roads had never been designed for heavy traffic and large sections disintegrated into soggy mud ponds through which our sappers tried to keep vehicles moving. In retrospect, we may have contributed to this state of affairs because we had put up posts in the road verges to protect them and to prevent vehicles skidding off the road. The only way of digging post-holes in the deeply frozen soil was by explosives, and this may well have disturbed the road foundations.

'My platoon worked on night shift, dusk to dawn, while the traffic was lighter, and a partial solution to the problem was to mix cement with the mud. Whether this formed some sort of mud concrete or just dried out the moisture I was never quite sure, but it seemed to work. The roads were kept open but it was a tiring, sleepless business. My day started with a personal clean-up and breakfast, followed by a few hours sleep. Then I would go to the Company Headquarters for lunch, to report progress and to carry out the inevitable administrative chores, including my share of censoring outgoing letters. I would get back to my platoon about 4.00 p.m., in time to get them moving for the night's work.

'The "Veritable" offensive started on time on 8 February, sweeping south through the Reichwald Forest. On 12 February, our Royal Engineer Company started bridging the Maas at Gennep with two other companies. My initial task was to clear the building area of mines and set out the home bank construction site. It was pouring with rain, and intermittent mortar fire seemed to have little effect as the mortar bombs buried themselves in the mud before exploding. In fact, this was the start of the flooding, and by the time the river bridge was completed it was isolated in a stretch of water from flood-bank to flood-bank. Before long the sight of a motor boat and a military lorry using the same road became quite common. Pontoon causeways were constructed from each flood-bank to an eventual length of nearly one mile. It was open to traffic on 20 February, only to find the floods abating, and by then the battle had moved southwards. We built two more bridges across the Maas. One at Venrai on 8 March at a site heavily mined with wooden anti-personnel mines, undetectable but capable of removing a man's foot, the second at Venlo, a massive floating bridge, strong enough for tank transporters.'

Allied forces for 'Veritable' were drawn from the Canadian 1st Army and consisted of the 2nd Canadian Corps under General Simmonds and the British XXX Corps commanded by General Sir Brian Horrocks, for the Canadian Army contained a large number of British and other national units, including a Polish armoured division. The German forces facing the Veritable–Grenade assaults were in a state of flux following the fighting in the Ardennes and the Schnee Eifel. The front was split between two German army groups, Army Group B opposite the Americans and Army Group H opposite the British and Canadians, with the V Panzer Army in the north and the XV Panzer Army in the south.

The only reserve available to either army was the Panzer Lehr Division, but there were formidable units in the German front line, 116 Panzer, 15 Panzer Grenadier, 9 Panzer, and other hard-fighting units, though all were short of men, munitions and equipment. Horrocks's XXX Corps would also be opposed around Wesel by the tough and tenacious German Ist Parachute Army commanded by General Schlemm, which had five well-trained divisions forward – each a mixture of infantry, panzer and panzer grenadier units – and four more divisions in reserve.

The only German weakness was a shortage of air, tank and artillery support, but their troops were in well-prepared positions and greatly aided by terrible weather and the sodden terrain of the flood-plain west of the Rhine, between the cities of Nijmegen and Wesel. This flood plain and the streams and woods on the low hills of the Reichwald and Hochwald just to the west would prove a formidable barrier to the British and Canadian troops and armour, and a great deal of the subsequent movement and supply was made in boats or amphibious vehicles.

The attack on the Reichwald was preceded by a massive artillery bombardment, from more than 1,000 guns, and a raid by 437 RAF bombers on the cities of Goch and Cleve, which lie south and west of the Reichwald Forest. During one of these air attacks Canadian pilot Bill Baggs from Mississauga had an unusual experience:

'I was serving as a Typhoon pilot with 164 Squadron RAF at the time and on 13 February I was on patrol over the Reichwald. The weather was poor with a cloud base at around 1,500 feet, and the flak was murderous. During one "cab-rank" attack on a ground position, four of our eight aircraft went down in flames, and with instruments toppling and compass spinning I set course for our base in Holland.

'Suddenly, a V-1 buzz-bomb filled my windscreen; it was coming straight at me, head on. I pushed the stick forward and the missile missed me by just a few feet. Realizing that I was heading in the wrong direction into the heart of Germany I violently altered course and tried to close up on the rapidly disappearing V-1, which led me back right over our fogged-in airfield. While the V-1 had a high priority on our squadron "hit-list", I often chuckle when I think of the one that saved me from flying in the wrong direction, to a very uncertain future.'

Clem Irving of Ridgeway, Ontario, remembers the start of Veritable and the infantry fighting in the Reichwald: 'I was a private in C Company, the Royal Regiment of Canada, 2nd Canadian Division. The start of Veritable was the end of the platoon's vigil at listening posts where we had spent the winter forward of our main defence lines. It was cold and wet and frightening and we were so far ahead of our lines that we would have been beyond help if we came under attack. The terrain was such that our only way back to the main lines was by boat.

'The casualty rate in the infantry was too high for real friendship to develop. It was dreadful to see the man next to you torn to pieces, and it would have been much more difficult if we had been real pals ... so we had no friends. How could you see a good friend fall and leave him to die alone while you carried on with the attack?

'I had several platoon sergeants in the short time I was in action. One of them got careless in the Hochwald Forest during 'Veritable' and was hit by mortar bomb fragments. I bound him together the best I could and shoved a dose of morphine into a large muscle that was still intact. The sergeant was quite alert when he was sent back but I have no idea if he survived. I knew that the surgeons would have to finish the job of severing his right arm. We had no stretcher-bearers to provide any assistance. The last one we had was killed by a burst of machine-gun fire, aimed exactly in the centre of the Red Cross on the back of his jerkin.

'Another sergeant left us in irons after having raped a German girl. He went crazy when he got a letter saying that the wife he had not seen in three years had given birth to a baby girl.

'There is no person in all of human history who knows everything about a war, a battle or an attack. Two men standing side by side and ordered to fix bayonets and charge a position would have different experiences as the action takes place. No two men sharing a slit-trench would have identical things occur as they fight off a counter-attack. The non-combatants behind the fighting men would have an entirely different perspective of what took place.

'Our last listening post duty of that terrible winter came to an end on the evening of 7 February 1945. The land in front of me sloped in the direction of the enemy and the German city of Cleve was off to the right, not many miles away. We had spent weeks without hearing a sound from the defence lines behind us, but for the past few days and nights we heard the sounds of engines moving up, more numerous every night and ever closer to the front. The enemy must have known that a major attack would come any day and responded with artillery fire on targets behind us.

'During the late evening of 7 February we began to hear the sounds of bombers, just two or three at first, about 30 degrees off to our right. An anti-aircraft barrage and the slender fingers of searchlights soon lit up the sky. The aircraft continued to approach in waves and before very long Pathfinder aircraft were releasing parachute flares. A large number of bombers then flew in and released their bombs within the targeted area. When the flares went out, new ones were released and the bombing continued: the ancient and historic city of Cleve was being obliterated. I watched it with a good deal of pity for the people as the bright flashes of exploding bombs were slowly replaced by the red glow of a city in flames.

'In the early dawn, the enemy positions to our front came under barrage from our artillery, hundreds of guns firing all at once. I had never heard such a barrage before; I was certain that the will of the enemy was being broken and before daylight we were ordered to fire everything we had into the enemy position as well.

'With daylight came the cutting edge of the offensive. British infantry from XXX Corps, which was then part of the 1st Canadian Army, arrived at our position and waited to start the offensive, for our defences were the Start Line for their attack.

'While their objectives were being softened by artillery and mortar fire, the infantry quietly went about their business and made themselves tea. I knew why they were quiet. Many thoughts go through a man's mind just before battle and we did our best to tell them about the defenses we had learned about on fighting patrols into the enemy lines. We felt that if the British knew exactly where the German machine-guns, mines and other weapons were, some lives would be saved, but the British officers stopped us from talking to their men and even accused us of trying to demoralize them. It became apparent that the Canadian Army's philosophy, one of treating the fighting troops like mushrooms – keep them in the dark and drop them in the shit – was shared by the British Army.

'The British infantry started their advance about 10 o'clock in the morning and the artillery and mortar bombardment continued as the two sides engaged and kept moving forward as the British infantry advanced.

'A lot of men died that morning. The sides of the road were littered with damaged and burning vehicles and the cab of one truck was dripping blood onto the road. The road at the bottom of the hill was raised as the low land and the wet season did not permit overland travel by tanks and heavy vehicles. Damaged vehicles had to be pushed aside so that the road could be used. The cross-roads ahead had traffic trying to move forward and another line trying to move across. Suddenly I heard an unfamiliar *swoosh*, a big explosion and the crossroads and everything on it was destroyed. Then I saw a strange aircraft – without a propeller – go into a vertical climb which it maintained until it disappeared into the clouds ... my first jet. I had never seen an airplane like that before, but I sure hoped we had some jet-planes too.

'This operation, which began on 8 February 1945, was called "Operation Veritable" and aimed at reaching the river Rhine in forty-eight hours and clearing the Germans from the country between the Maas and the Rhine. One of the tasks was to capture the Nijmegen–Cleve road and another was to force a corridor through the Reichwald Forest. Battlefield conditions could not have been worse because most of the area was low-lying and the spring thaw had begun. The Germans, occupying well-fortified positions in the Siegfried Line, resisted our advance with fanatical resolve. Breaking through the strong outer defences, the Allied forces found that the Germans had blow up the dykes, thus submerging a large part of the Nijmegen–Cleve road which turned the assault into an amphibious operation.

'The troops had to advance under the most terrible conditions, through mud and water more than 3 feet deep. The Army's amphibious vehicles were unable to handle it all, so the Navy with its boats and sailors was needed. It seemed strange to see trailers taking Navy boats and sailors towards the flooded areas, but Cleve was reached on 10 February and by 12 February the town was in the hands of the Allies.'

Patrick Hennessey of the 13th/18th Hussars fought in the Reichwald battle. 'Now that the trouble in the Ardennes had been settled, it was the intention to make a drive from the Nijmegen area into the North German plain and the industrial region of the Ruhr. For us this meant the completion of the clearing of the Reichwald Forest, which had started while I was on leave, pushing on through Goch, down into Germany, and crossing the Rhine. I felt very honoured that Major Cordy Simpson should take the trouble to brief me so fully – me, a mere sergeant – but he was a very likeable man and I got the impression he was thoroughly enjoying himself. My squadron was already in the forest, so I stayed the night at HQ and went on next morning by jeep to rejoin my tank.

'The Reichwald Forest was not an easy battle, particularly for the infantry, who once more had to bear the brunt of it. The Siegfried Line of prepared defences did not, in fact, extend as far as the forest, but the Germans had had time to make preparations to meet the attack which they must have known would come that way.

'When the attack had started, they had breached the banks of the river and had flooded the area. Also, although it was still very cold, the rock-hard, frozen ground had begun to thaw. This, combined with the constant movement of men and vehicles, and the results of artillery and mortar fire, had reduced the tracks in the forest into seas of mud. It was very hard going. I had missed most of the battle by being on leave, and returned just in time for the tail end of it, but that was bad enough.

'Finally, we emerged from the forest and began to fight our way against still determined opposition towards Goch and Cleve, both of which were fortified towns, so they had received severe aerial and artillery bombardment. Sergeant Ron Hepper, who was the leading tank of his troop, had got rather far ahead when he hit a mine which blew one of his tracks off. He was advised to leave his crippled tank and make his way back on foot, but he answered that he thought he could keep his guns firing for a bit longer. However, with one track gone and unable to move, his tank was an easy target for the German anti-tank destroyer and he and his gunner were killed. The rest of his crew managed to escape and make their way back. It was typical of Ron Hepper that he would not give up easily. He was a regular Tank Corps man who had come to us on mechanization. A very efficient and popular NCO, he had won the Military Medal on D-Day. He and Trooper Tom Cowen now rest in the Reichwald Military Cemetery at the edge of the forest.

'When we got to Goch we found the town in a shambles after the massive bombardments it had received. Surprisingly, many of the inhabitants were still there, living a troglodyte existence in the deep cellars which every house seemed to have. We were not sure how we should deal with these people. There were strict orders about non-fraternization and the dangers of trusting them, but most of these presented a pathetic picture of shock and bewilderment. The fighting was by no means over yet, the town was regularly subjected to enemy artillery fire and we were constantly on the alert for snipers.

'We paused at Goch to let the supply echelons catch up with us. We cleaned the tanks, got replacement clothing and generally caught our breath. We took over a number of houses as billets, reinforcements arrived to replace casualties, and to our surprise the regimental band came out to visit us. The Germans shelled quite heavily on the evening of their arrival and the band suffered a number of wounded. Nevertheless, they played several times for us at Goch, and the German civilians emerged from their cellars to watch them with something approaching respect. It seemed they were quite unable to resist the music of a military band, and indeed we were all quite sorry to see the band leave us as we prepared to move on once again.

'After a few days, refreshed and refitted, we moved out of Goch on our way to the Rhine. We went through Cleve as best we could. The whole town was a heap of rubble, bulldozers had to clear paths for us to get through – never have I seen such complete destruction. It had been known that Cleve was fortified as a strongpoint, and that is why it had been bombed before the initial assault on it by the 15th (Scottish) Division. The air bombardment had been extreme, some 1,300 tons of high explosive had been dropped on the town, and the resulting ruins and craters had impeded the attacking force, allowing the Germans to recover and put up a very savage resistance. However, by the time we got there, the town had been taken and we pushed on, leaving the Royal Engineers to clear up the chaos.'

Burton Simpson of Dunchurch, Ontario also remembers the start of Veritable: 'I was then a corporal in the Royal Regiment of Canada and around 8 February the British 51st Division went through our positions by Grosbeek. They were a famous Highland Division who had fought in North Africa and Sicily with the 8th Army. Anyway, this division went through us and we sure had some schmozzle for a while, especially from artillery and mortars.

'The Germans had multi-barrelled mortars, which screamed overhead and sounded like thunder when they hit. Quite a few of the British stepped on mines as well and came back with one leg. The bombers destroyed Cleve completely, there was nothing left of Cleve but a bunch of rubble, and three or four towns were like that. The attack when the 51st came through was our last big offensive for there were no really big solid battles after that.

'The German defenders were finally cleared out of the Reichwald by 13 February, and on 16 February we moved closer to the front line at Cleve, which was now in Allied hands. I had never seen a city immediately after it had been attacked by bombers and it was a never-to-be-forgotten sight. Cleve was in such a state that paths had been bulldozed through the rubble to open up the streets for our vehicles, and we were told that the bombing had added rubble to the defenders' bunkers so they had been even tougher to clear. I wondered what had happened to the civilian population.

'On 17 February my regiment moved off along the edge of the floods to Calcar, a move delayed for days because of fierce German resistance. On 19 February we started a period of real, tough, blood-and-guts infantry work, attacking well-defended enemy positions all along the Goch–Calcar road. Attacks and counter-attacks kept us busy for two days, always under heavy German fire. To make matters worse we were being assaulted by tanks and had to rescue another battalion of our brigade that had been overrun by German tanks and infantry. The last German attack came on the evening of 20 February; this was broken up and although heavy shelling and mortars continued, the Goch–Calcar road was ours. The three battalions in our brigade alone had over 400 casualties, killed, wounded and missing.'

The German wrecking of the sluices on the Roer dams and the subsequent flooding of the river valley held up the launching of the 9th US Army's 'Grenade' assault for two full weeks, and in that time the full weight of Von Rundstedt's armies was flung against the British and Canadians in the Reichwald.

The fighting for the Reichwald mirrored that experienced by the American infantry in the Hurtgen Forest during the previous November: mud, mines, inpenetrable woodland thick with wire and snipers, wide fire-breaks covered by machine-guns, heavy casualties from artillery and mortar tree-bursts, and the sheer exhaustion caused by fighting in continuous rain and cold, over broken ground.

All three British infantry divisions of XXX Corps, the 51st (Highland), the 53rd (Welsh), and the 15th (Scottish) met with stiff opposition in the Reichwald, but with the aid of air and artillery support they pushed steadily forward. By midnight on 8 February the 51st (Highland) Division had reached the edge of the Reichwald, and the 53rd Division had broken through the German front line and got beyond the town of Kronenburg, which fell to troops of the 15th (Scottish) Division. Meanwhile the Germans were bringing reinforcements north from the 9th US Army front with Panzer Lehr and troops of the German 6th Parachute Division coming into action against the Canadians.

The task of opening the main road down the axis of advance from Nijmegen to Cleve was allocated to the 2nd Canadian Division from General Simonds' 2nd Canadian Corps, which had advanced five miles by nightfall on 9 February and taken the town of Wyler. So far, so good; but on their left flank the 3rd Canadian Division – charged with clearing the flood plain between the Reichwald Forest and the west bank of the Rhine – was having a terrible time. Much of their area was under flood water even before their advance began and only on the right, on the slopes of the 300 foot Reichwald hills, could their tanks and infantry advance at all; out on the plain the only way to advance was by storm-boats and amphibious tracked vehicles called Buffaloes. Even so, the 3rd Canadian Division pressed forward and by the evening of 9 February had cleared the Reichwald up to their first objective, the town of Donsbrugger.

These attacks were supported by the specialized armour of the British 79th Armoured Division, flail tanks clearing minefields, flame throwers operating against German machine-gun posts, bridge-building tanks to clear the streams and deep water. Without this armoured support from the Specialized Engineer tanks, the advance would have been very costly.

Ray Knight continues his story with an account of a Crocodile flame tank in action: 'We were crouched in our slit, popping up to have quick look to our front between mortar bursts, when I became aware of a new sound, a rather screeching, clanking noise, almost muffled by the roar of an engine. It came from our right and there was no doubt in my mind that we were going to have our first meeting with either a Tiger or a Panther. Fearfully, I glanced in the direction of the noise, saying another little prayer to add to the ones I had already uttered.

'First the barrel emerged from behind the building that housed the wounded, followed by a squat, flat-topped turret ... whatever it was it didn't look like one of theirs. Then I recognized the shape – whoever said those Tank Recognition Classes were a waste of time! The driver hauled her round the corner and brought her to a stop, right in front of us. That's when I spotted the trailer towed behind. Although I had never seen one in action, I was awed by the fact that I was finally seeing a Crocodile, the flame-throwing tank.

'As though to confirm my thoughts, the flame-gun operator picked that very moment to either test or clear his weapon. From the spot where the coaxial machine-gun had once been, came a gush of roaring flame, spreading down the road before him. As the roar of the burning fuel died away, the flame projector silently continued to send out a streak of flame. Then he prepared to move on to his real objective further down the road.

'One of our companies had run into a devoted pocket of defenders who were going to have to be winkled out with something more impressive than standard infantry weapons, and after our little demonstration we knew they would be suitably impressed.

'It wasn't until the Crocodile had moved well clear of us that a thought hit me. Up to the time that it had made its appearance, the enemy had no real reason to waste any 88 mms on us now that we were dug-in. However, when the Crocodile came along, lighting up the countryside like a beacon, every anti-tank gun that the Germans had west of the Rhine could have zeroed in on it and, of course, on us. Sitting there beside the road with only a very shaky brick wall behind us, a near miss would have dropped tons of bricks on our heads. Even worse, if a shell had hit the Crocodile's trailer and it brewed up, we would have been flooded by the devil's brew that it contained. It wasn't until my buddy asked, "Did you see what that stupid son-of-a-bitch just did?" that I realized we had both had the same ugly thoughts at the same time. So much for armoured support!'

The weather, never good, broke completely on the afternoon of 9 February and low cloud prevented air support for the next few days. This left the infantry to fight it out unsupported against a stubborn enemy, fighting on their home ground.

John Craig was with the 1st Battalion, the Argyll and Sutherland Highlanders of Canada in the 4th Canadian Division, which came up to support the advance through the Hochwald: 'Gone now were the friendly faces of Belgium and Holland. In their place sullen, shocked faces of a people once dedicated to world domination, realizing their dream had become a nightmare, with khaki-clad troops pouring across the frontiers of the Reich.

'There were many tough fights for the Argylls in Germany, like the struggle in the Hochwald Forest. This forest lay in a picturesque piece of real estate, all rolling hills and open plains filled by masses of pine trees – an ideal spot for booby traps and anti-tank guns. The defenders were in the scattered farm buildings that dotted this part of the famous Siegfried Line, and the battle was a terrible ordeal. Rain fell on the war-torn forest, turning the ground into a quagmire that halted man and machines.

'The Argylls – along with the Algonquin Regiment, the Governor General's Foot Guards, the South Alberta Regiment, the Canadian Grenadier Guards, Lincoln and Welland Regiment, Lake Superior Regiment and other units of the 4th Canadian Division – combined to throw the enemy out of the Hochwald Forest and send him back towards the Rhine. The town of Veen beyond the Hochwald, south of Xanten, was the last town on the west bank of the Rhine to fall into Allied hands, but not without sacrifice. In twelve days' fighting in Germany, our regiment alone lost 260 men killed and wounded.'

On the evening of 9 February, General Horrocks ordered his corps reserve, the 43rd (Wessex) Division to move out of Nijmegen, and hook east through the Reichwald Forest towards Goch and Cleve. The leading brigade was at Cleve by first light on 10 February, where they were confronted by German paratroops supported by 88 mms and self-propelled guns. Street fighting went on in Cleve throughout the day and a huge traffic jam built up around the villages of Materborn and Nutterden, where the 43rd and 15th (Scottish) Division troops, tanks and supply trucks became hopelessly intermingled.

The Germans were very determined to hold onto Cleve, putting in parachute troops and elements of 15th Panzer Grenadier and 116th Panzer Divisions to bolster the hard-pressed garrison. The 15th (Scottish) battered their way into Cleve on 11 February, to find the town totally shattered but the ruins well supplied with snipers and machine-gun nests. These were eliminated by the evening of the 12th, when the town was handed over to troops of the 3rd Canadian Division.

General Crerar could not at first bring the full weight of his army to bear as the front around Nijmegen was too narrow. As the British and Canadian troops advanced south, so the front gradually widened and more divisions could be brought into the line, and by 15 February XXX Corps had three divisions around Goch, which fell on the 19th after four days of heavy fighting. Meanwhile, the Canadians had battered their way into Calcar, across a countryside carpeted with mines and covered by 88 mm anti-tank guns, facing stiffening resistance from German troops brought up from the American front further south.

On 19 February the 4th Canadian Infantry Brigade was attacked at night by the newly arrived Panzer Lehr division, which soon had tanks and companies of panzer grenadiers roving about the Canadian positions. In two days of fighting the 4th Canadian lost four hundred men, killed, wounded or missing; but Panzer Lehr had been the armoured reserve for Army Group B, facing the Americans to the south, so the Canadians had the consolation that in bringing troops north to oppose them, the Germans were weakening their front against Simpson's 9th US Army which was now about to attack.

By 23 February, after two weeks of hard fighting in terrible conditions, the British XXX Corps and the 2nd Canadian Corps had extended their front to a width of twenty miles, but still the German defenders showed no real sign of cracking. Fortunately, the floods on the Roer had now subsided sufficiently for General Simpson's 9th Army to launch the second phase of the Roer–Rhine assault, Operation Grenade.

For this operation General Simpson's 9th Army had been increased to ten divisions, with the 95th US Infantry Division in reserve, the support of four divisions of Collins' US VII Corps of 1st US Army bolstering their right flank, and a great quantity of artillery and air support.

Operation Grenade began on the morning of 23 February with a 45-minute bombardment of the German positions by 2,000 guns, followed by an assault in storm-boats across the Roer on a seventeen-mile front between the towns of Linnich and Jülich by three full corps, each with two divisions up. Simpson's task was to cross the Roer, and then drive north and east through München-Gladbach and across the Cologne plain, to link up with the Canadians and reach the west bank of the Rhine around Duisburg.

The German forces opposite Simpson's army had consisted of some ten infantry and Volksgrenadier divisions, supported by a considerable amount of artillery and mortars and about 230 tanks of the V Panzer Army, but this force had gradually been depleted during the Veritable fighting, and the XV Army, which held the southern part of the front, was anyway much less formidable than the forces further north. The terrain was not unduly difficult, for once the Roer had been crossed there was only the river Erft and the low hills of the Hamnbach Forest near Jülich barring the way to the Rhine plain, though the Germans had prepared three defensive lines, one on the east bank of the Roer, one on the Erft, and one between the two, each a mixture of minefields, bunkers and machine-gun posts. 'We are going to have some stiff fighting,' said General Simpson before the attack, 'but I think we are going right through.'

Sergeant Robert J. Slaughter from Roanoke, Virginia, of the 116th Infantry Regiment, 29th Infantry Division, tells of his part in Grenade: 'I well recall that on 3 February 1945, the 116th Infantry Regiment celebrated the fourth anniversary of its induction into Federal Service by firing every weapon at its disposal on enemy targets.

'On 23 February the 29th Division attacked the city of Jülich, which had been heavily bombed. The operation had been scheduled for 10 February but the Germans had opened the dam gates upstream, flooding the river banks. After a thirteen-day delay, the 175th Infantry smashed across the river at 0445 hrs and met comparatively light resistance. Our 3rd Battalion, 116th Infantry, was attached to the 175th in reserve to mop up after the assault. K Company was ordered to attack the citadel in Jülich, an ancient thick-walled and moated fortress. The streets of Jülich had to be cleared of debris by bulldozers for the armour to support our attack on the citadel.

'With the aid of 155 mm self-propelled guns, the Jülich citadel fell to the task force. This skirmish was symbolic of the ultimate Allied victory over the strongest of Hitler's strong points. The 29th Division's whirlwind offensive on the Cologne plain was brought to a successful conclusion on 1 March when units of the 116th Regiment, working with the 175th Infantry in what was later described as a "superbly co-ordinated attack", wrested the industrial city of München-Gladbach from enemy hands.

'I remember the capture of Gelsenkirchen and Holz and then village after village, for we were moving so fast that the German populace were still shopping in downtown stores when we came in. We invaded one restaurant and ordered a sumptuous meal from the menu ... well, as they say, "To

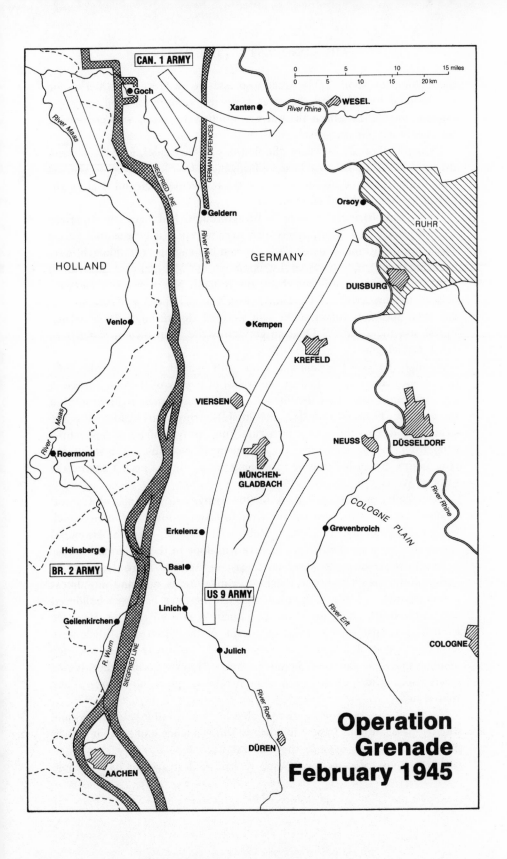

CAN. 1 ARMY

Goch

Xanten ● River Rhine **WESEL**

GERMAN DEFENCES

SIEGFRIED LINE

River Niers

River Maas

● Geldern

Orsoy ●

RUHR

HOLLAND

GERMANY

DUISBURG

Venlo ●

● Kempen

KREFELD

VIERSEN

River Maas

NEUSS

DÜSSELDORF

Roermond ●

MÜNCHEN-GLADBACH

River Rhine

COLOGNE PLAIN

Erkelenz ●

Grevenbroich ●

BR. 2 ARMY

Heinsberg ●

Baal ●

Geilenkirchen ●

Linich ●

US 9 ARMY

River Erft

R. Wurm

SIEGFRIED LINE

● Julich

River Roer

COLOGNE

DÜREN

**Operation
Grenade
February 1945**

AACHEN

0   5   10   15 miles
0   5   10   15   20 km

the victors, the spoils". My squad also assaulted a German barber's shop and ordered haircuts and shaves at gunpoint. Looting and pillaging was rampant during this phase; the war was winding down and we were making the enemy pay for past sins.'

By nightfall on 23 February, the first day of 'Grenade', four divisions of the 9th US Army had established a bridgehead four miles deep on the east bank of the Roer and captured most of the towns of Jülich and Baal for the loss of less than a hundred men.

Rapid exploitation, following a breakthrough, had been an American speciality since St Lô. Simpson's men were to repeat it here as they thrust ahead for the Rhine. On the 24th the combat engineers building bridges over the Roer were harassed by bombing but the gunners shot down eighteen German aircraft and drove the rest off. Nor were the Americans delayed by the arrival of IX Panzer which joined the XV Army on that day. The 30th US Infantry Division stormed east through the Hambach Forest and the 29th US Division got across the main road running from Jülich to Cologne.

Though the 35th Division had a very stiff fight at Hilfarth on the 26th, the advance continued, aided by the arrival of twenty of the new American Pershing tanks mounting the 90 mm gun that could match the 88 mm on the German Tiger. Within days the 9th US Army were hustling the XV Army back against the 1st German Parachute Army, which was now falling back from the north before the advancing Canadians, so that all the remaining German forces were now being pressed into a pocket around the town of Wesel.

Meanwhile, on the right flank of 9th Army, two divisions of General Hodges' 1st Army had crossed the river to take the town of Düren, which fell on 25 February. Lieutenant Robert Brooker of the 9th Armoured Engineers saw what the Allied offensive had done to these German towns:

'When we crossed the Roer river, east of Aachen, there was a lot of destruction. Aachen had been fought over many times now and was almost totally destroyed. Most of the roads through the town had been bulldozed so that the traffic could use them, but when we crossed the Roer river we learned just what total destruction meant. Both Düren and Jülich were levelled to about 4 feet high. The towns had been on the front lines for months and they had been bombed, shelled, blown up and then blown down again. There were no walls, no streets, no glass, no *nothing*. They were gone.

'As I was leaving Düren on a road that had been bulldozed, I noted one pane of glass still intact and I just had to throw a stone and break it. When people speak glibly of war, they should have seen those two towns to understand just what we mean when we say we destroyed a city. If people today saw what I saw back then, they might lose their enthusiasm for fighting.'

Within two days the Americans had a dozen divisions across the Roer and by the 26 February were making steady progress towards the Rhine. Keeping up the pressure from the north, the 2nd and 3rd Canadian Divisions, supported by the 4th Canadian Armoured Division and the British 11th Armoured Division, struck the German positions before Udem and Xanten on 26 February. The German resistance was as stiff as ever: over 100 tanks were knocked out and more than 1,000 Canadians were killed or wounded in the battle, including Sergeant Coseons of the Queen's Own Rifles of Canada (QORC), who gained a posthumous Victoria Cross. Four days later another Canadian, Major Frederick Tilston of the Essex Scottish Regiment, received the Victoria Cross for gallantry in an action in which he lost both his legs.

Percy Ball of McKellar, Ontario, recalls what happened to him in the Reichwald fighting: 'In March 1945 I was a signaller in the Algonquin Regiment, when I was wounded. Our B Company was cut off and had no communications, so I was asked to get a telephone line in to them. I had not seen the territory before – I didn't have a map and was only told the general direction, and I couldn't find them. The next time the lieutenant went with me and we got a line in. Next day it was blown up and I had to go in with another chap and fix it. From a shell hole I saw a platoon of soldiers hunkered down, and I made a run for them. As I did so a shot came from a sniper, but I reached the platoon – some of the South Saskatchewans – and said, "I gotta go across that field and get a telephone line in." I knew if I could get there and lie down, from 600 yards I wouldn't be much of a target. Their lieutenant said, "I wish you luck."

'He didn't wish hard enough. I thought that if I could run fast enough maybe the sniper wouldn't be able to hit me, for he was, maybe, five or six hundred yards away. At that time I didn't know where our line was – nobody knew and I was going pretty fast when he hit me, and he hit exactly where he aimed, in the stomach.

'The bullet took me right squarely in front, and came out by my spine. It was just like you picked up a sledgehammer and hit me right across the back. I had no sensation of being hit in the front. I can remember going through the air and coming down, and the next thing I can remember is lying on my stomach with blood running down my back. In the meantime, unknown to me because I have no memory of it, I had repaired the line. I had left my rifle and tape and pliers and everything else, so I left word with the doctor to tell my lieutenant what I had done. They went out the next day, after they had cleaned the Germans out of that piece of bush, and got it.

'Later the lieutenant came to see me in hospital in England, and he asked me, "When did you fix the line? You fixed it before you got hit, did you?" I replied, "I never fixed the line." He said, "Oh, but you did." "No," I said, "I got hit before I got to the break." "Well," he said, "the line of communications was established at the time you were out there, and when we got there your tape and your rifle and your pliers were lying with a fresh splice in the line, so you had to have fixed it." But I had no memory of fixing it, none at all, and I know I hadn't got to it when I was hit. I was no hero – you just don't think it's going to happen to you.'

As Sergeant Bob Slaughter has described, on 1 March 1945, the 9th US Army took the town of München-Gladbach and surged on towards the Rhine, hoping to capture a bridge. By 5 March they had reached the Rhine at Orsay, north of Dusseldorf, where the bridge had already been blown. Even so, Simpson's men wanted to press on and throw bridges over the river. They were only stopped by a direct order from Field Marshal Montgomery. General Simpson was a calm and contained officer who got on well with the Field Marshal but he was more than a little annoyed at this order. Other less well-disposed Americans saw Montgomery's actions as an attempt to hold the Americans back until Monty could make his own crossing and hog the credit for the British.

This is not likely, as General Simpson soon came to appreciate. There was and would remain a difference between the British and American approach to battle, but there were more specific reasons to call a halt here. Having reached the Rhine, Veritable and Grenade were over. Montgomery was now thinking of the next phase, an all-out assault across the Rhine, one of those set-piece battles at which he was the acknowledged master. He was also a firm believer in a 'tidy battlefield', and though the Veritable and Grenade forces had reached the Rhine by 5 March, there was still some tidying-up to be done.

The Reichwald fighting continued into March, as the British and Canadians fought their way through the Hochwald, another forest to the south of the Reichwald and on to the town of Xanten, northwest of Wesel. Ray Knight was a Bren-gunner with a Canadian Regiment, the Essex Scottish Regiment during the attack on Xanten. 'The date of my initiation under fire was 6 March 1945 and the objective was Xanten. At 0300 hrs we were quietly awakened and told to have breakfast as fast and as silently as possible. We gathered up our porridge, bread, jam and coffee, got it down quickly and were ready to move off within minutes.

'As we formed up we found that the overcast weather of the previous night had turned into a steady light drizzle which, if anything, muffled any noise we may have been making. Then, at the wave of our section leader's hand, we moved off. As we moved up the track, a couple of loaded jeeps passed us, heading back towards the farm, filled with the men who had prepared things at the "Start Line", wherever that was.

'Unable to smoke, there was nothing to do but stand in the rain and wait. Some us, probably through tension, took the opportunity have a final "nervous pee", adding to the steady pattering of the rain. Then, the wave came down to move forward. After a groping advance of about 100 yards, a faint white glimmer appeared on the ground. Stretched out as far as I could see was the taped-down "Start Line"; for some of us, the point of no return. Told to crouch down, we huddled in the mud, waiting for the barrage to begin. Other than our Bren-gun team, everyone else spread well apart. My Bren group kept close enough to be in constant contact; Whitey to lead us, me as the gunner, and Maudsley, my No. 2, spare barrel and all, to help me as best he could. The .303 Bren light machine-gun was the main infantry weapon, and we had to support the rifle section. Then it began.

'The entire sky behind us lit up, an orange-red wall of flame, followed seconds later by the sound of the shells, their moaning wails turning into screams as they thundered to earth in front of us. All across our front the ground heaved with 25-pounder bursts, mixed with a new sound to me, the whining of shrapnel.

'With the bursting of the first rounds we were signalled to move forward towards that wall of hot steel fragments. With my heart in my mouth, I followed Whitey, almost blindly, flopping when he did. As I lay there clutching the bipod of the Bren, I became aware of what seemed to be a stream of glowing onions arching through the night on our right flank. Seeing that, I remembered from the briefing that the 40 mm Bofors cannon were firing their guns ahead to mark the outer boundary of our advance, and although we couldn't hear them, they seemed to be doing their job.

'Up to that point, maybe halfway across the fields, the sounds of shells had been almost deafening. Then the roar took on another note – that of incoming shell fire. The enemy had had time to register his artillery and now, alerted by our cannonade, threw in his counter-barrage. Until that very second, I had wished I could have been farther back, out of the first wave. Now, with the German shells tearing up the ground behind us, I could only pity the poor bastards caught up in the maelstrom that chewed into their ranks. Still scared almost blind, I moved on with the Bren-team.

'After what seemed like a nightmarish eternity, something other than clinging mud appeared ahead. It was the orchard. We had made it – but not quite. Whitey, who was several yards ahead, suddenly threw up his arms and completely disappeared. Then, like Lazarus, he rose from the dead. First, his helmet came into view, accompanied by two pairs of upraised arms, each joined by a coal-scuttle helmet. Corporal White had taken two prisoners!

'There seemed to be a lull in the firing. Taking advantage of the relative calm, we started through the orchard towards the burning barns. Suddenly all hell broke loose. The enemy seemed to have caught his second wind and began to pour mortar fire in upon us. Bombs exploded through the apple trees, striking branches and throwing masses of splinters in every direction. This new phase of our ordeal turned out to be even worse than the one we had just been through.

'As the 81 mm mortar bombs screamed in, we crawled and skittered across the ground, trying to keep as low as possible. Then there was another lull. In a mad dash several of us rose and started towards the barns at a dead run, only to be caught upright by the next salvo. One poor bugger 20 feet to my left disappeared, completely engulfed in a tremendous blast. Thrown off my feet I felt a blow to my left hand as I was falling, but managed to hang on to the Bren. As I lay there, half stunned, I saw that the man on my left was down. He lay there gasping and writhing in a heap, one leg completely gone, the other only attached to what had been his waist by a mass of his own intestines. Christ, what a sight!

'Whitey, who had been ahead of us, had been struck too. He lay in the mud, groaning and clutching the calf of his left leg. As we reached him, we saw to our horror that most of the calf of his leg was gone and he was spurting blood from a severed artery. I snatched the shell-dressing from under the cammo-net on my helmet and poured on the pressure while Maudsley tried to wind the tape in place. When the pulsing blood slowed, we pulled and shoved Whitey over the ground, finally dropping into a ditch on the far side of the orchard. Realizing that Whitey was in a bad way and needing help immediately, it seemed up to me that I should go to seek help. Telling Maudsley to stay with Whitey, I headed back for the barns which were engulfed in flames.

'When the next mortar bombs came down I dived over the fence, straight into a manure heap. The top of the pile was about even with the height of the fence, so I found myself sliding face-down back to ground level through tons of maturing cow-pats, and God knows what else. The stench was unbelievable and there I was, drenched with it. To hell with the bombs, I dragged myself out and floundered to the safety of a brick wall where, safe but stinking, I looked around.

'The first person I saw was a stretcher-bearer. I called for help, but he just shook his head and pointed towards the front of the buildings. Hoping I would find help there, I left my corner and headed in the direction indicated, to the door of the main house. I found myself in a room full of wounded waiting for medical help. Not seeing another Red Cross, I picked my way through the jumble of legs towards a light shining through another door and found it led to the basement. Forcing my way down the steps I entered another room, the floor of which was covered with wounded. Thankfully, I spotted our platoon stretcher-bearer bandaging up someone's head. I caught his eye and explained what had happened to Whitey. He told me to grab the other end of a stretcher and off we went, back into the hell outside.

'We reached Whitey and the first thing "Stretch" did was to plunge some morphine into his arm, straight through his uniform. In seconds Whitey was out of it. While our rescue mission was taking place I realized that the sound around us had changed. The 81 mms seemed to stop, but within minutes they were replaced by other, even more frightening sounds – those of the "Moaning Minnies", the German multi-barrelled mortars.

'"Stretch" and I lugged Whitey back to the basement and there I left them both. That's when the first of the screaming "Minnie" bombs started to come in. Luckily for me, it didn't take too many minutes to figure out that the bombs were being fired in groups of six, all landing close together in rotation. Therefore, between the half-dozen lots, and carefully skirting the manure heap, I made my way back to my Bren. When I arrived at the site I found my gun and webbing but no Maudsley. He had disappeared.

'Puzzled by his disappearance, I started back towards the barns, then paused when I heard the grunting of a pig. There, snuffling around among the remains of the poor bastard who had been struck by the mortar bomb, was this great sow, making a meal of him. The ghastliness of the sight was unbelievable. In a fit of rage I ran at the pig, firing the Bren from the hip. Even as the pig went down, I calmly put on another magazine, and kept firing until the beast lay twitching in the mud.

'By that time I was completely disoriented. I did not have a clue where the rest of my section had dug-in. Not knowing what else to do, I sheltered behind a wall and started to shake, and that's where our platoon commander found me. I noticed that he had been sliced up too. His left arm was in a sling and there was a field dressing wrapped around his right thigh. He rapped out the location of my section and sent me on my way, still shaking.

'As it happened, the section was dug-in around the barn I had been sitting behind. Having lost my own partner, I jumped into a slit with another man who was by himself and started helping him to deepen the trench between "Minnie" bursts. Soon we were deep enough to be protected by anything but a direct hit. That done, I lit my first fag since the whole bloody mess had started, hours before. No cigarette ever tasted so good!'

General Schlemm, commanding the 1st German Parachute Army which with elements of other units now totalled 50,000 men, was still out on Simpson's left flank occupying a west bank bridgehead from Duisburg to just south of Xanten. While he was there, crossing the Rhine was hardly practicable. Schlemm had been ordered to hold a bridgehead west of the Rhine 'at all costs' – not least because down the Rhine went barge traffic carrying coal from the Ruhr to the arms factories of northern Germany – and General Schlemm was a formidable soldier.

Schlemm and his men did all that they could to obey this instruction, fighting hard for every foot of ground in what came to be called the 'Wesel Pocket', turning every house into a defensive position, every village into a strongpoint, but the relentless build-up of American, British and Canadian forces finally proved too much. Schlemm's forces were gradually pushed back, first into the pocket around Wesel and then across the Rhine. By 9 March Schlemm's forces were safely back over the Rhine, and when troops of the British 52nd Division entered Wesel on 10 March they found the Rhine bridges were down.

The month-long fight for the Reichwald and the Roer had cost the Allies – American, British and Canadian – some 23,000 men. German losses exceeded 90,000. It also cost Field Marshal General Von Rundstedt his post of Commander-in-Chief West. Furious with the loss of the west bank of the Rhine, Hitler once again dismissed Von Rundstedt and summoned Field Marshal Wilhelm Kesselring from Italy to defend the last natural defence line of the Reich.

While Simpson's 9th US Army was battering its way towards Duisburg, the divisions of General Hodges' 1st US Army were heading for the city of Cologne further south. One of these soldiers was Haynes W. Dugan of the 3rd Armoured Division.

'We knew that the German defences began just across the Roer, first a foxhole, then a single trench, later to be connected with others until finally an entire network line of entrenchments. So, when the jump-off attack across the Roer began on 23 February 1945, it was a welcome surprise to find these defences unmanned.

'Not that the advance to Cologne – captured on 11 March with the help of 104th Division and 8th Infantry Division – was easy, but the Bulge fighting had clearly taken some of the stuffing out of our opponents.

'I have some memories of that period: Seeing a human foot, so clean it was apparently just washed, lying at the side of the road ... no body, just a foot. The finding of the bodies of three members of a German family, all suicides, hanged at Berrendorf. Infantrymen of the 104th Division riding in farm trailers drawn by German trucks, or any other vehicle capable of being driven, looking like a pack of gypsies, but keeping up with the advance without walking.

'On 2 March a temporary Command Post (CP) had just been put up when the Germans began shelling us. We took cover and a bursting shell put a fragment through the situation map, right on that day's objective. The G-2 (Intelligence) portion of the CP on the outskirts of Cologne was in a series of workers' apartments built by the Reich. That winter, with freezing weather, it was as good as a refrigerator.

'In the closing part of the battle for Cologne the crucial question was, could we take a bridge before it was blown? I worked my way as close to the battle area in front of the cathedral as was safe, but there was no good vantage point. Finally, we entered a church which had a high tower. No clergy or custodian could be found and a door with a glass top barred our entrance to the tower. I regret to say I broke the glass with my pistol butt, and we reached the tower in time to see the last bridge blown.

'Our cameraman took motion pictures of the fighting in the cathedral plaza, where a lone German tank, probably a Panther, took on several of our lighter-gunned Shermans. These would advance around a corner from a side street, shoot once and back up. One of our tanks was hit and the movie shows the commander emerge from the turret, slide down the rear deck, fall to the ground and die. Damage to Cologne Cathedral was minor, quite remarkable in view of the fact that the British had bombed all the buildings round about almost to the ground, including the rail station.

'After the fall of Cologne, the Signal Corps turned searchlights on the clouds at night to provide artificial moonlight. This enabled us to walk around the unlit, rubble-strewn streets without stumbling into things. Our engineers put up water points on reservoirs once used to combat incendiary bombing. They purified the water and we could take showers in school buildings, though broken glass and rubble was all over the place and the sewerage system was not working. One huge bomb shelter, almost the size of a football field, had been built above ground, with a concrete roof about a yard thick. It had been much used and lacked adequate ventilation and stank.'

The Allied armies had now closed up to the west bank of the Rhine from Nijmegen to south of Cologne but found all the bridges down. Further south, the rest of the 1st US Army and Patton's 3rd US Army were also closing in on the river, Patton pushing hard up the Moselle valley hoping to find an intact bridge, for though the Saar-Palatinate south of the Moselle river remained in German hands, all eyes now were on the Rhine.

Patton's 3rd US Army had been attacking continuously in the Saar–Moselle Triangle, which ran from the meeting of the Saar and Moselle rivers at Trier to the southern border of Luxembourg, where the base of the triangle was thirteen miles wide. Fighting here had begun in early January (see Chapter 4) and went on throughout February into March.

Along the Moselle valley and in the Saar-Palatinate terrible winter

143

weather, heavy rain and thickly sewn anti-personnel mines caused a steady drain of casualties and slowed the American advance, but the push for the Rhine continued.

Sergeant Howard Keller was in this advance and recalls the German resistance: 'In March 1945 our company, Company L, 301st Infantry of the 94th Division, was assigned the task of taking a strategic hill in the Saar-Moselle Triangle. It was needed to protect the flank of a future supply road, when Patton's tanks leap-frogged through us.

'It was early and visibility was zero. The clouds were thick and it was pitch dark, so you could barely see your hand in front of your face. We formed a skirmish line and started up the hill without the benefit of an artillery barrage, hoping to surprise the Germans. We were near the top when I and two others were sent to scout ahead. There was another three-man patrol about 100 feet to our left. We advanced about 100 yards and noticed other shapes in the dark, and at first I thought they were our other patrol.

'I whispered, "Is that you, Ernie?" Ernie had a Swedish accent and the voice I heard talking sounded just like him. We could see a tiny bit better now and we noticed were in the midst of about a dozen Germans. There was no doubt who they were but they were unaware that Americans were on the hill. We had come up the hill without any advance bombardment in the early morning darkness. Our patrol members were close together now and we could see them moving around so our group moved to one side and we made our way back to our platoon.

'Our men were behind a hedgerow and we opened fire when it got light enough to see. They immediately answered with machine-gun fire but after a bit our platoon advanced and forced them to retreat. A wounded German was on the ground. Many of them fell and in front of me three men were in a foxhole and they surrendered. I sent the prisoners back with Jesse Sollenberger, and we continued till we cleared a large area.

'For the next few days they attacked us at least twice a day. Each attack was becoming stronger; they were desperate to get the hill back. One night they went all-out, with tanks and a large number of infantry and they overwhelmed our company. The lieutenant said he was the last off the hill and he ordered a massive artillery barrage. It was so effective the German infantry retreated and their tanks withdrew. When the company retook the hill everyone was surprised to see six men who never left the hill. No one gave them the word to go and they said a big Tiger tank was parked right next to their foxhole during the German attack.

'Several days later we were relieved and moved on through more hills and more towns. We had a lot of resistance and artillery thrown at us. Several of our men were hit but all the while we were moving ahead a

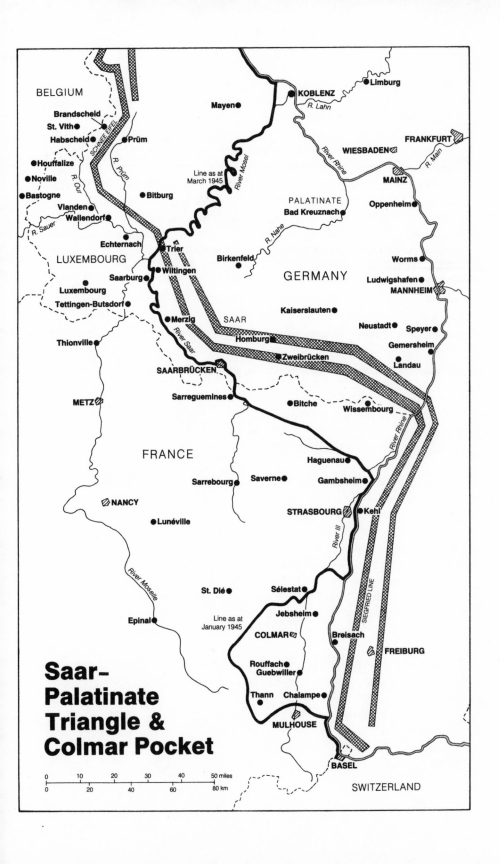

BELGIUM

Brandscheid
St. Vith ●
Habscheid ●   ● Prüm
● Houffalize
● Noville
● Bastogne
Vianden ●
Wallendorf ●

Mayen ●

KOBLENZ ●   ● Limburg

R. Lahn

River Rhine

WIESBADEN ▨   FRANKFURT ▨

R. Main

MAINZ ▨

Line as at
March 1945

Bitburg ●

PALATINATE
Bad Kreuznach ●

Oppenheim ●

R. Sauer

Echternach ●   ● Trier

LUXEMBOURG

R. Our

R. Prüm

River Mosel

R. Nahe

Worms ●
Ludwigshafen ●
MANNHEIM ▨

Saarburg ●   ● Wiltingen

GERMANY

Luxembourg ●
Tettingen-Butsdorf ●

Birkenfeld ●

● Merzig   SAAR

Kaiserslauten ●

Neustadt ●   Speyer ●

Thionville ●

River Saar

Homburg ●

Zweibrücken ●

Gemersheim ●
Landau ●

METZ ▨

SAARBRÜCKEN ●

Sarreguemines ●

● Bitche

Wissembourg ●

River Rhine

FRANCE

Haguenau ●

Sarrebourg ●   Saverne ●

Gambsheim ●

NANCY ▨

● Lunéville

STRASBOURG ▨ ● Kehl

River Ill

St. Dié ●

Sélestat ●

Line as at
January 1945

Jebsheim ●

River Moselle

Epinal ●

COLMAR ▨

Breisach ●

FREIBURG ▨

SIEGFRIED LINE

Rouffach ●
Guebwiller ●

Thann ●   Chalampe ●

MULHOUSE ●

Saar–
Palatinate
Triangle &
Colmar Pocket

BASEL ●

0   10   20   30   40   50 miles
0   20   40   60   80 km

SWITZERLAND

combat photographer was taking our picture; I thought he was very gutsy.

'I am proud of our division's accomplishments. I also would like to give a big thanks to our artillery. They did one helluva job. We were told to clear the Saar–Moselle Triangle, which is the Siegfried Switch Line. We crossed the Saar in two places, breaking through the Siegfried Line in two places and capturing the ancient fortified city of Trier.'

There were two bridges over the Moselle at Trier and as the American infantry entered the town on 1 March – a bright, moonlit night – they found one bridge blown, but the second, the ancient *Kaiser-Bruecke*, was still intact. By the morning of 2 March, the Americans had a bridge across the Moselle and General Patton had an open road before him, up to the Rhine at Koblenz.

LVT4 Buffalo

8 The Rhine Crossings

7–24 MARCH 1945

'Over the Rhine then, let us go, and
good hunting to you all on the other side.'

Field Marshal Montgomery
Message to 21st Army Group
23 March 1945

By the end of February 1945, with most of the Western armies on the Rhine and Patton forging towards it up the Moselle valley, Nazi Germany was clearly in *extremis*. With the last natural defence line on the Rhine now threatened, desperate measures were necessary to defend the remnants of the Reich and even schoolboys were recruited into the ranks of the *Volksturm*. One of these was Fred Rhambo.

'In 1945 I was fifteen years old, living in Hamburg and a member of the *Hitler Jugend* – the Hitler Youth – as we all were. We stayed in the *Hitler Jugend* until we were seventeen, doing a certain amount of military training. Then we were called up for the Wehrmacht, half-trained to be soldiers.

'My father had been a prisoner-of-war of the British in 1916 and he was a real pessimist about a German victory, especially after America entered the war ... that was, for him, the end.

'We boys were called up in February 1945 and sent to a training camp, a former concentration camp at Wedel. Our uniforms were old ones – a friend of mine had a tunic with five patched bullet holes in it. I was a Nazi then – and I am one of the few who will admit it today – but life in the Hitler Youth was fun and a challenge. We were young – what did we know?

'We trained with hand-grenades and the *panzerfaust*, and I was a squad leader. How we didn't blow ourselves up I will never know. One of my squad mates, Gerhard Ullner, had a 500 lb. British bomb split open in his

147

backyard. We would take some of the explosive to school and use it to burn our initials into the desks. The American bombers sometimes had records in them – gramophone records – and we would search the "shot-downs" for them. We liked American music – Swing – and some kids tried to dress like Americans, which the party hacks did not like at all.

'We got no news on the German radio. San Francisco could have burned down, they would not have told us. We all listened to the BBC under the bedclothes, though it was forbidden ... and those opening notes of Beethoven's Fifth Symphony – Boom–Boom–Boom–BOOM – sometimes gave people away to the Gestapo.

'So, we trained and waited, and the bombers came over by day and night. Then we heard the guns. There was electricity for just three hours a day but the street-cars were still running, sporadically, and the submarine yards and machine tool factories were still working. I was a fifteen-year-old with twelve young kids under me, and we waited for the British tanks.'

General Bradley and the two Army commanders in 12th US Army Group, Generals Hodges and Patton, intended to cross the Rhine 'on the run' if they could, without pausing to regroup for a formal assault. Such a plan would have been greatly eased by the capture of a bridge, but as the Allied armies raced up to the Rhine, bridge after bridge was found in the river or blew up in their faces.

Field Marshal Montgomery, on the other hand, intended to group the three armies – 1st Canadian, 2nd British and 9th US – of 21st Army Group on the west bank, bring up all his available forces and make a massive set-piece crossing around Wesel with all the impetus necessary to continue the advance right across Germany. This advance from the Rhine, north and east across the North German plain, would take the Ruhr, Bremen, Hamburg – and Berlin.

The SHAEF plan was for Bradley's Army Group to play a supporting role in this major assault across the Rhine, by crossing south of the Ruhr, which would be encircled rather than assaulted. This had always been the plan, recently confirmed in Malta. General Patton resented it, feeling that his fast-moving forces should be supported and supplied for a rapid advance to the east through Frankfurt.

Some Americans, like John Price of Astoria, Oregon, do not share Patton's views. 'No one has ever asked me what I did in the war, as I was a non-combatant personnel adjutant of the 33rd Armoured (Tank) Regiment of the 3rd Armoured Division of the 1st Army. The 3rd Armoured Division was the spearhead division of the 1st Army, which was commanded by General Courtney Hodges. General Hodges has yielded all the headlines to General Patton, whose 3rd Army was in a secondary role. You will do a

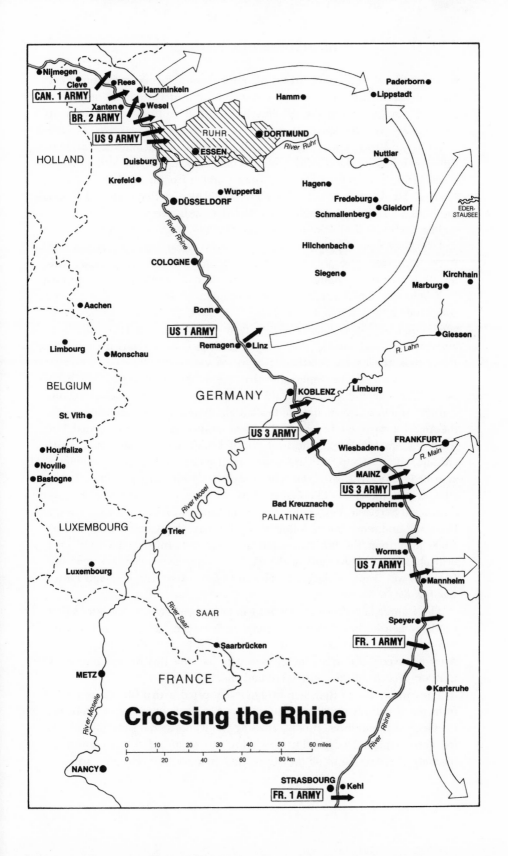

Crossing the Rhine

great service if you can correct the public's and media perception that General Patton won the war in Europe – and that if Patton had only been given the go-ahead and the gasoline he would have been in the heart of Berlin along with the spring flowers.'

Whatever Patton's wishes, at the end of February Eisenhower remained fully committed to the northern route. Then, on 7 March, the leading tanks of the 9th US Armoured Division, from Combat Command 'B' of General Hodges' 1st Army, reached a hill above the Rhine at Remagen and found the Ludendorff railway bridge across the river still intact.

The Germans had laid planks over the rail track and troops, trucks and horse-drawn supply wagons were now streaming east across the river. The officer responsible for the security – and if necessary the demolition – of the Remagen bridge had been a Captain Bratge. Bratge had under command a force of thirty-six infantrymen and some engineers commanded by Captain Friesenhahn, but on 6 March Bratge has been superseded by Major Hans Scheller from LXVII Corps HQ. All these officers were well aware that they would pay with their lives if the Allies took the bridge intact.

A prisoner told the Americans that the Ludendorff bridge had been prepared for demolition and would be blown up at 4 p.m. that afternoon, and the American troops did not hesitate. In spite of hearing defending fire, the Americans rushed the bridge. The demolition charges duly exploded, but when the smoke cleared, the Ludendorff bridge was still standing. Thus encouraged, a group of American infantrymen and combat engineers swarmed across the span, cutting every wire, throwing any unexploded charges into the river. The first men across were Lieutenant Karl Zimmerman and Sergeant Alex Drabik from Company A, 27th Armoured Infantry Battalion, and more troops followed. By the next day General Hodges had 8,000 men from the 9th Armoured and the 78th Infantry Division in a bridgehead on the east bank of the Rhine, covered by artillery and tank fire from the west bank of the river. The Americans were delighted and Hitler was furious.

The Führer had declared that no Rhine bridges were to fall into Allied hands. When he heard that the bridge at Remagen had been captured he had the officers tried for cowardice and treason by a 'flying court martial'. After a travesty of a trial, the officers who had not fled to the Americans were dragged from the court-room and shot.

The capture of the Remagen bridge was greeted with a barrage of praise from the American press and public, but it created a number of problems for General Eisenhower. Firstly, crossing the Rhine at Remagen was not in the current plan. Hodges' 1st US Army was supposed to turn south on reaching the west bank of the Rhine and link up with Patton's 3rd US

Army further south. Secondly, the terrain east of Remagen was hilly and wooded and unsuitable for rapid exploitation.

General 'Pink' Bull, Eisenhower's operations officer at SHAEF, was at 1st Army HQ when the news from Remagen arrived, and told Bradley bluntly, 'You are not going anywhere down there,' but since Hodges had seized a bridge, Eisenhower could hardly order him to abandon it. Eisenhower was already committed to the major Rhine crossing by 21st Army Group around Wesel, but the rapid capture of Cologne gave him five spare divisions to reinforce the Remagen bridgehead. More divisions were therefore rushed across the river into the Remagen bridgehead, which gradually began to expand.

Lieutenant Julian Van Buren of 9th Armoured Division remembers that time: 'We were to get to the Rhine and turn south, forming the north pincer of the envelopment and meet elements of the 3rd US Army coming up from the south. We were part of the 1st Army at the time, and along the way the forward elements came across the intact Remagen bridge, a railroad bridge with the ties covered with planks, making it passable to truck traffic. Because of some screw-up on the German side, they didn't blow it when our forward elements got there although it was charged with high explosives.

'On the east side of the river, the tracks went into a long tunnel through a solid rock mountain. Just a little to the north, closer to the river, there was the biggest wine cellar you could imagine. American GIs hauled wine out of there night and day, by the truckload. I took a truck up during the first days and got a load for our HQ. Lieutenant Hatoes and I drank a basket of it that night. It was the first time anyone ever drank Hatoes under the table, and boy! ... we were soused for days! It was Moselle wine, the same as champagne but without the bubbles.

'All roads to the bridge were one-way only. One could go east, but if you wanted to come back you would have to walk. In a very few days, engineer units had bridges across the river, so when the original bridge collapsed due to shell-fire, bombs and other things, it was really no problem for the bridgehead was already large and very secure. The 9th Division moved in a big hurry after that, becoming part of the south pincer round the Ruhr.'

Lieutenant Robert M. Brooker, of the 9th US Engineers, was attached to Combat Command 'B' on the drive from the Roer river to the Rhine. 'I was twenty-eight years old at the time, and I remember an officer of the 9th Engineers asking if I wanted to go across the Rhine river. Till this time I didn't even know that we had captured a bridge, so I went with him and we actually walked across.

'When I got back I told the two men in my jeep that I had been across the river and they did not believe me. In the morning we started for the bridge, but military police (MPs) were everywhere and we could no longer go that way. We had to go back a few miles, cut across country and come on the main road leading towards the bridge.

'When we reached the hill overlooking the Rhine, we could see the bridge still standing. We drove into town and found B Company of the 9th Engineers. We also found a basement to stay in, for artillery shells were falling all around, trying to hit the bridge, though this was almost impossible without a spotter to give directions.

'When the spotter planes came within range, our 90 mm gun radar would start the guns firing. Everybody would start firing over the bridge before the plane got there, and when the plane came into view it had already been hit. I don't remember how many planes came over but very few escaped. One bomb did hit the bridge but it failed to explode. The danger with everybody firing was that pieces of steel were flying all over. One medic would pull off his Red Cross brassard and start firing the 50-cal. machine-gun. If the plane disappeared behind a building, he would keep firing right through the building, making pieces of brick fly dangerously close, so we went to the cellar – it was safer there.

'Nobody was in a rush to get on the bridge with all that shooting and bombing. We moved slowly but every once in a while had to dismount and take cover from all the flying bullets. We saw a shell land on the bridge near the eastern end, and just as we got near the hole in the bridge, another shell hit close the same spot. The fragments from this shell hit our jeep and wrecked it. It blew a big piece of the shell through the motor block and through Verna's head. It also wrecked our windshield except where I was. The pieces hit me on the shoulder, head and leg, but nothing too damaging.

'A small piece of the shell came through the windshield and went between my arm and body, and the concussion blew Peterson out of the jeep. When he came down the jeep was not there. Our bedrolls were damaged beyond repair. Peterson ran west to the bank and I ran east to the tunnel.

'When I got to the tunnel, an MP lieutenant asked me if I was sure that Verna was dead. I told him that I was. He then asked if I had checked to make sure. I told him "No." He then went out there in the midst of the shelling to see if I was right, came back and told me that I was. It took a lot of guts to go out there.

'I spent the night in the tunnel alongside Verna's body. During the night some Graves Registration people came to remove the bodies and grabbed hold of me, but I assured them I was not dead. Since my jeep was wrecked, my driver killed, my sergeant gone, and I was in no condition to do anything, it was decided that I should go back to the other side of the river.

I knew that I was going to spend the rest of my life on the east bank of the Rhine; I was *never* going back across that bridge.

'We found that Corporal Verna was being listed as "missing in action". I was afraid to go back across the bridge, but I went anyway, found the Graves Registration office and got the records changed. I did not want his wife to think that there was hope when there was none.'

The German reaction to the taking of the Remagen bridge was swift but inadequate. On 8 March Kesselring ordered a counter-attack against the Remagen bridgehead which went in on 12 March but failed to achieve any significant result. Attempts to destroy the bridge by floating mines down the river, by shell-fire, or bombing or V-1 rocket strikes, proved equally ineffective – though the explosions weakened an already shaky structure – and on 17 March the Ludendorff bridge collapsed suddenly into the Rhine.

By then US army engineers had constructed other bridges into the 1st Army bridgehead, which was now twenty miles wide, eight miles deep and contained nine full divisions. The Remagen expansion continued as Field Marshal Montgomery prepared for his massive assault in the north, now set for 23 March 1945.

Hodges was not the only general anxious to get across the Rhine before Field Marshal Montgomery. General George Patton's 3rd US Army was now fighting its way up the Moselle to Koblenz and thrusting across the north of the Saar-Palatinate. The Saar was an industrial region, second only in importance to the Ruhr, and taking it would deliver a further devastating blow to the German war machine, but Patton lusted for the glory of a Rhine crossing. He had been beaten out of first place by Courtney Hodges but he fully intended to cross before Montgomery. Eisenhower insisted, however, that Patton must now turn south and overrun the Palatinate before crossing the Rhine.

The main effort to capture the Saar-Palatinate region, east of the Rhine, was made by General Devers' 6th US Army Group, and specifically by Patch's 7th Army, before Patton's forces took a hand. There was an element of military politics in this, for Bradley and Patton wanted to get the 3rd Army involved in more fighting, if only to stop more 12th Army Group divisions following Simpson's 9th Army into the grasp of Montgomery's 21st Army Group. After three days the German resistance along the Moselle began to crumble, and by 19 March Koblenz on the Rhine had fallen to troops of the 87th Infantry Division.

'Meanwhile, on 15 March, Patch's 7th Army had launched a supporting attack on a seventy-mile front from Saarbrucken to the Rhine. Squeezed by pressure from two American armies, the German 1st Army front in the Palatinate gradually crumbled. By 22 March the Americans were in sight of the Rhine at Oppenheim, with Patton urging General Eddy of the XII

Corps to push General Irwin's 5th Division across the river at all costs, just so long as his army got across here in the south before Montgomery got across in the north.

Irwin's troops duly reached the Rhine at Oppenheim, twelve miles south of Mainz, on 20 March. Two days later six battalions of the 5th Infantry Division crossed the Rhine in assault boats against light opposition, and by the evening of the 23rd, Patton had a bridgehead six miles wide and as many miles deep. A bridge was then thrown across the river and the rest of Patton's 3rd Army began to flow across the Rhine ... which Montgomery had still to cross. Patton's assault might have been much more costly, but most of the German defenders were now mustered around Wesel, waiting for Montgomery's attack.

War correspondents were coming up to see the Rhine crossings, some of them escorted by Haynes W. Dugan of the 3rd Armoured division. 'Things must have seemed pretty safe around 1st Army, for women reporters began to show up. There was Lee Carson of INS, who was very pretty and wrote well, but was often in trouble with the censor, and Iris Carpenter, an attractive British blonde who wrote for the *Boston Globe*. Among the correspondents was Jack Thompson of the *Chicago Tribune*, who had grown a magnificent chestnut-coloured beard. We nicknamed him "Mr Hemingway" because Ernest Hemingway was in France, winning the war with the FFI (French Forces of the Interior).

'Then Martha Gellhorn – the separated wife of Hemingway – showed up. I introduced her to the correspondents and when I got to Jack Thompson I could not resist, "... and this is Mr Hemingway". Fortunately the Germans put a few shells in our area just then and that took her mind off the matter; I hid under a half-track while the 88 mms hit the corner of the building.

'Another correspondent was Peter Lawless of the London *Daily Telegraph*, whom we called "Peter the Lion". Peter was a huge man, formerly in the British Army but now over age, who wore large mittens connected by a string around his neck. He was immensely likeable but was killed in a shell blast at the Remagen bridge.'

With the Americans across the Rhine, Montgomery poised to attack the Ruhr, and the Russians already on the Oder, it was now clear – even to Adolf Hitler – that the armies coming from the east and west were going to crush his forces between their steel fists. Still rejecting any thoughts of surrender, on 19 March the Führer ordered a 'scorched earth' policy throughout Germany. When the Allies overran Germany, said the Führer, they would inherit a wasteland.

Everything was to be destroyed. Factories, hospitals, canal locks, roads and bridges, railway tracks, autobahns ... everything. This proposal appalled many of his generals and met with particular resistance from Hitler's Minister of Production, Albert Speer. Speer was the most intelligent of Hitler's acolytes and knew that if this destruction took place, it would immensely increase the inevitable sufferings of the German people. Speer therefore took to his car and toured both Eastern and Western Fronts, begging the German generals to ignore these orders. In spite of their Oaths of Loyalty to the Führer, most of the generals agreed to ignore any 'scorched earth' orders coming from Hitler's headquarters.

Speer made no secret of what he was doing. He told the Führer on three separate occasions that the war was lost, even when warned that such remarks could cost him his life. On 18 March he had sent the Führer a detailed memorandum, listing the collapse of Germany's military and industrial capacity: '... in four to eight weeks the final collapse of the German economy is certain', he wrote, '... after that the war cannot be continued.' Another man might have been shot, or handed to the SS for transfer to a concentration camp, but Hitler had an affection for Speer. They were 'fellow artists', and on those grounds Speer was allowed his say but ignored. Besides, there were now other worries: the British, Canadians and Americans were crossing the Rhine in force at Wesel.

Field Marshal Montgomery's crossing of the Rhine on 23 March 1945 was made in two phases: a river crossing, codenamed 'Plunder', and an airborne assault codenamed 'Varsity'. The combination was a typical, meticulous set-piece Montgomery battle, planned down to the last detail and put into effect with overwhelming force. For the 'Plunder' assault, Montgomery had the Canadian 1st and the British 2nd Armies, together with the American 9th Army; and for the 'Varsity' assault two parachute divisions, the American 17th Airborne under Major-General Miley, and the British 6th Airborne Division (of Normandy fame) under Major-General Bols. Such a carefully planned assault was necessary for the 21st Army Group had neither the advantage of surprise as at Remagen, or the hope of an unopposed crossing as enjoyed by Patton's troops at Oppenheim.

The Germans around Wesel were fully aware of the northern thrust to the Ruhr and ready for what was coming. The Rhine here was more than a quarter of a mile wide and the east bank was ably defended by five German infantry divisions in well-prepared positions. Beyond the Rhine lay the town of Wesel, a major communications centre. The British would land north of Wesel by boat, parachute and glider, and fight their way through the Diersfordterwald Woods to the village of Hamminkeln and the Issel river. This area was defended by the tough, experienced troops of the German 1st Parachute Army: the 2nd, 6th, 7th and 8th Parachute Divisions, the 84th Infantry Division and the XLVII Panzer Corps. The US 17th

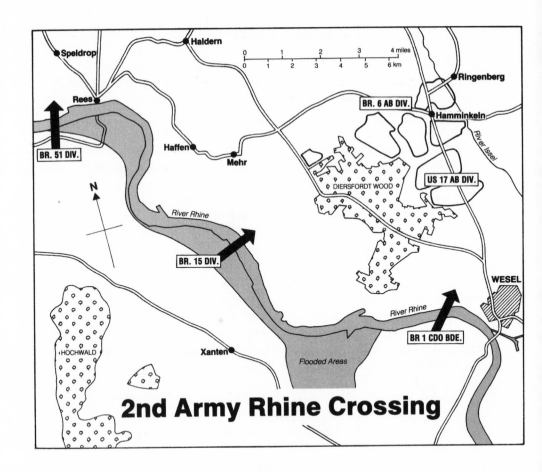

2nd Army Rhine Crossing

Airborne would land just south of the Diersfordter Wald and head south to link up with the 9th US Army and the British 1st Commando Brigade in Wesel.

South of Wesel, the 30th and 79th Divisions of Simpson's 9th US Army would spearhead the river crossing, opposed by the German 180th Division and troops from the LXXXVI Corps.

'Plunder' would be a night river–crossing, while the airborne assault was to be made in daylight, after the river had been traversed. The confusion of Normandy and the failure of the Arnhem landings had taught the airborne forces a useful lesson. This time both airborne divisions would land in daylight and in one lift.

Operation Plunder, 21st Army Group's assault across the Rhine, began at 2100 hrs on the night of the 23rd. After a barrage from over 5,000 guns, the Black Watch and the Argylls (from the 51st (Highland) Division of Lt-General Sir Brian Horrocks' XXX Corps) – supported by the 9th Canadian Infantry Brigade – went across the river in 'Buffalo' half-tracks. The

Highlanders landed at Rees, ten miles north of Wesel, supported by D-D swimming tanks, under the covering fire of 3,500 guns. The Highland Division landed in the face of slight opposition, but were swiftly counter-attacked by the German 8th Parachute Division, which held their ground at the village of Rees and cut off the Highlanders in the village of Speldrop.

Lieutenant Ian Wilson, with the Royal Engineers, takes up the story: 'The assault across the river Rhine began at 0200 hrs on 24 March, and by 0500 hrs 3rd Platoon was on the west bank unloading equipment. Shortly afterwards I was afloat to mark out the lines on which to drop anchor. Mortar and shell fire on the bridge site made us feel very exposed. The rest of the platoon was building a floating platform to drop the anchor assemblies.

'Crafts of all sorts were crossing the river, including landing craft manned by sailors. Some of our anchor lines were cut by propellers, so more anchors had to be laid and part of my platoon was laying anchors after the bridge was completed – there must be a lot of metal at the bottom of the Rhine at Xanten. Ours was the first British tank bridge across the river Rhine. Our armour started crossing at 5.00 p.m. on 25 March, and Winston Churchill visited the bridge site on the following day.'

The Highlanders were followed across the Rhine by the men of the 1st Commando Brigade. The Commandos landed two miles north of Wesel and just after they swarmed ashore, Wesel was rocked by 1,000 tons of bombs dropped by aircraft of RAF Bomber Command.

Trevor Walmsely was flying with 105 Mosquito Squadron, Pathfinder Force during this period. 'On 23 March, my navigator, Ted Povey, and I were sitting in the ante-room of the mess when I spotted our CO, "Slim" Somerville coming through the door, obviously looking for someone. I nudged Ted and said, "Slim's looking for volunteers; let's get out of here."

'Too late – down to briefing. We were seldom given the names of targets, and this briefing was very casual indeed. "You'll be marking for heavy bombers. Our troops are very close, so if there is any doubt about accuracy, don't drop." That was it, so we did the job and came home. The next day there was a signal on the notice board thanking Bomber Command for the attack on Wesel, stating that our troops had crossed the Rhine with minimum loss of life. It was signed "Montgomery".'

John Buckingham of 45 (Royal Marine) Commando, gives an account of his unit at the Rhine: 'The units which made up 1st Commando Brigade were Nos 3 and 6 Army Commandos, and 45 and 46 (RM) Commandos. No. 3 Commando was the leading unit for the crossing, and Wesel the objective; 45's target was a factory at the eastern side of the town while the other three units occupied various parts of the town and secured a bridgehead for a pontoon bridge.

'We had studied maps and aerial photos until we were familiar with the terrain, our route and the objective. A few days before the assault we left Venlo and moved to a point not far from the west bank of the Rhine. The Royal Artillery were moving into position, more and more guns lined up behind us until thousands of guns were in position to give us the big send-off.

'On the evening of 23 March the barrage opened up and we set off in single file for the bank of the Rhine. Finding the way was easy because the Royal Artillery had a pair of Bofors guns firing two lines of red tracers to mark our route. We marched under the tracer and thousands of shells screamed over our heads and hit the enemy positions on the far bank. Before we cross, the RAF had a part to play. Spot on 2045 hrs, the artillery fire ceased and precisely on time the Pathfinders dropped flares over the town of Wesel, marking the target. More than 200 heavy bombers then plastered the place.

'We must have had the best ever view of RAF heavies doing their stuff. The ground shook with the exploding bombs, but we were surprised to see the Germans fighting back, sending up a barrage of anti-aircraft fire. Then it was our turn. We embarked in Buffaloes, tracked vehicles which could traverse ground or water, and set off across the Rhine. There was little resistance, and although some German fire came our way and one craft received a direct hit from a mortar bomb, the landing was relatively unopposed.

'We landed dry-shod and set off, following the white tape to the forming-up position. Then came the difficulty. The RAF had devastated the town, whole streets lay in ruins, the railway was a twisted lattice-work against the night sky, fires were raging out of control, and the Germans came out fighting. Even the general commanding Wesel came out of his bunker, pistol in hand, refused to surrender and was shot dead. All our study of maps and photos was not much use amid such a shambles, and we scrambled around bomb craters and over rubble, following the man in front, hoping someone remembered the way.

'At this point I made contact with the Brigade commander, Derek Mills-Roberts. He did not suffer fools gladly, or indeed at all, and anyone who was not doing what he ought to be doing was a fool! There was the Brigadier, standing on a pile of rubble, illuminated by the light of a burning building, urging his brigade to "Get a bloody move on." A Commando soldier, ladened with all the paraphernalia of war, was hanging back a bit too much, and Mills-Roberts hopped off his pile with a cry of, "Close up, you bastard", and took a swipe at the chap's head. We speeded up and closed-up after that, my first experience of a wartime Commando Brigadier under the stress of battle.

'Next morning came the drone of aircraft engines and the skies filled with the parachutes of the 6th British and the 17th American Airborne Divisions dropping within our perimeter. My own memory is of a large American paratrooper landing almost on top of me, looking up and saying, "Am I glad to see you!" The Americans all sported at least a week's growth of beard. It seems the first thing they do in action is to stop shaving, so at least we greeted them as Royal Marines should, with clean shaves.'

Ken Adams also crossed the Rhine that night with 45 (Royal Marine) Commando. 'Being in F Troop (Heavy Weapons) we normally fired the Vickers MMG, but on this occasion we took a Bren, and as we scrambled out of the Buffalo, Jock dropped the Bren in the river. Imagine it ... the smoke and gunfire and us groping in the bottom of the Rhine for our weapon. However – success – we recovered it, full of mud of course, but Jock fired a few rounds and said, "I think it's OK ... I've got rid of the sludge."'

Four hours after the Commandos landed, at 0200 hrs on 24 March, the divisions of the 9th US Army and the 15th (Scottish) Division of the British XII Corps began crossing. The 15th Division landed north of Xanten, where they were met by the German 84th Division and the 7th Parachute Division, while the 30th and 79th US Divisions of the 9th Army crossed the Rhine south of Wesel against light opposition from the German 180th and 'Hamburg' Divisions. The Americans then flung a bridge over the river and had tanks across by mid-morning. This fight for the Wesel bridgehead was continuing when the glider and parachute forces arrived overhead at around 1000 hrs on 24 March.

Lt-Colonel Clifford Norbury, MBE, MC, was on the staff of the 6th Airborne Division. 'In 6th Airborne we reckoned we had nothing to learn from the 1st Airborne Division, as we were better at planning our operations and always considered it essential to jump or land as close to our objectives as possible. After Normandy we also appreciated that on a night drop a high percentage of kit and troops went astray – hence the daylight drop on the Rhine. In fact, there was a lot of smoke over the DZ's but at least we knew roughly where we were, and fortunately we had enough aircraft for us all to go in one lift.'

George Butler went in with the 13th Battalion of the Parachute Regiment. 'The flight was in daylight and over the drop zone we met with intense anti-aircraft fire, which fortunately caused very few casualties. Immediately on landing we swapped our helmets for red berets, rallied to the officers blowing the "tally-ho" on their hunting horns, took our objectives and secured the left flank in just over two hours. This position we held, in spite of German counter-attacks.

'Two days later, we struck out for the Baltic. The battalion policy was to wear our red berets and go for the Germans as hard as we could, wherever we found them. Provided the enemy were given no rest, the advance continued.'

Among those jumping that day was Gunner Jim Purser, with a Royal Artillery Fire Control party attached to the 8th Battalion, the Parachute Regiment. 'About 8 o'clock we were airborne. A vast fleet of aircraft headed towards the Rhine, but the journey was uneventful. There was little conversation, with everyone wrapped in his own thoughts. Once over the continent we could see our fighter aircraft diving and circling on our flanks, and this gave us confidence. Somewhere over Belgium the 17th United States Airborne Division, which had taken off from bases in France, took up position on our right. The sight of so many aeroplanes, some towing gliders, must have given great joy to onlookers on the ground who had been liberated from Nazi oppression only in the last few months.

'With thirty minutes left it was time to check our equipment. We were stood up and faced the rear of the aircraft. I watched the American crewman remove the large door near the tail. It was a perfect spring day outside – not a cloud in the sky – and pleasantly warm. Then the Rhine river – difficult to make out in detail because of the smoke that had been used to cover the ground attack. The red light went on, followed by the order "Stand in the door!" Only two to three minutes left. All seemed quiet outside. Perhaps we had taken the Germans by surprise. Someone behind me yelled, "Here we come, you square-headed bastards!" The green light came on and we staggered towards the exit door. My watch registered four minutes past ten. Out in the slipstream my parachute snapped open and I felt very vulnerable. My kit bag slipped from me and tumbled to the ground. There seemed to be no Germans beneath me but I was drifting into trees. Pulling hard on my lift webs I landed on the edge of the wood and dived under some bushes to orientate myself and plan my next move.

'I had to move back along the drop line until I saw blue smoke – the rallying mark for 8th Para. Bn. About a dozen paras came out of the woods. I was glad to see them, and together we made our way quickly and cautiously to the rallying point. One hundred yards to our right was an old farm building – the only building left in sight. It did not seem to be occupied, and we left it alone. Beyond this building was a small copse where I met up with Captain Hastings and Jackson, but no sign yet of Jarvie.

'Things were beginning to hot up in the vicinity of the dropping zone, as the Germans started reacting. Some 88 mm shells were bursting in the trees above us, and we dug for all we were worth into the sandy soil. Jackson's nose began to bleed. He thought that he had been hit but was quickly reassured that it was due to pressure from the bursting shells. Soon news came through that Jarvie had been killed. Rumours later circulated on the circumstances of his death. He has no known grave but there is a plaque bearing his name among the lists of others with no known graves in the Canadian War Cemetery in the Reichwald Forest. I assume he must have been hit by an 88 mm shell as he was coming down in his parachute.

'Late afternoon the whole battalion moved to take up position in the woods on some high ground about a mile distant. Our OP party remained attached to A Company, commanded by Captain Bob Flood. His conduct that day did much to help the morale of those of us who were in action for the first time. Digging-in and lining our trenches with discarded parachutes, we tried to make ourselves comfortable, but the night was cold and sleep was impossible. At about 8 o'clock on the Sunday morning there was the rumble of tanks, and lining the track we cheered as the 2nd Army tanks came up to us from the Rhine.

'From now on events began to move fast. The chase was on. In order to keep up the momentum of the advance into Hitler's Reich the 6th Airborne Division commandeered just about any vehicle that could be pressed into service. In addition to riding on the backs of tanks and in service vehicles, horse-drawn carts, steam rollers and fire engines could also be seen among the long convoy of transport. The Germans were still full of fight and were able to mount local counter-attacks. I remember that the SS made one determined attack in the Celle area, outside Hanover.'

Also arriving on the Rhine bank that morning was Peter Elliot Forbes of the 9th Battalion, Parachute Regiment. 'I was a twenty-eight-year-old lieutenant. We took off from an airfield in East Anglia at about 0730 hrs and prior to take-off an American flight engineer took some snapshots of my "stick" of twelve paratroopers attached to 3rd Para. Brigade HQ. The engineer sent copies of the snaps to my wife, though I didn't see them till well after the war. There was a US crew in the Dakota and the Jump-Master (despatcher) was an excitable little man in a baseball jacket and flak-suit, who dashed about a great deal after takeoff.

'The British half of this airborne armada set course for a drop zone in the Diersfordter Wald, a wood north of Wesel. Over Belgium I opened a bottle of whisky to flavour a half-warm tea canister someone had scrounged. The journey was passed in singing, card games and dice until H-Hour (1000 hrs) approached and we prepared to "stand-in-the-door", where I was second in the queue. The turbulence as we approached the Rhine could have been caused by the smoke from artillery supporting the ground forces, but there was heavy flak at our level, about 1,000 feet.

'The red "stand-by" light was on and we were waiting for the green "Go!" when the port engine, only yards away from the door, burst into orange flames and black smoke, either hit with flak or overstressed. The Jump-Master screamed for us to get back from the door and ran up to the cockpit; fortunately the "green" didn't come on. This was accompanied by a violent bank to the left which almost chucked us out of the door and through the flames. Over the shoulder of "Number One" I saw the ground getting rapidly nearer.

'The pilot did an excellent job, flying the machine on one engine, the flames were put out, we scrambled back to our seats and I consumed what was left of my whisky. We landed an hour later at Louvain, where I spent some time organizing transport to catch up with our division, and we rejoined the 3rd Parachute Brigade near Hamminkeln on the following day.'

Dixie Dean jumped with his "stick" of the 13th Parachute Battalion: 'Our Jump-Master was a talkative, scruffy New Yorker. Shortly after take-off he came round with cigarettes, and finding that few of us smoked, disappeared into the cabin, to come out again and offer us candy. That was the last we saw of him until he announced, "Twenty minutes to go."

'You couldn't criticize the pilots: their airmanship was first class. We flew in a very tight battalion box of forty aircraft and the formation they adopted – nine abreast – gave the impression you could jump from one wing-tip to another. Approaching the drop zone, flak was encountered and instead of descending to a dropping height of 600 feet, with engines throttled back to stalling speed, we raced across the DZ flat out, at around 1,000 feet.

'Visibility was poor, no more than 200 yards, with smoke drifting across from the burning town of Wesel. There was a certain amount of small-arms fire, and following heavy casualties during the Ardennes campaign in January we had a lot of young soldiers in the unit who dived for cover when the first shots were fired. To their credit, it required only a few words of encouragement to get them on their feet again. The black rectangle with a white border painted on the back of our jumping jackets concentrated 13th Battalion personnel in woods along the road at the edge of the drop zone.

'As I arrived there, prisoners were already being rounded up. Arthur Higgins, one of my sergeants, was busy disarming a group of twenty or more. "What'll you have?" he called. "A Luger or a Schmeisser?" Since I already had a Sten and 9 mm pistol, to say nothing of a fighting knife and several grenades, I settled for a pair of German binoculars with a mag-nification of 10 × 50 – far superior to Army issue. I still have them.'

Troopers of the American 17th Airborne Division were also landing, among them Jack Ariola of the 194th Glider Infantry: '24 March 1945 was the day we were to invade Germany. They took us to the marshalling area on 21 March and there we were oriented on our landing area. On the morning of 24 March they got us out of bed two or three hours before daylight.

'When we went to eat, I couldn't believe what I was seeing: there were crates of eggs stacked as high as a man's head. We hadn't seen a real egg since we had left the States, all they had given us was powdered eggs. I stepped up to the cook and when he asked me how many I wanted, I told him to cook me a dozen. I sat down and ate every one of them. I had forgotten that every time I got in a glider I was air sick.

'After breakfast we got all our equipment together and headed out to the airfield. That was truly a sight to behold. Gliders and C47s were lined up on the air strip as far as we could see. I believe that this was just one of nine or ten airfields they were using in France and England. The British 6th Airborne were also going with us. There were a total of more than 16,000 airborne troops in that invasion, and the air armada was over 500 miles long. It was the largest airborne invasion of the Second World War.

'The day before, my platoon leader, Lieutenant Dillon, asked me if I wanted to carry a machine-gun across the Rhine river. I told him "Hell, no", though he was a good leader and a fine man and we would do just about anything for him. He explained that Lieutenant Webb refused to load in his glider unless there was an automatic weapon in the glider. I told him that I would carry it, on one condition, that just as soon as we landed, I could leave the machine-gun and return to my squad. He agreed.

'When I went through basic training, I had trained as a machine-gunner, and I was the only one qualified for that job, so that was how I was elected. Reluctantly, I went over to the other glider and got the machine-gun and a belt of ammunition. I threw the belt of ammunition across my shoulders and got ready to load on the glider. Finally, we loaded and took off. The glider I was in had a glass or plastic bubble in the top and we could look up into the sky. I saw a bunch of fighter planes flying overhead.

'We got to the Rhine and just before we crossed the pilot cut us loose from the tow plane. This was also the first time they had used a double tow on an invasion – one C47 was towing two gliders. When the pilot cut loose we started down. The ack-ack – anti-aircraft fire – was so thick I believe we could have got out and walked on it. Bullets and flak were coming through the glider, and every time one hit the bottom of the glider and went out through the top it sounded like the crack of a whip, only ten times louder – very demoralizing.

'All around us we could see planes shot down, gliders falling from the sky, nose first, wings shot off and tails gone. Every one of them had fifteen good men inside. After we had glided about eight miles into German territory, we landed. We jumped the canal and went through a barbed wire fence and came to a stop about 50 yards from the road. I was sitting next to the door, so I was the first man out. I opened the door and started firing the machine-gun at a farmhouse off to my left. I didn't know if there were any Germans in it or not, but I meant to make them keep their heads down and not be able to fire at the guys as they unloaded out of the glider.

'I headed for the canal and set up the machine-gun position. While I was lying there I saw a woman running down the road like her house was on fire. There was small-arms fire and gliders still coming down, and ack-ack still in the air. I saw one glider coming down on fire, burning from one end to the other. Later I learned that one of our lieutenants was in it, Lieutenant Loomis.

'A wing of one glider fell off as it passed overhead and down came the glider. It was horrible, knowing that a bunch of men was inside. I could see C47s catching fire and crashing to the ground, but there were fewer men in those C47s than there were in the gliders.

'After everybody had unloaded and all the guys had got over to the canal, I hollered at Lieutenant Webb and told him that here was his machine-gun and I was going to take my leave. He didn't seem to like it too much, but that was the deal I had made; he just nodded his head and I walked away. We landed near Wesel. In our first twenty-four hours we took about 3,000 German prisoners. As near as I can recall, during the first twenty-four hours we lost about 394 killed and several hundred wounded. That was just in our division; I don't know how many people the British lost.'

The combined airborne assault, Operation Varsity, by 17,000 men of two divisions, carried in 1,500 aircraft and 1,300 gliders, required considerable precision. The airborne drop zones lay northwest of Wesel, around the woods of the Diersfordter Wald, 6th Airborne landing north of the village of Hamminkeln, 17th US Airborne to the south – and many men were scattered in the drop.

Lt-Colonel Crookenden gives his account of Varsity. 'I was CO of the 9th Parachute Battalion. Our brigadier was James Hill, who had commanded the 1st Parachute Brigade in North Africa, winning his first DSO and an MC. On 23 March, D minus 1, everybody wrote their so-called "last letters" for posting after the drop. Company officers had the job of censoring the company's mail and the OC of B Company was not amused by a lance-corporal who wrote no less than eleven "last letters" to eleven different women, swearing undying devotion to each one.

'I was getting into my jeep for a final tour of the battalion's aircraft, lined up round the perimeter track, when I heard the sound of a shot. Driving down the line I found one of my sergeants lying on the ground, looking ruefully at the ugly mess of his right foot. He was whisked away in a jeep and subsequently faced a court martial for a self-inflicted wound – a sad business as he had done well in Normandy. I later discovered he had done it because his wife threatened to leave him if he ever jumped again.

'Then we emplaned. The American aircraft captain and the crew chief, a warrant officer, came into the fuselage and checked that the pilot would give us the standard 4-minute "red" and then the "green". Then the engines started and we began our taxiing towards the runway, a long queue of thirty-six Dakotas. Our aircraft turned onto the runway, lined up with two others, and all three set off together. Thirteen minutes later all eighty aircraft from Wethersfield were in the air and had formed up into their nine ship elements – a fine piece of flying discipline.

'Next thing was the order, "Stand Up! Hook Up!" Each man fastened the hook of his strop on the cable, fixed the safety pin – rather carefully, as we had no reserve 'chutes in those days – and turned aft. Just aft of the door the crew chief in his flying helmet listened to the pilot. I was jumping No. 3. The "red" came on and we shuffled forward to the door. I could feel the slipstream and saw the river below us. Seconds later the "green" came on and out we went.

'Once my canopy developed, I could see the DZ exactly like the briefing photos. There was a double line of trees along the road to the west and square wood in the middle. The ground was covered with parachutes of the other battalions and I could see men running towards their objectives. There was a rattle of machine-gun fire, the thump of a mortar bomb and the crack and thump of two near misses. It was a most concentrated and successful drop and I felt a great surge of confidence as I sailed down to earth.

'In fact, we had reached the Rhine 9 minutes early, and the guns firing on the AA defences had to cease fire to let us fly through their trajectories. A good many of our aircraft were hit by 20 mm cannon and machine-gun fire, but only the lead ship was shot down. Happily all the crew bailed out.

'I landed in the middle of the DZ, banged my quick release and stood up. I could see our blue smoke going up at our planned rendezvous in the northeast corner of the DZ and a lot of men moving towards it. The square wood was the scene of a brisk battle, but my aim was to get to our rendezvous as fast as I could. There was no sign of my batman, Lance-Corporal Wilson, or of CSM Harrold, who had jumped after me.

'A few minutes later I reached the rendezvous, where RSM Dusty Miller was standing by his blue smoke canister, grinning broadly and guiding men into their positions in a tight circle round the rendezvous. I wanted to get the mortars' baseplates set as soon as possible and grabbed a passing mortarman, saying, "Any sign of Mr Jefferson?" (the platoon commander). "He's copped it, sir", came the reply. "Right through the head, a horrible mess." Two minutes later, Alan Jefferson came bouncing in – he had been a ballet dancer and walked like one – with a broad smile and a cheerful, "Good morning, sir."

'By 1330 hrs we were dug-in on our final positions, a picnic compared to Normandy. The next excitement was a counter-attack by a German assault gun and a few brave infantry, who came straight up the road through B Company's position; the gun reached B Company's HQ. Everyone dived into their slits or the ditch, but the company clerk, Tillotson, jumped up as it passed and banged a Gammon bomb on the engine covers. The gun stopped, a German put his head out of the hatch, Tillotson shot him and the rest surrendered. The SP gun was still a runner, so two ex-RTR men in the battalion took it over and it rumbled along with us for a week or so as we marched on into Germany.

'The Canadian Parachute Battalion succeeded in clearing the south side of the DZ, but they met stiff resistance from men of the German 7th Parachute Division. Their CO, Lt-Colonel Nicklin, was killed, still in his parachute, when caught in a tree. The gamble of dropping on top of the enemy positions paid off, as most of them were too shocked by seeing 2,000 men landing on top of them to cause us any major damage. The brigade loss on the DZ was some eighty killed and wounded. It was in bringing in some of these wounded under fire that the Canadian Corporal Topham won the Victoria Cross.'

Rifleman Paddy Devlin from Galway, an Irishman serving with the British Army, landed by glider with the 1st Battalion of the Royal Ulster Rifles. 'About 10.30 a.m. we cast off from the aircraft tug and on our own. The glider could only fly a mile, fully loaded, for every thousand feet in height. I sat alert and ready, gripping my machine-gun, intent on getting out fast as soon as the glider landed. The two lads on either side of the door stood up and slid the door into the roof, and before anyone could move I was out that door like a jack rabbit. I jumped to the ground and ran to the tail to cover the rear as I had often done in training. As I ran I saw German soldiers in the two-storeyed farmhouse about 50 or 60 yards away, and one of them was firing a Schmeisser submachine-gun in our direction. I threw myself down, positioning my gun, and brought it into the aim position, at the same time releasing the safety catch. This only took seconds but the Germans nipped back into the house. I put a few quick bursts after them through the door and windows to keep them pinned inside while the platoon got out and unloaded our spares. They say that only one in five gliders landed undamaged of the 400 or so used by our division. I was in one of the undamaged.

'I continued firing short bursts through the windows and doors, and as I was changing a magazine there was a shout that the Germans were running for the village – Hamminkeln. I looked up and saw about a dozen of them, legging it for cover behind a tall hedge. In my excitement I fired before I was properly into the aim and my burst hit the ground in front of me. I had to wait a few seconds before I could aim and fire again. This time I sprayed them as they reaching the cover of the hedge, but I could not say if I hit any of them. As I looked about me at the platoon lying beside the glider, everybody was flat on the ground and I seemed to be the only one firing. Then there was a shout that two German tanks were coming up the road. This road ran north–south and bounded the landing zone, about 70 yards or so away.

'I repositioned my gun so that I could fire at them as they came up opposite the glider. I would only have fired if the tank commander had his head exposed from the turret. In the event they weren't tanks but armoured personnel half-tracks. The Germans were standing up in the first one, shoulder to shoulder. They had obviously packed it as much as possible to get back to their own troops on the other side of the river Issel via the village of Hamminkeln. As they came opposite me I let them have a burst and they all collapsed behind the armoured sides. I couldn't have hit them all but there was a lot of shouting and screaming.

'The troops in the second vehicle were concealed behind the armour, and having seen what happened to the first vehicle they were travelling about 50 yards behind it. I sprayed it with a burst anyway, hoping to hit the driver. Both vehicles continued on towards Hamminkeln.'

Although the drop and glider landing zones had been bombed and strafed by Allied aircraft, the aircraft and gliders met fierce anti-aircraft fire as they came in low across the river. The US Transport Group dropping 6th Airborne lost forty-seven aircraft shot down or damaged out of the 120 Dakota C47s taking part, and over a quarter of the glider pilots taking part in 'Varsity' were killed or wounded.

Frank Haddock, an RAF pilot, had been moved onto gliders after Arnhem. 'At briefing it sounded so simple. We would be in one large formation with the 9th US Air Force and 2nd TAF giving top cover – flak would be negligible because 2nd TAF had blasted everything in the area during the previous two weeks, but German records show that there were 712 light guns and 103 heavy guns in the landing areas.

'We climbed away into a clear blue sky, across the river Orwell. The sight of 120 tugs and Horsa gliders was exhilarating, and we saw people in the streets of Herne Bay waving as the aerial armada moved across Kent. We crossed the French coast and later the message came from the Halifax captain that we were within sight of the Rhine.

'At that moment a Stirling bomber came across our formation in a shallow dive, its starboard engines and wing on fire, the crew bailing out in quick succession. We saw five bodies in space before their parachutes developed. It was an awesome sight and we felt that all was not well. The tug pilot called out that we were crossing the river and we were immediately aware of flak bursting around us and the smell of cordite. Another call from the tug crew – "Good luck and come back safely, lads" – followed by "Flapjack, flapjack", our signal to cast off.

'The glider became very quiet. Even at 2,500 feet we knew a considerable battle was in progress. The visibility was hopeless – a heavy smoke haze blanketed the landing area. We reduced our air speed to 100 m.p.h. and watched the other Horsas ahead as another Horsa came diving in our direction. It was necessary to take evasive action and we found ourselves heading back into our own aircraft. It was reminiscent of a dog fight – aircraft weaving all over the sky – except that we couldn't gain height and the all-up weight did not aid manoeuvrability.

'My colleague, Cec Law, called out, "I've got it. Look out for a space to land." Peering through the smoke, I pointed out a clear field to port. A stream of pink 20 mm tracer shells came towards us and followed us through the turn, getting closer. It was within a yard of the cockpit when it ceased. Whether the gunner ran out of ammo or came under attack from the paras, we never knew. We completed the turn, full flap down, and in we went.

'Immediately we landed I was to jump out with Bren-gun while the Army lads off-loaded their gun. I heard Cec bawl at the Royal Artillery Staff Sergeant "What? Are you telling me you don't know how to get the bloody gun out?" There we were with shooting going on and nobody knew how to get the load out; the load was disgorged in about 15 minutes.

'As I lay underneath the aircraft, I watched the crew and passengers of another glider being taken prisoner by German paratroopers. We could see a farmhouse which we approached warily, only to discover a large pool of blood in the hall, some wounded Germans in the cellar, and the family in a bunker in the garden. It had been captured by our paras and abandoned because of its isolated position. I remained at the window in the kitchen as a strange whooshing, whistling noise went across the top of the house, followed by a second and a third. They were US gliders going in to land about a mile away. This confused the situation even more, as we were unaware that any Americans would be in our area.

'At about 1500 hrs I sighted a lone figure in a red beret, rifle slung on his shoulder, strolling along the edge of a field: the first friendly face we had encountered since landing. Our visitor turned out to be Staff Sergeant Andy Kerr, an Army glider pilot from our own squadron.

'He suggested that we might consolidate with the paras who were dug-in near Hamminkeln. As we returned to the house a US paratrooper appeared with a terrible face wound. He was able to walk but his lower jaw was badly shattered and his ragged dressing was completely soaked. We used my field dressing to patch him up, loaded him on the jeep and headed across fields scattered with dead and a burned-out C47 Dakota.

'It was a relief to find ourselves in good company again – a motley crew of about sixty British and US paras, air landing brigade soldiers and glider pilots, including several from our own squadron. We settled down for the night, taking watches of one and a half hours and a similar period of "rest". It was going to be bitterly cold but, come what may, we were with friends and our spirits were high.'

Another RAF glider pilot was Dickie Taylor. 'During the summer of 1944 there were a number of trained RAF pilots at the Grand Hotel in Harrogate, Yorkshire, occupied with various odd-ball postings. I was one of these but the disaster at Arnhem that September altered all that. We were told we were going to see some action and would be transferred to the Glider Pilot Regiment of 6th Airborne Division. On the Rhine crossing, our glider was loaded with a jeep, a 75 mm Howitzer, ammo trailer, and a gun crew of three. There was thick smoke everywhere and we could hardly see the ground as we went down. We saw some parachutes coming down. The glider was soon unloaded and the gun crew left us. This was about 11 o'clock in the morning. There was no resistance from the enemy, though we could hear the chatter of German machine-guns around us and learned later that a good many of the airborne troops had run into opposition. We also learned that our flight commander, Captain Strathern, had been killed soon after landing.'

By the end of the day, the 6th Airborne Division had taken 1,400 casualties among the 7,220 men who dropped that morning, but had linked up with the 15th (Scottish) Division advancing from the river, and their landing and drop zones were secure. The US 17th Airborne Division, landing 9,650-strong, had about 1,300 casualties; twenty-one parachute or tug aircraft were shot down and sixty more damaged over the drop zones. The two airborne divisions took 3,500 prisoners and by the end of the day had linked up with the ground forces all around their perimeters.

The fierce resistance to the Plunder–Varsity assault removed any idea that the German Army was ready to give up the fight. A good indication of the severity of the fighting around Wesel comes from that day's casualty figures. The 51st (Highland) Division had 859 men killed or wounded during the assault phase of Operation Plunder the 15th (Scottish) Division, 824. Total 21st Army Group casualties for Plunder and Varsity – British, Canadian and American – came to 6,781 men killed or wounded. This can be compared with the 10,000 men killed or wounded landing on a fifty-mile front on D-Day.

While the assault troops and the paratroopers were fighting to secure their objectives on the east bank, more troops – American, British and Canadian – were coming across the river. John Melmoth crossed the Rhine with the 'Desert Rats' of the British 7th Armoured Division: 'I was at the Rhine crossing with 1st/5th Queen's of 131st Brigade. We crossed in a "Buffalo", so full of troops and so low in the water that we could dangle our fingers in the river. Being a non-swimmer, I was concerned that it would sink and totally disregarded the considerable amount of enemy fire until admonished by our sergeant to "Get your bloody head down." I was wounded shortly after the landing and did not rejoin the battalion until a week before the German surrender.'

Casualties on 'Plunder' were not restricted to the lower ranks. Major-General T. G. Rennie, commander of the 51st (Highland) Division, was killed during the day, as was the German commander in Wesel, Major-General Freidrich Deutsch.

There are various accounts of how the German general met his end. One American account states that he fell 'leading his men in a desperate counter-attack against the Commandos.' A British account states that General Deutsch was killed in the bombing. A third and rather more vivid account comes from Philip Pritchard of No. 6 Commando:

'In the middle of the battle, passing through Wesel, we found a Commando lance-corporal digging a grave in a garden. This seemed strange and we asked him why he was doing it. He said his section had been searching a house when they were confronted by a German officer. The lance-corporal immediately said, "Hands up!" but the German replied, "I am General Deutsch and I will only surrender to an officer of equal rank." The lance-corporal was fed up with all this and said "Well, this will equalize you", and fired his Tommy-gun at the general, with fatal results.

'Brigadier Mills-Roberts was furious, and as a punishment he ordered the lance-corporal to bury the general. Anyway, that was the gist of his story. As we went off, the unfortunate lance-corporal was still digging.

Another man in action that day was Lieutenant Hugh Clark of the Oxfordshire and Buckinghamshire Light Infantry. 'The company had a "*coup de main*" task to seize and hold a road bridge over the Issel. We evacuated the glider quickly but realized that we were not within sight of the bridge. In fact, there were no landmarks we recognized and while we were trying to locate our position, the glider came under fire. This was returned by our two pilots manning a Bren-gun.

'We made a run for the cover of the river bank, section by section. We made that safely but then one of our section commanders was killed by a sniper. We saw our glider hit by mortar bombs and catch fire, so our small packs and reserve ammunition were lost. We had, in fact, landed a mile south of the bridge, between the river and the autobahn.

'As we made our way back to our regimental area, we were joined by men from other units who had landed off-target. As I had a complete platoon, those who had joined us took position in the centre. Moving along the railway line we suffered a further casualty, a man shot in the leg. As he was unable to continue we applied a field dressing and left him, with the assurance that we would send stretcher-bearers for him as soon as possible. Apart from a good deal of machine-gun and sniper fire, the rest of the route back was uneventful. We passed through the Royal Ulster Rifles' positions to the HQ at the railway station.

'After reporting there, I continued with my platoon to B Company HQ at the level crossing. There I reported to my company commander, Major Gilbert Rahr, who asked me where I had been and why I had taken so long. He told me the bridge had been captured intact just after landing. Casualties in the battalion had been severe. No. 17 Platoon's glider had crashed with no survivors. No. 18 Platoon crashed into the edge of a wood on the east side of the autobahn; there were nine survivors, two of whom were badly injured and six of the survivors rejoined the company forty-eight hours later.

'My platoon was in reserve and ordered to dig-in along the railway line towards C Company on our left. We spent an anxious afternoon consolidating our positions, avoiding sniper fire and checking on our ammunition. By late evening the company were down to our last box of .303 ammunition. German tanks were reported on the other side of the autobahn and from time to time we called for fire from a troop of 5.5 inch guns supporting us from the west bank of the Rhine.

'Unfortunately, one of the guns was firing short, so one round in four was liable to land in the company position. On one occasion a group of Royal Engineers with a trailer-load of demolition charges arrived to mine the bridge; as we dived for cover from the shells, we realized the consequences if the trailer was hit, for one of the engineers who made it to a slit-trench just before I did, remarked, "I hate to tell you, sir, but there is half a ton of explosives just 6 feet from your head!"

'At about 2200 hrs, a German tank edged its way to the far side of the bridge. Lt David Rice, with one of his platoon, manned a 6-pounder anti-tank gun while my platoon supplied illumination with 2-inch mortar parachute flares. Although they scored several hits, they made no impression on the tank, but caused it to withdraw. At about midnight the Germans attacked again, their infantry crossed the river and forced No. 16 Platoon to pull back. The company commander ordered me to lead my platoon in an immediate counter-attack and retake the house by the river bank and the bridge. I led two sections in a bayonet charge, firing from the hip as we covered the 120 yards to the river bank.

'One amusing incident ... we had covered half the distance when a corporal on my right said, "Hold it a minute, sir, you're on your Jack", for having started in a straight line, we had gone into arrowhead formation with me in front. We arrived to find the Germans had pulled back but we could see two tanks no more than 100 yards away and could hear their infantry moving round them. The platoon took up position on the river bank and engaged the leading tank with our PIAT. We scored at least five hits and I can recall our disappointment when the tank did not "brew up". Both tanks pulled back out of range but after a brief interval began to creep forward again, and shortly before 0200 hrs a decision was taken to blow the bridge. The engineers had done a good job and the bridge went up with a tremendous bang.

'On the Sunday morning we reported our company strength as two officers and forty-five other ranks, all that remained out of a total of more than 120. Breakfast next morning was our first proper meal since we had left England forty-eight hours before, and later that day we commenced our advance to Wismar on the Baltic.'

Lt-Colonel Clifford Norbury continues his story: 'The ground troops had used a lot of smoke to cover the assault across the river and this had drifted east. My glider arrived safely over the area and dived into the smoke, the pilots hoping they would see the ground before we hit it. They did, but levelling out to land, we hit a bank which took off our undercarriage and a large portion of the floor. We came to rest with us looking at the ground under our feet. We had opened the door before landing, so I ordered everyone out double-quick. Within a few yards I saw a long, large hole, presumably dug by the farmer. We dived into this and as we did so, a shell hit the remains of our glider, and the jeep, trailer and all our kit went up in flames. Miraculously, my whole team was unscathed.

'Having collected my wits, I saw we were within 20 yards of a railway line. As there was only one railway line in the area, this told me that we were about 500 yards south of where we had planned to establish Rear Division HQ. We set off northwards, finding the farmhouse I was looking for without difficulty. On the way we passed some German and American dead and I realized that at least one stick of American parachutists must have been dropped too far north and had dealt with the Germans who would have been there to receive us. I always felt I owed my life to that mis-dropped stick.

'Not many members of Rear Divisional HQ had reached our location, but one party was the Royal Signals team with our wireless link to the UK. We commenced setting this up. In those days, wirelesses were nothing like as efficient as they are now, and I wasn't very optimistic about getting through, but amazingly, when the signallers opened up we heard the UK Airborne Corps at Moor Park loud and clear. I confirmed that the re-supply drop should go ahead in the late afternoon as planned, and recognized the voice on the wireless as that of John Darlington, with whom I had shared an office in England. I therefore terminated my transmission by saying, "Tell Eileen I'm OK", and before she had finished her lunch that day, my wife received a phone call from dear old John!'

Rick Hall of 67 Company, Royal Army Service Corps, had come all the way from the Western Desert with the 7th Armoured Division and kept a diary of his time in Germany: 'I had been in Germany in 1936, when a group of us cycled there from England to see the Berlin Olympics. We didn't have tickets so I didn't see the Games, but I saw some Blackshirts smashing a Jew's head against a brick wall. I thought then, "One day these people will have to be sorted out", and here we were to do it.

'Anyway, some entries ... 23 March 1945: Slept in cab at Kevelaaer, Germany. Railway station really bashed about. 24 March: Rhine crossing. Big paratroop concentrations going over. Took a dozen carriers of ammunition over the Rhine that night on pontoon bridge, bucking and swaying with the current. Sunday, 25 March: Went to pictures, saw *Adam Had Four Sons*.'

With the bridgehead secure, the engineers of the 9th US Army had the first pontoon bridge over the river by the evening of 24 March. More bridges followed in the British sector and by 25 March, 21st Army Group were pouring across into the heart of Germany.

The war went on across the Rhine, the Allies driving deeper into Germany day by day. Four days after the assault the bridgehead over the Rhine at Wesel was twenty miles deep and thirty-five miles wide. With three Allied bridgeheads over the river – at Wesel, Remagen and Oppenheim – the last German defences began to come down with a rush. The III Corps of Hodges' 1st US Army began to advance rapidly from Remagen heading east, along the south face of the Ruhr, while Patton now had a full corps across the Rhine at Oppenheim; and on 26 March Patch's 7th US Army crossed the Rhine near Mannheim. In the 21st Army Group area, the British 2nd Army, supported by the 9th US Army, was pushing north towards the Elbe, Bremen and Hamburg. On 27 March, the plan was still for 21st Army Group to head for the North German plain, Hamburg and Berlin, while Bradley's 12th US Army Group overran the Ruhr. Then, on 28 March, came a change of plan, and with that change, controversy.

Albert I. Schantz from Reading, Pennsylvania, arrived in Europe at this time. 'On 7 March 1945 I arrived in Prüm, Germany, and was assigned as a rifleman to Company 'A', 22nd Infantry Regiment, 4th US Infantry Division. The 4th Division had suffered many casualties after 199 consecutive days in combat during and after the Ardennes campaign and required about a 50 percent replacement.

'After retraining and re-organizing, we boarded trucks and travelled south through Luxembourg to Metz and Nancy in France, then east to Luneville and north to Worms in Germany. There we crossed the Rhine and engaged the enemy again on the front line on 29 March 1945.

'During our first battle we were pursuing the Germans when the 60 mm mortar gunner collapsed from exhaustion and I became the gunner. That meant carrying a 60 mm mortar and a .45 pistol in place of the M-1 rifle. The mortar weighed about 60 lb. with the base plate, but the promotion and the Combat Infantryman badge gave me a rise in pay. I can't remember exactly how much the increase was but I do remember that the Private rating paid $30 per month and the Combat Infantryman badge paid an additional $10 per month. I suppose the promotion rise was about $5 per month, all of which raised my monthly pay to about $45.

'During one of our battles we encountered sniper fire and our platoon leader spotted the sniper in the steeple of a church on top of the hill we were trying to take. He asked me to set up my mortar and knock the sniper out of the steeple. I set up and knocked the sniper off the church with the first shot and the rest of my platoon cheered. I don't know if this shot was the reason for my first stripe, on 1 April 1945.'

German Panther D tank

9 From the Rhine to the Elbe

23 MARCH–APRIL 1945

'I am the first to admit that war is
waged in pursuance of political aims.'

General Dwight D. Eisenhower
Cable to General Marshall
6 April 1945

On 28 March 1945, the very day that 21st Army Group broke out of the Wesel bridgehead and started its drive for the Ruhr and the North German plain, General Eisenhower had decided to swing the main thrust of the Western armies away from the north onto a new axis of advance, east towards Erfurt, Leipzig and Dresden, with the aim of linking up as soon as possible with the Soviet armies and cutting the German forces in two.

The Canadians were to clear Holland, the British were to advance to Hamburg, the lower Elbe and the Baltic coast, while the 9th and 1st US Armies, having first surrounded and then eliminated German forces in the Ruhr Pocket, were to thrust east towards Leipzig. Meanwhile Patton's 3rd US Army and Devers' 6th US Army Group were to clear Bavaria and advance into Austria and meet the Russians on the Danube. This change of direction meant that the Russians, who had already taken Belgrade and Budapest and were about to take Vienna, would also take Berlin.

From the purely military point of view there were several good reasons for Eisenhower's change of plan. In the first place it had already been decided that Berlin would be well inside the post-war Russian zone of occupation. Though Berlin would subsequently be partitioned between the Four Powers, Eisenhower saw no point in fighting for ground he would

175

eventually have to hand over to the Russians. Secondly, the Russians, having reached the Oder, were far closer to Berlin than the most forward of the Western armies, and would probably take Berlin anyway.

Finally, and perhaps conclusively, Eisenhower, Bradley and the SHAEF intelligence officers had become convinced that the Germans were pulling their forces back into the mountains along the Austro-Bavarian border aiming to set up a fortified 'National Redoubt' where SS troops and *Hitler Jugend* 'Werewolves' would fight to the end and prolong the war. It therefore made sense to chase the Germans swiftly south and overrun these positions before the National Redoubt could be manned and munitioned.

This plan neglected post-war political considerations and without consulting the combined Chiefs of Staff, Roosevelt or Churchill, Eisenhower then cabled this decision to Marshal Stalin in Moscow. Eisenhower's cable to Stalin re-ignited the barely dormant dispute between the British and American Chiefs of Staff. The British pointed out, quite correctly, that Eisenhower had no business reaching such a momentous decision on his own and even less business communicating it to Marshal Stalin without reference to his superiors on the Combined Chiefs of Staff Committee.

Prime Minister Winston Churchill, deeply concerned, at once contacted President Roosevelt, but Roosevelt was now very ill and leaving most of the strategic decisions to General Marshall and the American Joint Chiefs who, as ever, supported General Eisenhower. So, too, did Marshal Stalin who hastened to reply that the western swing away from Berlin met with his full approval and support. That alone should have caused the Western Allies to think again.

At this stage in the war military considerations were being – or certainly should have been – influenced by post-war political considerations. This is not historical hindsight based on fifty years of Cold War experience. There were plenty of voices raised at the time to warn the West of Soviet ambitions, not all of them British. Apart from Winston Churchill, the American ambassador in Moscow, Averell Harriman, was also warning Washington about post-war Soviet attitudes and intentions. It was already obvious that Soviet Russia had no intention whatsoever of keeping to any of the agreements reached at Yalta, over Poland or democratic elections or free speech, in Eastern Europe or the Balkans or anywhere the Red Armies or Russia's Communist partisan allies could gain control.

Communist influence was already a factor in Western Europe. Behind that influence came armed men seeking or seizing power, as they had already done in Yugoslavia, and had barely been prevented from doing in Greece. Communist parties were striving to seize power in Italy and Hungary while Austria and France contained large armed Communist parties. In early spring 1945 democracy in Western Europe hung by a thread.

Winston Churchill therefore wanted the Western armies to meet the Soviets as 'far east as possible' and 'deny the Communists the prestige that must accrue from capturing Berlin'. Winston Churchill was right to take the long view, but British influence was waning in Washington and the Kremlin. Eisenhower's plan was therefore approved and the die was cast in Europe for the next forty-five years.

Controversy was not lacking behind the German lines. After months of arguing with the Führer and disputing his policies, General Guderian was dismissed from his post on 28 March and replaced by General Krebs, formerly Chief-of-Staff to Army Group B, now defending the Ruhr.

Guderian could do no more. Most of the Eastern Front was crumbling and the Western Front was breached in four places. In the centre, along the Oder–Neisse Line, the spring thaw and a stoutly defended German defence line had brought the Red Armies to a halt, and there would be no advances here until the shattered railways and roads through Poland could be repaired and the ground dried out enough for tanks. In other parts of the '*Ostfront*' – in the Balkans, East Prussia, the Baltic coast and Pomerania – the Soviets were pushing ahead, their path still marked by rape, pillage and murder. Hundreds of thousands of Germans and '*Volksdeutsch*' were fleeing east before this fury, cluttering the roads, prey to strafing fighters and bombers, jamming the reinforcements trying to reach the front and the wounded trying to get away. Everyone who could, soldier or civilian, was trying to head west to the safety of the American lines.

In the south, Budapest had fallen and the Red Armies were pushing around Lake Balaton for the Danube and the Austrian frontier. In the north the Germans were evacuating their troops and citizens from Danzig. Kustrin fell on 12 March and German forces had been driven out of East Prussia by 19 March, evacuating most of the wounded and civilians by sea – though many ships were sunk by Russian aircraft and submarines, the passengers drowning by the thousand in the icy waters of the Baltic.

By 21 March Marshal Konev had a bridgehead over the Oder. Gdynia fell to Marshal Rokossovsky on 28 March and Danzig on 30 March, each capitulation being followed by terrible acts of rape and slaughter carried out on the civilian population and the prisoners. The Russians crossed the Hungarian frontier into Austria at the end of March, while in Czechoslovakia the armies of the Second Ukrainian Front advanced on Bratislava and Prague. On 1 April 1945, Adolf Hitler's 'Thousand Year Reich' had about five weeks left to live.

Among the infantry units crossing the Rhine was the 6th Battalion, the Royal Scots Fusiliers, and one of their number was Harry Holder. 'We crossed the Rhine about 0200 hrs on 24 March. At 10.00 the parachute and gliders came over, a glorious sight, but there was also the horrible sight of gliders being hit by anti-aircraft fire and the lads inside tumbling to earth and certain death. Soon we spotted what appeared to be a giant approaching, which turned out to be an American mounted on the shoulders of two German prisoners. He was the pilot of crashed Dakota who had broken both ankles and forced the Germans to carry him to our lines. He begged us not to shoot them – as if we would – as they had saved his life.

'We held our positions until next day and then began to force a crossing of the river Issel. On the way there we came across a group of paratroopers who had obviously been disarmed, lined up and shot. They lay in a line, their limbs distorted, and I am sure if we had encountered any Germans in the next hour or so, we would not have taken any prisoners.

'We pressed on to the sound of the pipes, as Colonel Mackenzie had ordered the pipers to play and let the paratroopers know we were on the way. Red berets soon popped up all over the place and they were very pleased to see us, especially after the Arnhem cock-up when 2nd Army failed to get through.

'I can only recount the action on the Issel from the point of view of a humble section leader. We got into a ditch with about 100–200 yards of open ground between us and the river, and Major Gray gave the order to attack. We were out of our ditch like a shot and going hell for leather for the river, firing as we went. Major Gray led the charge and was the first into the river. I was right behind and I remember pausing to let him jump in as I wanted to see how deep it was. It came up to my chest.

'Men were dropping all the time, but we waded the river and crossed into some woods, codenamed "Elizabeth", where we dug-in. I think there were only about twenty-seven of us left. Major Gray was assessing the situation and we were under fire from three sides, with bullets snapping all about.

'Eventually I was sent back across the river with a message for Colonel Mackenzie, telling him we were across and holding. I got back under a tremendous downpour and I remember coming across a slit-trench with a single soldier in it, either a Royal Scot or a KOSB (King's Own Scottish Borderer). I could not persuade him to come with me; he insisted he had to stay, though he was on his own, in case his comrades came through. I often wonder what happened to him.

'This action for the bridgehead over the Issel is one action that remains clear in my mind after all these years. I can close my eyes and remember it as though it were yesterday.'

Lieutenant Ian Wilson of the Royal Engineers remembers crossing the Rhine and the advance to the Elbe: 'As we crossed the Rhine, we crossed into springtime. The sun came out, the grass was green and blonde German girls in colourful dresses provided a great contrast to the drab winter we had just spent; but there was a strict no-fraternization order. The Germans were to be ignored. 73 Field Company RE had moved to Lingen, where we built a bridge over the Dortmund-Ems canal. We moved to Celle on 21 April to build another bridge and while there we became involved in one or two minor tasks at Belsen concentration camp, an unforgettable experience with which I was thankful to have had only superficial contact.

'We left Celle on 27 April to prepare for the Elbe assault and I made the bridge reconnaissance the night before the crossing. I remember the bridge transport officer who was with me on the reconnaissance, because he was one of the clumsiest men I have ever met. He seemed to kick or trip over every stone, and the Germans were on the far bank, but no harm came of it. The infantry crossed the river at 0430 hrs on 29 April, the bridge construction parties moved up at 0500 hrs on 29 April.

'Due to enemy fire, bridge building did not start until after midday, and was interrupted several times by air attack – the German Air Force's last fling. The bridge was completed in the afternoon of 30 April, and the 11th Armoured Division started crossing. I met my cousin as he was moving up and climbed into his vehicle to talk as we crossed the bridge. Shelling on the narrow exit road caused a number of hold-ups until the following day, but crossing the Elbe was really our last event. My company saw in VE Day near Lübeck on the Baltic, after which, ironically, we were called on for security patrols to protect Germans from marauding DPs (Displaced Persons) seeking vengeance.'

Gunner Jim Purser was still with the 8th Battalion of the Parachute Regiment. 'My first impression was how well fed the German people were, so different from the thin and hungry people of Occupied Europe. Also how effective the bombing had been: most of the large towns had been completely flattened – Coesfeld is one such that comes to mind – and in Hanover we could not get through the streets for rubble.

'When there was a lull in the fighting, souvenir hunting became very popular. I picked up a German helmet, a discarded American reserve parachute – the silk was worth a mint – two Nazi dress swords and three pistols. Jock Smith actually found a Nazi dress uniform that fitted him perfectly but this was not the time to swan about the countryside dressed as a high-ranking Nazi.

'Later in the campaign troops were stealing cameras and other equipment from unoccupied houses, and the problem became so serious that the battalion was mustered for an address by Brigadier Faithful, commanding the artillery in 6th Airborne, who explained to us the finer points of looting.

' "Anything which helps me win the war is legitimate loot", he explained.

"For example, I have nicked a razor – that keeps me clean shaven and helps me win the war. Any other form of looting is a military crime." '

The soldiers of 21st Army Group were neither the first nor the last Allied troops to cross the Rhine. On 26 March, General Patch's 7th US Army crossed the Rhine near Worms, followed on 31 March by the French 1st Army, which crossed at Speyer and had advanced south to Karlsruhe by 4 April, heading towards Stuttgart. By 2 April the whole 6th US Army Group was running into stiff opposition from the German Army Group G, but Eisenhower now had five bridgeheads across the Rhine from Wesel to Speyer and a wide choice of options for future action. He also had overwhelming force at his disposal.

By 1 April SHAEF had under command more than 10,000 aircraft and land forces totally ninety-four divisions, spread across seven armies in three army groups, with more divisions arriving from the United States at the rate of one a week. Though on a smaller scale, the British and Canadian armies were also being reinforced, with the transfer of a Canadian corps from Italy and a British infantry division from the Middle East.

The Germans had little left with which to oppose them. On 1 April, Allied estimates of German strength in the west came up with a figure of sixty-five divisions but most of these were divisions in name only. At least four 'divisions' consisted only of the divisional staffs trying to scratch together some forces to command. Another dozen were little more than battle groups, *ad hoc* collections of tanks and infantry. Most of the rest were the remnants of units worn out or shattered in heavy fighting west of the Rhine. Since the start of the Reichwald offensive, the Germans had lost over 350,000 men, killed, wounded or taken prisoner, but even with their Rhine defences breached the Germans fought on.

Their guns continued to take a steady toll of Allied strength, not least in the air where the aircraft supporting the Allied armies were meeting plenty of anti-aircraft fire. Among the young men killed in the last weeks of the war in Europe was Louis (Lou) Parker, a Canadian Typhoon pilot with 175 Squadron, RAF. His commanding officer duly wrote to his mother, one of many thousands of such letters written to relatives of fighting men during the six long years of the war:

Dear Mrs Parker,

By the time you receive this letter you will have been officially informed that your son, Flight Lieutenant Louis Holmes Parker, is missing from air operations over Germany on 13th April 1945.

Lou was leading a formation of eight rocket-firing Typhoons to attack a mortar position near the village of Verden, southeast of Bremen. At twenty minutes past four he led the formation down in a dive through some anti-aircraft fire, but as he fired his rockets, the pilot immediately behind him saw a steak of flame under the wing of Lou's plane. He warned Lou immediately by R/T and then saw Lou's plane pull out of the dive, climb up and then it turned onto its back still flaming, dived and hit the ground, bursting into flames immediately.

No one saw Lou bale out, or saw a parachute at all, and he was only out of sight of his Number 2 for a second or two, so the chances of his having got out are, I'm afraid, negligible. I think that Lou was probably killed instantaneously when the aircraft hit the ground, and in that case he would not have had any suffering to bear.

We are all very sad that Lou has gone, as he was a very popular member of the squadron and everyone feels they have lost a personal friend. As you probably know, Lou came to my squadron as a flight commander at the beginning of the year and since then he has done invaluable work for the squadron, both in flying, in training new pilots and in helping me with the running of the squadron. We all appreciated very much that he had come so far from his own home to join in our common cause.

His kit and belonging are being collected, listed and will be sent to the Royal Air Force Central Depository...

Flight-Lieutenant Louis H. Parker, RCAF, lies in the British Military Cemetery at Limmer, near Hanover.

With the suspension of strategic bomber operations in April 1945 many of the British 'main force' bombers were now engaged in the start of Operation Manna, flying in food to the starving people of Holland behind the German lines, usually without opposition from the German artillery.

W. B. Garnowski of 300 (Polish) Squadron remembers this time well: 'A flight I remember with great pleasure was on 28 April 1945. Our Lancaster bomber was loaded with flour, potatoes and so on, to drop over specified aerodromes in Belgium and Holland where people were starving. The Germans were still in occupation and the flights were by agreement. At 200 feet over the coast we could see the strength of the German defences and their AA crews watching us in our Lancasters.

'On the way back, it was most pleasing to see Dutch and Belgian people waving their thanks to us in their thousands, but I was relieved to finish the flight safely.'

Denis Haines was Assistant Adjutant with the 28th (Royal Marine) Battalion. He also remembers the final days of the war. 'I can remember how young we were. In February 1945 I was twenty years old and the colonel of 28 RM, John Taplin, was twenty-four. It was obvious that the end was not far off and there was much speculation as to the Germans' final action. There was talk of a Nazi withdrawal to a "Redoubt" on the Bavarian–Austrian border, as well as of the introduction of "Werewolf" teams within the occupied areas of Germany which were said to specialize in dealing with traitors and lone motorcyclists.'

Having got his army group across the Rhine, Montgomery issued orders for the advance into Germany. The 2nd Canadian Army was to wheel north and eliminate the German garrisons along the Friesian coast and West Holland, while Dempsey and Simpson were to 'drive hard for the river Elbe and gain quick possession of the plains of North Germany'. Simpson's 9th US Army was to advance along the north side of the Ruhr and make contact with Hodges' 1st US Army coming round the Ruhr from the Remagen bridgehead. All this was according to the previous plan, but then, on 28 March, came the thunderbolt from SHAEF.

Eisenhower had changed his mind about an advance north towards Berlin in favour of a thrust in the centre towards Leipzig by the 12th US Army Group moving out from Remagen. To put this plan into effect, and add weight to Bradley's thrust, Simpson's 9th Army would revert to Bradley's group as soon as the encirclement of the Ruhr had been completed.

Eisenhower's intention now was to effect an early link with the Russian forces advancing from the Oder and so cut the remaining German forces in two. It has been said that in proposing this Eisenhower was making a purely military decision and was unaware of the political implications. This seems unlikely. Politicians were in and out of SHAEF all the time and it is impossible that the politicians or Eisenhower, who after the war became President of the United States, kept their discussions exclusively to military matters.

However, it is possible that Eisenhower was unaware just how much the political accords forged at Yalta had already been breached by the Soviet Government. For all he knew, the Allied alliance still held and a rapid junction with the Red Army was therefore a valid military objective, even if it meant abandoning the chance of capturing Berlin.

Eisenhower's second reason was the National Redoubt in the Bavarian and Austrian Alps, but an American general later described the National Redoubt intelligence as 'pure moonshine'.' Anyway, the Redoubt, real or imaginary, was clearly not the main reason for Eisenhower's change of plan, for in his letter to Montgomery – outlining his future plans and the redeployment of his forces – Eisenhower added:

'You will see that in none of this do I mention Berlin. So far as I am concerned, that place has become nothing but a geographical location; I have never been interested in those. My purpose is to destroy the enemy forces and his powers to resist.'

Their different approaches to war had underpinned many of the disputes between British and American commanders since D-Day. Eisenhower's approach was traditional American military strategy, a concept dating back at least as far as Grant's campaign against Richmond and Atlanta during the American Civil War. This concept regards the capture of strategic or political objectives as secondary to finding the enemy forces, pinning them in position, destroying them and getting the fighting over with quickly.

Unfortunately, Western Europe in 1945 was not the Southern Confederacy of 1861–65. The objective now – apart from defeating Adolf Hitler and his criminal regime – should have been to avoid abandoning large parts of Europe and many democratic states to yet another totalitarian dictator, Joseph Stalin, and his equally odious rule. That thought was not paramount among senior American military men in April 1945. Expressing his support for Eisenhower's change of direction, General Marshall, the US chief, wrote to SHAEF: 'Personally, and aside from all logistic, tactical or strategic considerations, I should be loath to hazard American lives for purely political purposes.'

These American actions and statements, while very understandable, overlook the point that wars are started for political purposes, and as well as military victory, seek to achieve some lasting political solution. In April 1945 the United States had yet to realize that it would not be possible to bring the boys home and forget about the rest of the world when this conflict was over, whatever the private wishes of her political and military leaders. The United States had assumed a world role and must soon confront the challenge posed to the democracies by Communism.

Simpson's 9th US Army duly reverted to Bradley's command on 4 April and began to reduce Field Marshal Model's forces of Army Group B in the Ruhr. A fresh series of orders were then issued from SHAEF. Montgomery was to continue to the northwest, to the river Leine, the cities of Bremen and Hamburg, and the Elbe. His forces would then cross the Elbe, which was not the Stop Line between the Eastern and Western armies in the north, and occupy a bridgehead on the far bank.

Bradley would take the Ruhr and then advance east on Leipzig and Dresden to meet the armies of Marshal Koniev, while Devers' group was charged with advancing on the Nuremberg–Regensburg–Linz line and preventing any attempt by the Germans at establishing their National Redoubt in Bavaria or Austria. The link between the 12th and 6th US Army Groups would be Patton's 3rd US Army.

Eisenhower's view of the situation ignored the benefits that were rapidly accruing from the various Rhine crossings. The Western armies had torn open a 200-mile-wide gap in the centre of the German defences and once Model's forces in the Ruhr had been rounded up, the way was clear for the advance of both 21st and 12th Army Groups north and east into Germany. With sixty strong divisions available, little coherent opposition, and no natural obstacles, the capture of Berlin was certainly within Eisenhower's grasp, not least because the Germans were still holding the Russians on the Oder.

The American Joint Chiefs, however, had already endorsed Eisenhower's plan, telling the British Chiefs that it offered the best way of 'crushing Germany as expeditiously as possible'. On the matter of consulting Stalin, the Joint Chiefs added that Eisenhower 'should continue to be free to communicate with the Commander-in-Chief of the Soviet Army'.

This ingenuous snub to their British ally chose to overlook the fact that Marshal Stalin was rather more than 'Commander-in-Chief of the Soviet Army'. He was also the political leader of Soviet Russia and head of the Communist Party, a body dedicated to the political domination of as much of the Continent as the Red Armies could subdue. Taking this last point, the ever-reasonable General Eisenhower was careful thereafter to consult the Combined Chiefs before communicating with Stalin, but the damage had been done. The Russians would take Berlin and Prague and most of Eastern Europe, where their surrogates would seize power, with grievous effect for the post-war world.

Though dismayed at this change of plan, Field Marshal Montgomery was more concerned with the loss of Simpson's 9th US Army, which represented a third of his Group. With his Canadians ordered away into Holland he begged Eisenhower to let Simpson's forces remain under his command, at least until 21st Army Group reached the Elbe.

This request was denied. Before it left 21st Army Group, the 9th Army advanced along the northern face of the Ruhr to join with Hodges' 1st US Army at Lippstadt on 1 April, duly reverting to Bradley's group on 4 April. Having driven a wedge through the German 1st Parachute Army, the two American armies now encircled Model's Army Group B in the Ruhr; 1st US Army thrust into the Ruhr Pocket north and east to Solingen, Wappental and Dortmund, while the 9th US Army swept on across the north face of the Ruhr against steadily crumbling opposition, often no more than road blocks.

Having delivered his protest to SHAEF, Montgomery now turned his forces towards the Baltic and in the next two weeks flung them across a series of rivers, the Leine, the Weser and the Ems, in his rush to reach and cross the river Elbe.

The British 2nd Army had made a rapid advance towards Bremen. On

8 April the forward elements of 2nd Army crossed the Leine and reached the river Weser near Verden, after an advance of 180 miles from the Rhine bridgehead. This advance, though rapid, was not without loss and Lieutenant Gush, of 7th Battalion, the Parachute Regiment, gives a vivid account of what happened to his men when crossing the Leine at Neustadt:

'At about 6 o'clock on the evening of 7 April, I was told to leave my platoon position and march on the road to Neustadt. As it was getting dark, the battalion halted along the road, about two miles south of Neustadt, where orders were given out. The three platoon commanders at that time were Captain Woodman commanding 4th Platoon, myself with 5th Platoon, and Sergeant Keilly 6th Platoon. Briefly, our orders were that the battalion was going to move into Neustadt and capture the bridge over the river Leine. Our company's particular job was the bridge. While A and C Companies moved off up the road towards Neustadt, B Company was to move off the road, march across country to the river and then follow it to Neustadt, enter the town near the bridge, then cross and hold it.

'It was a fairly dark night but the going was easy and we had no difficulty finding the river, and we began to follow it towards the town. There were many small steams and large patches of water and we had to take a very winding course which was confusing in the darkness. At last we could make out the shapes of the houses ahead and we could hear Germans walking about and shouting on the other side of the river. It sounded as if they were pulling out.

'We found our way between some houses and gardens and filed out into the main street. We followed this in the direction of the bridge, moving in single file as quietly as we could, but there seemed to be an awful lot of people about. No one could see who they were and we hoped they were all civilians. Since we did not know where we were, the map was not much help, so Captain Woodman and Major Reid asked some civilians where the bridge was.

'We were shown the way and told that German soldiers had been preparing the bridge for demolition, but had left without blowing it up. When we were certain we were close to the bridge, Major Reid called Captain Woodman and me and pointed out that the best plan would be to rush the bridge with 4th Platoon on the left and my platoon slightly behind to the right. I told my three PIAT men, Privates Lloyd, Jones and Lees, that because of the weight of the PIAT and its bombs they had better wait and come over when we had consolidated.

'All the men knew that the bridge might blow up at any moment and no one knew whether there were Germans on the bridge or on the other side. There was a shout from Captain Woodman and 4th Platoon set off a full speed. My platoon followed on the right of the road and we quickly came to the bridge and crossed it, running as hard as we could go. There were no signs of any charges and no one firing at us.

'Then I heard Captain Woodman shouting that there was another, bigger bridge ahead. Once more we ran forward and immediately came on to a large concrete bridge, definitely prepared for demolition, for I ran into a low, wide wall of explosive laid across the bridge and up the sides. Immediately beyond this wall was a second one. I shouted for even greater speed and we ran so fast that as we reached the other side of the bridge, we had caught up with 4th Platoon. At this moment we were checked. The leading men of 4th Platoon had been fired on and were firing back with their Sten-guns. One man had crossed the road and was in front of me, firing into a house on the right. Then there was the most terrific cough and rush of air and many thousand coloured lights – the bridge had exploded.

'It occurred to me that we were all being killed. I remember hearing a voice, and the exact words were: "Come on, B Company!" The voice sounded distant and rather feeble, but I recognized it as Captain Woodman's. I thought what a very peculiar thing to say, when it was obvious that most of B Company were blown to pieces. I got up and went over and found that he was hit in the knee. I was hit in the middle of my back and behind my left knee. However, we could both walk.

'We looked on a scene of utter destruction: small fires, bits of wood and corpses were burning, which gave out a flickering light. Then some men appeared – Privates Crofts, Wylie and Elliott – there were about two more but I cannot remember their names. There seemed to be no Germans about but it didn't matter much to us whether there were or there weren't. Captain Woodman then recce'd a house a few yards from the remains of the bridge. The house was badly knocked about but we decided to carry the wounded men in. How many were wounded and how many were dead we did not know. I asked if any of the unwounded men could swim back across the river. Private Crofts volunteered and swam back with a message for the company commander, Major Reid.

'The rest of the night was such appalling chaos that it is impossible to describe. We sorted the wounded from the dead, carried them into the house, dressed their wounds as well as we could and injected morphia into the ones in great pain. We knew that the people on the other side of the river would be making repeated efforts to get over to us, but we found it hard to understand why they couldn't get across. After a while we found we could spare two men to act as sentries in case we were attacked. The other men acted as medical orderlies and attended the wounded. I can only remember Privates Wylie and Elliott. There were about two more and all these men did extremely well. They kept their heads and went calmly from room to room, dressing wounds, adjusting bandages, taking round drinking water and doing their utmost to help the wounded.'

This rapid advance to the Leine had been in the face of opposition at various towns and rivers along the way, most noticeably at Ibbenburen, where troops of the British 11th Armoured Division were engaged by students from the German NCOs' and Officers' Training School.

Robert Davey was at Ibbenburen as a platoon commander in the 2nd Devons. 'Our brigade was told to take a town by the name of Rheine, which had a big aerodrome and was by the Dortmund-Ems canal. The ridge at Ibbenburen was very adequately defended by Hitler Youth officer cadets, mostly from Hanover. We went in riding on tanks, which is only partly useful; you cannot hear the sound of firing because of the noise from the engine and the tank tracks. One of the men was kneeling between my knees, speaking to me when he was shot and fell dead.

'We advanced behind a creeping barrage, but the cadets were well dug-in and we had to winkle them out with rifles, bayonets and grenades. When it was over and we were collecting the wounded, I found one German boy under a bush. He spoke perfect English and asked if the stretcher-bearers had been and gone. I said they had, and he said, "Then I think I will die." It was just as well he did, for he had no arms or legs.'

As the British advanced to the Elbe, other Allied soldiers – POWs – were making their way towards the river, hoping to reach the Allied lines. Among them was a Canadian from Fallingbostel POW camp, Richard Copley of Milton, Ontario.

'After a rumour that once across the Elbe all POWs would be held hostage, Bill and I decided to strike off on our own in a southwesterly direction, through very dense bush, where we stole some potatoes from a farm and slept out. The next day we pushed on and were at the edge of a country lane when a cart, drawn by two horses and with two men on board, passed by. Some minutes later an RAF fighter attacked the cart with a rocket and destroyed it. We took off from that scene, and forgetting caution stepped onto the lane – right in front of a German soldier. He was old, and when we asked him to accompany us, on promise of safe conduct through the Allied lines, he not only agreed but commandeered a horse and cart. For Bill and me it was a wonderful feeling, being chauffered by an armed German. Getting onto wider roads we were dismayed to see German tanks, but they ignored us. Following the tanks were German personnel carriers, and as they passed the soldiers waved and even threw handfuls of biscuits into our wagon.

'We saw Tiger and Panther tanks in farmyards and assumed that they were setting up for battle. On we went, until all hell broke loose, machine-gun fire, cannon fire, tracer bullets everywhere, and the horse and German bolted, separately. Bill and I dived into a shallow ditch and shared our last cigarette. When everything had quietened down, we made for a bend in the road and there was a tank with a big white star on it. As we approached, the lid flipped up and a British sergeant popped up and said, "Who the hell are you?" We told him RAF escapers, and he flipped a florin at us and said, "Have your first pint on me, but find a place to stay because we are moving out right away." We chose the most prosperous farmhouse we could find, and as we approached it a young German civilian offered us his girlfriend. In no uncertain terms, Bill told him where to go!

'As we were the only Allied personnel in the village we demanded a chicken for our dinner, and accommodation in a proper bedroom. The farmer and his wife were very willing and hosted us well. We left the farm to walk west and south and were surprised to see a jeep occupied by two RAF pilots. They were visiting farms right behind the front line and confiscating shotguns and, they said, flying them back to England. Bill and I walked on until we got to an Army establishment, where we scrounged some white bread, which to us was just like having birthday cake. I have noted in the diary for 18 April 1945: After marching for twelve days, Bill and I managed to escape and get back to our Lines. On this day finished my "Kriegie" service.'

Another prisoner on the run at this time was H. S. Grey of the 9th Battalion, the Parachute Regiment, who had been wounded and captured on the Rhine crossing and escaped from a German hospital:

'From D-Day to the end of the war at Wismar my section had three killed and five wounded – not bad for a section of ten men. Well ... to cut a long story short, I woke up in this German hospital and promptly escaped. Everything was confusion and I stole a German staff car and just drove off in it. I eventually ran into the Canadian Parachute Battalion of 6th Airborne Division and two days after that I was back with my own battalion. The funny part is that when I opened the boot of the staff car looking for loot I found a case full of German marks, all brand new. I bet the German officer was surprised when he found his car and money gone. I took the money and just threw it away, which might sound daft but the whole lot would not have bought you half a loaf of bread at that time.'

The British XII Corps, having reached the river Ems, turned south to cross the Dortmund-Ems canal, where the 7th Armoured Division took up the fight. Osnabruck was captured on 4 April by the 1st Commando Brigade, then attached to 7th Armoured Division.

Bill Sadler of 6 Commando takes up the tale: 'I have always been intrigued by those accounts where the narrator states in great detail who shot who, and where. I was far more concerned that no one shot me. Anyway ... the brigade entered Osnabruck in the early hours of Sunday morning, suffering some casualties from Spandau fire which produced the usual Commando reaction: "Bash on regardless." We sprinted across the open ground in groups and the Spandau was knocked out by a well-placed PIAT bomb. We had completed the capture of the town by 10.00 a.m., mopping up a few pockets of resistance and taking about 400 prisoners, including some Hungarians. The local Gestapo chief was shot dead in his office by our Field-Security officer, Major Vicomte de Jonghe – then we went on to the Weser.'

The river Weser was reached by VIII Corps on 5 April, while the 52nd Infantry division fought its way across the Dortmund–Ems canal at Rhine. Lieutenant Alan Gibson of the Royal Marines recalls this part of the advance into Germany:

'I was a platoon officer in 10 Company, 116th Independent Infantry Brigade. Of the journey into Germany I can only remember being scared out of my wits, riding on top of a Bren carrier with faulty brakes and faulty steering, clinging on like grim death. I recall an overnight stop somewhere near Osnabruck. Russian POWs had been liberated and were begging for food and cigarettes, and the local mayor told us, in no uncertain terms, that we had to protect the populace from these savages. We reached Hamburg and took over part of the docks on the south side of the Elbe.'

The 7th Armoured Division found the bridges over the Weser destroyed and had to turn west for Wildeshausen and Delmenhorst to cut off the retreat of the ever-pugnacious German 1st Parachute Army, now pulling back from the Ruhr Pocket towards Bremen. Wildeshausen fell on 10 April and on the same day the 11th Armoured Division secured a crossing over the river Aller after a stiff fight against the 12th SS Training Battalion and the German 325th Infantry Division, a unit hastily evacuated from Denmark.

John Tough and his Sgt-Major George Morrice MM, and Terry May DCM, were of the 1st Battalion, the Gordon Highlanders; Tough recalls part of their advance to the Baltic:

'We came across the Rhine near Isselburgh were the Germans were using airbursts and mortars. We were joined here by two Seaforth Highlanders looking for mortar bombs to fire back. We then fixed our bayonets to clear a wood but the Germans had cleared off, though there was quite a bit of shelling and MG fire and our new corporal, Lance-Corporal Kilgallon – a Yorkshireman – was hit in the hip. The next day the Guards' Armoured Division came through to us and we moved on to Delmenhorst – but we can't remember the dates though it must have been in mid-April.

'The Germans had declared Delmenhorst an open town as there were more than 2,000 wounded Germans there. Terry May had already been wounded. He got his DCM in the fighting for Rees in March, where the platoon commander and two section commanders having become casualties, Terry – who was a private – took over the command of both sections and led them for the next two days against German paratroopers. We spent a

189

week or so around Delmenhorst before the Canadians came through heading for Wilhelmshaven. There was a place called Ebersdorf and we took a hammering there with mortars and heavy stuff and we had a few skirmishes with German Tiger tanks and infantry. On the day the war finished we went into Bremerhaven in TCVs (Troop Carrying Vehicles) and took over the town from the XV Panzer Grenadiers. It felt strange to stand and watch the German officers shouting orders to their men and marching them away to the POW camp.'

H. Trew was with the 13th Battalion of the Parachute Regiment. 'I was on the Rhine drop and carried on to Wismar, to a place called Bad Klienan where we set up a road block within hailing distance of the Russians. There was a "No-fratting" order to stop us talking with the Germans, but at the end of the war I was on guard duty and playing football with some local lads when one boy ran over the road to retrieve the ball and stood on a mine or a booby trap. I ran over to pick him up and found he had a severe wound in his throat.

'The medics heard the explosion and came up with the ambulance to take the lad to hospital. My partner in the battalion was a German Jew who had taken the name Edwards to fight with us, and he took me to the lad's mother to tell her what had happened. I was never able to find out if the lad lived or not.'

The British advance towards Bremen was going well in early April, aided by good weather and the 2nd Tactical Air Force – which flew more than 4,500 sorties over the front during the first two weeks of April. Mosquitoes of Bomber Command continued to bomb Berlin – raiding the city fifteen times as the Russians approached from the east – and there were many heavy bomber raids in support of Allied ground operations. These included an attack on Bremen in support of 21st Army Group and the bombing of several towns in front of Bradley's 12th US Army Group.

Throughout April Allied air attacks on German cities gradually subsided, partly through a lack of targets, partly because of the ending of the Strategic Air Offensive on 16 April, and partly because the damage caused to the cities actually hindered the advance of the Allied armies, who needed bulldozers to clear rubble from the streets before their tanks could advance.

Ted Beswick was a mid-upper gunner with 61 Squadron RAF and remembers his final raid: 'Our last raid was on Hamburg on 9 April 1945, the target being the oil storage and U-boat pens. There was an intense box barrage over the target and we were hit in the nose on the bombing run, but only slightly damaged – though we had a 1,000 lb. bomb hung-up in the bomb bay. The skipper made two more runs before giving up and heading for home.

'Clear of the target, small specks could be seen diving down on the

Lancaster behind us. Suddenly this Lancaster climbed steeply, then exploded and our rear gunner opened fire on an ME262 jet coming through the debris. I yelled to the skipper to "Corkscrew 2" because of other Lancasters in the vicinity. This was a limited manoevre but on levelling out we saw an ME262 quite near. I could see the pilot's head and the black cross on the fuselage. The jet must have been throttled back, so I was able to give him a short burst from the mid-upper turret. All my crew saw black smoke come from it, then it moved down vertically and dived out of sight, pursued by Mustangs from our fighter cover.

'I don't know what happened to it, as we were too busy watching out for further attacks. The hand-up still could not be dislodged over the sea, but on landing it dropped into the bomb bay. I could hear it rattling about and reported my suspicion to the skipper. Our fears were confirmed by our bomb aimer shining a lamp through the two windows into the bomb bay. The skipper turned off the runway and held till the armourers arrived with a bomb trolley and all the crew assisted in unloading the bomb.'

Air operations still continued at full vigour over the Baltic, where Allied aircraft pressed home their attacks against German Type XXI snorkel-equipped U-boats, working up for a spring assault on Allied convoys or heading out to the Atlantic and bases in Norway. Bomber Command, the 8th Air Force and both Tactical Air Forces took part in this final offensive. The Germans lost 151 U-boats in the last five months of the war, more than half of them to air attack.

While the British 2nd Army was pushing towards Bremen and the Elbe, the 1st Canadian Army was clearing the Germans from the north of Holland, with the 2nd Canadian corps thrusting towards Wilhelmshaven. These advances went well in the face of stiff opposition from the German 6th Parachute Division on the Twente canal, and by five other German divisions in North Holland, including the 34th SS Division, a unit largely comprised of Dutch Nazis. The 4th Canadian Armoured Division crossed the Ems on 8 April and took the town of Friesoythe, where Lieutenant Grove Proulx of the Argyll and Sutherland Highlanders of Canada had a curious experience – recalled here by his wife:

'My husband, Lieutenant Grove Proulx, was wounded and taken prisoner on 23 April 1945 near Osterscheps, a small town east of Friesoythe. What is unique about my husband's wounding is that the young German lad, Heinz Brune, who shot my husband in the leg, then went out into the line of fire and pulled my husband back into the ditch, on his side of the road. In doing so Heinz was wounded in the arm.

'My husband and Heinz were both taken to the same German hospital and while in hospital Heinz was very good to my husband, cadging food and acting as an interpreter.

'Before being liberated by the British, they exchanged addresses. About a year later my husband received a letter from Heinz, and they corresponded for about five years, though eventually we lost touch. However, in 1979, when we were going to attend the 1980 "We Do Remember" celebration which the Dutch gave for the Canadian forces who had helped to liberate Holland, we asked a young German friend to try and find Heinz. He did so and we learned he was living in Gummensbach. I wrote to tell him of our visit to Holland and he and his wife invited us to visit them, which we did. Our German friends, who live in Bielefeld, drove us down, and Heinz and his wife Oola entertained us for two whole days.'

On 16 April the Dutch town of Groningen fell to the Canadians after four days of street fighting. Troops of 1st Canadian Corps were equally successful around the Zyder-Zee, though there was still fighting around Apeldoorn and at Barneveld, where the corps took nearly 9,000 prisoners. By 18 April the 1st Polish Armoured Division, under command of 2nd Canadian Corps, had reached the German border; and by 19 April the Germans in Holland were cooped-up in a pocket on the Ems estuary, and effectively out of the war.

To the east of the Canadian corps the British XXX Corps was pushing on to the Ems, led by the Guards Armoured Division which had crossed the Twente canal on 1 April. Then came a long series of blown bridges over rivers and canals between the Twente and the Ems at Lingen, but the Royal Engineers were now expert at bridge building and the British advance hardly slowed. The Ems was reached in the early morning of 3 April and crossed in the face of fierce opposition, during which Captain Ian Liddell of the Coldstream Guards won the Victoria Cross.

There was more fighting east of the Ems, where the *Grossdeutschland* Training Regiment and elements of the 7th Parachute Division were dug-in at Lingen, but after two days Lingen fell and XXX Corps pressed on towards Cloppenburg.

On 10 April, having largely subdued the German forces in the Ruhr, General Bradley and General Simpson came up to meet Field Marshal Montgomery and General Dempsey of the British 2nd Army, to discuss co-ordinating plans for the next phase of the campaign. Montgomery intended to push on to the Elbe without delay, outflanking Bremen which would be dealt with later by XXX Corps. Bradley agreed that Simpson could protect his own flanks as 9th Army pressed on towards the Elbe further south, and could take over a section of General Dempsey's front when that river was reached. Montgomery's forces were then reinforced by the attachment of General Ridgeway's XVIII Airborne Corps and the advance towards the Baltic continued.

Sergeant Rick Hall of 67 Company RASC supplying the 7th Armoured Division, kept a diary of this time: 'The entries show the lack of reality during April 1945. One minute we were at war in a strange country, the next minute we were bargaining for presents to send home to our wives.

'Friday, 6 April: Osnabruck – civvies looting the joint all day. 7 April: Moved up to village and collected eggs, also weapons from Volksturm. Searched house in company of Russians. Sunday, 8 April: Had a day in company of French and Belgians. Had a look around town in their company. I believe that the town was Solingen. Friday, 13 April: Moved from Solingen. Anchored in birch woods by farmhouse. Surrounded by "Werewolves".

'Saturday, 14 April: Listened to international football. England 6, Scotland 1. Played solo – lost 2s.6d. Tuesday, 17 April: Moved 0700 hrs. Spent day talking to liberated prisoners 11B Fallingbostel. Got mouth organ. A remark by one of the ex-10 Company lads has stayed with me all these years. He spotted me while he was still inside and I was outside the wire. His remark was, "There's that ruddy canteen corporal. The thought of his bloody doughnuts has haunted me every *blankety* night", or words to that effect.

'Wednesday, 18 April: I think that this must have been the day that we took the drums of insecticide down to Belsen, which was located among trees. There were bodies along the sides of some roads through the pine trees. It seems unbelievable that they were rushing to eliminate as many prisoners as possible before they were overrun. Was it dementia or hatred or hoping to remove the evidence?'

That question would not be easily answered. On 12 April the 15th (Scottish) Division reached Celle, where resistance stiffened again as they ran into a mixed force from the scratch Panzer Division 'Clausewitz' outside Uelzen, which fell after hand-to-hand infantry and tank fighting on 15 April. Meanwhile, the British 11th Armoured Division had crossed the Aller near the town of Winsen where, on establishing a bridgehead on the east bank, they were approached by a group of German soldiers asking for a local truce.

This request for a local cease-fire was not due to any particular military necessity or humanitarian impulse, but because of a health hazard. A few miles to the north of Winsen lay a large concentration camp and the Germans wished to hand this camp over to the advancing Allies, because many of the inmates had typhus. The stench from this camp was already drifting in the wind as the 11th Armoured Division captured Winsen and advanced across the tank training grounds at Hohne towards a place called Belsen.

The entrance to Auschwitz

10 The Concentration Camps

'The day the British tanks first appeared, we were
transferred to a new block ... I think to make a good
impression on the British Army. There had been some grass
growing around this block and when the tanks passed through I
was eating my first food for five days; I was eating grass.'

H. O. Le Druillence of Jersey, CI
Belsen Concentration Camp 1945

On 6 April 1945, American troops of General Walton H. Walker's XX Corps liberated the concentration camp at Ordruf near Erfurt. On 11 April the Americans overran the notorious 'Dora', the slave labour camp at Nordhausen in the Hartz Mountains. On the same day troops of the 5th US Infantry Division entered the concentration camp at Buchenwald. On 15 April 1945, troops of the British 11th Armoured Division entered the concentration camp at Belsen.

What the Allied troops discovered in these places shocked the civilized world. At Ordruf more than 3,000 emaciated corpses lay in the bunks or rotted in the lines between the huts. Among the corpses, naked survivors, swarming with lice, clung to what remained of their lives. Ordruf, like the 'Dora' camp at Nordhausen, had supplied slave labour to underground factories for the production of V-weapons – a programme directed by Dr Werner Von Braun, later the architect of the American space programme. Workers at Dora were routinely beaten, hanged for lack of vigour or worked

194

to death ... as long as the V-rockets were produced their lives were expendable.

The capture of Dora was described in the 3rd Armoured Division's war diary:

'NORDHAUSEN was entered on 11 April by Combat Command "B". The enemy offered little opposition in the town itself. Perhaps they feared being connected in some way with the notorious NORDHAUSEN concentration camp near the city. This camp was uncovered in all its depravity by the 3rd Armoured Division and steps were taken to insure that photographic and other evidence was collected before any changes were made. Even the great piles of starved dead were left as found.

'Division medical personnel quickly removed the hundreds of starvation cases to emergency hospitals where they could be cared for. Many of the less severe cases were cared for on the premises while systematic arrangements were made to save as many lives as possible by organizing the facilities of the camp. Medical Officers of the 3rd Armoured remained in charge until relieved as the division moved on.

'North of NORDHAUSEN, at a place called "Dora", the 3rd Armoured uncovered one of the Germans' most extensive and elaborate underground factories. This factory, devoted to the construction of V-1 and V-2 weapons and Junkers airplane motors, as well as extensive experimentation with a super-secret V-3 anti-aircraft weapon, was completely underground. Some of the tunnels were at a depth of six hundred feet and extended for two miles. Here and at the V-2 Assembly plant at KLEINBORDUNGEN, the most able-bodied of the inmates from the NORDHAUSEN Concentration Camp were forced to work at manufacturing and assembling parts. Both of these plants were taken and secured by the 3rd Armoured.' The killing at 'Dora' had continued to the end; six slave workers had been hanged in the factory on March 31.'

Other workers were executed at Dora – for lack of zeal or to encourage the work force – by being strangled on a six-noose gallows; fifty-seven prisoners were once hanged at Dora in a single day. Of the 60,000 slave workers sent to Dora, 40,000 had died by the end of the war, and they were still dying when tanks of the 3rd US Armoured Division rolled into Nordhausen. Only 400 were still alive in the Dora compound, lying in their own excrement, surrounded by corpses, some of them, according to an eyewitness, 'stacked up in heaps, like firewood!'

When the sound of American artillery reached the camp on 5 April 1945, the slaves of Dora were hurriedly evacuated, many to the camp at Belsen. Over a thousand of them did not get that far. Their SS guards marched them into barns at Gardelegen in Northwest Germany and set the barns alight.

Many of the tormentors were far more fortunate, escaping punishment or being spirited away to safety. Werner Von Braun and Arthur Rudolph, the head of production at Dora, were taken to the United States and richly rewarded for their part in the American space programme. Many other Nazi murderers, like Adolf Eichmann and Dr Mengele, the 'Angel of Death' of Auschwitz, escaped to South America or hid for a few years before resuming their lives in Germany and Austria. Other war criminals and murderers were caught by the Allies and a number of concentration camp commandants and guards were tried and executed after the war. Before justice could deal with the killers though, the Allies had to help the victims and this task was immense.

At Belsen, where the camp was formally handed over to the British by the SS Commandant, Joseph Kramer, the troops found 40,000 men, women and children crammed into accommodation built for 8,000. A good number of these people had recently arrived from camps further east, such as Auschwitz and Buchenwald. All were emaciated and starving; many had typhus. Anne Frank, just fifteen and author of the famous diary, had died of typhus in this charnel house three weeks earlier, and the dying continued. No attempt had been made by the Germans either to help the sick or bury the dead until the British guns announced imminent retribution. There were some 10,000 unburied bodies lying about the camp when the British troops arrived, many in such a state of putrefaction that the soldiers had no option but to scoop them into grave pits using bulldozers.

As soon as Belsen was liberated, a hygiene section, a field ambulance and a casualty clearing station of the Royal Army Medical Corps arrived to help the survivors, while men from the Military Police began to round up the SS guards, the men and women who were responsible for all of this. Two of the most notorious of these were the Commandant, Joseph Kramer, who had had ten years' service in a variety of concentration camps and became known as 'the Beast of Belsen', and a twenty-one-year-old woman, Irma Grese, whose career of sadism in the SS had taken her to the women's camps at Ravensbruck and Auschwitz-Birkenau before she arrived at Belsen in January 1945. Grese routinely amused herself by slapping, whipping and clubbing women prisoners, setting a guard dog on those who fell down, forcing sick prisoners to kneel for hours in the snow holding heavy stones in their outstretched hands, and from time to time shooting them dead with an automatic pistol. According to one prisoner, Anita Laskar Wallfisch, who knew Grese in Auschwitz and at Belsen, Grese, though one of the worst, was just one of many.

'She become known because she was young and pretty, well ... prettier than the rest; but she was no worse – and no better – than a lot of the others. Most of the guards were stupid and this job, this power over others, simply went to their heads. Grese was a small-town girl and she joins the SS and gets this smart uniform to wear and shiny boots and then she goes to a camp and there are all these Jews she has heard about and all she has heard about them is true.

'They *are* ugly and they *are* dirty and they don't keep themselves clean. She is too young and too stupid to realize that if you shave someone's head and starve them to skin and bone they don't look pretty, and if you deny them soap and water and make them live in filthy huts running with vermin, they will not be clean. She thinks they are just like that – dirty Jews – and she can do what she likes. And yet ... I can remember in Belsen, maybe the day the British arrived or the day before, she said to me "Perhaps now we can both go home", as if she had suddenly realized we were the same species.'

The wonder is that anybody survived this constant brutality, but Anita Wallfisch survived years in Auschwitz and Belsen: 'I cannot explain Auschwitz to you. It was another world. We were tired, we were dreadfully hungry, we were shaved, we were ugly. You did not think of the future, you think of what is happening to you *now*. You don't think of tomorrow, you think only about *now*. And you learn ... you learn how to avoid punishment, to stay out of trouble. Auschwitz was hopeless, grey, the ground churned into yellow clay which would stick to your shoes – and you were not allowed to have dirty shoes.

'We were not people to them: we were numbers, tattooed numbers. My number was 69388 but at least I was somebody. I played the cello, so I was the girl who played the cello in the orchestra. Is that not bizarre, an orchestra in Auschwitz? The Germans are a very sentimental people you know. They would go to the sidings and send thousands of people to the gas chamber and then come back and ask us to play for them. Dr Mengele and Dr Klein, who was later the doctor at Belsen, were both very fond of music.

'So it helped to be known, to be somebody, not to be just a number. It helped my sister to find me when she arrived in the camp. I had kept a pair of shoes, a sort of tan pigskin, and one day, at home, I spoiled them with a stain – I remember my mother was very cross. Anyway, to improve them I decorated my shoes with little bobbles, but when I arrived in Auschwitz a girl took my shoes away. Then, some time later, my sister arrived and saw this girl wearing them and asked her where she got them. "From the girl in the Camp Orchestra ...", and so my sister found me. My parents were taken away early in the war, to Isbica, and shot into a mass grave ... I do not hate the Germans ... I will not join them in that trap of hating people.'

Joseph Kramer, Irma Grese, Dr Klein and nine other Belsen guards were tried by a British military court at Hameln in November 1945 and executed by hanging in the following month.

At Buchenwald, a large camp near Weimar, the sights which met the shocked American soldiers were almost beyond belief. Naked, rotting corpses lay about in the spring sunshine. In the huts lay more dead and the emaciated living, crawling with vermin, lying in pools of vomit, excrement and urine.

At Buchenwald, aside from the beatings and hangings and the usual torments, the prisoners had to endure the particular sadism of the commandant's wife, Ilse Koch, who earned the soubriquet of 'the Bitch of Buchenwald'. Frau Koch had developed a taste for unusual household ornaments: lampshades made from tattooed human skin. Any prisoner with unusual tattoos was soon marked out for execution, but the rest died in time of brutality and neglect.

When the Americans arrived there was no food, no water, no facilities of any kind at Buchenwald. Nor had there been any need for them. The people who went to the concentration camps of the Third Reich went there to work and die.

Some people, however, did not die. Robert Sheppard was a young English officer in the French Section of the Special Operations Executive (SOE). Taken by the Germans he survived brutal treatment at the hands of the Gestapo and imprisonment in three camps – at Natzweiler, Mauthausen and Dachau – as well as the prison at Frenes near Paris and a holding camp at Neue Bremm near Saarbrucken.

'I was about twenty-one when they picked me up. My codename was "Patrice". When the transport got to Neue Brenne, I was the only Englishman, and an SS corporal ordered me to undress – they were always doing that – gave me a wooden shovel and said, "Englander, Komm." I was put naked into the latrine pit and ordered to shovel it out, though the prisoners were still using it.

'Our contact with the SS was usually slight. Most of the dangerous people were the "Kapos" – the prisoners who did the dirty work for the SS. The SS guards appeared to be the sort of people who would be unsuccessful in any other life.

'People remember the big ones, Belsen, Auschwitz, Dachau, but there were a lot of camps. Dachau had 174 satellite camps, some worse than the main lager; there was one at Allach where 3,000 slave labourers worked for BMW. Natzweiler was dangerous for me as I was sent there for "Nacht und Nebel" treatment – Night and Fog – to be shot or hanged, or quietly disposed of, like a lot of SOE people. Four of our girls in SOE were killed in Natzweiler and another four in Dachau. For me the worst camp was undoubtedly Mauthausen, where I worked in the quarry. Another SOE colleague, Bloom, was killed in the quarry. There were 186 steps from the quarry at Mauthausen and we manhandled rocks up and down all day on a slice of bread, a bowl of weak soup and a slice of sausage if we were lucky. Many men died in the quarry of exhaustion or beatings.

'I don't hate the Germans either; there were plenty of Germans in the camps. I don't think the Germans outside really knew what was going on inside; maybe they knew enough to be frightened, but nothing more.

'How do you survive? Well ... luck. Luck in where you were sent, what shoes you got to wear, in the guards you met. Age helped. A camp was not a place to be too young or too old – you aged fast enough. Health was important. If you were ill or sick or had a chronic illness, like cancer, you were soon killed, or gassed. There were hospitals – *Reiver* – but no treatment. You went in, you recovered or you died. You had to keep clean, for dirt meant lice, and lice brought typhus. There was a saying in the camps, "*Ein Laus, ein Todt*" – "one louse, one dead" – and it was true. I was actually in the *Reiver* at Dachau when a tall SS man said to me, "Your comrades have landed in Normandy but we have thrown them back into the sea." So that was 6 June 1944, and at that news I felt better.'

Ordruf, Belsen and Buchenwald were not the first concentration camps to be discovered by the advancing armies; Germany was littered with these places (see the map on p. 200; which shows only the main camps). On 23 July 1944, Russian troops advancing through Poland had discovered the death camp at Majdanek with the gas chambers and crematoria still intact. The Soviets publicized this discovery and showed this camp to Western journalists, but very few accounts or photographs of Majdanek appeared in the Western press, even though half a million people, mostly Jews and Russians, had been done to death there. Only 1,000 inmates were still alive when the advancing Russian infantry ran in among the huts.

The Western media and politicians tended to dismiss the evidence of Majdanek as either exaggeration or Soviet propaganda, and this view prevailed throughout the summer months of 1944, even when the Soviets overran the death camps at Sobibor, Belzec and Treblinka. These were extermination camps, and having completed the task of exterminating the Jews of Poland, they had been closed down in 1943 – though the slaughter of tens of thousands of people had left evidence the Germans were unable to completely destroy. Then, on 27 January 1945, Soviet troops entered Auschwitz.

Concentration camps fell into various categories. There were death or extermination camps, where the inmates were slaughtered on arrival or soon afterwards. There were labour camps, where they were fed the minimum and worked to death; and experimental camps where 'scientific' and 'medical'

Concentration Camps

experiences were carried out on the hapless prisoners. There were sick camps for those who were to die when the guards decided and not before, and training camps where the SS passed on the techniques of brutality and mass murder. There were even recuperation camps, where Jews were kept in case they were needed as hostages or for exchange or sale.

Many camps combined two or more of these functions. At Neuengamme, a slave labour camp, Dr Heissmeyer performed medical experiments on healthy people, on one occasion injecting twenty-five adults and twenty children with TB bacteria. Dachau, the first of the camps, was mainly used to detain political prisoners but the inmates were also used for experiments by German scientists and doctors, among them a Dr Rascher.

Rascher's experiments included freezing prisoners to death in a cold-water tank to see how long a shot-down Luftwaffe pilot might survive in the Channel; placing prisoners in a decompression tank to test the effects of altitude until their lungs burst; and amputation of limbs – without anaesthetics – letting the victims bleed to death to check the efficiency of coagulant drugs. Dr Rascher's reports regularly concluded: 'The experiment was successful but the patient died.'

Auschwitz, perhaps the worst of the camps, combined most of these rôles – including the last. The guards at Auschwitz were fully trained murderers and had honed their skills to a fine art – in three years they murdered well over a million people; some estimates give the total at over four million.

Dr Ada Bimko gave an account of Auschwitz at Kramer's trial in 1945: 'I am aged 32 and am a Jewess of Polish nationality. I am a qualified Doctor of Medicine. I was arrested in August 1943 because I was a Jewess and I was taken to Auschwitz where I worked as a doctor. I set out hereafter what I observed myself with regard to the mass exterminations of prisoners and I will name the persons, each of whom individually selected persons for extermination. I have examined the records of the numbers cremated and I say that the records show that about 4,000,000 persons were cremated at the camp. I say that from my own observation I have no doubt that at least this number were exterminated.

'The selections of persons to be exterminated were made in three ways: (1) on arrival, (2) on selection parades held two or three times a week on average, (3) in hospitals.

'For example, I arrived in a batch of 5,000 persons. SS Doctor Rohde, SS woman Drechsler and SS man Tauber were waiting at the station. They made a selection at once. First of all the children and the old people were picked out, then those who looked ill, and after that anyone was picked out until 4,500 people had been selected. These went to the gas chamber and were never seen again.

'In this way died my father, my mother, my brother, my husband and my son aged six. My sister was not selected then but she was selected and killed at a later date. I have been present at many other station selections where the same procedure was adopted. The number selected was always a round figure, which might amount to as many as 10,000 persons on one day.

'Persons were also selected for execution from those detained in hospital. The patients were made to run naked past the selectors and those who could not run quickly or looked ill or poorly developed, or in the case of women, were ugly, were picked out by the selectors. There were often as many as 4,000 patients in hospital at a time, and I have known as many as 1,000 taken from hospital and never less than 500. I particularly remember 1 December 1943, when there were 4,124 women patients in hospital. There was an outbreak of typhus and 4,000 patients exactly were sent to the gas chamber. The selectors on this occasion were Doctors Tilot, Klein and SS man Tauber and SS women Mandel, Drechsler and Brandel.

'Selections were also made at roll-calls in the camp as and when desired by the SS when sick-looking people and old persons were picked out. Sometimes, during the winter months, the women were compelled to remove all their clothing whilst SS selectors walked round the ranks and chose individuals who were thin or ill. At other times they had to hold out their hands, and those wearing bandages or having visible wounds were chosen. On other occasions a selection of the parade, without any sorting, were detailed for the gas chamber.

'Whilst at Auschwitz I saw SS male nurses Heine and Stibitz inject petrol into women patients. All five of these died within three to ten minutes. Though I have not seen operations on women done for experimental purposes, I have been informed that such operations were carried out. Thus, experiments were made with regard to sterilization and artificial impregnation. I myself spoke to a women who said she had been fertilized in this way.

'In August 1943 I saw SS man Tauber knock down a girl who arrived late at roll-call, beat her and kick her and stand on her stomach for ten minutes until she died.

'In the Birkenau section of Auschwitz Camp there were five brick buildings all similar in appearance. These were different from the other buildings in the camp. They were commonly known by all the prisoners as crematoria. I saw the condemned persons driven to these buildings in lorries. I did not see the persons actually enter the buildings as it was not possible to get sufficiently close. Both men and women were in the parties taken to these buildings. The condemned women were ordered to undress and leave their clothes behind in Block 25, and sometimes they undressed at the gas chamber. Occasionally they were allowed to take blankets with them to the gas chamber, but this depended on the SS man in charge. The crematorium and gas chambers were in an area of the camp known as Brzezinki.

'One day in August 1944 I was able to visit one of these buildings. The visit was arranged with an SS *Unterscharführer* who agreed to show me around. If anyone stopped us we agreed to say that our visit was in order to fetch blankets. The SS man took me in through a door and inside we met a Polish prisoner named Josef Goldberg who comes from my home town. He was employed in this building. The door through which we entered the building led into an undressing room, for there were hooks on the walls. This was on the ground floor. From this room there was another door into another room which appeared to be a shower-bath room. I noticed that there were five or six rows of spray fittings in the roof, with about twenty sprays to each row. The floor, walls and ceilings were made of concrete. The room was about 48 ft square and 10 ft high. There were no drains; if the water came through the sprays it could not drain away. With the floor being on the same level as the other rooms, the water would flood right through the building. The SS man told me that this room was the gas chamber.

'Walking through the gas chamber we went through another door which led into a passage pointing directly ahead. There were two rails leading from the door of the gas chamber and on these two rails was a flat-topped wagon. The SS man told me that the wagon was used to take corpses from the gas chamber to the crematorium at the other end of the passage.

'We then walked back through the gas chamber and undressing room to the door through which we had entered the building. Near this door were some stairs. We went up these stairs and came to a room above the gas chamber. Across this room were two pipes, each about three inches thick. The SS man told me that the pipes, which were in the floor, were connected to the spray fittings in the gas chamber below. In a corner of the room were two large cylinders, but I did not notice whether these cylinders were connected to the pipes. The SS man told me that the cylinders contained the gas which passed through the pipes into the gas chamber.

'With reference to the gas chamber, there were also hooks on the walls in this room. The SS man told me that they were there to hang towels on, as condemned prisoners were led to believe that it was a shower room, and were given towels to deceive them.'

The 67,000 surviving inmates of Auschwitz had been marched away to the west ten days before the Russians arrived, many destined for the camp at Belsen. The crematoria had been dynamited and the staff records of the German industrial giant, I. G. Farben, which had used slave labour from Auschwitz, had been carefully burned. Dr Mengele, one of the doctors who had 'selected' those suitable for work and those only fit to be gassed, had fled, taking with him the records of his 'experiments'. Many of these 'experiments' had been perpetrated on children, especially twins, usually without anaesthetic. Between experiments, Mengele kept these children in cages, like laboratory animals.

In spite of all their efforts, years of systematic murder by the SS could not be entirely concealed. In the camp storerooms the Russian troops discovered 340,000 men's suits, 836,000 women's coats and heaps of sacks containing tons of human hair ... So what had happened to these people? They had been gassed and cremated by the million, as part of a deliberate policy approved by the German Reich.

The systematic destruction of 'unwanted' people was part of the creed of the German Führer, Adolf Hitler. Hitler had laid out his political aims and intentions quite clearly in his book *Mein Kampf*, written during his brief stay in prison in 1925. In this dreary work the future Führer described '... the sacred mission of the German people', which, according to Hitler was 'to establish the superiority of the Aryan race' over the lower orders, the *untermenschen*. These included any Slavs, Poles, the Russians, gypsies, the mentally feeble, homosexuals ... anyone who did not fit the blond, blue-eyed, Nordic norm idealized by the Führer must be swept away. Most of all, the future glory, even the survival, of the 'Aryan race' depended on the destruction of the Jews.

Adolf Hitler came to power as Chancellor of Germany in January 1933. In March 1933 the Reichstag, the German parliament, granted Hitler dictatorial powers. His war against the Jews began just ten days later, on 1 April 1933, and was cruelly effective. In 1933 there were some 600,000 Jews in Germany. Sixty years later, in 1993, there are about 40,000. By the time the war ended, in May 1945, six million Jews, two-thirds of all European Jewry, had been killed by the SS and their adherents.

Two points should be made about this act of genocide. Firstly, this enthusiasm for racial slaughter was not directed only at the Jews. Millions of other people passed through the camps and into the gas chambers. The Jews stand out because of their numbers, because of the peculiar savagery with which they were hounded, because the philosophy invented to justify their destruction – though devised by madmen – was accepted by normal people, and because the aim of this philosophy was their total extinction. Neither were all, nor even a majority, of the German people party to this policy; there were exceptions, as Ben Halfgodt, a Jew from Poland, recalls:

'Of course there were decent guards, decent Germans, even in the camps. If there had been no decent guards, none of us would have survived. There were also those who let us survive because they could make money by sending Jews out to work, or selling our labour to help the German war effort. The Jews of the ghetto at Lodz lasted longer than most because they were useful. Biebow, the German Commandant of Lodz, was getting six marks per Jew, per day, from the Wehrmacht for providing Jewish labour. He spent 80 pfennigs per day per Jew on food, so he was making a profit of 5 marks 20 per day on every Jew; that was good money. Of course the Jews starved to death in the end, and Biebow was tried and hanged for it in Poland after the war.'

The war against the Jews could not have been maintained without the co-operation of many other nations allied to the Reich. This war was not conducted only by the Totenkopf – Death's Head – members of the SS, the usual alibi offered in defence of the German people. The Austrians, who were – and remain – notoriously anti-Semitic, attacked their Jewish fellow citizens of Vienna with enthusiasm and ferocity after the Anschluss in 1938. Hitler was an Austrian, as were a significantly large proportion of the concentration camp staff. It is notable that although the Austrians provided only about 10 percent of the Reich's soldiers, these soldiers committed a very high percentage of all recorded war crimes.

The Latvians, Lithuanians and Hungarians were notably brutal towards their Jewish populations, and many served as 'trusties' – or 'Kapos' – in the camps. The Poles continued to murder Jewish refugees even after the war was over. The French police actively participated in rounding up French Jews and shipping them through the camp at Drancy just north of Paris, to the camp at Auschwitz in Poland, or the women's camp at Ravensbruck, some miles north of Berlin. The only Axis or occupied nations which emerged with any real credit from the Holocaust were Denmark, Italy and Finland. Among the defeated nations, Denmark alone flatly refused to implement the anti-Jewish Nuremberg Laws. When Danish Jews were ordered to mark their clothes with the yellow Star of David, the King of Denmark put one on his uniform; within hours most of the citizens of Copenhagen had followed his example. Working together, the people of Denmark saved their Jewish fellow citizens and only fifty Danish Jews died in the concentration camps.

Among the Axis Powers, Italy alone showed no enthusiasm for anti-Semitic action. Finland, an ally of Germany for much of the war, also declined to deport or act against their Jews. Hitler finally persuaded Mussolini to pass anti-Jewish laws but the Italians showed no willingness to implement them – for 'an Italian Jew is first and foremost an Italian citizen'. While Mussolini was in power, no Italian Jews were deported to the camps, but after he fell the German garrisons and the SS swiftly began to implement Hitler's policies. Some 8,000 of Italy's 40,000 Jews were sent to the death camps where most of them died by the end of the war. The Finns, when pressed to deal with their 'Jewish problem', replied briefly that there was no problem, and their Jews were left in peace.

Though he loathed the Jews, Hitler did not plan their destruction immediately on taking power in 1933. His original intention was to remove the Jews from Germany by making it impossible for them to live or work within the expanding frontiers of the Reich.

The first steps towards this end were the 'Nuremberg Laws' passed in September 1935. These codified what was already happening – the removal of Jews from German public life. The Nuremberg Laws condoned the dismissal of Jews from posts as newspaper editors or university lecturers, and extended these acts to cover racial purity and citizenship. Sexual relations and marriage between Jews and Aryans was forbidden. German women could not work in Jewish firms or homes. Jews could not fly the German flag. Jews could not be citizens of Germany. From September

1935, German Jews were simply 'subjects of the state', nothing more. Jews had no rights of any kind in the new Germany.

The laws were implemented by German employers, religious leaders, university chancellors and professional associations. They were later extended to cover gypsies and other '*untermenschen*' throughout the German Reich and in the territories conquered by the German Army from 1939 to 1943.

These laws, and the blind eye turned by the German people to the brutality meeted out daily to Jews in the streets of Germany, soon had the desired effect. Every German Jew who could do so applied to leave the Reich, and between 1935 and the outbreak of war in 1939, two-thirds of all German Jews emigrated. One of these was Walter Lowenstein.

'I had a good business in Weisbaden, and many friends, not all of them Jews by any means. Life got very difficult from 1933, but I loved the town and, after all I, too, was a German, so I did not want to leave. Then, one night a friend of mine – and a member of the Nazi Party – came to my house and said, "Walter, they are going to arrest you in the morning."

'That night I left for Holland. I wanted to go to England, but the British were not accepting Jews; this was 1938. The Hitler people had a scheme to get rid of the Jews, so that for every day you travelled away from the Reich you were paid three marks. I decided to go as far as I could, maybe to New Zealand, but in the end I went to Chile. Life there was hard because most of the businesses were run by British or German people. The British would not employ me because I was German and the Germans would not hire me because I was a Jew. This was good for me because I started to work for myself and I did well. I got most of my family out of Germany, but those of my friends who remained in Weisbaden all went to Auschwitz. You can see their empty graves in the Jewish cemetery in Weisbaden – their bodies are in the dust of Poland.'

So, by one means or another, Hitler got rid of the German Jews. Those who could afford to, or were helped by Jewish agencies, fled to safety beyond the seas. Those who remained lived in fear or were arrested and sent to camps like Dachau, the first of the concentration camps, opened on 20 March 1933. Many German Jews committed suicide, worn out by fear, brutal treatment, constant insults, hopelessness, but by one means or another, Germany began to be '*Judenrein*' – Jew free.

In March 1938 came the annexation of Austria. Austria has since presented itself as the first victim of Nazism, but the photographs and newsreels of Viennese crowds cheering the arrival of Hitler's troops and swiftly brutalizing their Jewish fellow citizens gives the lie to this claim. With Austria, Hitler acquired both an ally and a problem, for Austria contained 200,000 Jews. The Führer's rapidly emptying pool of German Jews had been replenished at a stroke.

The immediate answer was to establish a concentration camp at Mauthausen on the Danube, near the pleasant town of Linz, and turn the Austrians loose on their native Jews, but the 'Jewish Problem' went on growing. As the Germans occupied Czechoslovakia, Poland, France, Belgium, Holland and the rest of Western Europe, so they acquired more Jews. France had 350,000 Jews, Belgium 66,000, Holland 140,000. When the Germans overran Poland in 1939 – and with it another two million Jews – the task of dispersing the Jews was clearly becoming impossible. Moreover, the western Jews were generally well integrated with the local population. To cut them out from the mass would take a little time and cunning. With the Jewish population of Poland, where anti-Semitism was already rife and the Jews lived in their own communities, the Germans could be far less subtle.

Ben Halfgodt again: 'In September 1939 I was not quite ten and living in the town of Piotrkow, near Lodz, with my mother, father and two younger sisters – Mala who was then eight and Lusia who was five. Piotrkow was a town of about 55,000 people, and contained about 15,000 Jews.

'The Germans arrived in our town on 5 September. The first thing they did was to set fire to the Jewish houses and shoot those who ran out. They also burned the sacred books from the synagogue and Jews with beards were attacked, their beards cut or burned off. Jewish bank accounts were blocked and the Germans then imposed a fine, levied on the entire Jewish community, taking twenty-five hostages until the money was handed over. How do you raise money when everything has been taken away? Jewish shops were, of course, looted and there were shortages of food. Soon afterwards we were ordered into a ghetto, the first ghetto set up in Poland.

'Into a poor part of the town, which had held maybe 3,500 people before the war, they crammed all 15,000 Jews. These houses were not good. They had no electricity and little sanitation, and we were subjected to constant raids by the SS who came at night to take people away for forced labour. Before long there were 28,000 Jews in our ghetto. The poor suffered most, and those who arrived late who were already destitute. We all had to wear an armband with the Star of David on it, and from the age of fifteen people were rounded up for forced labour.'

German troops invading eastern Poland and Russian in 1941 were accompanied by squads of SS troops and Gestapo called *Einsatzgruppe*, or Special Section Squads. The *Einsatzgruppen*'s business was murder, and their victims were Jews. After the German Army had overcome any resistance and occupied a town, an *Einsatzgruppe* then moved in. All the Jews would be rounded up, taken out to a forest nearby, ordered to dig a large grave, stripped of their clothing and shot. Over the weeks, as the Germans advanced, the effect was like that of a large broom, sweeping the

Jews away by the thousand. To give one example, at Piryatin in the Ukraine on 6 April 1940, one *Einsatzgruppe* killed 1,600 old men, women and children in six hours, shooting even babies in the back of the neck. The work was over by 5 p.m., after which the Germans got drunk.

Ben Halfgodt remembers this time: 'In 1941 a thousand of the most able-bodied men were sent to the river Bug, which was the new border with Russia. We were living now in what was called the "Warthegau" in western Poland – the part of Poland that had been absorbed into the German Reich. The men who were taken away to the Bug worked all day on a ration of 500 calories. You cannot work and live long on that but there were others who fared worse; it was better than in the Warsaw ghetto where the daily ration was 185 calories, and 100,000 people died of starvation.

'The worst of it was the constant round-ups, constant raids, taking people from the ghetto for work parties ... anything to make life even more difficult for us. I was eleven, so I was not taken for work parties, but children of fourteen were. My father, who was in his thirties, would hide on the roof at night when we heard the commotion below that told us the SS had come into the house and were dragging people away. We lived on the third floor and he had time to escape onto the roof before they reached our room.'

During the Russian campaign of 1941–2, some 3,000 Germans served in the *Einsatzgruppen*. There is no evidence that these men were psychopaths. Indeed, a substantial number seemed to be drawn from the middle and professional classes; all the officers and many of the NCOs had university degrees. This may have been part of the reason why, by the spring of 1942, the senior German officers charged with overseeing the work of the *Einsatzgruppe* had to report problems in the ranks.

Murdering men, women, children, babies, day after day is not to everyone's taste. There were reports of heavy drinking and disorder in the *Einsatzgruppe*, of failure to kill victims efficiently, of refusing to continue the slaughter, even of suicide. The task of shooting tens of thousands of Jews was having an adverse effect on 'pure Aryan' men, and the accepted execution method, a bullet in the nape of the neck, was failing to make any appreciable dent in the problem. If Poland and the other eastern territories were to become '*Judenrein*', fresh methods would have to be found. The Germans therefore did what anyone would do when confronted with a management problem: they set up a committee.

The committee to organize the Final Solution – the extirpation of European Jewry – met in a villa at Wannsee, a suburb of Berlin, on 20 January 1942. The 'Wannsee Conference' of 1942 was called by the head of the Main Office of Reich Security (RSHA), SS General Reinhard Heydrich. Also present was SS Lt-General Heinrich Muller, head of the

Gestapo and a dozen others led by SS Lt-Colonel Adolf Eichmann, then head of the Gestapo office handling Jewish Affairs. Also present were representatives from the German Foreign Office, the department of justice, the SS, the police and the Gauleiter of Poland. These were not uneducated brutes: more than half of those present at the Wannsee Conference held doctorates from German universities. So, with coffee and notepads at their elbows, these senior representatives of the German Reich sat down to discuss the systematic destruction of a whole race of people.

Various solutions were discussed, starting with the slow but sure method – the sterilizing of all Jewish males. It was pointed out that the Jew takes his race from the mother, so clearly Jewish women must be sterilized as well or a more practical method had to be found. These wide-ranging talks moved on to shooting, gassing, starvation and forced labour. The experiments with Zyklon-B gas at Auschwitz were reported to be going well, and if gas chambers and crematoria could be provided and installed in camps, the pace of the solution could be stepped up. The only real worry was transport. There were Jews all over the Reich and the task of shipping them and other undesirables to the death camps was a vast logistical problem, but this task was entrusted to Lt-Colonel Adolf Eichmann. With the slaughter of the Jews thus organized and entrusted to a senior officer, the delegates to the Wannsee Conference called for brandy and cigars.

The decision of the Wannsee Conference to destroy the Jews of Europe were soon put into effect, as Ben Halfgodt recalls: 'From January 1942 rumours became more insistent that deportations were going to take place to settle us in the east. There was also talk of people being taken away and gassed. This was very difficult to believe, but there was nothing we could do about it; we had been abandoned. The Poles, at best, were not prepared to help. Some did, of course, but many more were prepared to denounce Jews living outside the ghetto. Many Jews did go out to bring in food – my father among them – otherwise we would have starved.

'In September 1942 we heard of towns from which Jews had been deported, and the rumours grew that our town would soon be among them. Only those who worked for the administration, in the Jewish police or the sanitary police, or those who worked in a factory run for the benefit of the Germans, would be allowed to remain. We had a glass factory and a woodworking factory in Piotrkow and by 1942 some 600–700 Jews worked there; some even earned money and could buy food.

'In September 1942 my family planned that we would go into hiding among non-Jews. My two sisters were given away to non-Jews, but I was now twelve and I told my father I wanted to work in the glass factory and I finally got a permit to work on 12 August 1942.

'For the next two months we lived under the Sword of Damocles. We knew the deportations were coming but we did not know what to do. People were making hiding places or getting ready to flee. Then we heard that the Jews of Warsaw had been liquidated. The deportation to Treblinka from Warsaw started on 21 July, and by 10 September 310,000 had gone to the gas chambers. It was a frightening time when we heard of this.

'I worked on the night shift at the factory. I reported in the evening and we were marched to work, where we were handed over to a foreman. On the first day I worked with a party of Poles – glassblowers – and I had to collect the liquid glass for them in wooden moulds. Every time I made a mistake they would kick me in the head, and I got kicked and beaten all the time. It was not what I expected, and it was Poles who did this, not Germans.

'On 7 October 1942 they said the deportations would begin the next day, but nothing happened. Then they said it would be the next day, and then the one after that. On the night of the 14th I went to work as usual. My mother and father were now outside the ghetto and I worked all night; in the morning, around 8 o'clock – I was now twelve years old, remember – we left work, were counted outside and about to march back to the ghetto when someone from the factory came and stopped us, and I knew the deportations had started. It took seven days to clear our ghetto of 22,000 Jews. All of them were sent to Treblinka, and within a week all had been gassed.

'My mother and sisters went into hiding, and what survived of the ghetto, the 'legal Jews', were moved into a small ghetto of two half-streets. There were only 2,200 'legal Jews' who had work; but there were more Jews in hiding, or outside the ghetto. Then the Germans offered an amnesty to the 'illegals'. They said if they would come out they would give them ration cards; but this was a false amnesty. Five hundred and twenty people gave themselves up, including my mother and sister Lusia, who was then seven. All 520, including my mother and my sister, were marched into the woods outside the town and shot on 20 December 1942.'

One question remains largely unanswered to this day: Did the German people know about the camps and what was done to the Jews and others in these places? Dr P. J. Dobias, a prisoner in the camp at Mauthausen, near Vienna, has no doubts on this score.

'Did they know? Of course they knew. How could they not know? Look, you think there were just a few camps? Dachau, Bergen-Belsen, Mauthausen, Buchenwald ... in Germany and Austria. I don't speak now of the camps in Poland or the east. There were many more camps in Germany, maybe thirty big ones and scores of smaller ones. Dachau had more than 140 work camps in the surrounding Bavarian countryside, all full of prisoners. Nearly every large town had a concentration camp, and every camp had satellite camps round about. They, the Germans, now say they did not know because they are ashamed ... and so they should be.

'Mauthausen was a small camp, and not only for Jews – though there were many Jews there – but it was mostly a political camp. There were Spaniards there, Republicans picked up in France after the Occupation. At any one time there were 20,000 prisoners in Mauthausen and during the war more than 160,000 prisoners were murdered there or died of overwork in the quarry or of brutal ill-treatment. The local people saw us being herded to work every day and they saw our condition. They could – they must have – smelt the smoke from the bodies burned in the crematorium, and at Mauthausen there was a small town nearby of maybe 4,000–5,000 people. The citizens saw us every day, they saw the transports coming in. Of course they knew, and so did most of the rest of the Austrians.'

A typical day in a concentration camp is described in the records of Neuengamme, a camp near Hamburg: 'In summer reveille was at 4.30 a.m. After washing, a frugal breakfast and bed making, to which the SS attached great importance, the inmates assembled for roll-call. Work began at 6 a.m. whatever the weather, and continued with only an hour's break until 6 p.m. or dark.

'On return to camp there was another roll-call. This could take up to two hours to complete and only then were the prisoners fed, though the roll-call was usually followed by the meting out of punishment, e.g., flogging at the whipping block. Flogging – twenty-five strokes with a whip or rod on the bare buttocks – was frequently administered. Other punishments included beatings, solitary confinement, transfer to a penal company or hangings from a stake. The Gestapo used Neuengamme for executions and more than 2,000 people were shot there, apart from those who were often driven beyond the trip wires by the SS, when they would be shot by the guards.'

Prem Dobias saw this last activity at Mauthausen: 'One cold, rainy day in the late fall of 1942, I was working with a group of other prisoners in the granite quarry in the camp at Mauthausen near Linz in Austria. We were all soaked with rain, shivering, but most of all, hungry ... very hungry.

'I had just been transferred to a Kommando where I did not have to load heavy rocks into wagons, but I had to shovel earth. While working I looked with envy at a farmhouse, which was partly hidden by a hill. There lay freedom, a home with a roof to protect people from rain, but most of all there was food, and it looked so close. There was a little hill, separated only by no-man's land, where SS guards in high towers with machine-guns watched that strip of land which separated the quarry from freedom.

'During the early afternoon two SS guards walked towards our Kommando. We watched them coming with apprehension. When they reached our group we took off our soaked caps and stood to attention, according to camp regulations, but the guards appeared friendly.

'One of them told us that they were looking for ten prisoners to form a special Kommando. Such prisoners would have to know German well, would have to be experienced farm hands, and they would have to know how to feed pigs. They would start working right away and go from the camp daily to "that farmhouse", and they pointed to the farm on the hill.

'The fact that I had never fed a pig in my life seemed unimportant. I wanted that job. I stepped forward and said I was born on a farm and all I had done for a living was to feed pigs. I was not the only one. Suddenly every man in our Kommando knew how to feed pigs, but not all of them knew German, and I was persistent. Finally, one guard chose a dozen men and when our small group was assembled, the guards chased the remaining prisoners back to work.

'We were ready to go when the other guard remarked that his companion had too many. They counted us, then looked us over carefully and I was pushed out of the line with another prisoner, a Spaniard. I started to plead with the guard, but I was silenced with a kick.

' "*Reichts um, ohne Tritt, Marsch!*" ("Right face, March!") was the order, and the lucky ones were on their way towards the farm. I never thought I was capable of such envy as I watched them march away. The group reached the meadow separating the quarry from the farm grounds with the guards a considerable distance behind the group, and I had turned back to work when I heard the sound of machine-gun fire.

'The whole trick dawned on me. As soon as the group of "pig feeders" crossed the border between the watch towers they were shot down. The official cause of death would be declared, as with similar shootings, as "*Auf der Flucht erschossen*" – shot while attempting to escape.

'I leaned on my shovel and looked in the direction of the bodies of our former fellow prisoners who were among us only a few minutes ago. I could so easily have been one of them. The SS guards who had selected the volunteers were now returning. When they reached our Kommando we stood to attention, our dripping caps in our clenched fists. "Who among you knows how to feed pigs?" asked one of the guards, and both of them were laughing while we stood there in the rain.'

The concentration camps were organized on a continent-wide system, and thousands of people were needed to make it work. Even if what went on behind the wire was cloaked in mystery, the endless 'transports' – those long, clanking files of cattle trucks, crammed with victims, stinking of human waste and dead bodies – could hardly pass unnoticed as they trundled across Germany through the towns and marshalling yards to the camps. Apart from simple observation, the staff of the German railway system, the Reichsbahn, organized the transport for the SS and made a good profit from this trade in human misery.

The Reichsbahn charged the SS four pfennigs per kilometre for every prisoner transported to the camps. Children under ten were transported in cattle trucks, without food or water, often for days, at half price. Discounts were allowed for groups of more than 400 people. Tickets for the guards were paid for in advance, and according to the United States Holocaust Museum, '... *railway employees used the same forms to send Jews to Auschwitz as they did to send tourists on vacation.*'

Ben Halfgodt was 'transported' to Buchenwald in 1944. 'After my mother and sister were killed, I was left behind with my father and my elder sister. The first months of 1943 were a terrible time. People were being killed by the SS for no reason at all. A man clearing a house dropped a lamp, and an SS man went into the house and shot him. A Jewish policeman was helping his mother across the road and they shot him. My uncle and other relatives were taken and shot ... it was a constant nightmare. Finally, in April/May 1943, they decided to liquidate what was left of our ghetto, the 1,600 or so who were left – though my father, my elder sister and my three-year-old cousin Hania worked in the woodworking factory until November 1944.

'There was a small camp within the precincts of the woodworking factory at Piotrkow, and we lived there while working in the factory, but in November 1944 the Russians were getting near and they decided to deport us. I was now fifteen. My father and I were sent to the camp at Buchenwald, while my sister and her cousin were sent to the women's camp at Ravensbruck, north of Berlin. We were transported to Buchenwald in December in cattle trucks. It took five days. It was very cold but when you cram a hundred people into a cattle truck meant for forty, the crush keeps you warm.

'In comparison with the other camp I went to later, Buchenwald was not too bad, and at first I had the company of my father. On our first day in the camp he vanished from the roll-call and came back to hand me two loaves of bread. As a result, they did not allow us to be together in Buchenwald and we were separated. This was a dreadful moment in my life.

'My father was a very wonderful person; he took a lot of risks and he could not be subdued. He always took his life in his hands. He went into the woods where my mother was shot and found the clothing of the people, and items that the Germans had not taken away. He brought back our photographs. When we were in the ghetto he would go out and get food, though my mother begged him not to. She said, "I would rather be hungry and have you alive than you take these risks", but he said, "I married you

213

to look after you and the children and that is what I will do," and he always did.'

There is no need to continue with this litany but there are plenty of people who say that none of this ever happened. There were no concentration camps, no cattle-truck transports crammed with victims, no mass executions, no crematoria or gas chambers, no Wannsee Conference, no Final Solution. That people can say this today should come as no surprise.

In 1945 Sidney Bernstein was a war-photographer with the British 2nd Army in Germany. 'When we entered the camps at Belsen and elsewhere – there were plenty of them – it felt wrong to take pictures. You wanted to vomit or run away or try to help, but I kept on filming, partly because it was my job to record all this, but mostly because, as a realist – and a Jew – I knew that one day, maybe in ten years or twenty or fifty, people would start to say, "None of this ever happened."'

That thought occurred to others at the time. Many Allied commanders ordered their men to round up German civilians from nearby towns and bring them to the camps, to see what had happened, to help the survivors, to bury the dead. Having seen the sights at Buchenwald some Germans went home and killed themselves.

Having viewed the camp at Ordruf, where even the tough General Patton vomited at the sights, General Eisenhower ordered that all US troops in the vicinity should be given a chance to see the camp. 'They sometimes wonder what they are fighting for', he said. 'This will show them what they are fighting against.'

Marcus Willard of 12th Infantry Regiment, 4th US Division, remembers some concentration camp survivors. 'It was in April 1945 and we were parked in a secondary road near Bad Tolz, having coffee and doughnuts, when this group came along in clogs, wearing black and white striped clothes, looking starved. We passed them a box of doughnuts but in the rush the bottom dropped out and the doughnuts fell into a puddle of dirty water. No matter. They pounced on the doughnuts and in seconds the doughnuts, water and mud had been consumed by those poor starving people. I was nineteen when I saw that and I won't ever forget it.'

Ben Halfgodt remembers how his war ended. 'We were working with German women in a weapons factory, making *panzerfausts*. By April 1945 the German women were becoming very depressed; they were worried that they were going to be raped by the beastly Russians. For the first time they were worried that they might become the victims in this war. We all knew the end was coming and the prisoners were sent away. We were put into cattle trucks and shunted from pillar to post for days, until we arrived on 20 April 1945 – Hitler's birthday – in the camp at Theresienstadt, north of

Prague. We were the first to arrive from Buchenwald, but more arrived from other camps, exhausted, emaciated, in a terrible state. At least we did not go out to work any more and we could sleep. Finally, on 8 May, rested but famished, we were liberated by the Russians. I was then fifteen and weighed 50 kilos, about 110 lbs.

'The Russians were very good to us; they brought food and told us we could do what we liked. A lot of people took revenge. Those guards who were caught were beaten to death, either by us or by the Czechs. The Czechs took other Germans and drowned them in the river. That is how my time in the camps ended, but my father was killed a few days before the war ended, in a camp called Buchau.'

Colonel Richard Siebel was in charge of the group that liberated the camp at Mauthausen. 'On 5 May 1945 we dispatched a patrol from Combat Command 'B', of the 11th Armoured Division, to find any German troops in the area or to make contact with the Russians, since we had been halted due to the International Restraining Line.

'Our headquarters received a message from the patrol that they had discovered what appeared to be a large camp or jail. They briefly described what they observed and were told to return at once in order to provide a more detailed report. Upon their return, they brought with them one of the prisoners, a United States naval lieutenant by the name of Jack H. Taylor. Lieutenant Taylor gave us detailed information about the camp. I returned to the camp with a reinforced patrol to make an inspection, and report on the number and condition of the prisoners. Upon my return I made a telephone report to Division Headquarters. A short time later a message was received from General Dager that I was to return to Mauthausen with a number of troops and all medical assistance necessary and take command.

'We returned to the camp in the late afternoon of 5 May 1945. The camp was bedlam, prisoners running all over in utter confusion. On entering the headquarters we found a Russian major, a former prisoner, seated at the commandant's desk. He stated that he was in command of the camp and had established a tribunal for the execution of certain "Kapos". After considerable explanation that the Americans were now in command, he still insisted that the Russian prisoners were in command and refused to leave.

'It was necessary to point a pistol at him and escort him and his followers to the Russian compound. It was getting towards dusk and with our available troops the task of getting the people back into the main compound seemed almost impossible. Here were thousands of people who had been starved, beaten and cruelly tortured, suddenly freed. However, they had no food, electricity, clothing or sanitation. The tension that existed was unbelievable and erupted the next day with a riot in which four "Kapos" were executed, having their throats cut by the prisoners.

215

'We segregated the entire population of the camp by nationality and housed them accordingly. At this time all the weapons – knives, rifles and grenades – which they had acquired from the armoury before our arrival were collected and destroyed.

'After this action we were able to bring order to the camp and make a survey of the people and physical equipment. It was found there were approximately 18,000 prisoners representing twenty nations. The task then was to dispose of approximately 700 bodies by establishing a cemetery in the sports platz.

'Immediate action had to be taken to save the remaining prisoners, as we had to locate food, establish a water supply, sanitation, electricity, medical assistance and other basic items. We located German warehouses with dehydrated vegetables, found a German potato storage facility, and were able to use a crop of oats for the making of bread. We butchered horses from the surrounding area and took milk from the farms for the prisoners. At the beginning many prisoners' digestive systems were so debilitated or sensitive that any type of food made them sick.

'We brought in mobile hospitals with the necessary medical personnel to render aid to those prisoners who were dying or ill. The original food we gave the prisoners was weak potato soup and a small piece of oat bread. This was done in order to prevent their systems from going into shock by feeding them too much or too rich food. Gradually the diet was increased, the soup thickened, larger slices of bread being given, and eventually their diets were supplemented with vegetables and meat. Despite the valiant efforts of our medical personnel, approximately 1,500 of the prisoners were beyond help and eventually died. They, too, were buried in consecrated graves dug on the sports platz.

'In order to facilitate the running of the camp, several hundred Wehrmacht soldiers (not SS) were brought to assist in the reconstruction and operation of the camp. These were POWs and were treated as such, and it should be noted that many of them appeared appalled or stunned by what they observed. Their co-operation greatly assisted in the operation of the camp. On one occasion a squad of German prisoners was set upon by the Mauthausen prisoners, an understandable response when one considers the horrible torturings and sufferings the Mauthausen prisoners sustained at the hands of the SS. It was only after the threat of force that the Mauthausen prisoners withdrew and the Germans were allowed to work unmolested.

'During our stay we had restored order, established medical assistance, provided food, buried approximately 2,000 people in consecrated graves, and repatriated approximately 13,000 people to their homelands.

'The commandant, who was later shot by American soldiers while attempting to escape, denied any wrongdoing, and to his death stated that he had never hurt anyone. The crematoria did exist as I personally viewed them. I saw the courtyard immediately to the right of the front gate to the prison where prisoners would be sprayed with fire hoses in winter and left to die of exposure. I viewed the gas chamber where people were packed in so tightly they couldn't move and little children were thrown on top of their heads before they were gassed.

'I saw the dissection room and the cooling room where the bodies were stacked like bundles of wood awaiting dissection or cremation. I viewed the private execution room where prisoners were hanged or shot by order of the commandant and learned from a prisoner that an American lieutenant had been executed by the commandant with a shot in the back of the head.

'I saw the electric fences where prisoners who could no longer endure the suffering threw themselves for a swift death. I saw the bunk-beds in the barracks, bunks made for one man, where emaciated prisoners could sleep three to a bed. I saw the people and what had been done to them and know the ways in which they had been mistreated.

'Mauthausen did exist. The world must not be allowed to forget the depths to which mankind can sink, lest it should happen again.'

Martha Gelhorn, an American war correspondent, was in Dachau when the war ended. 'Dachau seemed to me the most suitable place in Europe to hear the news of victory. Surely this war was fought to abolish Dachau and all the places like Dachau and everything that Dachau stood for and abolish it for ever.'

P47 Thunderbolt

11 The Americans to the Danube

APRIL 1945

'The battle of Germany is now at the point when it
is up to the Field Commander to judge what measures
should be taken for a quick and complete victory.'

General George Marshall
31 March 1945

It is now necessary to go back in time and look at the operations of the
American armies after they crossed the Rhine in March 1945. By the end
of the month, with three full army groups across the river, Eisenhower could
now complete three major tasks following the change of plan announced by
SHAEF on 28 March. The 21st Army Group would, as already described,
thrust northeast for the Baltic while the 1st Canadian Army cleared Holland;
part of Bradley's 12th US Army Group, the 1st and 9th Armies, would
eliminate the Ruhr Pocket and then thrust east to meet the Russians along
or beyond the Elbe; and finally, Devers' 6th US Army Group and
Patton's 3rd US Army could head south to Bavaria, Austria, and the
borders of Italy and Czechoslovakia, overrun the 'National Redoubt' and
advance towards the Danube. The stage was now set for a final thrust into
Germany, and the Western Allies went about the task with overwhelming
force.

Eisenhower now had under his command no less than ninety divisions,
including five airborne divisions and twenty-five armoured divisions. These
were made from sixty-one American divisions, twelve British divisions,
eleven French divisions and a Polish division, plus a number of independent
brigades. The American armies had recently created a new force, the 15th
US Army – a formation of six divisions in Bradley's group, currently

218

deployed west of the Rhine – with the task of taking over occupation duties for the other American armies as they advanced further into Germany. In early April, after the Rhine crossing at Wesel, the 15th US Army closed up to the west bank of the river to prevent any German formations recrossing or escaping to the west as the Ruhr Pocket was eliminated.

On 25 March, the day after 21st Army Group crossed the Rhine at Wesel, Bradley's men broke out of the Remagen bridgehead. The Germans had little left with which to stop them. The German Order of Battle around the Remagen bridgehead listed five infantry divisions, two parachute divisions and a panzer grenadier division, but these 'divisions' were in reality little more than battle groups of about brigade strength. General Bradley, on the other hand, had divisions to spare.

Bradley had thirty-four divisions in his group, including the 15th Army, and would soon have another twelve when Simpson's 9th US Army reverted to his command. One of these was the 7th US Armoured Division, in which James 'Ed' Thompson was serving.

'I was with the 38th Armoured Infantry Battalion and on 26 March 1945 we were back in action. The Ludendorff bridge at Remagen had collapsed before we broke out of the bridgehead, so we made a night crossing of the Rhine on a pontoon bridge, not a comfortable drive across under blackout conditions.

'After getting across, we broke out of the bridgehead and drove on unchecked for several days. We changed direction several times, covering approximately 150 miles of beautiful countryside with quaint villages. We left it littered with remnants of German equipment, including some which had been drawn by horses (the German Army was running low on gasoline and had begun using all the available horses).

'The only damage to our half-track was when a German shell made a direct hit on it, but the shell, luckily for us, was a dud. However, the impact tore a large, gaping hole in the armour. By this time, we had become quite attached to "Holy Hell II", and affectionately referred to it as our "home away from home".

'We were also taking many prisoners. In one five-day period the 7th Armoured Division took 13,071 prisoners. General Van Fleet described the attack of the 7th Armoured as one of the most rapid advances ever executed by American forces. We often had long lines of prisoners marching back to POW cages. The division drove south to Limburg, then across the Dill river, captured Giessen, then Kirchain and the Eder See dam.

'On the drive it was always reassuring when weather conditions permitted our bombers to make their attacks. They looked powerful, passing over us in such large numbers on the way to their targets. I compared those pilots to the ones who flew the small Piper Cub planes in combat as observers for our artillery. I remember watching one as it floated overhead, when it was struck by a German shell and completely disintegrated.

'On 3 April one of the men shot a deer and we had venison to eat. Three of the men went fishing with a hand grenade and netted about 75 lb. of fish, so we had a little variety to supplement the K and C rations, as well as the army chow. In Germany we didn't have civilian barbers, so we got to be a pretty ragged looking group. I started cutting one fellow's hair and had him about half-finished when the Germans began shelling us. We had to move out in a hurry and it was three days later before I got around to finishing that haircut, and I never did become a good barber.

'By 5 April we had captured Schmallenberg, Gleidorf and Fredeburg. In one of our drives we advanced thirty-five miles in thirty-four hours right through the enemy lines, and several times had Germans on both sides of us. I recall when our half-track was the lead unit, and I happened to see a German poke his head out of a hedgerow, then disappear. My buddy and I sprayed the hedgerow with machine-gun fire, and when our medics checked later, they found six dead Germans. That same day, several Germans came out of the woods with white flags and their hands up and surrendered.

'We were now travelling so fast, gas and food supplies were often in short supply. We relied on K rations and food we found in houses in the towns we captured. We found chickens, eggs, canned vegetables, fruit, ham and so on. In one house a couple of the fellows and I took over, we found a beautiful layer cake with icing, probably made for someone's birthday. We celebrated for them, whoever it was. We found jars of peaches and cherries to go with it. The people had fled the house only a short time before we took it, and we probably took some chances but nothing appeared booby-trapped.

'All this was going on near the battle front. We were staying in a different place almost every night since we were rolling at such a rapid pace, and a lot of the German troops were not able to get out of our way. The stench was awful after the snow melted and the ground thawed and there were many decaying bodies, both humans and animals.

'Fifty years later, having seen movies about the Second World War, I realize that often they do not, and cannot, depict all that occurred. Many of them over-dramatize. This is only a personal opinion, but others who saw more combat that I did appear to agree.'

By 28 March Bradley's troops were pushing hard for Paderborn and the link-up with 9th US Army, their advance spearheaded by 'Task Force Richardson', a battalion of the 3rd US Armoured Division equipped with some of the new and powerful Pershing tanks. By the end of the day this task force was within fifteen miles of Paderborn, but on the following day it ran into a defence line manned by SS troops in battalion strength supported by around sixty Tiger and Jagdpanther tanks. The fighting here went on all that day and for much of the following night. An attempt to out flank the German position was lead by the 3rd US Armoured Division's commander, General Maurice Rose, who ran into a column of German tanks and was shot dead while attempting to surrender. General Rose was the second Allied divisional commander killed in four days, following the death of Major General Rennie, the commander of the British 51st (Highland) Division who was killed at Wesel on 24 March.

The American troops were aided in the breakout by tactical bombing from the Allied Air Forces. Group Captain Robert Law DSO, DFC, was then commanding 109 (Mosquito) Squadron in RAF Bomber Command. His account, and that of Bill Morrison of the 8th Air Force, describe some typical air operations in April 1945.

'After some accurate attacks on Dusseldorf, Bremen and Mainz in February, Squadron Leader Bowman DSO, DFC (Navigator), and I were detailed to mark Paderborn in the Ruhr. We dropped our ground markers through 10/10th cloud, within two minutes of our Time-on-Target and with a ground error estimated at 100 yards. The Master Bomber was Wing Commander S. P. Coulson DSO, DFC, CO, of No. 582 Squadron; he controlled the bombing of 268 heavies. The target was very accurately attacked, with 3,000 separate fires and very extensive destruction. We also saw German jet fighter contrails, an unusual and unwelcome occurrence.

'8 April – Berlin: With Squadron Leader Bowan as navigator, using ground stations located on Continental Europe, we were to drop our markers on Berlin from 33,000 feet, but did not get a release signal. It was a fine, clear night, but no searchlights and no flak. We climbed to 35,000 feet for a second run but again ran out of signal. At the end of that run we saw the twin exhausts of a German jet fighter, probably an ME262, obviously being controlled to look for us. He was weaving from side to side, and I can imagine his ground controller telling him where to look. We kept in formation below and slightly behind him, shadowing him. This continued for some three or four minutes, but seemed interminable. Then the jet opened his throttles wide and climbed sharply to the right. We opened up our throttles and dived sharply to the left! After some anxious minutes, we concluded we were not being followed and returned more sedately to base. We could easily have shot him down had we had guns.'

Bill Morrison was flying daylight missions over Germany with the 323 Bombardment Squadron (H), 91st US Bombardment Group, and could see the devastation on the ground: 'Most big cities like Nuremberg, Kassel, Berlin, Leipzig, etc, showed the effect of four years of heavy bombing, mostly by area bombing RAF attacks. By 1945 there weren't too many roofs left on houses or buildings in major cities. They would appear as waffle-irons, just blocks of grey, gutted buildings.

'I never thought much about the German civilians down there and I don't think many other combat crewman did either. We didn't hate them. Most of what we felt was impersonal; they were the enemy and they were shooting at us. Depending on what kind of bombs you were carrying, usually 10 × 500 lb., GP and two 500 lb. clusters of incendiaries, the actual strike would be devastating; a whole area would boil with smoke.

'Sometimes you would be carrying incendiary clusters, and when they struck the target area would sparkle like diamonds in the sunlight. At other times, if your group was flying at the end of the attacking force, fires would be raging everywhere below and the target covered with black and grey smoke. As the war progressed to the end in March and April, bombing altitudes sometimes came down to 8,000 or 10,000 feet and you could really see the detail of destruction in Germany.

'I have heard it likened to a lunar landscape, and I can agree with that, but the German flak gunners never faced an ammunition shortage. There were few Luftwaffe pilots left and a great shortage of fuel, but there never seemed a shortage of shells for them to shoot at us. By February, most of our targets were oil and synthetic fuel refineries and railroad marshalling yards. Germany always had a thin grey veil covering it from all the fires and devastation, and our P51 fighter escorts were turned loose to attack anything that moved below. The 8th Air Force could have stopped carrying out attacks by the end of March since there were very few strategic targets left undamaged. Instead, a 100-mile long stream of four-engine bombers left England daily to attack German targets that would be in the Russian Zone when Armageddon came to an end.'

The effect of this bombing was apparent to the troops advancing on the ground. Most of the smaller German towns along the front were up to 90 percent destroyed, while some 75 percent of Berlin lay in ruins even before Russian shells began to fall on the city.

Robert Slaughter of the 29th US Infantry Division recalls the advance into Germany: 'In spring 1945, we sensed the war was beginning to wind down and attitudes changed. Back in Normandy no one expected to go unscathed and the prayer was for the "Million-Dollar Wound", the one that got you home more or less in one piece. Now that the war was about over, we were a bit less gung-ho.

'German civilians were friendly and generally co-operative. They had lost faith in Hitler and were tired of war, as were we. Many would have starved if Allied troops hadn't given them food and warm clothing, and although it was forbidden to fraternize with Germans, many ignored the ban.

'Families were desperate for food, firewood, medical supplies and warm clothing. Some of our company were unforgiving but the vast majority, including me, were sympathetic and generous though a few were ruthless in their quest for valuable "loot". Many packages mailed home had gold jewellery, silver, flatware, deutschmarks, works of art and other booty in them. Nazi memorabilia – souvenirs such as flags, uniforms, weapons, medals, books – were what most of us sent. Front-line soldiers didn't have the means to store booty for shipment home, so were forced to leave treasures for rear-echelon soldiers. Many infantrymen were fleeced of their precious souvenirs by unscrupulous rear-echelon medical personnel while under sedation on the operating table. Many wallets, watches and rings were stolen at Army evacuation hospitals.

'German prisoners also were stripped of rings, wallets, watches and fountain pens, as were Allied prisoners unlucky enough to be captured by Germans. As the war wound down the tough attitude of the German military waned. They had become disillusioned with the war and began surrendering in droves. We found them hungry, ill-equipped, scared of their leaders and not well trained. There were a few good officers left who forced these Volksturm-types to fight against their will. Fewer tanks and less artillery were now being used and pockets of resistance were harder to find.

'We were moving so fast that many villages and towns were being captured without firing a shot. We charged into Holz, Germany, while downtown merchants were still conducting commerce. My squad captured a barber shop and each of us ordered a haircut and shave. We didn't trust the barber with a straight razor, so we watched over each other while he shaved us. We also found a savings and loan bank and filled our knapsacks with brand new Deutschmarks. They were legal tender and I was very rich for a few days. A day or two later the added weight of my illegal wealth almost cost me my life. We were ambushed going into Setterich and I was very slow reacting because of this burden. The next German family that looked like they could use the money became recipients of several thousand deutschmarks. All the money in the world is of little use when one is dead.'

The rapid advance into Germany by the Allied armies in March and April 1945, was accompanied by a sharp rise in looting, rape and desertion. On the American front only thirty-two men were arrested and tried for rape in January and February combined, but this jumped to 259 in April, when the armies were in Germany – minute in comparison with what was happening along the Eastern Front but not to be tolerated. In 1945 American military courts sentenced hundreds of men to prison for crimes ranging from robbery and desertion to rape and murder, and seventy were executed.

Although the Ludendorff bridge at Remagen had collapsed on 17 March, fresh bridges had by then been flung across the river and the 1st US Army bridgehead had expanded to a length of 30 miles – from Bonn south to Koblenz – and to a depth of 9 miles from the river. Into this area, Bradley had packed most of the 1st Army and his initial breakout was made by three full Army corps.

By 28 March the Americans from Remagen had reached Marburg on the southern flank of the Ruhr and were starting to wheel north to meet Simpson's 9th US Army, pushing forward on the right flank of the British 21st Army Group. This junction was completed on 1 April and on 4 April, following Eisenhower's directive of 29 March, Simpson's 9th Army reverted to Bradley's command. With encirclement achieved, Bradley's next task was to eliminate Field Marshal Model's army group in the Ruhr, but he had sufficient forces to spare in 1st Army for the advance to the Elbe and the link-up with Patton's 3rd US Army coming up from the Oppenheim crossing in the south.

Lieutenant Robert M. Brooker was with the combat engineers of the 9th Armoured Division during the Remagen breakout and the fighting for the Ruhr Pocket. 'As we broke out of the bridgehead on the east bank of the Rhine, we headed south along the river for about thirty or so miles and then east on the autobahn to Limburg and the Lahn river. The bridge across the Lahn had been blown and my orders were to build a bridge so that part of our combat command could go and meet 3rd Army coming up from the south. We would cut off a few thousand German soldiers by this manoeuvre.

'I was attached to Battalion Headquarters and had gone to bed about midnight. I was wakened at about 1 a.m. and ordered to go to Limburg, pick a bridge site, come back to our C Company of the 9th Engineers and take them back to build the bridge. At the same time I was to tell Division Headquarters when the bridge would be completed. We picked the site, returned to meet the company, sent the message and took the company to the area. It was beautiful; there was plenty of space for our vehicles, gravel to build approaches, a wide river with a slow flow, and as far as I could discover, no enemy on the other side.

'The next step was to find out what was on the other side. The only solution was for me to take a five-man patrol across the river in a boat and check it out. We reached the other side and found that we were building the bridge into a cliff. We decided to swing the bridge a little to the right but first we had to clear out any German soldiers. We found about eighteen, captured them and took them to our side. I asked one of them why they gave up so easily, and he pointed to the blown bridge where one of our Pershing tanks was sitting, the 90 mm gun aimed right where these Germans had been. I doubt that the tankers even knew that anybody was across the river. While taking the Germans across I covered them with my carbine and even threatened to shoot one of them. When we got back I discovered that my gun had no bullets in the chamber.

'Later, I took a foot patrol across the river to check out a rail crossing. On the way back we had to climb a hill and as we reached the crest we met about fifteen armed German soldiers, all looking at us. I knew that if we started shooting they would slaughter us and I came up with one of my more stupid statements. I said to my sergeant, "If we ignore them, maybe they will go away." We did so and walked right through their formation.

'These Germans were guarding a British and American prisoner-of-war hospital. One of the American POWs came running out and started to tear down Sergeant Schearer's pants. He explained that he had promised to "kiss the ass" of the first American soldier he saw.

'I put a British colonel in charge of the hospital, ignored the Germans and brought our patrol back to the other side of the river in time to meet my commanding officer, who told me that the site I had picked was bad. I told him that I could not find a better one. I think that after the General complimented him on the bridge, he felt somewhat differently.'

Patton's 3rd US Army had also broken out of their Oppenheim bridgehead and apart from coming north to link up with 1st US Army, on 26 March the 3rd Army entered Frankfurt – their advance assisted by a massive raid by Mitchell medium bombers of the 9th US Air Force.

During the advance on Frankfurt, Patton's Army was diverted by the curious 'Hammelburg Mission', when Patton decided to send a task force under the command of Captain Abraham Baum. Consisting of sixteen tanks and about thirty half-tracks full of infantry from the 10th Armoured Infantry and the 37th Tank Battalion, it sought to liberate American prisoners at a POW camp at Hammelburg, thirty-five miles behind the German lines.

Many officers on Patton's staff and in Task Force Baum were less than happy about this mission, but Patton was adamant and the force set out shortly after midnight on 25 March. During 26 March the task force made good progress, shooting up German transport and taking about 200 prisoners. When they reached the town of Hammelburg, however, the Germans were alert and ready for them, and three of their tanks and a number of jeeps and half-tracks were lost before the Americans reached the POW camp and drove their tanks through the wire.

Then matters started to go seriously wrong. There were nearly 5,000 prisoners in the camp, of which about 1,400 were American, and there was no means for Task Force Baum to evacuate them the thirty-five miles back to the American lines. Some prisoners swarmed onto the tanks and half-tracks while the rest prepared to march.

Meanwhile, the German troops in Hammelburg had been rallied by a Wehrmacht major home on leave, and he sent men with *panzerfausts* running to the prison camp where they knocked out Captain Baum's tank just beside the main gate. Baum then lead his much depleted force round the town only to run into more resistance, and more *panzerfausts* at Hessdorf, five miles to the southwest. Low on fuel and ammunition Baum withdrew to a hilltop where his force was attacked at dawn on 27 March by twelve Tigers and two companies of panzer grenadiers supported by artillery.

After a brief but gallant resistance Baum ordered his men to escape in small groups and try to get back to the American lines. Baum, who had already been wounded twice, was wounded again and captured. Only fifteen Americans escaped; fifty-seven were killed or wounded and the rest taken prisoner.

The disaster to Task Force Baum then gained a lot of media attention when it transpired that Patton's son-in-law, Lt-Colonel John Waters, captured in North Africa in 1943, had been a prisoner at Hammelburg, and indeed still was, having been wounded in the breakout. Patton denied knowing that his son-in-law was in the camp, though Patton's aide – a Major Stiller, who was on the mission – had told several people that Lt-Colonel Waters was at Hammelburg before setting out. This affair eventually petered out and Lt-Colonel Waters regained his freedom a few days later on 6 April, when tanks from the 14th US Armoured Division re-entered Hammelburg.

Frankfurt was secured by 28 March and Patton then began to force a passage past Weisbaden towards Kassel and the Thuringian Forest. The axis of advance for the various American forces can be seen from Map 7 (p. 149), but from the north, 9th US Army units were advancing east on a front from just south of Magdeburg, north to Wittenberg. South of 9th Army, Hodges' 1st US Army were advancing on an axis through Dessau and Leipzig, while further south still, Patton's forces were thrusting east through Gotha, Weimar, Jena and Chemnitz.

Meanwhile, strong forces of the 1st and 9th Armies were mopping up in the Ruhr Pocket. To avoid confusion, the fronts of these two armies set along the Ruhr river, which runs west from the Rhine to the town of Nuttlar. The 9th Army took on the industrial belt to the north, the 1st Army fought through the more open but rugged country to the south. The 4,000 square miles of the Ruhr were defended by two armies – 5 Panzer and XV Army – both of Field Marshal Model's Army Group B, plus two corps of the hard-fighting German 1st Parachute Army from Army Group H. Both groups had been reinforced by large numbers of troops formerly employed manning the numerous Ruhr anti-aircraft batteries; the first

American Intelligence estimates had calculated Model's forces as totalling about 150,000 men.

Model was a good general, well able to put up a fight, but his ability to defend the Ruhr was hampered by Hitler's usual orders to hold every metre of ground. Field Marshal Model was a loyal Nazi but in spite of the Führer's orders he did not want to see his troops pinned in position and destroyed, and during the first days of April, he ordered a series of breakouts to the east. All these were repulsed by the encircling Americans. Then followed ten days of heavy fighting in and around the industrial cities of the Ruhr, the Germans often putting up a fanatical resistance as the Americans closed the ring. It took four days of stiff fighting to capture Hamm, though Duisberg fell to the 17th US Airborne Division after only token resistance. Essen, with the famous Krupp steelworks, was also captured without difficulty, but the German troops fought fiercely to hold Dortmund against the 75th and 95th US Infantry Divisions.

Ken Kennett fought in the Ruhr with the US 86th (Blackhawk) Division. 'We went south along the Rhine and crossed below Bonn on the pontoon bridge they put up when the Ludendorff bridge collapsed. We stopped in a small town called Hilkenbach and got ready for our drive to cut the Ruhr Pocket in half. We rode in trucks to Seigen, and then up to meet the 9th US Army coming down from the north. Our battalion wasn't in the lead until we got about thirty miles from Hagen, but I will never forget the night of Friday 13 April. We were on trucks all night, our forward elements hitting road blocks, and we were catching sniper fire. This made the entire convoy stop and start.

'Buildings were burning all along the road and it seemed every time we stopped one was right beside us. This made us a beautiful target, and we all held our breath until we moved again. A sniper decided to take a shot at a truck behind us, but luckily everybody was awake and they all opened up on him with about twenty-five rifles plus a couple of BARs. What a racket they made! After about half a minute of this, somebody sneaked up to the building and tossed in an incendiary grenade. The building was a barn filled with hay, so in about a minute we had plenty of light to knock off the two men who ran out. Another time, a truck ahead of us was hit by a German bazooka. It made a mess of the truck and caused a few casualties. We were glad when daylight came and Friday 13 was gone.

'When we got to the outskirts of Hagen it was time to get off and walk, because we were coming into enemy artillery range. About half of us were off our trucks when a machine-gun opened up on us from a railroad bridge to our right front. I was standing beside the truck with a half-opened can of peaches in my hand, so I hit the ditch before I finished eating the peaches. We hadn't eaten in eighteen hours, so I was damned hungry and

I knew the gun couldn't get me in there. One of our .50s on a jeep opened up and knocked the German gun out, and then we started into town.

'We hit a machine-gun once in a while but by then our tanks had come up, so they didn't give us much trouble and by noon we were in the centre of town. The Germans opened up with 88s and an anti-aircraft gun, but we ducked into doorways and all they did was knock some cement around. They did, however, hit the truck I had left my pack on, so my pack was kaput. At about 2 o'clock, we met the other outfit and the battle for Hagen was over except for isolated sniper fire. We took a terrific number of prisoners. I helped search about fifty who had come out of some woods. They were a sorry looking bunch, mostly kids and old men of the Volksturm. We took up a defensive position on the flank, where we stayed until relieved by one of our other battalions. Then we returned to Hagen and spent a week in an apartment house for a well-deserved rest.'

Ralph Teeters was still with the 4th Division which was now part of 7th US Army. 'We crossed the river at Worms, a town south of Oppenheim. I remember we stayed in German houses for several days; we forced the residents to get in their basements and stay there. Finally, the mayor got permission to butcher a horse and the Germans came and got portions of the meat. We would not share our rations with them and they were pretty hungry by that time.

'We had crossed the Rhine and that had been a big deal; everybody talked about the Rhine. We crossed it with little incident and went into a pursuit to the east and to the south. Here we again got on tanks, from our own tank battalion. Sometimes we would move as far as fifty miles in a day. One of the places we went through was Bad Mergentheim, and I remember how many prisoners we took. We sat in defensive positions and they'd walk in and surrender. Either before or just after this, there was an incident that netted several of us Bronze Stars.

'We had gone almost forty-five miles on tanks that particular day, and late in the afternoon, we headed into the town on the Tauber river. We found the tank ahead of us, with Johnny Latvamaki, who had been badly machine-gunned, and Johnny was terribly wounded with a bullet through his pelvis, his lower abdominal cavity and out the other side. Johnny was a special guy for me and I was very unhappy about this. This story proves that the emotions take over. We were made unhappy by the surprise of the attack as much as anything else, and we considered ourselves salty, experienced veterans.

'When we came under fire, our tanks didn't fire back and we were swearing at them. We were stuck behind the tanks, and behind us was the company clerk. A bullet had gone through the windscreen of his jeep, and he was close as he'd ever been to any kind of combat.

'Kind of showing off, and because Johnny had been wounded, I organized guys to go on up. Crane, one of my sergeants, jumped into the tank and kicked the guy in the turret out of the way and started firing the .30 calibre machine-gun. We went up this hill, maybe 25–50 yards, and saw several Germans in foxholes, and we ordered them to surrender. Some of the guys shot them in their holes.

'I was carrying an M-1 and I jumped into a slightly sunken road, and found three German soldiers pinned down because of the .30 cal machine-gun that Crane was firing from the tank. It was all rather stupid, emotional, and showing off, and certainly did not show good judgement. I ordered these three Germans out and one refused. The others got up with hands up and I sent them back and said to the guy with me, "Get their watches and pistols if they have any." This third German would not get up, and I fired my rifle at him and I think I hurt him ... I don't know.

'We went back with these prisoners, and later on found that about a battalion of Germans had surrendered on that side of the hill. I don't know how we escaped. I only know that what we did was stupid, without anyone ordering us to do it. We were just so goddam sick of what was going on and unhappy with our own tank battalion and the way they were performing at the time.'

The 1st and 9th US Armies were still battling in the Ruhr Pocket where on 14 April, after ten days of fighting, the two armies met near the town of Hagen and cut the German forces in two. After that, resistance in the Ruhr rapidly petered out, with thousands of prisoners coming into the American lines each day. By 18 April all fighting in the Ruhr had come to an end and the Americans discovered the scale of their victory, for the forces in the Ruhr far exceeded the original intelligence estimates.

Within the Ruhr Pocket the Americans destroyed twenty-one German divisions, including the remnants of the battle-worn 9th Panzer Division, and captured 320,000 German troops, including thirty generals, among them General Bayerlein, who had commanded a division in Normandy, and General Harpe of the V Panzer Army. The prisoner-of-war cages set up to accommodate these captives covered an area of several square miles.

The Americans did not, however, capture Field Marshal Model. Model held the view that 'A field marshal does not surrender', and when the time came he was as good as his word. On 21 April 1945, following the defeat of his Army, the field marshal went into the woods north of Dusseldorf, lay down on a swastika flag and blew his brains out. Model's body was recovered by his son and re-interred at the German military cemetery in the Hurtgen Forest.

Eliminating the Germans in the Ruhr had only employed part of Bradley's forces during this period. By 18 April the 9th US Army had already pushed two corps across the river Weser and assaulted the city of Hanover. On 19 April, 9th Army had crossed the river Leine. Further south, 1st US Army had also crossed the Weser and the Leine and was already in the western foothills of the Hartz Mountains, heading for Nordhausen. In the south, Patton's 3rd US Army had taken Gotha and most of the Thuringian Forest, besides protecting the left flank of General Patch's 7th US Army as it fought through the Hohe Rhon Mountains.

All these advances were greatly aided by the cover and support provided by the Allied air forces, and one of the P47 pilots covering the American ground forces was Tom Miller. 'I flew forty-two missions in my P47 "Thunderbolt" fighter plane between 25 March and 6 May 1945. The area was southern Germany, flying mostly close air support for General Patton's 3rd Army from the Mannheim–Frankfurt region, east and south to the Nürnberg–Munich area.

'I was first stationed at Toul in France in late March, after spending a few days touring London and Paris en route. Our armies were just crossing the Rhine river on my first mission. I remember a vast panorama of level green fields appearing almost like a huge park but with tanks a few hundred yards apart lined up for miles along the west side of the Rhine. The tanks had large panels on top painted bright orange to identify them as friendly to us fighter pilots.

'Germany is a beautiful country from the air, as is England. The only evidence of war was an occasional column of smoke in the distance, which on close inspection, turned out to be a burning tank, truck, or town. In early April my Fighter Group, the 358th "Orange Tails", moved to a captured German airfield at Mannheim. It once had many fine buildings but was pretty much in ruins, as was the city of Mannheim.

'Most of my missions were ground attack, providing front-line support and air cover for the armies and preventing any German rail or truck supply movement. We destroyed quite a few trains, trucks and even anti-aircraft guns, which were being used against the ground troops, and we lost a number of planes and pilots to anti-aircraft fire. Most pilots who flew both air-to-air combat and ground attack have written that ground attack is much more dangerous. I once watched three planes out of a flight of four shot down while attacking a train. The train was later found to have been Hermann Goering's private armoured train, with some of Germany's best anti-aircraft gunners on it. My flight of four was to go down next, but much to my great relief the flight leader terminated the attack, announcing over the radio, "That's enough planes for that train."

'I flew missions in which we attacked airfields, dive-bombed 88 mm anti-aircraft guns which were being used against troops entering Nürnberg, destroyed tank-truck supply columns, and even bombed small villages when requested by the Army. Some of these blew up like fireworks because they were being used as ammunition dumps. On two missions we circled over prison camps to discourage the guards from shooting at the approaching Army troops or shooting prisoners. We found out later that one such camp was Dachau, the notorious concentration camp near Munich, so perhaps I helped a few of those who might have been exterminated.

'One day that was rather Armageddon-like, was about 1 April. The small city of Ashaffenburg was taken after two or three days of house-to-house and street-to-street fighting, with heavy losses on both sides. My fighter group made the short flight from Mannheim several times that day, where we were directed to bomb just a block or two ahead of our infantry of the 45th US Division who came from my home state of Oklahoma. General Patton did not like to have his infantrymen killed in house-to-house fighting. If a town resisted he would line his tanks up in a half-circle around the town, call in us fighter bombers and start shelling and bombing. The town would soon put out white flags.

'Air combat seemed to happen in slow motion, not at all like the flash of twisting, turning, exploding planes portrayed in the movies. The sky is vast and planes a few miles away seem small, almost like a flock of birds in the distance. When we turned to intercept the jets the turn was slow, almost graceful, and the minute or two it took to get close seemed for ever. Then the jets which were much faster than our "prop jobs" increased power and slowly left us behind.

'From the air you do not come into direct contact with the dead and the destruction. From the air you do not even see people – they mostly hide in some sort of shelter when a plane comes over, so you do not see death and killing. Even when your plane is hit you usually don't know. When my plane was hit the worst, with sixty-five holes in the back part, I only felt it lurch and heard a "whump" sound. I am alive today because of a thick plate of armour behind the pilot's seat, and because I was flying the P47. We "Thunderbolt" pilots grew to love that big, strong airplane with the big round engine in front and the armour at the back giving us protection.'

With the Ruhr secured and the Germans' ability to resist much reduced, Bradley now concentrated his forces for the drive east towards Leipzig and the Elbe. This advance had begun on 10 April when 9th US Army pushed two corps towards Braunschwig. By the following day Simpson had the 2nd US Armoured Division across the Elbe at Schonebeck, just south of Magdeburg, having advanced more than fifty miles in a single day.

This advance put Simpson's leading elements within fifty miles of Berlin and, had General Eisenhower so wished, in a strong position to compete with the Soviet forces for the prestige of entering the German capital. Many Americans believed that 9th Army would spearhead this drive, not knowing of Eisenhower's change of plan. That it would be a race was obvious from Marshal Stalin's actions in April, for in spite of agreeing with Eisenhower that 'Berlin has lost all its strategic significance', Stalin had ordered two Army Fronts (groups) to cross the Oder and advance directly on the German capital. This attack across the Oder did not begin until 16 April and in those intervening six days the road to Berlin was within Simpson's grasp.

Anticipating that the 9th US Army might still be ordered to Berlin, Bradley told Simpson that once he had a bridgehead over the Elbe he was to 'be prepared to continue the advance to Berlin or the northeast'. Simpson now had such a bridgehead, but the Germans seemed determined to hold the country east of the Elbe, and a fierce counter-attack on 14 April drove the 2nd US Armoured Division back across the river.

A 'Stop Line' – the line on which their advancing armies would meet – had already been agreed between the Western and Soviet forces. This ran from Bayreuth, north to Chemnitz, passing just east of Leipzig, then along the river Mulde to the point where the Mulde flowed into the Elbe. The 'Stop Line' then followed the Elbe north through Magdeburg to the boundary with Montgomery's 21st Army Group at Wittenburg. In the north, Montgomery's group had been ordered to advance to the Baltic.

Since the Russians were still well to the east of the Elbe, Simpson re-crossed the river in the face of stiff opposition from German infantry, artillery and aircraft, and expanded his bridgehead on the east bank around the city of Magdeburg.

Hodges' 1st US Army to the south was having a much harder time. Hodges' axis of advance towards Leipzig lay through the Hartz Mountains, difficult terrain running up to beyond the 800 m mark and ably defended by several divisions totalling 13,000 men of the German XI Army. These divisions were shadows of their former selves but the terrain was favourable to defence and the Germans were still fighting hard. Taking the Hartz Mountains and the wrecked industrial towns of Halle, Dessau and Leipzig was a stiff task which kept the 1st Army busy until 21 April.

Ken Kennet continues his story of the US 86th (Blackhawk) Division: 'During this time things were kind of screwed up. We were moving fast but other outfits were doing likewise. We would come to a town expecting to find Germans in it, but after taking precautions in approaching it, we would find it full of GIs from some other outfit. It made us rather mad, and there was a lot of bitching going on. Empty stomachs didn't help things either.

'The next real action was when we crossed a small river called the Altmuhl. We had driven down to the river and found the bridge blown up. We had tanks and tank destroyers with us, so we stopped at the edge of the river for the night, in a town called Eichstatt. Early next morning, while the fog was down, we infantry crossed on a footbridge which the engineers had put up during the night. The idea was for us to cross and make a bridgehead, so the engineers could put up a larger pontoon bridge to get the tanks across. We didn't know it, but the 14th Armoured had crossed the day before, before the bridge was blown, but were driven back because they hadn't any infantry with them. They had to leave one half-track and a tank behind because the Germans blew the bridge before they could get them back.

'Everything went well at first. The fog covered us while we crossed the bridge, hit the woods and found nothing, so the engineers started work on the bridge. However, an 88 mm was zeroed on them, and every time they started work, the Germans would open up and drive them into holes and throw a few more rounds to undo what they had done. This went on all day. We had gone as far as we dared without the armour and around 4 p.m. we were ordered to pull back to some buildings near the river and set up a defence position. We had just pulled out of the woods and started back, when the missing half-track showed up, only it wasn't on 'our side. The Germans had taken it and put it in working order. They opened up with the 50-cal. and the only thing that saved us was that they were very inaccurate – thank god!

'We hit the ditches and crawled into the woods. Then the Germans started circling, to cut us off from the river. We tried to dig in, but the ground was hard, and we couldn't organize so we kept pulling back until we could make a dash for the houses. We made it and set up a defence line, and that night the engineers got the bridge across. In the morning the armour came over and started the drive to the Danube.'

The path into the Ruhr and towards East Germany had been flattened out by Allied bombers ranging far ahead of the armies. Such missions were not without loss even at this stage of the war, as B17 pilot Lieutenant Noel 'Robbie' Robinson of 751 Squadron, 94th Bomb Group recounts:

'Mission No. 30 took us to Hopsten in the Ruhr valley. I was alerted at 0200 hrs and the briefing was at 03.45. We took off at 06.30, carrying 38 × 100 lb. GP bombs and 2,300 gallons of gas. There was a patch of ground fog on the field as we started our takeoff run, so I had to go on instruments while Don Neilsen, my co-pilot, tried to keep visual contact.

'We entered the Continent at Zyder Zee, climbing to an altitude of 25,600 feet. Just before we reached the IP, the Germans started putting up flak which was concentrated in the 'Low' box of our squadron. I was in the

'High' box. The leader of that box was knocked out and the deputy took over.

'Our bomb run took us over the cities of Munster and Rheine, both famous for the amount of flak they could put up, and those German gunners were having a field day. The aeroplane right below me took a direct hit, rolled over, and exploded. The force of the explosion almost blew me out of the sky, but we managed to maintain control, and went on to the target. The ball turret gunner on that ship, flying as 'toggelier' on this mission, had flown with us on the Fulda Mission on 19 March. A straggler was flying close to us, trying to get to the target to drop his bombs and get credit for the mission, but the gunners started tracking on him and he went down. The leader of our box was hit and had to leave formation.

'The deputy had just taken over as we arrived at the target, but dropped his bombs on schedule and we all dropped on his release. By the time we cleared the target, there was pure pandemonium throughout the formation. Most of the aircraft had damage – some severe, others minor – and many wounded crewmen. Trying to dodge crippled aircraft became almost as difficult as trying to dodge the flak. We were all pretty shaken over the intensity of this anti-aircraft barrage. Our ball turret gunner, Rick, had been ill for about two weeks and we were using a replacement gunner. It was a rough indoctrination for the replacement gunner, and he was so scared he messed his pants.

'Things finally settled down enough for us to assess our damage. We had been hit, but fortunately no one was injured and there appeared to be no major damage to the plane. We retraced our path back across Holland, the Zyder Zee, and the North Sea, where we let down to 4,000 feet and came on into Glatton, landing at 12.15. This was mission no. 100 for my aeroplane No. 123. We had saved four bottles of Scotch whisky and intended to have a celebration in honour of the event, but no one was in a party mood, so we saved it for later. We found out about a week later that the ball turret gunner on the ship that exploded had been blown free when the plane blew up and he survived and made his way back to the group. He said that all he really remembered was that he suddenly found himself falling free in the sky. He was wearing his parachute, so pulled the ripcord and rode the parachute to the ground.'

The task of mopping up the snipers and machine-gun nests in Halle, Dessau and Leipzig was largely left to the infantry divisions while an armoured spearhead forged east to Hodges' Stop Line on the river Mulde, where they seized two bridges on 15 April.

The Americans were now overrunning a number of concentration camps in the Leipzig area, including Ordruf, which fell to the 4th Armoured Division and Buchenwald near Erfurt which fell on 11 April. Other concentration camps liberated at this time included those at Landsberg, Weobblein, Gunskirchen, Ebensee, Ludwigslust, Dora and Flossenberg.

Although the garrison of Leipzig still held out, the Americans now straddled all the road and rail communications with southern Germany, thereby isolating Army Group 'H' from Kesselring's control and leaving the remnants of Army Group 'G' in the east and Bavaria – the German 1st VII and XIX Armies – to face the combined night of Patton's 3rd US Army, pushing east through Weimar and Chemnitz, and Devers' full US army group, marching on Munich, without any possibility of support.

Lieutenant Robert M. Brooker of the 9th US Armoured Division was back with his combat engineers as the 1st US Army advanced on Leipzig and the Mulde river just to the east. 'When I got back we were getting ready to go around Leipzig. We drove around the city within the anti-aircraft belt. Every so often there was a group of four 88 mm or larger guns and it went like this: We would attack the guns and have our artillery drop shells on them. When they turned to fire at us, our P47s would dive in and attack them. When they fired up at the planes we would advance on the ground. By doing this we were able to capture each set of guns. We then went onto the Mulde river east of Leipzig. Company A of the Engineers held three miles of the road west of the river but we set up our guns to fire both east and west, since we had not taken all the ground behind us.

'I did some sniping across the river but I hit nothing. Once we drove down into a field near the river, set up a mortar and a 50-cal. machine-gun and started firing at a haystack. The bullets bounced off it so we cut and run. Sergeant Schearer and I went into a town and checked the blown bridge over the Mulde to see what was needed to fix it. We were caught in a crossfire of snipers and had to retreat behind a house. The man fired through the house at us. When a man started firing at us on our side of the river, from a house that had a white flat on it, Schearer wanted to go into the house and clean it out. When we got back to the tank company, I asked them to burn the house down. They blew a hole into the house, then fired some phosphorus shells into it.

'The 69th US Infantry Division came up to take our place. A platoon of one of the companies took our house and started to form a patrol to cross the river. I explained that each time I tried it, they fired at me and so I thought it best not to upset the Germans. They ignored me, went over and got shot up. Eventually this division met the Russians east of this point. When the 69th Division took our place on the Mulde river, we moved down into Czechoslovakia.'

The Americans of the 12th Army Group were now pushing east on a broad front, while Patch's 7th US Army had come forward to protect Patton's right flank in a line west through Nuremberg and Neilbronn, ready for their thrust south towards the Danube through Stuttgart. On Patch's right flank, General Lattre de Tassigny's 1st French Army had advanced along the east bank of the Rhine towards the Black Forest and the city of Stuttgart.

During the first two weeks of April, Devers' 6th US Army Group made good progress, with the 1st French Army taking Stuttgart on 22 April, capturing 28,000 Germans for the loss of less than 200 Frenchmen killed and wounded. By 14 April the 3rd and 45th US Divisions had taken the town of Bamburg and on the following day the French secured the town of Kehl, just across the Rhine from Strasbourg. This move was welcomed by the citizens of Strasbourg as it finally silenced the German guns which had been firing into the city from across the river.

Germany's situation was now desperate and most of the German Army knew it. The Western Allies were taking up to 30,000 prisoners a day, many of them anxious to surrender quickly to the Western armies rather than take the risk of falling into the hands of the Russians if they fought on. Even so, many Germans, especially those in the SS units, continued the fight. An Intelligence Review from the British 21st Army Group states why:

'Thousands of German troops continue to fight bravely and well, not merely because they are fanatics but because they are good soldiers; but there are not enough of them, nor is their equipment sufficient to turn the scale.'

This was the nub of it: the German armies had little left with which to fight. They were short of tanks, guns, fuel and ammunition, and as their slender resources declined, so the fighting petered out.

On 15 April, General Simpson again proposed to General Bradley that he should advance from his expanding bridgehead over the Elbe at Magdeburg and drive those last fifty miles into Berlin. Bradley passed the message on but this proposal was turned down flat at SHAEF. Simpson was directed to hold his line on the Elbe and await the arrival of the Russians.

The British 21st Army Group was to continue advancing towards the Baltic at Lübeck in the north and seal off the Danish peninsula from the advancing Russians, while Hodges' and Patton's armies, and Devers' full army group pushed east and south towards Bavaria and the Danube. A fresh directive giving orders for this phase was still being drafted at SHAEF when the Allied armies in the west received an unexpected blow. Franklin D. Roosevelt, the President of the United States, died at Warm Springs, Georgia on 12 April 1945.

Roosevelt's death sent a wave of sadness across the world and Wayne S. Traynham of the 311th Infantry Regiment, 78th US Division, remembers how he heard the news, when fighting in the Ruhr Pocket: 'I was given a three-day pass to Belgium, where I got a bath, clean clothes and one night's good rest. I was expecting three days of this, when a guy came around telling us that all men from the 311th Regiment were to get back to their company, as the 311th was jumping off across the Sieg. The first thing I saw after crossing was a dead German soldier. We were now in the Ruhr Pocket where the 311th Regiment covered 149 square miles, cleared 266 towns and captured over 15,000 prisoners. Half the time I didn't know where we were or where we were going, but it wasn't my job to know so I didn't worry about it. The German Army was the most confused bunch of men I had ever seen.

'A surrendered German soldier told the lieutenant that twenty German soldiers were in the next town and wanted to surrender. The lieutenant let him go and told him that when he came back with the twenty men their password was "Kodak". That night, about midnight, the sergeant took six of us to the outpost to relieve the other men and he reminded us that the Germans were supposed to surrender and their password was "Kodak". About two hours later all hell broke loose. The Germans had come back but they didn't come back to surrender! They came back fighting.

'Everything was lit up from the tracers coming from the machine-guns. I broke for a run and when I got to the CP, I charged to the telephone. We had a telephone line strung out from the CP, to the outpost and all I could hear on the phone was the clatter from the machine-guns. What I remember most is that next morning I was sitting in the sun outside the CP, and someone came by and told me President Roosevelt had died.'

Donald B. Straith, Snr, of Warren, Michigan, wounded in the Bulge fighting, had just returned to the 101st US Airborne Division. 'The unfamiliar faces were a depressing factor. Out of about 140 men in Company A when it left for Bastogne, only forty-eight had returned. The company commander, Captain Meason, had been wounded and shipped out. His replacement, Captain Roy Kessler, was dead and had been replaced by Lieutenant William C. Kennedy. Sergeant Shoemaker, my squad leader, had been wounded, but Sergeant Crusan and Jerry Janes had come back safely.

'My platoon had been particularly hard hit, and most of the men I had known were gone. Dave Bahus and Dave Diener were both dead. Lou Braasch had been captured, Rose, Bednar and Duke Stewart, whom I had last seen in an ambulance, had all been wounded and shipped out, never to rejoin the division. Jack Bran, in spite of going to Bastogne without a helmet, had survived and was now a sergeant and squad leader. Likewise, my two companions from the observation post at Noville, Cavanaugh and Cunningham, had made it back.

'I made inquiries and found that happy-go-lucky Corporal Leo Padlovsky had been killed on the road into Noville by an artillery shell. Another man, to whom I had loaned some money, was also dead. About the only ones left in the company whom I knew were one of our cooks, Bob Duffee, and Bill Martin from Dearborn, who had come with me in November.

'As we awaited our next mission, my mail began catching up with me again. I knew there must be quite a backlog but I certainly wasn't prepared for the avalanche which came the following week: fifty-six letters, Christmas cards, valentines and birthday cards, four high-school newspapers and a postcard. It was all I could do to read it, much less answer it.

'American troops had finally crossed the Rhine river and everyone thought that the 101st would parachute into Germany to link up with these troops. Then one morning, great flights of C46 and C47 transports passed over camp, returning in the afternoon at low altitude with static lines streaming out the doors. We learned that the 17th US Airborne Division had made the jump instead, so it came as no surprise when, on 2 April, we climbed into our large trailer-trucks and headed north.

'We were now with the 15th US Army, on the west bank of the Rhine keeping German troops penned up in the Ruhr Pocket, and half-expected German troops to leap on us across the river, but apart from seeing a movie one rainy afternoon, all we did for a week was a little training with *panzerfausts*, the German equivalent of our bazookas. We each got one shot at a brick tower but found the accuracy not very good. The idea of our using *panzerfausts* must have been dropped because when a night combat patrol was announced a couple of days later, Charlie Syer was issued with a bazooka and I was made his assistant.

'After dinner on 11 April we went back to our quarters and with much laughter and horsing around, blackened our faces for the raid. Minutes later we were briefed on our mission: cross the Rhine in small assault boats, proceed along a road and through a village – later identified at Himmelgeist – take what prisoners we could and return in boats that the engineers would have waiting at the river edge of the village.

'As we assembled on the opposite shore a short time later, I became concerned about the amount of noise we were making, and felt that a lot of the men weren't taking this raid very seriously. When Syer said in a loud voice, "Where the hell is Straith?" I angrily hissed back, "Right behind you! Keep your damn voice down!" When the last boats had landed a couple of minutes later, the company moved out on a road paralleling the river.

'It's hard to say how long we waited there in the dark, the only sounds being distant shouts and an occasional shot from the rest of the company as they swept through the town. Suddenly, with only a fraction of a second's warning, a salvo of shells bracketed our position, showering us with dirt.

The Germans must have really zeroed in on us, because a couple of minutes later there were explosions all around us as another salvo landed in our midst. I was frantically trying to stretch my steel helmet to cover all of me when a shell burst a few feet to my left rear, and a chunk of compressed clay and stone from the road hit my head. Through all the noise, I heard Syer call out, "I'm hit bad!" and he fell over on his side and lay there groaning. Elkins yelled, "Quick, Straith, put a tourniquet on my leg and get this damned machine gun off me." The concussion had blown his 42 lb. weapon, tripod and all, on top of him. To our surprise, Red and I were untouched, having been so close to where the shell landed that its fragments had arched just over us, one hitting Elkins and a bunch more tearing open Charlie's back.

'The shelling had stopped, and as I moved the machine-gun, one of our medics ran up. After taking Syer's pulse and listening to him groan and gasp for air, the medic decided to take care of the other casualty instead. Syer's groans were becoming weaker and then stopped altogether. I could see the luminous dial of his watch, so I reached for his wrist and felt his pulse, but after only a few beats it stopped. When I reported this to the medic, he reached over to check it himself, and confirmed that Charlie was dead.

'When the medic finished working on Elkins, we moved to the ditch and found that the other medic, Alex Abercrombie, was also a casualty, bleeding from a temple wound where a shell fragment had pierced the side of his helmet; but he was mobile so we sent him ahead to the boats. A short time later, the command was given for the rest of us to head through town to the boats, so we loaded Elkins onto a stretcher and started out.

'As we moved along the road, I noticed the glow of a cigarette in the ditch and in a whisper asked the others who it was and why he was still there. Someone replied that it was Roberts, that he was dying, and that the cigarette was all that could be done for him. His partner, Santillan, had been hit in the middle of the back by one of the shells and blown in half.

'The boats were waiting and we loaded the wounded man into one of them. Then we knelt in the bottom, shoved off and began paddling like mad. It was so dark that we couldn't see a thing, and we had no idea how far we had come or had to go when an explosion and a big orange fireball a few feet above the water lit up the river to our left. Whether it was from a tank or from a fieldpiece we didn't know, but the Germans had apparently rushed in some kind of artillery, presumably an 88 mm, which was firing point-blank with shells timed to burst over our heads. Luckily the current had carried our boat to one side of their line of fire, so we just crouched lower and paddled faster. After half a dozen rounds the firing stopped. Moments later our boat ground to a sudden stop, and I had visions of us being stranded on a sandbar like sitting ducks. To our relief, we had safely reached the western shore and dawn was breaking as we straggled back into Nievenheim.

'Later in the day we learned the net results of the raid: three men dead, eleven others missing, three German prisoners taken. No one had seen Alex after he had been sent on ahead to the boats. The other missing men were presumed to have drowned when their boats capsized. We heard that one machine-gunner had his tripod around his neck and sank like a rock. The prisoners were all old men who could provide little information of any value and certainly weren't worth the men we had lost.

'In later years the division's history stated: "The raid cost the company three killed and four wounded, mostly from small-arms fire ... Two boats capsized in midstream ... and eight men were missing ..." Having been there, I know this to be at least partially inaccurate.

'There wasn't much time to rest. That same day the company packed up again and moved a mile north to the small village of Norf. Nothing eventful happened to us there except the announcement of the death of President Roosevelt. In spite of being in a combat zone, we were ordered to attend a memorial service for him that afternoon in full dress uniform.'

Roosevelt's death had not been entirely unexpected among the higher echelons of American political life, or among those of the Allied leaders who had seen the President at Yalta, but it came as a terrible shock to the American people and their allies.

The Nazi leaders were delighted. Some saw Roosevelt's death as a sign of divine intervention, a portent of a change for the better in Germany's fortunes. Dr Goebbels, the Reichminister of Propaganda, certainly took this view when he first heard the news, calling for the best champagne, congratulating the Führer on a "miracle", and reminding Hitler of an astrological forecast that the war would turn in Germany's favour during the second half of April. His public reaction was rather more muted. Goebbels was very careful to remove any sign of gloating from German broadcasts, and these adopted a neutral tone when referring to Roosevelt's successor, the former Vice-President, Harry S. Truman.

Winston Churchill received the news of the President's death with "a sense of irreparable loss". In spite of their differences over Russia, the future of the British Empire and the shape of the post-war world the two men were more than colleagues, having been deep personal friends for many years.

Roosevelt had been Britain's staunch supporter in the difficult years from 1939, through the defeats in France, the Battle of Britain and the Blitz, and the long bitter struggles in the North Atlantic and the Western Desert before Pearl Harbor and America's entry into the war in December 1941. Roosevelt had steered the Lease–Lend Bill through Congress to ensure Britain a steady supply of war material, ignored gloomy forecasts of Britain's inevitable defeat from the US ambassador in London, Joseph Kennedy, and over-ruled the wishes of the non-interventionist lobby. Roosevelt, like Churchill, had seen Anglo-American solidarity as the cornerstone of victory, and in spite of all the strains and pressures that solidarity held until the end.

If the German people or their Nazi leaders had hoped that the death of Roosevelt would lead to peace overtures from the new administration in Washington or any slackening of American resolve to finish the war fast, they were swiftly disappointed. President Harry Truman made it clear that his intention was 'to continue the work of his predecessor', get the war over and get the United Nations established during the forthcoming conference at San Francisco on 25 April. The only major change was a sensible and long overdue stiffening of American attitudes towards the aims and ambitions of Marshal Stalin, though this change came too late to affect the Soviet domination of Eastern Europe.

The soldiers at the front heard of Roosevelt's death with sadness, but they lived with death every day. The only way forward was to finish the war and they pushed on to that end, through a succession of shattered towns and cities, greeted with relief by sullen German citizens and with joy by tens of thousands of newly liberated men, the former inmates of the prisoner-of-war camps.

The wire

12 The Prisoners of War

'We were unloading Red Cross parcels,
when one of the German guards rode up on his bike.
He told us he loved cycling, adding: "When this
terrible war is over, I shall get on my bicycle
and ride all round our Great German Reich."'
'Oh, yes?' said one of the Kriegies, 'and what
will you do in the afternoon?'

Robin Ross Taylor
Stalag Luft 3

As the Allied armies moved into Germany in March 1945, they began to overrun prisoner-of-war camps or catch up with long columns of POWs being marched away from their liberators. Some of these prisoners had been captured in recent battles. Others had been prisoners since the early days of the war. Even now, with the end in sight, every ebb and flow of battle, every bombing raid or strafing attack over the Reich added more prisoners to the tens of thousands awaiting freedom behind the wire.

When an appeal went out for contributions to this book, there was a large response from POWs anxious to tell a little of their time in captivity. They were the 'Kriegies', a title taken from the German '*Kriegsgefageners*' – prisoners-of-war. Although some of the best books to come out of the Second World War – like *The Great Escape* or *The Wooden Horse* – are exciting tales, life in a POW camp was not one long round of concert parties, 'goon' baiting and escape attempts. Nor were all the prisoners kept in idleness in well-run camps. A great many of the 'other rank' prisoners were used for forced labour or sent to work on farms; and whatever their rank, for the great majority of POWs their years in a prison camp were a time of deprivation, hunger and not a little danger.

A description of daily life behind the wire comes from RAF rear-gunner Ron Eeles, who after being shot down in 1944 was imprisoned in one of the best-known camps, Stalag Luft 3 at Sagen in Southwest Germany. 'Stalag Luft 3 was a detention camp for airmen. The camp was built in a vast clearing in a pinewood forest and the inmates of the outer compounds had no vision beyond a vast impenetrable panorama of trees.

'There were five compounds, each containing between 500 and 1,000 men. All prisoners were Allied aircrew, including Naval airmen, but the Americans were segregated and occupied a compound of their own. I was in the East Compound, which by the end of 1944 housed close on 1,000 men.

'East Compound consisted of eight wooden huts, each split into ten rooms with fourteen men in a room the size of a household living room. The "furniture" consisted of a table, a bench and a small stove. Sleeping arrangements comprised two-tier bunks with wood slats supporting a palliasse of straw. The upper bunks collapsed if the occupant was unduly restless, thus causing havoc below. Another reason for collapse was a shortage of bed-slats, for a levy was imposed on each bunk during tunnelling operations as slats made ideal supports for tunnel structures.

'An issue of one blanket per man was totally inadequate during the winter months, and a ration of coal bricks was normally reserved for cooking only. The compounds were surrounded by barbed-wire fences with sentry boxes on stilts, referred to by us as 'goon-boxes' – goons being our name for the guards – sited at intervals along the boundaries of the camp. These were manned at all times. During darkness searchlights constantly swept the compounds.

'Ten feet inside the barbed wire was a single trip or warning wire. If anyone crossed this the nearest sentries would automatically open fire. Every new entrant had the importance of this wire instilled into him upon arrival. The compounds were continuously patrolled by guards nicknamed 'ferrets'. These men wore overalls and carried a steel rod and a torch. They were on the lookout for tunnelling activities and frequently disappeared under huts where they hoped to find evidence of tunnelling or overhear conversations of an incriminating nature.

'To counteract the attentions of the ferrets, the camp had a "duty pilot" system in the hut nearest the entrance. His responsibility was to keep a record of all ferrets inside the wire so that their whereabouts were always known. The ferrets became aware of this practice and one of the regulars was in the habit of walking over to the "duty pilot" to request that his arrival and departure be recorded. They were also after the illicit camp radio on which we obtained the BBC news.

'The camp inmates were a cosmopolitan lot with many civilian vocations. A small cross-section included a tram conductor, a millionaire's son, a waiter, a lord, a publican, a racehorse trainer (Marcus Marsh), a politician (Aidan Crawley), a dance-band leader, a professional dancer, a cowboy, a veterinary surgeon, a university don, a detective, a cobbler, a jockey, a dietician (I think he had a lean time of it), a radio announcer, a Texas Ranger, a Canadian mounted policeman, a professional gambler, a bookie, a piano tuner, and – believe it if you will – a self-confessed burglar, pickpocket and pimp.

'Our typical daily ration was ⅑th of a standard loaf of black bread, a bowl of soup, two potatoes and a small quantity of ersatz margerine and jam. Occasionally there was a handout of vegetables and a small quantity of meat, often rumoured to be horsemeat, but consumed without undue complaint.

'Fortunately, an issue of Red Cross parcels took place weekly which supplemented the diet. These parcels were primarily of American, British, Canadian and New Zealand origin. The normal issue was one parcel per person, and this added considerable interest to an otherwise drab menu.

'Cigarettes were the camp currency, and regular auction sales were held. Among goods offered for exchange were tinned foods from the Red Cross parcels, clothing, and any article capable of barter.

'No reference to prison camps would be complete without reference to escape efforts. The East Compound was considered the most difficult to escape from, partly due to the light, sandy soil. Although close on forty tunnels were started from mid-1942 onwards, not a single one was successful. This lack of success promoted thoughts in other directions, and in July 1943 the "Wooden Horse" escape began, when three officers, after digging a tunnel beneath a vaulting horse, made a clear getaway and all returned safely to England.

'This escape involved a homemade vaulting horse being placed in the same spot each day, within ten yards of the camp boundary. Two men were concealed inside, and while other inmates of the camp were invited to keep fit by vaulting over it, a tunnel was dug below it. The whole "Wooden Horse" escape took some four months. In March 1944, a mass outbreak of seventy-six RAF prisoners took place through a tunnel nicknamed "Harry", which exceeded 350 feet in length and 30 feet in depth. It was this "Great Escape" which led to the shooting of fifty RAF officers by the Gestapo. Following this tragic event, all future attempts were prohibited by the Senior British Officer (SBO).

'It was common practice to walk round the warning wire for exercise –

known as "circuit bashing" – and a complete circuit of the East Compound measured 932 yards. One had to walk warily as some danger lurked in the background. We had, for instance, a nine-hole golf course made by the golfing enthusiasts who performed quite creditably with homemade clubs and balls. Nevertheless, a raucous "Fore!" occasionally made one duck for cover. A homemade golf ball cost 200 cigarettes on the mart.

'Academically, one could delve into many subjects. A plentiful supply of books had built up over the years due to the Swiss Red Cross, our Protecting Power who looked after the welfare of Allied POWs. Dramatics also played a prominent part in camp life and productions took place monthly. The shows were normally accompanied by the camp orchestra whose signature tune, appropriately, was 'Time on my Hands'. In spite of continuous practice their performances left much to be desired and we could not always get out of earshot.

'We did not encounter many problems with the guards, who were either elderly or unfit for active duty. They did not interfere with us provided we complied with camp regulations. By mid-1944 most of them showed no interest in the war and gave the impression that the conflict was as good as lost.

'Two roll-calls, known as *"Appells"*, took place daily, but there were also random hut checks, when all the occupants were locked out for several hours while a thorough search took place.

'It was on such occasions that lectures for the politically minded by our budding MP or dancing lessons by our professional dancer held some appeal. I have often wondered what some of us must have looked like doing a "slow, slow, quick–quick–slow" to a record by Victor Sylvester.

'This was everyday life in Stalag Luft 3 up to early January 1945, when the Russian advance from the east necessitated our speedy removal elsewhere. In spite of the holiday camp image I may have unintentionally created, camp life was frequently boring and frustrating.'

Sergeant Hurst joined the RAFVR as a weekend flyer six months before war was declared. By April 1941 he was a sergeant-observer with 51 Squadron. 'We were shot down by flak while endeavouring to hit the submarine pens at Kiel in the early hours of 8 April 1941. I came down in Schleswig-Holstein on an estate owned by a German who spoke excellent English with a strong Canadian accent. From his mansion we were collected by the German Army and taken to a sea-plane base on the Baltic coast. The crews of the German planes were as friendly as one could wish, and we regaled them with exaggerated tales of the Whitley bomber.

'During four years in captivity I found the Germans to be better than I expected, except for a very few individuals. The commandant of Stalag Luft 1, near the town of Barth, had been a prisoner of the British in the

1914–18 war. His attitude appeared to be that since he had been fairly treated by the British then, he would do the same by us now. Before the Gestapo prohibited it, he would allow prisoners under escort to bathe in the nearby bay, and allow parties to go for walks outside the camp. He would also allow us to sing the National Anthem, but all this was stopped by the end of 1941.

'I also remember the camp interpreter, who had lived in North London before hostilities, and he gave us German lessons. The other guards were a mixture, all believing that England was "Kaput" – finished. One prisoner was shot in the heart while attempting to escape and I was shot in the chest and leg by a rifle shot – fired as a warning to keep me away from the wire – which splintered on hitting the ground ... but that was just bad luck!

'In 1941, a former BBC radio engineer managed to built a primitive radio receiver from silver paper found in cigarette packets, plus graphite from ordinary lead pencils, plus odds and ends, either stolen or bartered. This receiver was sufficient to pick up Morse transmissions containing news from England which was translated into plain language and read in each hut. As far as I am aware this was the first receiver to have been made in a POW camp during the 1939–45 war. In the course of time the receiver was reduced in size and concealed in a piano accordian, which still played in a restricted way. It was later conveyed to Stalag Luft 2 in April 1942 and remained in service throughout our captivity and can be seen today in the RAF Museum at Hendon in London.

'During this time we received British Red Cross parcels, with occasional Canadian parcels. The German ration for prisoners was the equivalent of 900 calories per day, mainly of rye bread, potatoes and swedes with the occasional thin meat soup – so we must consider our comparative good health as due entirely to the Red Cross. Even so, I lost two-and-a-half stones in weight during those four years in captivity.'

German treatment of POWs varied and much depended on their rank and nationality. Officers of the Western allies were not obliged to work, and their stories of their time in prison, their attempts to escape, successful or otherwise, and their baiting of the German guards has been the subject of many books and films. Russian and Polish officers were frequently shot on capture or, if taken alive, sent for slave labour.

The rank and file of the POWs were obliged to work, though by the terms of both the Geneva and Hague Conventions they could not be employed on work which 'gave direct assistance to the enemy war effort'. This caveat did not prevent many Allied soldiers being sent to work in coal mines and munitions factories or to build fortifications, but at least the Western POWs were fed. Russian POWs were usually treated as slaves, frequently beaten, starved and worked to death. Prisoners from the Western Allies relied for the bulk of their food on Red Cross parcels supplied under the terms of the Geneva Convention. Soviet Russia was not a signatory to the Convention and no one, including the Soviet Government itself, took any interest in the welfare of Russian POWs.

Of the nearly six million Soviet prisoners-of-war taken by the Germans between June 1941 and May 1945, only one million survived captivity. Two million died of starvation, overwork, brutality and neglect. A million simply disappeared, murdered on capture or later by the SS or SD (the Gestapo). At least another million served in one capacity or another in the German armies, some in front-line formations like the divisions of General Andrei Vlasov. There are many accounts of Russian prisoners serving in the flak-artillery detachments defending the cities of the Ruhr. All these Russians were shot or sent to labour camps on their return to Soviet Russia in 1945.

German prisoners captured by Soviet forces often suffered a similar fate. To give just one example, of the 90,000 soldiers of the German VII Army who surrendered at Stalingrad in 1943, only 5,000 returned from captivity in the Soviet Union, years after the war ended.

Following the proclamation of the notorious 'Commando Order' in 1942, British Commandos and American Rangers captured on small-scale raids were turned over to the SD for interrogation and execution. This order was used to shoot British paratroopers attacking the heavy-water plants in Norway, and the Royal Marines of Operation Frankton, captured after their canoe raid on German shipping in the harbour at Bordeaux.

If they survived the precarious moments of capture, the POW faced years in captivity – 'a sentence with no visible end and no remission' – in the words of one old Kriegie.

The stories which follow come from a broad cross-section of prisoners captured in many theatres of war and describe what their life behind the wire was like, and how it ended in the winter and spring of 1945.

John D. White joined the British Army in 1939. 'My unit was the 58th (Sussex) Field Regiment, RA, part of the 44th Division. I was captured outside Dunkirk in May 1940 and finished up at Stalag 88 at Lamsdorf – Upper Silesia. My POW No was 10722. From there we were "invited" to work for the Reich at an oil refinery. I worked for almost five years to see this project completed and then destroyed by US bombers, and we were released by General Patton's forces at Moosburg in Bavaria in April 1945.

'The early years of POW life were undoubtedly the worst. Up at 4 a.m. summer and winter, and on the job at 6 a.m. every day except Sunday. We worked all day from 6 a.m. to 6 p.m. without food. Poor health, hunger and exhaustion took its toll and it was not long before we became infested with lice. It should be added that British POWs did have a small trump card in the form of the Geneva Convention, which offered some "protection from hardship". This was only effective if your captors felt inclined to comply with the rules, but I felt for the Russian and Polish prisoners who had no one to help or protect them.

'After the first year, Red Cross parcels were sent to Allied POWs. When parcels did get through to us, the quantities were so small, as they had to be shared by eight to ten men. When conditions allowed, quantities increased and sometimes we were able to share a parcel between four men. The day we were given on parcel between two men was considered the next best thing to Heaven.

'Christmas 1944 saw the last air raid. On returning to camp we found everything destroyed, for Allied aircraft had bombed the refinery and the surrounding area and the advancing Russians had only stopped at Cracow to regroup. Some of us were sheltering in a destroyed bath-house when we heard the sound of visitors who turned out to be a Russian Reconnaissance group. This group went back unmolested by the Germans, but only after their vehicle fell into a bomb crater outside the gates of our camp.

'The next morning we were told to pack anything we could carry and prepare to march west, across the Oder before the Russians got there, after which the bridges were to be blown. I found a piece of wooden ladder which could be pulled like a sled and on this I packed as much food, clothing, cigarettes and water as I could, also a spare pair of Army boots which only just survived the long march from Upper Silesia to Moosburg.

'This walk took fourteen weeks to complete and is almost impossible to describe. Our only ambition was to survive each day; we had no idea where we were going, only that we were going in the direction of the Western Front, wherever that might be!

'On the first day we marched all day and all night in order to cross the Oder as quickly as possible. The guards were very nervous and urged us on with boots and rifle butts. On the way we passed a large number of concentration camp prisoners, clad in their striped pyjamas, some without shoes in the freezing snow. They were being beaten unmercifully by their guards.

'We usually marched all day, keeping clear of the main roads, covering about twenty miles from dawn to dusk. Each night we stopped at a farm and bedded down in straw in barns, where the farmer was forced to feed both the guards and us. Food was short and we were lucky to get a slice of black bread or potatoes. The weather continued bitterly cold and one night someone stepped on my left boot, denting it where it touched one of my toes. We always slept with our boots on for fear of losing them, or even not being able to put them on again in the morning. That night was well below zero and I contracted frostbite where the boot touched my toe. In a day or so my toe swelled up and was so painful I could barely walk.

'Overcome with weariness, our inclination was to sit on the side of the road. This did not please one of our guards, a moron with bright red cheeks, who we had nicknamed the "Farmer's Boy". Most of us rose to our feet quickly at his shout, except for one of our companions. The guard used his rifle butt on this unfortunate soldier, who raised his arm to ward off the blow. The guard then fired point-blank into the prisoner's chest, the bullet passing straight through his back and narrowly missing three of us in the next row. This soldier, a member of the Royal Sussex Regiment, was so close to freedom...

'His death did not go unavenged at Moosberg. Our guards had surrendered and we were questioned by Patton's troops as to whether we had been mistreated by the guards. We told them that one of our companions had been murdered and that was the end for the Farmer's Boy, who was taken away and shot.'

Charlie Leggatt of the Cameron Highlanders had been captured with the 51st (Highland) Division at St Valery-en-Caux in 1940. 'Our journey to captivity involved forced marches through Northern France to be displayed as "spoils of war". The French populace endeavoured to throw us a crust of bread, and after the first few days we were served with a small ladle of black bean soup; to gauge the quantity, a round fifty-cigarette tin, which was service issue then, more than held the ration. We slept in the open, in orchards or some similar place.

'We went over the border to Belgium, where my mate and I spent the time picking the lice off our shirts. The Belgians were so scared of the Germans they would not even give us water, unlike the Dutch, who put out buckets of soup on occasions.

'On New Year's Day 1945 I lay in the Stalag hospital with a damaged ankle, having fallen off a truck at a factory in Ottmachau, a small provincial town in the area while on *Arbeitskommando* (work party). Stalag was a grim place then. Red Cross supplies had long since ended because of Allied bombing of the railways.

'In the last days of January 1945, word was passed around that all had to parade with their possessions, little as they were, for a march west. Imagine a snake of, say, 10,000 prisoners, five abreast, a guard on each side. We were driven on with overnight shelter in the huge barns peculiar to the area. I learned to climb to the upper loft to evade the occasional shower of urine from above! One could not take off the frozen boots for two reasons; firstly to avoid the danger of stealing, and secondly, the difficulty of getting them on again in the morning. Onwards we trudged through Upper Silesia to Gorlitz in Lower Silesia. Places I remember were Bautzen, Dresden, Weimar, Erfurt, Mulhausen.

'On the morning of 8 April 1945 we awoke to find the guards gone. Shortly afterwards an American jeep drew up at the compound gate amid understandable jubilation, especially among those of us nearing the end of a five-year internment. We had a couple of American walking-wounded with us, who joined us when we passed through a Stalag occupied by Americans taken in the Ardennes offensive of December 1944. They were very low in morale, weary and dejected ... poor fellows, after only a few months "in the bag". On 13 April, twenty-nine of us flew from Kassel in a Dakota, landing on an American air base at Membury in Blighty.'

New Zealander Peter Christian was captured in Greece in 1943. 'I was with the 19th Infantry Battalion, 2nd New Zealand Division and left behind, wounded, when Greece was evacuated in 1941. The Greeks tended my wounds and I lived with a Greek family for eighteen months until "traded in" by another family for food. I ended up in Lamsdorf near Breslau and from there went to a working party in Bauerwitz.

'Our working camp, a brickworks, was situated in the village of Bauerwitz in the southeast of Ober Silesia near the Polish and Czechoslovakian borders. There were two work camps in the area, ours, consisting of a dozen or so assorted nationalities – English, South African, Australian and New Zealanders – at the brickworks, and another camp of similar size and composition at a dairy factory. The unmistakable sounds of war were growing daily. A large number of the local civilians had already moved away to the west and the American sphere of influence, and then, like many other POWs, we were marched west – away from the Russians.

'We were horrified to see numbers of striped-pyjama-clad bodies lying along the roadside, concentration camp victims too weak to continue the trek and shot by their guards. The sight seemed to upset our guards who were not SS but ordinary soldiers repatriated from the front after being wounded. We had something in common with these men so we were reasonably friendly towards each other. This concern was evident when a trigger-happy guard shot and killed one of our men who had left the column to scavenge an empty shed for anything edible. The other guards gave the killer hell, one guard even hitting him with a rifle butt. Our column now had about 200 assorted POWs and even at our slow pace we had overtaken two columns of concentration camp inmates.

'For the first few weeks of the march the war could have been a thousand miles away. We didn't hear bombing or shelling, we didn't see aircraft, not even vapour trails in the distance, nor did we see any troop movements. This was a change from our working party where every day we saw evidence of conflict. Bauerwitz was on a main rail link to the Eastern Front through Cracow, and troop trains passed the brickworks which were built alongside the rail line. Troops, tanks, evacuees, Russian POWs, we saw them all.

There was also plenty of action in the sky above and we were impressed with the way a couple of German fighters would attack three or four dozen Allied bombers before being shot down.

'The sounds of battle returned. Bombers flying high and fighters flying low were with us every day. In mid-March we marched to the German border, but we had little idea of dates or time. We had arrived at a place called Brux with an enormous POW camp alongside the Hermann Goering Werks, a factory completely wrecked by American daylight raids and night raids by British bombers. The Brits dropped flares at the limits of the factory and bombed within the markers. The Americans dropped their bombs as soon as the target came in sight and between raids we were employed in cleaning up the wreckage. It was a gigantic heap of twisted steel and powdered bricks covering mangled bodies. With two raids a day there wasn't much point in the clean-up. The Germans would shelter in concrete air raid shelters, or would head for the open country with the POWs, who weren't allowed in the shelters.

'We awoke one smoky morning to discover we had no guards and that there was hell to pay artillery-wise from the direction of the Russians. Some quick meetings were held by the POWs to decide what to do. Some were for staying until released by the Russians, others were for heading in the direction of the Americans.

'I teamed up with a Royal Marine, Harry Fry from Blackpool, and we took off heading west. The POWs who awaited the Russians were to spend some uncomfortable weeks with our Eastern Allies in the Crimea and were to arrive back in the UK six or eight weeks after we had been delivered to safety by the USAAF.

'Many Germans, both army and civilian, had the same idea – rather the Americans than the Russians – and no one gave Harry and me more than a passing glance. I began to feel that the large, red POW diamonds sewn onto our battledress jackets were potential bullseyes for some mean-spirited German soldier. I wanted to rip mine off but Harry said, "No, it's our only means of identification." The Germans were less likely to shoot a POW than they were some deserter from a labour battalion.

'Around midday we caught up with some French POWs who weren't very pleased to see us. It's strange that we never got along with the French, and whatever these had in mind they didn't want us with them. We felt a bit peckish so called at a farmhouse and asked for food. The occupants were an elderly couple looking as nervous as we felt, but in broken German we explained how hungry we were and the farmer told us all he had were potatoes. We accepted a bag and fled.

'The shelling was getting closer. Russian fighter planes were everywhere, shooting at anything that moved. We didn't make much progress that day

251

and by late afternoon we decided to rest up in a large barn half-filled with hay. We lit a fire outside to bake the potatoes, and a couple of our French friends suddenly turned up to help us eat them.

'Next morning we were aroused by the sound of whining gears, shooting, shouts and the clatter of tank tracks. A score of heads popped out of the hay. Men of half-a-dozen nationalities raced to the barn door to see a Russian advance party moving down the road in the direction we hoped to go. We crossed our fingers and set out after them.

'After a couple of kilometres a fresh burst of firing broke out ahead. We found ourselves in the middle of the Russian column. A Russian officer strode up and harangued us for a couple of minutes until we managed to convince him we were POWs. He then waved us on. We walked on through the Russians towards a village about 200 metres away. There were white sheets hanging from the windows but not a soul in sight. A couple of German half-tracks were smouldering on the outskirts of the village, obviously the target of the shooting we had heard.

'As we moved nearer we could see movement from the windows. I glanced back and right behind us were Russians with machine-pistols at the ready; we were being used as cover. I spoke to Harry and moved closer to the ditch. We saw a glint in one of the windows and Harry and I hit the ditch as both sides opened fire.

'From the shelter of the ditch we watched the Russians clear the village. There was nothing subtle about the house clearing but it was certainly effective. They just poured in through the doors and windows, mowing down anything that moved. When the shooting and yelling stopped, we eased ourselves out of the ditch and headed out of the village. We paused by a destroyed anti-tank gun to see if there was anything worth having as a souvenir of the occasion, but a yell from a Russian soldier indicated that he would claim whatever was available. Some of the German crew were still alive. Maybe the villagers would get to them when the Russians moved on. It must be one of the most lonely and helpless moments of a soldier's short life, to be left alone and badly wounded with only the enemy around him.

'Harry and I moved on towards Karlsbad and the Americans. A few kilometres on we were stopped by a German rear-guard wanting to know what was behind us. We told them there was a Russian column. They shrugged and headed back to their positions. We were stopped and questioned many times by German troops but they were not interested in us. One German officer told us we would be safer travelling in pairs rather than in a group that could be mistaken for Russians. We did break up the group but were still fired on by an SS road block.

'About three hours later we arrived in Karlsbad. The outskirts were completely deserted and Harry and I trudged the empty streets. As we approached the end of an avenue we saw four tanks ahead. We stopped and were about to retrace our steps when we were hailed from the direction of the road block by an unmistakable American voice: "Who are you?"

' "English POWs."

' "Advance one at a time with your hands on your heads."

'We had reached the limit of the American advance into this area of Germany. We learned that the war had ended five days ago, on 9 May 1945.'

Richard Clark, now of London, Ontario, Canada, saw what happened when the Russian troops arrived: 'I was in a work camp in eastern Germany. There were 400 POWs and we worked twelve hours a day making hydraulic cylinders and ball-bearings. Our meals consisted of one bowl of soup and two slices of bread every twenty-four hours. Before things got worse in Germany we used to get the odd food parcel from the Red Cross. We were kept informed of the progress of the war by German Communists who worked with us, and by the beginning of April we knew the Russians were massing not far away at Colbus. One Monday morning, as we were walking to the factory, we heard the guns and by noon more POWs from other camps had joined us.

'We reached the main camp, Stalag 4B, and knew the war was nearly over as the German guards had disappeared. On 23 April Russian Cossacks of the 1st Ukrainian Front rode into camp, going straight to the Russian POW compound where they armed all the Russian POWs. They then went berserk, going to the nearest farms, raping the women and killing all the livestock. Some Russian POWs who had been working with us went back into the town and killed over 100 people, including the town dentist and his daughter.

'The Russians put guards on the rest of us and marched us to a place called Reisa, where we were put in an old panzer barracks, but allowed to roam the town because they couldn't feed us. We depended for food on looting houses that the Germans had left in a hurry.

'On 23 May 1945 – two weeks after the war ended – we were marched into a field with large pictures of Stalin, Roosevelt and Churchill on three sides, and exchanged for Russian soldiers taken prisoner by the Americans. The delay was because the Americans knew their Russian prisoners would be shot as traitors for fighting for the Germans, but that was the only way the Russians would let us go.'

Many American and British POWs were detained for weeks by the Russians, as Raymond Heard, an RAF navigator, wrote in his diary: '30 April: Liberated on 22 April but our continued detention in this prison camp – Stalag 3A – by the Russian authorities has now passed the bounds of being irksome. Getting home is all we can think about and the roadblocks which have been put in the way are calculated to cause us to do something desperate to ease our frustration. We have been told that there is a large pocket of German resistance in the area; occasionally we hear gunfire and shells have come near the camp.

'Last night the Russians issued an order that we must all report – 10,000 of us – to be identified and fingerprinted before we can be sent home. We can't see the relevance or value of this operation but we are willing to succumb to it if it will help our release.

'The next morning, when we reported to continue the dreary process, we were informed that the order had been countermanded and the procedure cancelled. During a walk through the woods near the camp this afternoon, a friend and I were accosted by a Russian soldier who raised his rifle and demanded our watches. Mine had been confiscated by the Germans after we were shot down but my friend was wearing his wristwatch, which he refused to hand over. The Russian blustered and threatened until finally he was given the watch, which he put on his arm to join the other nine he had stolen and which stretched from his wrist to his elbow. After the good reports we had heard about the behaviour of the occupying troops, this came as a blow; but we had to admit that every army has its gangsters.'

Milton Wroblewski of Portage, Wisconsin, was captured in Italy in 1944 while serving with the 335th Infantry Regiment, 88th US Division. 'Twenty of us were captured in a farmhouse in Vedriano in the northern Appenines. We were taken north, about twenty miles, through our own artillery fire, and interrogated by a German captain. Then we had a five-day box-car trip to Germany, sixty men to a car. We were left in Munich during a bombing raid at noon and then taken to Moosburg and Stalag 5–2A near Dachau, until rescued by troops of General Patton's 3rd US Army.

'I used to go to Munich on ten-men work details with one German guard. Every noon the guard had to take us to a bomb shelter or to a cave while the raids were going on. On one occasion we were walking through the streets of Munich with a wheelbarrow when the two fellows with me said we should try to escape. I told them that we could take the wheelbarrow with us but we would not get far, and if caught by the SS we didn't know if they would take us back to camp or shoot us. That was a thing they loved to do.

'Some of them hated Americans, but the Austrian guard I used to go to Munich with treated us well, even though it cost me an American cigarette to have him look away while I talked to a *fraulein* and had her get me some of the black sawdust bread. I tried to get at least six loaves so that I could feed the ten of us Americans who ate together.'

Not every released POW simply went home. One British soldier,

Christopher Portway, captured in Normandy in 1944, fought with the American infantry of Patton's 3rd US Army after his release.

'Following my escape I made my way towards the American forces, being bombed and strafed continually, including a machine-gun attack by US Marauders which holed the pramload of Red Cross goodies I had "liberated" from a bombed Red Cross parcel train.

'The front line was extremely fluid but SS troops had formed some sort of stand against the advancing American tanks near a Bavarian village, I know not where, just as I got there pramless and foodless. Hiding beneath blackberry bushes in a wood, I watched the Germans prepare to defend the area with 88 mm guns being manhandled into position at the edge of the wood and Germans passed within a few feet of me. The Americans started shelling the wood, slicing the tops off trees, some of which promptly fell on me. I became distinctly unhappy until I noticed that the Germans were packing up to withdraw.

'When they had gone I emerged to be met by a hail of machine-gun fire from the Americans every time I showed myself. I shouted that I was British, whereupon they shouted questions about baseball teams and football teams, but as I knew nothing about either game it wasn't much help. Eventually the Americans relented on the grounds that I was so pig-ignorant I must be a Limey.

'I was then given my first decent meal for a year – fried eggs on white bread; I was as sick as a dog but it was worth it. When asked if I could operate a Browning .50 machine-gun I said I could and was invited to become gunner for a half-track instead of being sent to the rear as a released prisoner.

'The days ahead were easy enough, rolling forward and halting when opposed. The Americans were not risking lives at this stage of the war; not theirs anyway. At the slightest opposition we simply radioed for an artillery "stonk" or an air strike, the latter coming almost before we had finished giving the map co-ordinates. Crashes, bangs, fire and smoke, followed by a loud silence, and on we rolled again over a litter of broken masonry, scrap metal and rag-doll bodies. Prisoners came in with their hands in the air and we pointed the way we had come and left them to it. Only the old men of the German Home Guard fought to the bitter end. We all felt sorry for them, but not for the bastards of the Hitler Youth, who fought frantically until we pulverized them.

'We gave sweets to the children and made the adults work and cook for us. My American companions were perpetually grumbling about their K rations, but I found them manna from heaven – but then I would, wouldn't I? I certainly found them to be better than the British Army rations I had received in Normandy.

'Overhead, great fleets of aircraft passed en route to "take out" another town or city, and we cheered them on their way. We had lost all sense of pity. Then one day the sky was empty and we were informed that hostilities were to cease at lunchtime ... or whenever it was; and I hadn't even fired my Browning.'

Among many POWs from the Allied air forces was Australian George Haggard of 466 (RAF) Squadron, Bomber Command, shot down in February 1944. 'I was the flight engineer; with the exception of the bomb aimer the rest of the crew were Australians. We baled out over the German border on the way back from the Berlin raid on 15 February 1944, landed unhurt and were picked up within twenty-four hours. After a short spell in Dulag Luft, the officers went to Stalag Luft 3, and the rest of us to Luft 6, a five-day trip by cattle truck. This was not as bad as it sounds because at that time we were not partitioned by barbed wire. The thirty-odd prisoners were supposed to have half the space and the six guards the other half, but in practice a more equable arrangement ensued.

'About half the prisoners were US airmen from the 8th Air Force, some of whom had managed to retain their peaked caps with the cellophane covers – don't ask me how. I can remember as the train trundled through the night towards East Prussia (we had the lowest priority on the system), the guards looked on in amazement as the Americans had a barn dance to the music of a mouth-organ. Over five days in a confined space, tempers became frayed on both sides, and there were occasions when the Germans started calling the Americans "luft gangsters" and us "terror *fleigers*", and herded us back to our half of the truck, but after a couple of hours it would simmer down and they would retreat to their corner and we'd all spread out again. Surprisingly, I look back on that journey almost with pleasure.

'On the march out, either on 17 or 19 April 1945, we arrived at the small town of Gresse. I hadn't even had time to take my pack off when I heard a shout "Typhoons!" and two or three aircraft were seen banking round and lining up on the road. I dived behind the nearest tree. They came in with rocket and anti-personnel bombs and one of the rockets exploded just in front of my tree and blew back. If I had been on the other side I would have got the chop. They came in again and I got to the ditch at the side of the road just as they made another strike. I made tracks for the ploughed field at the side of the road and had got about 25 yards into it when I saw four or five shallow craters littered with British and German bodies. When one of the Typhoons lined up on the road again, I remember thinking, "If he fires he'll miss me. He must be out of bombs by now, and I'm damned if I'm going down in the mud again."

'It was an odd feeling because before becoming aircrew I had been a mechanic on 181 (Typhoon) Squadron. However, instead of firing, he flew along just above the treetops and waggled his wings, but by this time the damage was done. The padre had formed a party who had turned their RAF greatcoats inside out to form the letters R–A–F. The aftermath was typical: one minute there was total chaos, then about 30 seconds of complete silence, then shouts of "Stretcher-bearers!", and from the Germans, "All the wounded walk on to the next farm as quickly as possible." I think they meant walking-wounded! I heard there were thirty dead and I hope that figure is correct, because I understood it was nearer seventy with thirty wounded, the high death toll being due to the number who died from wounds later.

'On 2 May we reached a village called Kittlitz and the news of the surrender came through. The guards laid down their arms and said, "We are now your prisoners." I can't remember seeing them marched off. I think a lot of them dispersed into the countryside in the hope of making it home. From Luneburg we were transported by US Army trucks to Holland and thence back to the UK on 9 May 1945.'

Henry Freedman was a sergeant in the 442nd Infantry Regiment, 106th US Infantry Division when he was captured during the Battle of the Bulge. 'I was in a group of about thirty-five men pinned down by 88 mm fire from Tiger tanks. Next day we were marched through the town of Prüm and loaded into box-cars. On Christmas Eve 1944 we were bombed by the RAF while sitting in freight yards and on Christmas Day we arrived at Stalag 9B Bad Orb.

'The Germans wanted more information than name, rank and serial number and had us strip to the waist in zero weather, but they finally relented. The NCOs and officers moved out on 25 January and I was sent to Stalag 9A Zeigenhain. I weighed 165 lb. when captured and 110 lb. when liberated on 30 March 1945 by the American 6th Armoured Division.

'I kept a diary and noted the contents of the first Red Cross parcel I received, which included two cans sardines, corned beef, meat and beans, liver pate, cheddar cheese, grape jam, coffee, milk, margarine, cocoa, cigarettes, biscuits, sugar, prunes, vitamin C tablets, salt and pepper, soap.

'My diary entry for 5 March 1945 reads: Rations cut to a quarter, ten men to a loaf. March 9: English, French and Russian POWs arrived from Breslau area after forty-three-day hike. 14 March: First beautiful day – everybody went outside – played ball and enjoyed the sunshine. 21 March: Camp strafed by American pilot. French POWs hit. 22 March: Deloused. Commissioner representing the American Government arrived from Switzerland. 29 March: A day to remember! At 0800 hrs we fell out in formation so the Germans could move us out of the Stalag in groups. When the first group fell out, the Germans changed their minds and decided they wouldn't move any of us at all. We got a very thick barley soup and French bread.

By early evening the Germans had taken off or given themselves up. The camp was ours! The next day, 30 March, we were liberated. A 6th Armoured jeep was the first American vehicle to enter the camp. What a sight! We were told that we would leave at any time – America here I come!'

George Rosie of the 101st US Airborne Division had been captured in Normandy on D-Day 1944. 'In France we didn't run into many mean Germans, but in Germany it was different. When they said "Move!" we moved and we moved fast. The Germans treated the Russians particularly badly, and they didn't receive Red Cross parcels because the USSR did not recognize the Geneva Accord. That cost a lot of Russians their lives.

'When we got to the camp we received twelve cigarettes and a quarter of a British Red Cross parcel. The compound was primarily English with about twenty Americans to each barracks. The British ran the compound like it was a British colony and we all answered to their "Man of Confidence", who was elected by the men. Their sergeant-major was our direct representative to the Germans.

'Of the four camps I was in, Stalag 4B was by far the best-run camp. The Brits had everything organized. Believe me, their sergeant-major was in charge and he let you know it in no uncertain terms. Red Cross parcels and the food could be bartered at our exchange store. The money was cigarettes. Every parcel had a cigarette price. We didn't get fat, but after a period of time we began to get some of our strength back and a little bit of our weight. We could walk to the Canadian, Dutch and French compounds, but the Russian compound was off-limits.

'In November it turned really cold. We had no heat in the barracks. Bogie, Bradley and I were sleeping in a double bunk with six blankets. Each of us took turns sleeping in the middle – until we discovered I was the only one who didn't have to get up in the middle of the night to go pee. From then on I had the warm spot. In early January 1945, men from the Battle of the Bulge started coming into camp. Some of them were Airborne but a lot of them were from the 106th US Division, a very green outfit that the Germans chewed up during the battle.

'On 6 January we were taken down to the railroad station, put in German Army box-cars, which had a small stove in them and a small supply of coal plus three days rations. The old experienced Kriegies, Bradley, Bogie and I, volunteered to tend the stove so we could be closer to the heat. In a few days we unloaded at Stalag 3B at Fürstenburg. The barracks had not been used for quite some time and they were a mess. The next day we went into the compound and found other barracks that were empty and took all the bed slats back to our barracks.

'The next day we got a hot shower, clean underwear, which was a minor miracle, and one American Red Cross parcel between two men. We heard over our radio that the Russians were moving fast. In Stalag 4B we were worried about the Eastern Front. On 31 January 1945, 4,080 American NCOs started on a six-day march. It was colder than hell, down around zero. We had been given some old overcoats which was a blessing, but no one had hats or gloves or boots.

'We moved all day with a few short breaks. We stopped by barns around 5 o'clock. Again, no food. One POW walked over to an old German woman standing by a fence in the front yard and tried to trade a bar of soap for some food. One of the guards walked up behind him and smacked him on the back of the head with his rifle butt. He dropped like a sack of potatoes. As we were marched into the barn we walked by him but there was no sign of life, the back of his head was smashed in and he was bleeding badly.

'In the morning everyone was cold and stiff as hell. It felt like you were ninety years old. Our break was near a Jewish concentration camp. They looked like skeletons and we saw a guard beat them with clubs. The Germans got us back on the road and as we were moving out, one guy yelled out, "You lousy goddamed Krauts. God will get even with you some day. He will. He will. He will."

'Further on down the road we saw Jews digging gun emplacements. We saw a guard pull a revolver and shoot one of the Jews who dropped into the ditch. It was a day I'll never forget. To this day, when I see a photo or film about those concentration camps, I get sick all over again.

'Stalag 3A was about twenty-five miles southeast of Berlin. For about the last thirty days before we were liberated, hundreds and hundreds of US bombers flying very high would turn just as they passed the camp and head for Berlin. On 23 April one of the men in our tent was up early, probably to check the water tap, and when he went out he found there were no guards, not even on the main gate. Around 9.00 a.m. a Russian Sherman tank came down and flattened the barbed-wire fences. On one of the tanks was a big husky woman of, I'd say, around thirty-five. We found out she was the tank commander. At one point she jumped off the tank and ran over to one of the little half-starved Russian POWs, picked him up and hugged him. We later found out he was her brother.

'There were female soldiers carrying rifles and Tommy-guns. The Russians in the POW camp were given rifles and were back in the Army; half-starved but nevertheless they were back in the Army. I would have hated like hell to have been any German in the way as they marched on Berlin.'

Private David Thom was just nineteen when he was captured in 1940. 'I was with C Company, 5th Bn, the Gordon Highlanders, 51st (Highland) Division. I was captured on 12 June 1940 at St Valery-en-Caux and sent to Stalag 20A at Thorn, where I was put into a dungeon in one of the forts for not saluting a German soldier. The real punishment was missing food –

one-fifth of a loaf, roughly two slices, and a ladle of watery soup a day.

'I was then sent to work on a farm belonging to a Major Brandt. There were ten of us, nine Gordons and one Black Watch. Our normal working hours were 6 a.m. to 8 p.m., six days per week, but we were decently fed. On Good Friday 1942, the farmer came to us and said, "Your sergeant has been shot." Sergeant Ted Speake was our senior rank.

'Our guard was a brutal, sadistic pig, who would arrive at our billet in the morning and jab anyone slow with his bayonet. A day or two prior to the shooting he had beaten my pal Arthur with his rifle butt and only the intervention of the farmer saved Arthur from being killed; Arthur died a few months later as a direct consequence of this beating. On Good Friday the lads had returned to the billet and were sitting around when the guard appeared and chased them out, using his bayonet and rifle butt. He went up behind Sergeant Speake and shot him in the back, killing him instantly. He then bayoneted another man in the back, piercing his stomach. A German officer arrived and put the guard under arrest; the wounded man was taken to hospital and Sergeant Speake was buried in the local cemetery.

'On 20 January 1945, as the Russian Army approached, we were ordered to a flat area near the bridge across the Vistula. There was a continuous stream of Germans crossing the bridge: troops, tanks, motor transport, horse-drawn transport, the lot. We were kept standing around until late in the day and issued with a tin of meat between two, our first meal since we left Klein-Tromnau. When it was realized we couldn't cross the bridge, we were taken down river and sent across the ice.

'We eventually came to Magdeburg, a much-bombed city, and were put into a school. There were roughly a hundred men in our room and the floor was covered in straw and crawling with lice. After one night we were all crawling with lice too. We came eventually to a place called Gossa near Torgau, where the American and Russian armies met, and we were liberated by the Americans.

'After liberation we were taken by truck to Halle and smothered in DDT – boy ... did that shift the lice! We were looked after by the Americans who couldn't have been kinder, and flown by Dakota to Brussels and from there in Lancaster bombers to an airfield near Aylesbury, and a day or two later we all went home.'

Arley Koodenkauf was twenty-six years old in January 1945 and a corporal in the 377th Parachute Field Artillery, 101st US Airborne Division, when he dropped into Normandy at 0100 hrs on D-Day. 'On 31 January 1945 I was a prisoner in Stalag 3C. The camp was being evacuated so I escaped by hiding with three of my room-mates. We guessed that the Soviet forces were near and that the Germans would try to send all prisoners across the Oder. The column leaving the camp came under attack by Russian tanks a few miles from camp, sustained several casualties and eventually returned to camp. The second attempt was again interrupted by the Russians and most of the prisoners were liberated. One small contingent was double-timed towards Küstrun and spent several more months in captivity. I rejoined the others back at the camp which was now controlled by Soviet soldiers.

'On 3 February we were furnished with guides and headed east and told that we would get no Red Army escort, that we were to head towards Warsaw and that we would not be allowed to carry weapons; the Russian soldiers were so trigger-happy that they opened fire on anyone in a strange uniform who was armed. The attitude of the Soviets was not very friendly. Thus began our two-month trek to the east.

'We reached Landsberg on 6th February and stayed there until the 9th because of heavy fighting outside the city. It was here that I almost lost my life at the hands of a drunk Russian soldier armed with a Tommy-gun. He was sure I was an enemy and the only thing that saved me was a grand piano in the apartment where I had been prowling. I sat down and played him a chorus of 'Dark Eyes', the only Russian melody I knew, and made an instant friend.

'The Americans were amazed at the attitude shown by the Soviet soldiers. None was friendly and some were openly hostile. Some Americans lost all their possessions at the point of a gun, for discipline in the Russian Army was very poor, and the Red Army lived off the countryside. It was only well back from the front, at Wreschen, that we found any semblance of control.

We lived in a schoolhouse, and were issued with black bread, vodka, and occasionally some soup, supplementing our diet with raw carrots dug out of the yard. At Odessa we lived in a three-storey building on the main square and ate a lot of fish and pickle soup, but received some candy from American and British sailors in the port. Here we had our first showers in six or seven months. We reached Odessa on 16 March and left there on the British ship *Circassian*, and arrived in Naples on 2 April 1945.'

Many of the accounts received from Allied POWs attribute their eventual release to General George Patton's 3rd US Army, but Rifleman Dennis Halfin found his own way to the British lines: 'I was twenty-seven on 1 January 1945, a rifleman in the 1st Battalion, KRRC (King's Royal Rifle Corps). I was taken prisoner in Crete in 1941, several months after the Germans took the island, and in January 1945 I was in Stalag 2D at Stargard, Pomerania – the only English POW in a Canadian POW camp.

'I worked closely with the Canadian padre, Major John W. Foote, VC – we shared our Red Cross parcels – and Sergeant-Majors Cordner and Menzies of the Calgary Tank Regiment, in getting Red Cross parcels and clothing to Canadian POWs throughout Pomerania.

'When the Russian forces came closer in 1945 we were force-marched west. The German guards hurried us along, our feet sore and bleeding, and Major Foote's ankle had swollen badly. The Germans offered him transport but he refused, saying his place was with the men. En route we met up with a French working party who told us of the pitiful plight of some American POWs at Wismar. Major Foote and several NCOs decided to get permission from the German guards to allow Sergeant-Major Arthur from the Royal Regiment of Canada and me to go into Wismar and see for ourselves. We located the camp and found about two dozen American POWs in a very sorry state – wounds, sores, sick, and with very poor rations. Their condition so angered Sergeant-Major Arthur that he shouted at the camp guards and demanded medical attention for the Americans. The *Lager Führer* told us he would speak to his *Hauptman* (Captain) and next morning German doctors came from the Luftwaffe hospital. On seeing the plight of the Americans the doctors immediately sent those who could not walk to the hospital and looked after the remainder right there in the barracks.

'That evening we asked a farm woman for permission to sleep in her barn. When she realized we were British and not Russian – she was terrified of the Russians – her relief was so great she insisted we sleep in the farmhouse. She lived with her parents and two children, her husband being with the German Army. She warned us of German soldiers in the nearby woods. We did meet up with them but they ignored us.

'We continued to Luneburg, the dispersal point for Allied POWs, and that was the last time I saw Sergeant-Major Arthur, who died in Canada soon after the war. Major Foote was promoted to Colonel and I visited him when I emigrated to Canada in 1947. He eventually became a Minister in the Ontario Government and died a few years ago. He was a wonderful gentleman, the finest man I ever knew.'

Jonathan 'Dusty' Miller of Willowdale, Ontario, was a POW in Germany from October 1943 until he escaped in April 1945. 'I was held in Stalag 4F at Profen, between Leipzig and Zeitz. In our camp there were 120 British and 400 Russians. Six of us broke out to alert the Americans to our plight. Unfortunately, after getting only a hundred yards from the camp, one man looked up to see how far we had come. The guards opened fire and shot him through the head. After giving my solemn promise to the camp commandant that we would return, five of us tried to carry the wounded man to friendly forces, as there was no medical help in the camp. Two of us, holding up a white flag, walked until we made contact with an American armoured unit.

'After explaining that the Germans had artillery behind the camp and the prisoners were in danger if they tried to destroy it, the Americans gave us an ambulance, complete with a medical officer and driver, and we returned to pick up our wounded man. As we had given our word we would return to camp, we did return, much to the surprise of the commandant.

'I would like to mention that the German commandant was a very good type, a true soldier, who had been wounded on the Russian Front. He treated us very fairly and at dawn next morning he came and asked me if I would take him to the Americans so that he could surrender the camp. I agreed if he would give up his pistol. On reaching the American lines I handed the commandant over to the Americans. Two hours later the commandant returned to the camp with an American officer, the guards put down their rifles and surrendered to the American officer and the prisoners marched out of the camp, free for the first time in years. I might add that our wounded buddy died on the operating table.'

Canadian airman Reg Snell of Ontario, shot down in 1945, continues Miller's story. 'Because the Russian, British, Canadian and American troops were breaking through on all fronts, prisoners-of-war who were physically fit were evacuated from prison camps and put on "death marches" across Germany. They were well-named "death marches" because many prisoners-of-war who took part in them were reduced to the point of extreme fatigue and never finished. I cannot say with any accuracy how many prisoners in my group died on this march, but it was only by the mercy of God that I was able to make this difficult journey.

'There were some frightening experiences as we marched our way deeper into Germany. We were loaded into railway box-cars and about to pull out of a station when we saw planes approaching. We recognized them as American Thunderbolts, and I distinctly remember that on the rails next to ours were German soldiers who had deserted the German Army but had been recaptured. They were ordered to remain where they were in their box-cars. When the Thunderbolt mission was complete we went back to the railway yards to discover all the German deserters were dead.

'I was liberated on the morning of 29 April by General George Patton's American 3rd Army. One week later we were trucked to the nearest German airfield, from where we were flown back to England in a Lancaster bomber. On the way back the pilot flew over some of the German cities, one of which was Munich, to show us the bomb damage. Everywhere we looked there was destruction. It looked like some giant hand had swept across these cities, levelling everything in its path.'

Sapper Henry Lewis Little of the Royal Engineers was captured on Crete on 27 May 1941. 'On Sunday, 27 January 1945, I was a POW in Poland. At 10 p.m. the guards at the work camp compound told all the POWs to be ready to move in 30 minutes. They marched us out at around 11 p.m. –

about 250 men. Winter in Poland was − 10°F and we were then in Silesia, Southwest Poland. We did not know that the Red Army was breaking through east of us, and the goal of the German Army was to keep the POWs out of the hands of the Russians.

'The column of POWs stretched for miles, some English, some Russians, some prisoners from concentration camps in their striped uniforms. These prisoners and the Russians were shot if they fell out and could not get back before the executioner, riding a horse at the end of the column, caught up with them. Some of those who died of cold were Lascars from the Merchant Navy who had been captured by the German Navy. I remember seeing some huddled together, frozen by the roadside.

'We moved through Czechoslovakia, going right through Prague, where the Czechs tried to help us with bread thrown from the houses. We marched on into Germany, where things got harder, with no help from the people; they had nothing. We were strafed from the air, twice by Russian fighter planes and three times by US planes. I really don't know how many prisoners were killed because as soon as the planes left we were hustled away.

'A group of US POWs joined us and when they heard how long some of us had been captured they couldn't believe it. It's a good job these men were soon freed, for they were really despondent and going down fast. We were even joined by one US airman who was shot down in one of the raids and parachuted from a B25 right into our yard.'

Jack Poolton was a twenty-four-year-old private with the Royal Regiment of Canada when he was captured during the Dieppe raid in 1942 but his account begins two-and-a-half years later. 'The German treatment of the Russian prisoners was horrific, far worse than of us, which was bad enough. There was an epidemic of typhus in the Russian camp and the Red Cross demanded that the Russians be moved as it was endangering the lives of the British. However, British medical people volunteered to go into the Russian camp to help as the Germans would not enter the huts. The Russians were dying of starvation but would carry their dead comrades out to be counted at roll-call so as to draw their bread ration. We were always trying to help them and any of the German rations that weren't eaten we would try to get to the Russians, though this was strictly forbidden. The Russians were worked at least twelve hours a day on working parties, their feet wrapped in rags; it was a pitiful sight. At least we had uniforms, our British greatcoats and army boots. They had nothing.'

For the POWs too, the war was ending. Many old Kriegies rejoined their units, ready to continue the fight in the Far East, but most went home, to Canada, Australia, New Zealand, Britain or the USA, where many of them experienced great difficulty picking up the threads of normal life again after their time in captivity.

Some, like the Poles and Czechs, had no homes to go to, after the destruction of the war or the takeover of their country by Communists who did not welcome people from the West. Many Russian POWs, thought to have been corrupted by their enforced contact with the West, simply exchanged a German prison camp for one in Siberia. The war was ending and Great Power rivalries were starting to bear down again on the long-suffering people of Europe.

Overrunning Germany

0   40   80   120   160 miles
0   50   100   150   200   250 km

N

NORTH SEA

SWEDEN

DENMARK

COPENHAGEN

BORNHOLM

Flensburg

Heligoland

Wangerooge

Kiel

Neustadt

Barth

BALTIC SEA

Wilhelmshaven

Lübeck

Rostock

Groningen

Westerbork

Oldenburg

Hamburg

Wismar

Gresse

Friesoythe

Bremen

Lüneburg

Ludwigslust

Stettin

Stargard

Cloppenburg

Verden

Uelzen

Amersfoort

Lingen

Fallingbostel

Celle

Barneveld

Apeldoorn

Osnabrück

Hannover

HOLLAND

Bocholt

Munster

Braunschwig

BERLIN

Küstrin

Lippstadt

Magdeburg

Poznan

Cologne

Kassel

Nordhausen

Dessau

Torgau

BELGIUM

Ziegenhain

Halle

Leipzig

Bautzen

Sagan

Gotha

Erfurt

Riesa

LUX.

Weimar

Zeitz

Dresden

Görlitz

Breslau

Frankfurt

Bad Orb

Plauen

Chemnitz

Theresienstadt

Schweinfurt

Bamberg

Bayreuth

Karlsbad

Bad Mergentheim

Pilsen

PRAGUE

FRANCE

Nuremberg

Strasbourg

Stuttgart

Eichstatt

Brno

Belfort

Augsburg

Regensburg

Moosburg

River Danube

Dachau

Munich

Linz

VIENNA

Lake Constance

Garmisch

Salzburg

Innsbruck

Berchtesgarten

SWITZERLAND

Graz

Lake Balaton

Line as at VE Day

Klagenfurt

HUNGARY

Milan

ITALY

Zagreb

Genoa

Trieste

ISTRIA

CROATIA

Nice

LIGURIAN SEA

ADRIATIC SEA

River Rhine

River Weser

R. Leine

R. Ems

River Elbe

Neisse

River Oder

US Garand and British No. 4 Rifles

13 The End in Europe

'The mission of this Allied Force was fulfilled at
0241, local time, May 7th, 1945.'

*General Dwight D. Eisenhower
Message to the Combined Chiefs-of-Staff*

On 16 April 1945, three Russian armies advanced across the Oder and
Neisse rivers, two of them marching on Dresden, the third heading directly
for Berlin. By 25 April Berlin was completely surrounded and shells were
falling on the Reichstag, the Chancellory and the Führerbunker.

Hitler had returned to Berlin on 16 January and by all accounts the
Führer's physical and mental condition had deteriorated sharply in the last
few months. According to one observer, 'His head wobbled, his left arm
was slack, useless, and he trembled a great deal, his face and his eyes gave
the impression of total exhaustion ... his movements were those of a senile
man.' Living in his bunker, 60 feet below the ruined Chancellory, could
not have helped – for the atmosphere there, as recorded by William L.
Shirer, was that of a lunatic asylum. His one consolation was the arrival,
on 15 April, of his mistress, Eva Braun, who came to share the Führer's
fate.

As April gave way to May, Germany plunged ever deeper into a desperate
situation. Her people were ravaged by hunger and disease or trampled
underfoot by hostile armies, her cities were destroyed by shellfire and
bombing, her countryside was awash with roving bands of slave labourers
and displayed people, many of them intent on robbery and revenge – and
still the war went on. Helmut Stöcker barely survived the following
encounter in the closing weeks of the war:

'In April 1945 I was with 16th Panzer Division based at Troppau. On the night of 18 April 1945 the division was ordered to travel to Hoschtitz. The divisional commander, Lt-General von Müller, took the leading car as he had been commander in the region of Kremsier during the occupation of Czechoslovakia in 1939. He was accompanied by our radio car but travelled separately, and we were to meet in Hoschtitz.

'On 19 April 1945 we arrived at the castle of Hoschtitz as General von Müller had ordered. The four other men in my company waited outside the gate and I went to the nearby buildings. I had no suspicion about the general's car, which was already standing in front of the steps to the castle, and there were no signs of partisans.

'As I approached, the door was suddenly pulled open and somebody hit me in the mouth with a pistol. I was dragged into the hall where about twenty people, including three women, were standing around. All were wearing brown uniforms. I thought it was some misunderstanding with Hungarian soldiers. Suddenly a door opened and the divisional commander appeared, and behind him some men.

' "No, he is not somebody from the SS. He is one of my people, a man from the Panzer troop", said the general.

'I did have the panzer uniform on and wore the panzer emblem on the collar. Presumably, one of the Partisans had mistaken me for an SS man. They took me to the cellars, where the windows were guarded by more people. At my request they brought me a bowl of water so I could rinse out the wound in my mouth. Two men with guns stood by and watched me, and it was also explained to me that my lip would be treated later by a doctor. When I asked to which group the men belonged, they told me with pride that they were partisans.

'After a short time a large man appeared, wearing the general's leather coat, and I was taken, flanked by two men, further into the cellars, where I saw the bodies of the general's three companions. Then it was my turn ... I was shot by the man in the leather coat, but I had great luck. Because of a slight movement of my head, the bullet grazed the lobe of my ear and passed behind me, missing me by about 2 cm, but I fell to the floor. As I had not lost consciousness I could prop myself up and breathe without them noticing, and I could see, too, that the four other men of my troop had been taken into the castle. I do not know how they had been taken, but probably at the point of the bayonet. In any case, they were soon laid out on the floor, beyond all hope.

'One partisan stood in the cellar doorway and stabbed with his bayonet at the bodies on the floor. Extra straw and covers were thrown over the corpses. Later, when it grew dark, I checked on the bodies around me; I counted seven corpses, already cold and stiff. I could not get out as the guards were still in the castle, and the one guarding the door was passing by constantly; also it was bolted.

'I think I fell asleep then, but suddenly I was awake again as the door was being broken down – after about twelve hours. Around 3 o'clock in the morning, as SS officer stormed in. When I heard German being spoken, I sat up and before me stood this SS officer, a machine-pistol over his shoulder. As I sat up, he took a few steps backwards – I looked dreadful. As he explained later, had I not raised my arms, he would definitely have shot me.

'The SS officer had come to the castle the previous day, but because the vehicle standing at the front was displaying a divisional general's pennant, he did not inspect it any closer. He assumed General Schorner was inside the castle and the SS didn't want to interrupt anything.

'On 20 April 1945 I went into hospital. On the same day the bodies of the seven shot men were taken and placed in the hospital mortuary. It was established that the three companions of the general had been shot and bayoneted. They counted thirty-three wounds on one of them. There was one good thing about my injuries – they prevented me from being taken by the Russians as a prisoner-of-war.

'The Divisional Commander, Lt-General Dietrich von Müller, was handed over by the partisans to the Russian Army and he only came back out of a Russian POW camp in October 1955. He died on 30 January 1961 in Hamburg.'

The rapid Soviet advance into the Reich had matched that of the Western Armies. By 3 April the Russians had crossed into Austria and were pushing hard for Vienna, while other Soviet forces laid siege to Bratislava in Hungary. The siege of Vienna began on 6 April and fighting was soon raging in the suburbs of the city. Vienna fell to the Russians on 13 April, the surrender followed by the usual outburst of pillage, rape and violence. On the Baltic coast the city of Königsberg fell on 9 April. By 20 April – Hitler's fifty-sixth birthday – Russian forces had almost encircled Berlin and the leading elements of Marshal Zhukov's armies were already in the eastern suburbs and brushing aside General Gotthard Henrici's forces of Army Group Vistula, and destroying the German IX Army which lay in the centre of their advance.

Within the Bunker, the Führer continued to give orders for the destruction of his enemies and the movements of his non-existent armies while fretting about the loyalty of long-standing colleagues and the possibility of plots. In this, at least, he was quite correct; many of his colleagues, like Speer, pressed him openly to make some accommodation, perhaps with the vengeful forces now bearing down upon Berlin and certainly with the Western Allies, who were rightly regarded as more merciful than the Soviets. Others in the

Führer's entourage were already attempting to make their own, secretive arrangements with the Western Powers.

On 23 April, Marshal Goering, the Deputy Führer, sent a message from his refuge in Bavaria, suggesting that since Hitler was now besieged in Berlin, Goering should take over the leadership of the Reich. Hitler's response was to strip him of his rank and titles and order his immediate arrest by the SS.

On 24 April, Heinrich Himmler, Commander of the SS, opened secret negotiations in Lübeck with the Western Allies through Count Bernadotte of the Swedish Red Cross in Lübeck, while in Switzerland the SS General Kane Woolf had been negotiating with General Alexander for more than a month on terms for the surrender of all the German forces in Italy. These attempts at a settlement got nowhere, not least because the Germans would not negotiate with the Russians.

Himmler was certainly terrified of the Russians but the Western Allies refused to negotiate a separate peace. The German surrender must be unconditional and made to all Allied nations at the same time. The German armies must surrender to whatever forces they were fighting at the moment of surrender, and German soldiers could not fight off the Russians then flee west to surrender to the Americans or British. Since becoming a prisoner of the Russians was the fate most feared by all the German soldiery, the fighting went on. Count Bernadotte did use his negotiations with Himmler to extract some relief for the victims still held in the SS-run concentration camps, but this war would be settled on the battlefields.

On the Western Front the advance continued up to and beyond the Elbe. On 22 April Eisenhower, though offering to stop his armies on the Elbe–Mulde line, suggested to the Russians that – if it would be of assistance – he could advance beyond the Stop Line and take Dresden. The Russians hurriedly replied that they were happy with the Elbe–Mulde line and would clear all German territory up the the east bank of those rivers, adding that they also intended to clear the Moldau valley in Czechoslovakia – and take Prague.

Bradley was now pushing his forces up to the Elbe–Mulde line, mopping up strong but scattered German forces on the way. On 18 April, Magdeburg finally fell after rejecting an offer of terms and suffering a massive attack by all the medium bombers in the 9th Air Force as a consequence. The 9th US Army also closed up to the Elbe, by which time the 1st US Army to the south had already reached its Stop Line on the Mulde. American tank radios were now picking up transmissions from Russian tanks beyond the river, and on 25 April 1945 American and Russian forces met for the first time at Torgau on the Elbe, when patrols of the 69th US Division met advance elements of the Russian 58th Guards Division, a meeting which effectively ended the war for the soldiers of the 1st US Army.

The remaining German armies were split in two by this meeting at Torgau. Where, and if, the fighting continued, now depended on the willingness of the local German commander. The Western Allies had taken more than a million prisoners since the Rhine crossing three weeks before, and apart from containing and feeding these prisoners, and sifting out the SS and concentration camp guards passing themselves off as ordinary Wehrmacht soldiers, the Allied armies also had to cope with tens of thousands of displaced persons (DPs), many thousands of released prisoners-of-war and the care of a desperate and often starving civilian population.

Walter Schindler, now of Bolton, Ontario, was then an NCO in a German panzer unit. 'For me, the war ended on the Russian Front. I belonged to Battalion No. 33; we had four companies with fourteen or fifteen tanks each. We could hear the Russian Front, and six kilometres behind were the Americans, and they still told us that we were going to win the war. We moved back 1,000 kilometres and got kicked in the ass, and in those last four kilometres we were going to win the war! Finally, we started digging holes and throwing our guns and rifles and everything in, as we didn't want the Russians to get them. Pity the poor farmer who would have to blow the field after all this.

'Then we decided we would go to the Americans because nobody wanted to be taken as a prisoner of the Russians. The Americans didn't treat us rough, but they didn't treat us well either, with a kick in the ass here and there ... and then there was my watch ... he was a good-natured guy who took my watch. Then they took us on the truck and he kicked me in the ass again and said, "Let's go, *kamerad*." It wasn't a good watch anyway – it only cost four or five marks.

'They took us to a field near Stettin, and all the prisoners were there in the open field with jeeps at each corner, or Dodge trucks with a machine-gun at each corner, and there was an imaginary line here which we were not supposed to step outside, except to go for a crap, and then a guy with a machine-gun would go with us.

'This lasted only two days and then the Americans turned the whole prison camp over to the Russians, apparently because they had agreed that this was the dividing line and everything on the one side was Russian and everything on the other side was American. The Americans had advanced further so they had to retreat, but they didn't want to take us Krauts along with them, so they decided that we could go to the Russians. It was a disorganized commotion, I can tell you! The Americans moved out on one side and the Russians moved in on the other, with trucks and everything. We had a young lieutenant from a neighbouring company, and he had got hold of a Red Cross flag from somewhere, so he stuck this on one of the trucks and we took off with that truck. When the Russians moved in we just drove between them, and nobody stopped us because of the Red Cross flag.'

The main task facing Montgomery's 21st Army Group in the north was to push north, seize the port of Hamburg and then advance across Schleswig-Holstein to seal off Denmark from the Russians advancing along the Baltic coast. Bremen fell on 27 April and the Elbe was crossed on a broad front on 28 April, following receipt of a cable from Eisenhower urging Montgomery to press on with all speed to Lübeck on the Baltic. Among the units pressing north was the 1st Commando Brigade.

The advance of the British 1st Commando Brigade from the Maas to the Elbe is one of the great stories of the war, for this brigade of four Commandos, two Army, two Royal Marine, never stopped advancing and took every obstacle on the run, frequently at the point of the bayonet.

Philip Pritchard of 6 Commando gives one reason why: 'Our Brigadier, Derek Mills-Roberts, was a great commander and a thinking soldier. He was just thirty-six, and had started the war as a second lieutenant in the Irish Guards. He led from the front and you could always expect to see him where the bullets were flying. He did not suffer fools at all, never mind gladly, and was a totally professional soldier, representing all that is best in the British Army.'

Bill Sadler also of No. 6 Commando recalls one of the brigade's assaults in the closing days of the war: 'We crossed the river Aller at night over a ruined railway bridge, because the city road bridge was held by the 2nd Battalion of the German Marine Fusiliers. The brigade crossed in double file led by 3 Commando and got behind the German positions in complete silence, ready to engage the enemy.

'We took up position in a long, dry ditch, facing a wide-open space before the enemy line. This was *it*; bayonets fixed, nine rounds in the magazine and one up the spout, waiting for our mortars and MMGs to stop firing on the German positions. The moment they did, No. 6 Commando rose as one man and with the second-in-command blowing the "Tally-ho!" on his bugle charged forward at an all-out run, firing from the hip at anyone who rose in front of us.

'The enemy finally broke and ran, but not before their battalion commander, their RSM and two company commanders were lying with other dead among the trees. My immediate target was already dead as I reached the wood – luckily for me – he was well over 6 feet and weighed about 16 stones. He lay on his back, stone dead, smiling at some private joke.

'The Germans then counter-attacked, coming back through the woods shouting, "Cease firing", which we didn't. We held the ground we had taken and the Brigadier awarded us with the only concession of the entire campaign: "No one need shave for the time being." '

The 1st Commando Brigade were still forging ahead, crossing the Elbe–Trave canal to seize Lauenberg on 30 April, an assault led by 6 Commando in Buffaloes. They found the enemy dug-in on top of a 150 foot high escarpment, from where they engaged the commandos with rifles, machine-gun fire and showers of "potato masher" grenades; 6 Commando landed, deploying to the flanks, and drove the Germans back as Nos. 3, 45 and 46 (Royal Marine) Commandos swept up to take the high ground. The brigade swept into Lauenberg in time to take the bridge before the German engineers could fire their charges.

Bill Sadler was in this last advance: 'After Lauenberg the brigade continued to advance, virtually unopposed to Lübeck and Neustadt. Here we found the bodies of about 300 concentration camp people: men, women and children, in striped clothing, lying at the foot of the cliffs or washing about in the sea, all shot or drowned. Brigadier Mills-Roberts ordered the burgomasters to provide a burial party from the townsfolk and the dead were buried in a mass grave. Years later I read that the Germans had discovered a mass grave outside Lübeck, but no one in the town had any idea how it got there – an amazing example of collective amnesia.

'On 3 May the German commander in Lübeck, Field Marshal Milch, surrendered his army and his field marshal's baton to Brigadier Mills-Roberts. Disgusted at the sights we had uncovered at Belsen and Lübeck, the Brigadier broke the baton over the field marshal's head.'

Having crossed the Elbe at Lauenberg on 29 April – an assault spearheaded by a brigade of the 15th (Scottish) Division and Commando Brigade – the British and Canadian forces were picking up speed. The Elbe crossing was made in the face of slight opposition, and the advance continued in spite of some sudden attacks by a resurgent Luftwaffe against the Elbe bridges. Further south, two divisions of the US XVIII Airborne Corps, now attached to 21st Army Group, also crossed the river, where they were joined by the British 6th Airborne Division for a thrust north and west towards Wismar, where British and Russian forces met for the first time on 2 May 1945.

The Allied air forces were still bombing in support of the armies and still meeting enemy fighters. Wesley Southworth, a flight engineer with 76 Squadron, RAF, recalls some of the last operations: 'To Harburg (suburbs of Hamburg) – Target submarine pens about 5 hours. Quite an uneventful trip as far as I can recall.

'To Hamburg – not so good. I recollect we had a new bomb aimer and on approaching the target he missed the area and the pilot elected to go round again. Being at the rear of the bomber stream we were picked up by a night fighter – a rattle of gun-fire – a gunner shouting "Corkscrew starboard". This meant rapidly banking and losing altitude, then climbing up again, hoping the fighter would fly past us. This we did, but the cannon fire hit us, damaging the tail and port side; holes were torn between the fuel tanks and ailerons. On our return the wireless operator said, "I still say it's a piece of cake, Wes."

'To Wangerooge (Friesian island) – daylight raid on gun emplacements at approximately 8,000 feet. Flight path over Speekerooge Island, then on to target. Flak was average but two aircraft failed to return. I saw the aircraft in question for some reason come together behind and higher than us. I lost sight of one of them but the other spiralled down till it was out of sight. W/O Outersan and his crew failed to clear the aircraft and died. The other one crashed and the only one to survive was the pilot who managed to clear the aircraft and parachute down, only to be taken prisoner.

'To Heligoland in daylight. As we taxied round the perimeter, orders came to return to dispersal. I think some aircraft had got off but one aircraft, piloted by W/O Holmes, had veered off the runway with a full bomb load. The undercarriage collapsed and black smoke began to rise from it, but all the crew managed to get out before the aircraft blew up.'

Arden Bomeli of Pittsburg, Pennsylvania, was still flying missions over Germany at this time. 'I had arrived in England on 23 December 1944 on the *Queen Elizabeth* and by 1 January 1945 I was with the 487th Bomb Group (837 Bomb Squadron). I few thirty-one combat missions over Germany and Occupied France before VE Day. I was a pilot of a B17, although I trained in B24s – and had a crew of nine. We flew most of our missions together, and I am still in contact with all but four of them.

'In the last few months of the war the enemy was still very visible – we were not flying "milk-runs". The flak was horrendous and quite accurate, even at 22,000 feet, which was our average altitude. I was flying left wing on the squadron leader on a mission when they had a direct hit over the target. I will never forget watching the tail gunner struggle to get out of his escape hatch and succeeding in freeing himself just moments before the last blinding flash of the exploding Fortress.

'We were lucky as none of our crew was injured, although our plane had its share of battle damage. We were not shot down, taken prisoner, or did anything heroic, but I know that I experienced fright that can only be described as stark terror.

'Probably my only claim to fame was being "Tail-end Charlie" on my third mission on 3 February 1945, in the biggest air raid on Berlin. I had lost power going in (two of my superchargers were not functioning properly), but since I was beyond the point of no return I tried to stay in the bomber stream to avoid becoming a sitting duck. I straggled behind the last group just as the target appeared in front of us. We dropped our bombs at random in the target area, and were able to catch up with a group at the rally point. Except for running out of fuel and landing at an alternate field, the rest of the flight was uneventful.'

Here and there, even as the war ended, the German Army kept fighting, often in small infantry groups armed with *panzerfausts*, or in company strength accompanied by one or two Tiger tanks.

On 2 May, German resistance in the north effectively collapsed. Harry Upward was driving a Sherman Firefly tank in the 5th Royal Tank Regiment when he met a Tiger: 'The war was almost over but you couldn't take chances. I used to drive with the driver's hatch open, rather than trying to see through the visor or the periscope, but that day, for some reason I decided to let my seat down and close the hatch. The whole squadron was advancing near Luneburg, just a day or two before the war ended, and with our 17 pdr gun we were at the back, covering. Then we stopped while the commander went ahead for a look, and just as we went forward again – wallop! We got a direct hit from an 88 mm gun.

'It was quite an experience – terrific concussion – a great flash and a bang to make your teeth ache, and then the tank was on fire. I could not get out as the fighting compartment was full of flames, and – thank God – the gun was fore and aft, or I would not have been able to get my hatch open. As it was we all got out, and I was the only one hurt, with burns on my hands and face. They took me to hospital in Brussels and that was the end of my war.'

Lübeck fell after a small amount of sniping and over 15,000 German soldiers of the garrison began their weary march towards the prison camps. The US Airborne Corps swept through Ludwigslust to Wismar, which fell to the British paratroops of 6th Airborne Division, and the US Airborne took over 250,000 prisoners when the German III Panzer Army and XXI Army surrendered on 3 May. On that day, General Wolz, the garrison commander in Hamburg, formally surrendered the city to Lt-General Sir Miles Dempsey of the British 2nd Army; and tanks of the 'Desert Rats', the 7th Armoured Division, which had fought the Germans all the way from the Western Desert, rolled into the city.

SHAEF was still convinced that a major military threat could still come from German forces in that 'National Redoubt' the Germans were said to be establishing in Bavaria and the Alps. This Redoubt never existed in any significant form, but the task of finding and destroying it was entrusted to the 3rd and 7th US Armies as they turned south and east towards Bavaria and Austria.

Patton's army began its final march on 22 April, pushing along the edge of the Czech border to reach the Danube at Regensburg before heading towards Linz and Salzburg. By 26 April Patton had forces on either side of the Danube and was forging ahead in the face of light opposition, the 3rd Army suffering less than 100 casualties a day as they swept across Bavaria to Passau. Meanwhile, Bradley ordered Hodges' 1st US Army to extend its right flank to the south to cover Patton's advance.

General Patch's 7th US Army were having a much tougher time as they forced their way south towards Munich, reaching Nuremberg on 15 April. The garrison of Nuremberg held out for five days, engaging the Americans in the rubble-strewn streets with snipers, machine-gun nests and dug-in 88 mm guns. This city, the scene of the Nazi Party's flamboyant pre-war rallies, fell to the Americans on 20 April. On that day the French 1st Army took Stuttgart and on 22 April advance elements of both armies reached the Danube and forged across the river.

On 30 April the Americans of Patch's XV Corps entered Augsburg and advanced on Munich. On the way troops of the 45th US Division overran the concentration camp at Dachau, the first concentration camp set up in the Reich after Hitler came to power in 1933. A day or so later the Americans were entering the Alpine passes beyond Garmisch and heading for Innsbruck in the Tyrol, while the French 1st Army forged along the north shore of Lake Constance and turned south into Austria. The Reich was finished and even the Führer knew it. On that day, 30 April 1945, Adolph Hitler shot himself in Berlin.

The last days of Hitler have been fully recorded elsewhere and need only be summarized here. All the leading Nazis, Goering, Goebbels, Von Ribbentrop, Hitler's secretary Martin Borman, as well as the military leaders, Keitel, Jodl and Grand-Admiral Doenitz, had attended Hitler's birthday party on 20 April. Then they had hurriedly dispersed, Doenitz to the north, Goering to his estate at Karinhall, outside Berlin, Ribbentrop and Himmler to places of supposed safety. Over the next few days the Russians tightened their hold on the city and the defection of Himmler and Goering became clear to the half-demented Hitler. Himmler's treaty, revealed by the Allies in a radio broadcast on 28 April, was the last straw. Himmler was beyond the Führer's reach but Himmler's liaison officer, SS General Hermann Feyelein, was in Berlin; Hitler had him shot in the Chancellory garden.

On 29 April Hitler married Eva Braun and wrote his will and testament, appointing Admiral Doenitz as his successor and Martin Borman as his executor. On the following day, at around 3.30 p.m., the Führer and his new wife committed suicide; Hitler with a shot in the mouth, Eva Hitler, née Braun, by taking cyanide. Berlin fell to the Russians on 2 May.

With Hitler dead, Goering disgraced and most of the Nazi leaders on the run or in hiding, the task of running the Reich in its final hours and surrendering Germany to the mercy of the Allies fell on the Commander of the German Navy, Grand-Admiral Doenitz. Doenitz's first concern was to avoid surrendering more of the country and its people to the Soviets than he could avoid. On 3 May he sent a delegation of senior officers to Montgomery's headquarters, asking the British to accept the surrender of the three German armies now falling back on Berlin from Rostock on the Baltic.

Montgomery refused. These German armies, having fought the Russians, must surrender to the Russians, though – he added – his troops would accept the surrender of any individual German soldier who came into the British lines. He also asked for the immediate surrender of all the German forces '... on my western and northern flanks, in Holland and the Friesian Islands, in Heligoland, Schleswig-Holstein and Denmark'. It had been agreed that the German capitulation must be to all the Allies at once, but this could be seen as a tactical battlefield surrender of forces on his front and Montgomery had the powers to accept it. Having no option the Germans agreed. After consultation with General Eisenhower, Montgomery accepted the surrender of the German forces in the north in a tent on Luneburg Heath at 1830 hrs on 5 May 1945, the surrender to take effect from 0800 hrs on the following day.

Some of the German generals were confused by this surrender, making the point that they might be able to continue fighting the Russians and even the Americans. They were swiftly corrected on this point. 'They were my prisoners from 0800 hrs on 6 May, and I would not allow them to conduct operations against the Russians ... or the Americans,' said Montgomery, later adding, 'This caused some consternation but I do not think that the German delegation saw the humour in this situation.'

With the German surrender on Luneburg Heath, the British Empire's part in the European war was over and the war itself was almost finished. British forces in the north entered Copenhagen on 5 May to a tremendous welcome from the populace and the rest of Denmark was swiftly overrun by British troops.

Patton was still pushing ahead on the Danube Front, making his war last as long as possible. Patton's men crossed the river Inn on 3 May and met elements of the VI SS Panzer Army defending Linz and already under attack from Patch's 7th US Army, which took Salzburg on 4 May. On the following day Americans from the 7th Army and French soldiers from the French 1st Army took the Führer's summer retreat at Berchesgarten, much of which they found in ruins. What remained was then burned to the ground. At dawn on 4 May the Americans of the 7th Army reached the top of the Brenner Pass and the troops of the 103rd US Infantry Division shook hands with troops of the 88th Division of the American 5th Army coming up from Italy, where the German Armies had surrendered on 2 May.

General Eisenhower now ordered Bradley's 12th US Army Group to advance east into Czechoslovakia, at least as far as the town of Karlsbad, where at the request of the Soviets the American advance halted, leaving Prague and most of Czechoslovakia to the Russians, though Patton was still advancing towards Pilsen, having heard that the citizens of Prague had risen against the Germans in the city and were in need of help. With seven divisions of his 3rd US Army already in Czechoslovakia, Patton believed that he should have been allowed to advance to Prague and the Modau river, but in spite of a further request from Winston Churchill on 7 May that the Americans should take Prague, Patton was held back while the Czechs and Germans fought it out. The Red Army took the city of Prague on 9 May, after which the citizens of Prague took a terrible revenge on the German men, women and children left in the city.

Lieutenant Robert M. Brookes of the 9th Engineers, 9th Armoured Division, was with the 3rd US Army at this time. 'After leaving the Mulde river we moved back to a village. From there we were sent down to Patton's 3rd Army, though we had been in the 1st Army since the Battle of the Bulge. We were sent into Czechoslovakia and headed for Pilsen. As we drove, I noted that at each curve in the road there was an 88 mm gun aimed down our throats but nobody around to fire it. We were asked to carry a message to the other column of the Combat Command. Before, we had always taken such messages across the country through German territory, but this time I got the brilliant idea that the war was close to an end and I didn't want to take any more risks for my men.

'We drove back into Germany to start out the next day to the other column. As we drove into our headquarters we got word that we had instructions to "defend in place". This meant that the war was over. We would do no more advancing but we weren't to take any crap from the Germans either. This news came the night before the world knew that the was over in Europe. Instead of having a big celebration that night, we had had a tiring wait to see if there were any 88 mm gunners to fire the guns that day, so the three of us just went to bed.

'The next day we were sent to Bayreuth to find a home for the Headquarters Company. I found a hotel but when the hotel owner was asked by me to show us the rooms, he had an idea that if he said that he had no keys he would evade housing us. Each room we came to he told me he had no keys for that room. At the third room we came to, I put my back against one side of the narrow hall and kicked the door down with my good old army boot. The door went in all the way and along with it the frame. He found all the necessary keys. Then Captain Newman told me that this was my room.

'On the day before the end of the war, Company A had captured a tank car full of V-2 rocket fuel, almost 100 percent ethyl alcohol. We could not get messages from one column to another very rapidly but the message of the finding of the alcohol got out to the entire division in about 5 minutes. If you wanted any you had to rush for your share. One filled a five-gallon jerry-can and took it with him. The first three weeks almost everybody in the division was completely soused. I know I was. After three weeks the division general ordered that all the liquid be dumped down the sewer. I kept only about a gallon after that.'

With the Führer dead, her armies dispersed and her industry in ruins, Germany could fight no longer. On 4 May, Doenitz's plenipotentiary General-Admiral von Friedeburg went to Eisenhower's headquarters at Rheims, where he yet again attempted to surrender only those German forces fighting on the Western Front. Eisenhower promptly refused to discuss this proposal. His terms were unconditional surrender to all the Allies – take it or leave it. Von Friedeburg took these terms back to Doenitz's headquarters at Flensburg.

On the following day, 5 May, SHAEF heard that General Jodl, as head of the OKW, was on his way to Rheims to discuss the terms again, but by 6 May it was clear that the Germans were stalling, hoping to gain time for more of their forces to escape to the safety of the Western lines. Therefore, when they asked for a further delay of forty-eight hours on the evening of 6 May, Eisenhower refused, telling Jodl that he would 'seal off the Western Front to prevent any movement of German troops and civilians unless they agree at once to my terms of surrender'.

Surrender had already been anticipated. Lieutenant Dennis Haines of 27th (Royal Marine) Battalion remembers the end of his war: 'The evening of 4 May 1945 found me just outside a place called Bad Zwischenahn, a minor spa west of Oldenburg and about 35 km south of Wilhelmshaven. I was directing the B-Echelon vehicles into a field for the night. As I did so, the Canadian commander of a Sherman tank which was passing by shouted to me, "The Germans have surrendered! The war's over!" He had heard this over his tank radio, whereas we, in our soft-skinned vehicles, had been out of touch.'

The Germans surrendered to the Allies and Jodl signed the act of surrender soon after midnight on 7 May 1945. In other circumstances, one might pity General Jodl, for his last words at the surrender have a certain dignity: 'With this signature the German people and the German armed forces are, for better or worse, delivered into the victor's hands. I can only express the hope that the victor will treat them with generosity.'

Belsen, Dachau, Malmedy, Poland, the twenty-million dead in Russia, the six-million victims of the Holocaust ...? There was no reply – there could be no reply to Jodl's plea and six months later he was hanged at Nuremberg for war crimes. The German surrender was ratified in Berlin just before midnight on 8 May 1945 – VE Day.

B17 Flying Fortress

14 Epilogue
1945

'I wish I could tell you that all our
toils and troubles were over ... we have
to make sure that the simple and honourable
purposes for which we entered the War are
not brushed aside ... There would be little
use punishing the Hitlerites for their crimes,
if law and justice did not rule, if totalitarian,
or police Governments took the place of the German
invaders...'

Winston Churchill
May 1945

The Second World War did not end on 8 May 1945. The war still went on
in Burma and the islands of the Pacific, over Japan and in many parts of
Eastern Europe. It was not until 13 May that the Germans in Prague and
the countryside of Czechoslovakia stopped fighting, not least because they
were fighting for their lives against the local partisans and trying to protect
the *Volksdeutsch* of the Sudetenland from the vengeance of the Czech
population. There was also sporadic fighting in Germany and Austria as
SS units fought on or took to the hills.

Elsewhere in Europe the guns fell silent for the first time in six years,
and the people of Germany could emerge from their shelters and see what
had happened to their country. Apart from those places which had been
swiftly overrun, the villages, town and cities of Germany were heaps of
rubble.

Suicides floated in the rivers. Every wood and orchard had its crop of
dangling bodies – the apparent hopelessness of the situation driving people
to despair and death. People were already starving – there was no food;
bands of displaced persons (DPs) roamed the country taking what they
wanted; and the Allied armies were moving cautiously from their final
positions, as the euphoria of victory gave way to the problems of peace.

Map 10 (see p. 266) shows the positions of the armies on the day the war ended. The Western and Eastern armies faced each from Wismar on the Baltic, south to the Elbe and then down the Elbe to the junction with the Mulde. South of that river junction the Western and Soviet armies were still far apart. Leipzig, soon to be in the Russian Zone, was held by the American 1st Army. Most of Czechoslovakia and Austria was still unoccupied – though the American 3rd Army had Linz – and Patton's men were well inside the Czech frontier and probing towards Prague.

The European was over but the Continent was in ruins. Hundreds of thousands of German prisoners had to be sorted out, those guilty of war crimes imprisoned to await trial, the rest sent to POW camps or home. Roads had to be bulldozed through the rubble linking the city centres, and water, gas and electricity services restored, houses rebuilt, disease prevented, food brought in. An entire nation had to be taken apart, cleaned of the Nazi pestilence and rebuilt.

Not only were Germans suffering. The Dutch were starving, as Dennis Duffey recalls: 'From 29 April to 7 May we flew on Operation Manna. A large pocket in western Holland was still in German hands and the population was approaching starvation. Many old or sick people had already died, and a truce was arranged with the local German commander, and Lancasters of 1, 3 and 8 Groups started to drop food supplies for the civilian population. Pathfinder Mosquitoes marked the dropping zones; 2,835 Lancaster and 724 Mosquito flights were made before the Germans surrendered at the end of the war and allowed ships and road transport to enter the area. Bomber Command delivered 6,672 tons of food during Operation Manna.'

Dick Parkinson from Natal in South Africa was a prisoner in East Germany when the war ended. 'The Red Army took control. Quantities of black bread were issued to the prisoners who were then marched across the Elbe, to what appeared to be an abandoned city – Riesa. The Russian Army was everywhere, sturdy women soldiers in the turrets of tanks, long lines of well-kept horses being groomed by Cossacks. The Red Army rations appeared to be half a loaf of black bread each day and dried fish. Columns of soldiers came singing through the streets of the town, and the sound echoed off the walls with a haunting and frightening power.

'Slipping away from the increasing control of the Red Army some prisoners began to drift away across a sun-drenched Saxony, heading west. It soon became obvious that this apparently empty countryside was in fact full of people, snaking columns of ex-slave labourers, displaced refugees, and lone German soldiers, keeping away from the Russians, hoping to get to escape to the west. Every farmhouse was full of people keeping out of sight. Here was a Russian soldier, grinning, a knife between his teeth, straddling a sheep. Some girls scampered off to the shelter of a barn when horsemen appeared on the hill...

'At last the Mulde river, the bridge blown, the gap spanned by planks. On one side several hundred refugees with their prams and bundles, on the other noise and bustle, jeeps and lorries, stars and stripes, a GI reading a comic book. A Soviet soldier blocks the planks "*Niet* ... *Niet*", then an American officer calling across, "You guys wanna come over?" So over we go, plank to plank, out of the war.'

In their newly established Occupation Zones and in their various ways, the victors set about the task of rebuilding Germany. Twenty million Germans were homeless; 600,000 had been killed in the bombing. More than five million refugees were roaming the land looking for shelter or their families.

Fred Rhambo, the fifteen-year-old Hitler Youth soldier, survived the war in Hamburg. 'The city surrendered without a battle, and the British tanks just rolled in. By June I was an apprentice in a machine-tool factory, where our supervisor was a British staff-sergeant, Sergeant Henwood. Our job was to pack up the factory and ship it to England. The city itself was in ruins; we lived in caves, in the rubble, or in camps on the outskirts. It was 1952 before there were again enough houses in Hamburg.'

'When it was all over and we had a chance to look about,' said Sergeant Ted Smith of the Guards Armoured Division, 'they said that the Americans got the scientists, the Russians got the factories, the French got the women and the British got the ruins. That was about right, but although we had this "no fraternization" business – "no fratting" as the troops called it – it never stood a chance of working. Within days most of the lads had a German girlfriend, a "little bit of Frat." '

Not all the troops went onto occupation duties. The war in the Pacific and the Far East still went on, and within a few days of the war ending in Europe some of the divisions were on their way to the East. The 4th US Infantry Division went back to America, to shed some of the veterans and train new men, before heading for the invasion of Japan. The British 6th Airborne Division was also shipped out, en route for India and a part in Operation Zipper, the invasion of Malaya.

Don Neilsen, a B17 pilot in the 457th US Bomb Group, recalls his return home: 'When the war in Europe ended, most of the 8th went home, flying our own planes, and landing at bases in the West, waiting for redeployment in the Pacific, I guess. During this period the main claim to fame of the 457th Bomb Group came when our commanding officer, Colonel Rogner and his assistant, Colonel Smith, borrowed a B25 and flew it from Sioux Falls in South Dakota to La Guardia Airfield in New York City.

'Colonel Rogner lived in Baltimore and Colonel Smith somewhere in

Connecticut, and they flipped a coin to see who should take the aircraft and who should go home by train. Colonel Rogner lost and took the train; Colonel Smith picked up a sailor hitch-hiking a ride, took off in poor weather on Sunday morning 28 July, and flew the B25 right into the Empire State Building'.

Tragedy also struck elsewhere, as Dennis Duffey of 12 Squadron RAF recalls: ' "Exodus" operation, Order No. 1, was issued on 2 May. Two days later, Lancasters were landing at Brussels and Jurincourt to repatriate prisoners-of-war from Germany. Exodus went on during VE Day, 8 May. Next day came stark tragedy as RF230, loaded with twenty-five passengers and a crew of six reported, soon after take-off from Jurincourt, that an emergency landing was necessary. It appeared that the passengers were told to take up stations at the rear, and this upset the flying trim and the pilot lost control, for the aircraft dived to earth near Roye-Ami and all on board were killed. Apart from that tragedy, 74,000 ex-POWs were brought safely home in Lancasters up to 28 May, when the final evacuation was carried out.'

Lt-Colonel Clifford Norbury of the British 6th Airborne recalls what happened to his division: 'We finished up at Wismar on the Baltic but very shortly thereafter we withdrew to an airfield, handed in our transport and weapons and were flown back to the UK. There we had a few days leave and an Investiture at Buckingham Palace, where King George VI handed out the awards. Then to Salisbury Plain with orders to prepare for our immediate transfer to India and thence to Singapore and Malaya. Thus ended the first five months of 1945.'

For some people, like Jack Santcross, a Jewish boy just ten years old in 1945, the war has never really ended. 'My family had been sent to Belsen in 1944, but were transported east when the camp became too crowded. We were "Exchange Jews", not to be killed at once, because my father had British nationality, because his father had been born in England ... and that meant that since my father was British, I was British too. I was five when the Germans came to Holland and I spent five years in the camps, a large part of my childhood. Being British did not keep us from being transported to Belsen but it kept us alive – just – until the war ended.

'After the Germans came in 1940 we were moved out of our home to a suburb with lots of other Jews and then to the camp at Westerbork, a concentration camp in Holland. Every Tuesday morning at Westerbork there was a "transport" to the east, mostly to Auschwitz or Sobibor but we were "Exchange Jews", who might be useful, so we were kept back. In 1943 Westerbork got full so we were transported to Amersfoort, but after a month, back again to Westerbork.

'We were transported to Belsen in 1944, and you may find it hard to believe but Belsen was then a "privilege camp" – not for the Russian POWs but for us in the "Star Camp". The politicals had to wear the striped clothes but we were allowed to keep our own clothes, though we wore the yellow star. The Germans would not let Jewish children be educated but there was a lady there, a Yugoslav, Hanna Levy Hass, and she would teach the children. I remember 31 August 1944, when the Dutch Jews celebrated the birthday of our Queen.

'Joseph Kramer and his people arrived from Auschwitz-Birkenau in December and it got strict and much worse, though I don't think he did anything to make it worse – or to make it better. It was just his indifference and neglect. So we stayed on and the food got less and people got ill – soon there were bodies everywhere. I was ten years old and surrounded by dead bodies. People got spotted fever from the lice and that killed a lot of them.

'Anyway in April 1945 it was decided to ship us "Privilege Jews" east to the camp at Theresienstadt. This was near Prague in the east, and it was odd because most of the new arrivals in Belsen had just come from the east.

'We were shipped out in cattle trucks on 8 April 1945, a week before the British arrived, but we never got to Theresienstadt. We were shipped all over Germany in those cattle trucks, our train attacked frequently by Allied aircraft, until 23 April when Russian soldiers stopped the train near the town of Trobitz, east of Leipzig.

'The Russians were good to us but we had no home to go to. We had lost our home in Amsterdam, though we were eventually allocated a room somewhere. I had a touch of TB so I went to hospital for three months and then to Switzerland to recuperate. I stayed with some nice people there but they had no idea what I had been through. I was eleven, I had no education...

'I have never recovered from Belsen, from that time, from being shunted about like a parcel, from the fear and the neglect and ... all that. I have always felt out of step with others of my generation, but that is common to all the survivors; our problems are different.

'Belsen spoiled my life ... there is not a day I do not think about it. Perhaps that is my own fault, but there it is...'

Looking after the thousands of POWs and concentration camp survivors was a major task, as was hunting down the leaders of the Nazi regime and the major war criminals, though some of these were beyond reach. Mussolini, Hitler's first ally and leader of the Italian Fascists, had been shot by Italian partisans at the end of April, his body hung up by the heels in Milan. Joseph Goebbels, the Reichminister of Propaganda was already dead.

Electing to follow their Führer, Goebbels and his wife had first poisoned their five children in the Führerbunker in Berlin. This done, they had directed an SS orderly to shoot them both in the head. Their bodies were then burned in the Chancellory garden. Martin Bormann had been killed in a tank while attempting to escape. Most of the other Nazis were now being rounded up, among them the man directly responsible for many of the Nazi massacres and the horrors of the concentration camps, the leader of the SS, Heinrich Himmler.

Kenneth McKee, then with Headquarters, British 2nd Army, tells how Himmler was taken: 'On 22 May 1945, three members of the German Army in civilian clothes attempted to cross the Bremervole bridge between Bremen and Hamburg. Their papers aroused the suspicion of the MPs and they were sent to a nearby internment camp for further investigation. The next day one of these men requested an interview with the camp commandant.

'The request was granted and the prisoner, with a patch over one eye, duly appeared before the commandant. He then removed the patch and told the astonished commandant that he was Heinrich Himmler and the others were two members of his staff. He was immediately searched and placed under a special guard while 2nd Army HQ were informed.

'That evening Colonel Murphy of the General Intelligence Staff at 2nd Army HQ at Luneberg arrived, identified the prisoner as Himmler, which was confirmed by his party number, his SS number and recent photos.

'Colonel Murphy then took personal charge of the prisoner. He was ordered to undress, which he refused to do, saying he had already been stripped four times. Colonel Murphy insisted, saying that force would be used if necessary. Himmler then undressed and his civilian clothes were taken away. The only clothes available were a British Army battledress, vest, pants, socks and boots. These were produced but Himmler said he would not wear them at any cost, so Colonel Murphy said he would have to wear just an Army blanket. It was eventually agreed that Himmler should wear the vest, pants, socks and boots with an Army blanket round him, and in this garb he was driven back to 2nd Army HQ.

'Colonel Murphy had ordered a room to be made ready in advance, and a doctor was standing by to give Himmler a medical examination. The doctor started his examination at Himmler's feet, working up to his head. The examination had been completed except for his mouth. The doctor opened Himmler's mouth and felt around with a finger. Then he moved Himmler over to the light and looked in, seeing a small, dark blue object between Himmler's teeth. At that instant Himmler bit on it, shook his head and collapsed.

'At once a stomach pump was applied and other resuscitation measures taken, but all efforts failed to restore consciousness. The doctor said he died within 5 minutes, and nothing could have been done to prevent him taking his life in this way. Later, on searching Himmler's clothes, a small glass phial was found in a brass tube, about 1 inch long and $\frac{1}{4}$ inch in diameter, containing a concentrated solution of potassium cyanide. Colonel Murphy produced these objects and passed them round and then took us to a room where Himmler, ashen faced, was lying with the Army blanket over him.

'Several days later, a cast was taken of Himmler's face, a cast which can now be seen in the Imperial War Museum in London. Afterwards the body was wrapped in the Army blanket and taken to a lonely spot on Luneburg Heath by an officer and two sergeants of the defence company. Here a hole was dug and the burial took place, all three being sworn to secrecy regarding the location ... thus died one of the war criminals.'

Most of the other Nazi criminals got a trial before they died. War crimes trials took place all over Germany in 1945–46, with the trials of the major war criminals taking place before an international tribunal at Nuremberg towards the end of 1945. The charges ranged from crimes against humanity to the waging of aggressive war and the trials went on for months.

Those in the dock included Hermann Goering, Head of the Luftwaffe and Deputy Führer; William Frick, Minister of the Interior; Hans Frank the inquisitor of Poland; Grand-Admiral Doenitz, last Führer of the Reich and head of the Navy. There, too, was Dr Arthur Seyss-Inquart, an Austrian lawyer who had become ruler of Holland; and Dr Ernst Kaltenbrunner, who had succeeded Heydrich as head of the SD, the SS Security Service.

The half-crazed Rudolph Hess was back from his imprisonment in Britain; and Julius Streicher, the Jew baiter, editor of the anti-Semitic Nazi newspaper *Der Stuermer*, published in Nuremberg to stir up hatred against the Jews all over Germany. Hitler's roving Ambassador and Foreign Minister, Von Ribbentrop, the man who conspired with Molotov of the Soviet Union to carve up Poland and free Germany to attack the west, was in the dock with the rest.

There was Fritz Sauckel, organizer of the slave labour force, and Admiral Erich Raeder, head of the Navy – the man who had sent the U-boats to sink unarmed shipping. There was Albert Speer, the Reichminister of Production, and Alfred Jodl, Chief of Operations for the Armed Forces (the OKW); and Keitel, Hitler's toady, the man who had sent the 'flying court-martials' to hang exhausted German soldiers. There was Alfred Rosenberg, the philosopher of the Nazi Party, and Baldur von Schirach, head of the Hitler Youth. The men William Shirer had called 'an assortment of misfits' were gathered together for the last time. They had all been involved in conspiracy to wage war, of war crimes, or of crimes against humanity and now they were here at Nuremberg to answer for those crimes. Even some of those in the dock were shocked when it became apparent just how extensive and brutal those crimes had been.

Only Albert Speer showed any real contrition, any appreciation of what had been done by these people in Germany and elsewhere in the previous twelve years. The others blamed Hitler or each other or claimed they had only been obeying orders, but Albert Speer rejected such excuses. 'Even in an authoritarian system, the leaders must accept a common responsibility,' he said, 'and it is impossible for them to dodge that common responsibility after the catastrophe.'

In the end, the leaders of the Third German Reich got more justice than they deserved. Goering, Von Ribbentrop, Streicher, Sauckel, Frank, Jodl, Frick, Kaltenbrunner, Rosenberg, Seyss-Inquart and Wilhelm Keitel were sentenced to death by hanging. Hess and Raeder were given life imprisonment; Speer and Baldur von Schirach, twenty years in prison; Doenitz ten years. The hangings took place in the prison in Nuremberg on the night of 16 October 1945, but Goering died by his own hand shortly before being led out to execution, taking another of those cyanide capsules. Von Ribbentrop replaced him as the first one on the scaffold. The bodies were then taken to Dachau and cremated in the ovens of the concentration camp.

During 1945–46, war crimes trials went on all over Germany as part of a general process of de-Nazification. Whole professions – doctors, laywers, civil administrators – were purged of Nazi adherents. A great number of war criminals from the SS, the Gestapo, the armed forces and concentration camp 'Kapos' were tracked down, arrested and tried. The commandants of the various concentration camps were tried and sentenced to death. Those from the east were taken back to the camps they had tyrannized and executed before the eyes of the former inmates, but those who were not executed rarely served out their terms in prison. By 1950 the majority of German and Austrian war criminals had been set at liberty. Some, like Dr Mengele of Auschwitz, fled to South America and lived out their lives in hiding. Some met retribution many years later, like Adolf Eichmann, organizer of the Final Solution, who was kidnapped in Argentina by the Israelis in 1960, taken to Jerusalem, tried for his crimes and hanged.

Not all the Germans were criminals like these. There were many decent Germans, people like the famous Oskar Schindler who saved more than 1,000 Jews from the gas chamber. When the dust settled in Berlin, more than 8,000 Jews emerged from the places where their Gentile German friends had kept them concealed for years. But many Jews left at once for Israel, unable to live in a Continent where two-thirds of their people had been done to death.

While Germany was being purged and re-organized, the work of re-shaping the post-war world went ahead. The conference to establish the United Nations took place in San Francisco in April 1945 and, much to the relief of the Western nations, the Soviet Union was represented by Foreign Minister Molotov. However, the Soviets now had Eastern Europe in a firm grip and showed no sign of keeping any of their Yalta agreements.

Poland was already lost. Other Eastern European nations were now falling under the Communist sway. Tito's Yugoslav partisans were hanging on to territory in Austria, occupying Klagenfurt and territory around Trieste and the Istrian peninsula, where the Yugoslav border dispute with Italy would rumble on for years. East of the Elbe and in the Balkans, democrats and liberals were being ruthlessly purged, hunted down and liquidated, together with rulers of wartime governments like Ion Antonescu, the President of Romania, who was executed by the Communists on 17 May.

Poland continued to concern Winston Churchill, for now that war in Europe was over the Polish troops serving in the Western armies wanted to go home. Their fate on return might be uncertain and it had already been decided by the British Parliament that any Polish soldier unable or unwilling to go home should be offered British citizenship. As the weeks went by after VE Day, with clear signs that Poland had now become a Soviet satellite, more and more Poles began to consider this option.

President Truman, though taking a far harder line than Roosevelt, still wished to maintain cordial relations with Soviet Russia, not least in the hope that Russia would, as promised, send troops to attack Japan. Soviet Russia was far more interested in building up her forces in Eastern Europe and waiting until the American armies had gone home. Then, with the aid of civil unrest created by national Communist parties in Greece, Italy and France, the Communists would slowly overrun the countries of Western Europe.

The Soviet hope of dominating Europe received a setback on 18 July 1945, when the first atom bomb exploded on a test site near Alamogordo, New Mexico. The Soviets had no knowledge of the atom bomb and the possession of this strategic weapon by the West proved a considerable setback for Marshal Stalin.

The Americans dropped an atom bomb over the city of Hiroshima on 8 August. On 9 August a second bomb fell on the city of Nagasaki, killing 75,000 people and inflicting radiation sickness on a further 75,000. The Russians finally declared war on Japan on 10 August 1945 and the Second World War ended on 14 August, VJ Day, after nearly six years of global bloodshed.

Meanwhile the General Election of 1945 had taken place in Britain, and the result was a Labour Party landslide. The previous Tory majority of 393 seats was turned into a Labour majority of 146; thirty-one government ministers lost their seats, and Winston Churchill was no longer in power. He summed up his dismissal later with just a hint of bitterness:

'On the night of the 10th of May, 1940, at the outset of this mighty battle, I acquired the chief power in the State, which henceforth I wielded in ever-growing measure for five years and three months of World War, at the end of which time, all our enemies having surrendered unconditionally or being about to do so, I was immediately dismissed by the British electorate from all further conduct of their affairs.'

Many British people were sorry to lose Winston Churchill and grateful for his leadership in war, but they remembered the 1930s and the promises broken after the First World War; they wanted no truck with the Tories after this one.

Winston Churchill stepped down on 28 July 1945 in the middle of the last 'Big Three' conference at Potsdam, giving place to the Labour Party leader, Clement Attlee. Of the three great leaders who had directed the course of the Second World War, only Stalin was still in power. Other Western leaders got their rewards and honours: a Viscountcy for Mont- gomery, who later became Chief of the Imperial General Staff; the Freedom of the City of London for General Eisenhower, who was to follow Truman as President of the United States; a host of medals and knighthoods for the generals and the commanders. The simple soldiers went home again, and were content with that.

General George Patton never went home again. He stayed in Europe and on 9 December 1945 was severely injured in a car crash outside Mannheim. He died two weeks later and now lies with other soldiers of 3rd Army in the American military cemetery in Luxembourg City.

These Big Power manoeuvrings and the triumphs celebrated by their leaders were of little concern to the troops occupying Germany just after the war ended.

James Ed Thompson of the 7th US Armoured Division remembers that time: 'I was at Schoenberg, about twelve miles from Lübeck, restoring electricity to houses we had occupied. There was a great shortage of power at this time, and cigarettes were the currency. I remember that a pack of cigarettes cost 5 cents and yet you could get $200 – around £50 in British money – for a carton of cigarettes on the black market in Berlin.

'There was a hospital in Schoenberg full of wounded German soldiers, and we used to go round with a stretcher and collect all the weapons as the wounded were brought in. The area we were in was designated as the British Zone and ten of us were on an outpost guarding an Elbe river crossing. The Russians on the far side were friendly at first, with the usual

290

backslapping, rejoicing and toasts. Then one day on guard I saw bodies floating by, the first of many, and the Russians began using the bodies for target practice. Another night, my buddy and I heard a noise in the river and saw a German girl swimming towards us. We pulled her out and my buddy, who spoke German rather well, got her calmed down; she said she was running from the Russians who had raped her. We heard many stories like this, and of women and whole families who had committed suicide to avoid this threat. Many of our own troops were guilty of rape, justifying it as being one of the spoils of war.

'The big gripe now the war was over was what were we doing here and how soon could we go home? Weeks later, in July, we had pulled back from the Elbe and the Russian Zone into the American Zone. At Heilbronn I went to a USO show with Jack Benny, Ingrid Bergman, Larry Adler and Martha Tilton among the stars. It was also reported that the No-Fraternization ban might be lifted – it didn't work anyway. The girl I mentioned earlier, the one we pulled from the Elbe, became friendly with my buddy. He told me they had fallen in love and planned to marry when the No-Fratting ban ended. However, when we left Dessau he left her behind. Three weeks later she turned up, having travelled 300 miles across Germany on a bicycle. I don't know if they ever married.

'My company was getting pretty thin now. The points system for rotation to the USA was established to keep track of combat time. You got points for months of service, combat campaigns, wounds, etc., and senior soldiers got more points. We had already turned in our tanks and half-tracks. Men with less than 85 points were being shipped home now and I expected to be leaving soon. I finally got home on 23 March 1946.'

For most of the millions of men and women who took part, this is how the war ended, by going home again. That is how wars usually end. The defeated are punished, the victors rewarded, fresh alliances are concluded and the whole circle starts again. Nothing is finally settled.

By March 1946, less than a year after the war ended, Winston Churchill could say in a speech at Fulton, Missouri: 'From Stettin on the Baltic to Trieste on the Adriatic, an Iron Curtain has descended across the Continent of Europe...'

In 1948 the Russians imposed a land blockade on Berlin, hoping to drive the Western Powers from the city. Only Western resolve and the two-year long epic of the Berlin Airlift prevented that happening. In 1950 Communist forces invaded South Korea to begin the bitter Korean War; the British fought the Communists for ten years in Malaya. Then came Vietnam...

Thanks to the atomic bomb and the threat of global destruction none of these wars escalated into worldwide conflict, but though every war ends in peace, every peace holds the seeds of further conflict. That Soviet decision to move the Polish frontier to the Oder–Neisse line may yet return to haunt the continent of Europe, and with the break-up of the Soviet Empire the peace of Europe is again in the balance. A knowledge of what happened the last time Europe tore itself apart may therefore prove useful.

The stories of brave, ordinary people have made up the bulk of this book, so let three of them have the final say on the war in Europe.

Sergeant Ted Smith of the Guards Armoured Division: 'I remember the cost, I suppose. I didn't get a scratch but I was lucky. Doug Tamblin was wounded, and his driver got his feet blown off. Bob Jarvis and Jock, his mate, got machine-gunned on top of a tank; each thought the other was dead and they didn't find out different until they met at a reunion thirty-four years later. Lieutenant Edward Collins lost a leg and most of his crew were killed when an anti-tank gun hit his tank at a crossroads. Spider Edwards was killed, and not even in battle. He was cleaning his teeth when a shell splinter hit him in the head ... that shattered me. You lose mates, people you know well ... that's all I want to say.'

Freddie Fish of the RAF: 'I was on leave on VE Day because we had just finished our tour. I just breathed a sigh of relief and thought, "Thank God it's over." I did not rush off to celebrate VE Day, though the streets were full of crowds singing and laughing and the pubs did a roaring trade. I think I just went to a Working Man's Club with my father and had a quiet drink. There was no point in getting too starry-eyed as we still had the Japs to deal with and Bomber Command was preparing a force to help the Yanks bomb Japan.

'My thoughts were mainly relief that I had survived and gratitude for the marvellous comradeship, courage and spirit of my crew. I remember vividly the faces of those who did not come back, some in particular that I knew well, and just hoped that their sacrifice would not be in vain. All aircrew were volunteers and having taken it on, never shirked. The greatest disgrace was to let your comrades down, so although frightened or terrified at times, you pressed on, not to let yourself, your crew or your squadron down.

'We had no back-up or "counselling" as they do today. I was struck by the Gulf War which only lasted a few days – not six years – and yet some of the chaps needed "counselling" and lots of help. During our lot if you got the chop, your relatives were informed you were missing and they had to just get on with it. No one ever came up to us and offered help of any kind. You just had to make the best of it, and soldier along on your own.

'The war was over and our next task was to survive in Civvy Street. I went back to my old firm in 1946 at a weekly wage of £5 a week, an average wage for the time. On that you had to get by and maybe get married and build a home. I finally got married in 1949 and we started married life with two rooms and a bathroom in my parents' house.

'I don't think people today realize how hard it was fifty years ago. When I got back from the war I was told that I had to compete against younger men with more experience, and that my four-and-a-half years war service did not count. I was soon told, and it was perfectly true, "You can't use the war as an excuse any more." It was tough going and you had to work and study hard to get anywhere, but at least if we had to go back to rationing tomorrow, Spam and powdered egg, it would not bother me one bit ... and it might do this over-fed, over-indulged, feather-bedded nation a bit of good.'

Jack Capell of Portland, Oregon, went from 'Utah' Beach to VE Day in Germany with the 4th US Infantry Division. 'How do I feel about it, looking back? Well, I survived – a lot of good men didn't, so I must be grateful. I remember the hard times, in the Hurtgen and the hedgerows, but I remember a lot of real good people – the world could use them now.

'I saw the war through in the infantry, which is not the easiest place to be, but – and I said this when I got back – I wouldn't want to do that again – but I wouldn't have missed it either ...'

Many of the veterans who contributed to this book mention how hard the war was on their families, who had to stay at home, waiting and hoping, fearing the news that a telegram might bring. One of these relatives was Barbara Fozzard, who remembers her brother, Corporal Thornton Hitchen:

'He was a corporal in the 2nd Lincolns and was killed at dawn on Good Friday, 30 March 1945, aged twenty-six. He was in the D-Day landings where he was wounded and brought back to England. He was recovering when his son was born on 23 July 1944 and he applied for compassionate leave to see his wife and son, but for some reason it was refused. Though he wasn't fully fit, he was sent back to his unit in France, and so his travels began again.

'I don't have any official letters with regard to his death but if my memory serves me right he was killed either crossing or near a river at a place called Bocholt, just across the border from Holland. Four of his comrades were killed at the same time and they were buried in the village churchyard until moved to the military cemetery. It is ironic that our late mother's brother, also called Thornton, was killed on the Somme in 1916, during the First World War. We still grieve for my brother. I still have the letters and cards he sent to his sisters and it all seems such a waste of young lives. He never saw his son.'

BIBLIOGRAPHY

Bartov, Omer, *Hitler's Army*, Oxford, 1992

Bracer, William M., *Storming Hitler's Rhine*, St Martin's Press, 1985

Bryant, Sir Arthur, *Triumph in the West*, Collins, 1959

Eisenhower, General Dwight D., *Crusade in Europe*, Heinemann, 1948

Ellis, L. F., *Victory in the West*, HM Stationery Office, 1968

Gavin, General James M., *On to Berlin*, Bantam Books, 1979

Gilbert, Martin, *Road to Victory. Winston S. Churchill 1941–45*, Minerva, 1989

Harris, Sir Arthur, Marshal of the RAF, *Bomber Offensive*, Collins, 1947

Hawkins, Desmond (ed.), *BBC War Reports. June 1944–May 1945*, Oxford University Press, 1948

Jacobson, Ray, *History of 426 Squadron RCAF*, Toronto

Lucas, James, *The Last Days of the Reich*, Arms and Armour Press, 1986

Von Luck, Hans, *Panzer Leader*, Bell Books, 1989

Macdonald, Charles B., *The US Army in World War II. The Last Offensive*, Department of the Army, 1973

Macdonald, Charles B., *The US Army in World War II: The Siegfried Line*, Department of the Army, 1963

Montgomery, Field Marshal Bernard Law, *From Normandy to the Baltic*, Collins, 1950

Moorhead, Alan, *Montgomery*, Hamish Hamilton, 1946

Neillands, Robin, *The Raiders. The Army Commandos*, Weidenfeld and Nicolson

Neillands, Robin, *By Sea and Land. The Royal Marine Commandos*, Weidenfeld and Nicolson

Neillands, Robin, *The Desert Rats*, Weidenfeld and Nicolson, 1991

Norton, G. G., *The Red Devils*, Arrow Books, 1988

Patton, General George, *War As I Knew It*, Pyramid Book, 1948

Phillips, Raymond, MC (ed.), *The Belsen Trial*, William Hodge, 1949

Ryan, Cornelius, *The Last Battle*, Collins, 1966

St George Saunders, Hilary, *The Green Beret*, N.E.L., 1971

Shirer, William, *The Rise and Fall of the Third Reich*, Pan, 1964

Thorwald, Jurgen, *Flight in the Winter*, Pantheon, 1951

Toland, John, *The Last 100 Days*, Bantam Books, 1967

BIBLIOGRAPHY

Trevor-Roper, Hugh, *The Last Days of Hitler*, University of Chicago Press, 1982
The US Holocaust Museum, *The World Must Know*, Washington
Verrier, Anthony, *The Bomber Offensive*, Batsford, 1968
Werth, Alexander, *Russia at War 1941–45*, Barrie and Rockcliffe, 1964
Wilmot, Chester, *The Struggle for Europe*, Collins, 1952
Whiting, Charles, *Patton's Last Battle*, Jove Books, 1987
de Zayas, Alfred M., *Nemesis at Potsdam*, Bison Books, 1989

INDEX